COMMON LAND AND INCLOSURE

COMMON LAND AND INCLOSURE

E. C. K. GONNER

with a new introduction by

G. E. MINGAY

Routledge
Taylor & Francis Group
LONDON AND NEW YORK

Published by Frank Cass & Co. Ltd.,
by arrangement with Macmillan & Co. Ltd.

First published	1912
Second edition	1966

Published 2005 by Routledge
2 Park Square, Milton Park, Abingdon, Oxfordshire OX14 4RN
711 Third Avenue, New York, NY 10017

First issued in paperback 2014

Routledge is an imprint of the Taylor and Francis Group, an informa business

ISBN 13: 978-0-714-61311-6 (hbk)
ISBN 13: 978-0-415-76040-9 (pbk)

PREFACE TO FIRST EDITION

THE main object of the present work is to trace the process whereby the land of this country came into agricultural use under full individual control. That movement, as will be seen, is treated as continuous and as due in the main to the operation of large economic and, so to say, normal causes. While the rapidity and extent of inclosure varies from time to time, and while its kind undergoes certain changes, progress continues. Moreover, despite the particular features which appertain to different periods, the movement owes its impetus and direction to certain dominant though often undetected influences. Hence the emphasis laid in the following pages on such factors as the soil, the effect of the addition of new agricultural land on the use of that already in cultivation, the date of inclosure from the wild state, the influence of progress in farming, and of the new demands arising from an advance in industrial development. The connection of these with the progress of inclosure and with its results, differing as these often do from epoch to epoch, are treated of in detail.

But there is one subject touched on, with regard to which I may be blamed for not attempting any definite and general conclusion. I refer to the effect of the eighteenth century inclosures upon the condition of the labouring class. As a matter of fact the controversy of that period is subjected to very careful examination, and conclusions are reached which may be employed in support of varying views; but when it comes to a question of general approval or condemnation, I find a simple one-sided decision difficult. Inclosure is so much a part of a wider economic movement, and so often a consequence rather than a cause, that to set out its results as wholly bad or wholly good seems to me quite impossible. Some results, indeed, are fairly clear, but they do not point uniformly in the same direction.

Thus, on the one hand, it is pointed out that in certain parts of the country the inclosures of that century facilitated the operation of the forces which led to larger farming and so to the diminution and partial extinction of the yeomen and small farmers. Similarly, it seems probable that a considerable amount of common field inclosure in a district often led to a temporary pressure on poor relief.

On the other hand, the beneficial effect on farming taken as a whole is undoubted. This displays itself on all sides, and particularly in the increased utilisation of what is, after all, the distinctive agricultural wealth of England, rich grazing and dairy lands. Again, the examination attempted and the tables adduced seem to me to prove that rural population at the end of that century did not vary with inclosure, and that this movement was not at any rate the main cause of the increase in poor relief expenditure. Nor does the accusation of general arbitrary or unfair treatment of the small farmer or the poor owner appear to me tenable.

In my view the inclosure movement was an inseparable part of a much wider movement, and hence an estimate of its results must take into account not only the local disturbance and the individual consequences it entailed, but the broad general effects which it achieved or rendered possible. But for this, regard must be paid to certain facts or aspects which for one reason or another have received inadequate attention. Among such are the importance of inclosure to progressive farming, the strict geographical limits within which inclosure occurred, and the close connection between inclosure from the wild state and the waste and inclosure of land under arable. Of even greater importance was the change whereby agriculture from being a means of subsistence to particular families had become a source of wealth to the nation, a change in progress alike in the seventeenth and eighteenth centuries, and one which made improvement in its productivity momentous in a national sense. From this point of view the retention of a system which withheld land from its best use was an obstacle to general progress only to be defended by arguments equally applicable to any improvement or invention in a productive process.

On the other hand, the consequences of the alteration were manifold. Owing in the main to the circumstances of the time, and principally to the mechanical change which led to the disappearance of industries allied to and plied with agriculture, the allotments to the small holders were often inadequate as a sole means of livelihood, and in a large number of instances soon sold. As a consequence, small independent holders grew rapidly fewer, and in agriculture as in industry the proportion of those who work for and live by wages increased. But this occurred, it should be remembered, not only in counties or districts subject to inclosure in the eighteenth century, but in those where there was little trace of such; not only again in regions where at some time or other the open field had existed, but in those where there is reason to believe open field either never existed or played a very insignificant part.

I have purposely abstained from dwelling at length on the incidents of a few cases. Such a method, while it may make things more picturesque, is misleading when the instances are few out of many thousands, and not necessarily typical.

To touch further on this point would travel outside the province of a preface, and lead to a discussion of what forms the subject of the text itself.

A few words are needed as to the maps and tables appended to or included in the present work.

Of the five maps three require little or no explanation.

The one based on Ogilby's *Britannia* has been traced from the road plans and descriptions given in that book. The map may be taken as illustrating the condition of the country, open or inclosed, shortly after the Restoration, as far as that is reflected in the hedged, fenced, and walled or open condition of the roads. I think it is a reliable index, though no doubt some modification is necessary for reasons set out elsewhere. The two which depict actual inclosure by act, respectively of wastes and open field, need little comment. It must, however, be remembered that a certain proportion of so-called open field inclosures consisted of commons. The remaining two are attempts to represent the condition of the country towards the close of the seventeenth and the sixteenth centuries respectively. To arrive at them I have worked backwards, starting from the land inclosed in the eighteenth century and so open before, and making similar additions for other recorded inclosures, much on the lines of the tabular statement on pp. 268-9. Of course the treatment has been according to the registration district and not the county. In showing land as open they do not distinguish between waste or wild and open field. After some consideration I gave up any such attempt as too uncertain.

The main tables may be divided into three groups according to the particular aspect with which they deal.

Firstly, there are two treating of the progress of inclosure from the beginning of the sixteenth century either in general (pp. 268-9) or in respect of direct inclosure into individual use from the wild state (p. 285). These two tables should be read in conjunction with the statements offered as to the development in the separate counties in Book II., Appendix A. Thus studied it is hoped that they will afford some brief indication of the very important matter which constitutes the subject of Book II.

Secondly, there are the tables which attempt the geographical allocation of the recorded inclosures by act. For reasons given in the text the data on which these are based, though approximately accurate, are only approximately accurate, and therefore too much importance must not be attached to decimal points. Further, the mass of detailed computation involved in the tables in Book II., Appendices B and C, is so great that the occurrence of some error is possible. I believe them, however, to be substantially correct. In Appendix C, the percentage of townships affected is added in round figures. To do this the list of parishes or civil townships given in the Census Return is employed. As compared with the percentage of land this indicates the degree in which inclosures were widely spread over the district, a matter, as it seems, of considerable importance in interpreting the evidence furnished by the tables as to the previous condition of the land. This calculation was difficult, and cannot claim to be precise. One thing more, it must be remembered that where percentages of land are given these are calculated on the whole acreage of the county or district as if the whole area had been open to inclosure. As a matter of fact some deduction must be made for the site of the villages and for the surface occupied by road or water. Hence the percentages of available land brought under inclosure are greater than those stated.

Thirdly, the tables giving the comparisons between inclosure, population, and poor relief need a word. In certain cases towns had to be excluded. When this was done, it was done impartially; and I consider that the case is under rather than overstated with regard to the greater density or increase of population, and the less increase in poor relief expenditure in the inclosed parishes. The large number of tables constructed with reference to this general matter is due, I ought to add, to my surprise at the absence of evidence as to any effective relation between inclosure and both population and poor relief. But further calculation only corroborated the results already ascertained.

I have to thank Messrs. Longmans, Green & Co. for permission to use the chapter on the seventeenth century, originally published in the *English Historical Review*, and also the map prepared from Ogilby's *Britannia*.

In conclusion, I wish to express my sincere acknowledgment of the opportunities for study offered by the various libraries in which I have worked. In Liverpool I received much assistance from the officials in the Public Reference Library and the Athenæum Library, the University Library, partly by reason of its newness and partly owing to its inadequate funds, possessing few of the books or papers which I had to consult. But it is difficult to estimate my obligations to the officials of the British Museum Library and the Public Record Office. In this, as in other cases, I have found them not only willing but anxious to afford and extend facilities to the genuine worker.

E. C. K. GONNER.

UNDERCLIFF, WEST KIRBY,
11*th Jan.*, 1912.

CONTENTS

BOOK I

COMMON AND INCLOSURE

I

COMMON AND INCLOSURE

III

THE METHOD OF INCLOSURE IN THE EIGHTEENTH AND NINETEENTH CENTURIES

APPENDICES

BOOK II

PROGRESS OF INCLOSURE

I

PROGRESS OF INCLOSURE

II

THE SEVENTEENTH CENTURY

III

EIGHTEENTH CENTURY

APPENDICES

BOOK III

EFFECTS OF INCLOSURE

I

GENERAL EFFECT OF INCLOSURE

II

EFFECT ON AGRICULTURE

III

EFFECT ON PARTICULAR PRODUCTS

IV

EFFECT ON AMOUNT OF ANIMAL PRODUCTS AND GRAIN

V

EFFECT ON CONDITIONS OF RURAL LIFE

VI

EMPLOYMENT AND POPULATION

BOOK III

APPENDICES

LIST OF TABLES IN TEXT AND APPENDICES

MAPS

(At end of volume)

NEW INTRODUCTION

By

G. E. MINGAY

INTRODUCTION TO SECOND EDITION

by G. E. MINGAY

PROFESSOR GONNER'S book, here reprinted after more than fifty years, belongs to a period remarkable for its scholarly and influential contributions to English agrarian history. The richness of that time is amply exemplified by the names of Maitland, Vinogradoff, Gay, Leadam and Gray, to mention but a few of the most distinguished, and may be further illustrated by the appearance in the one year of 1912 alone, not only of Gonner's authoritative study, but also of Ernle's well-known *English Farming Past and Present*, and not less important, Tawney's celebrated masterpiece, *The Agrarian Problem in the Sixteenth Century*. These works were among the finest fruit of a strongly-rooted historical growth stretching back to Thorold Rogers' pioneer work in the 1860's, one vigorous branch of which had come to concern itself very largely with the problem of the decline of the English peasantry.

In the late nineteenth and early twentieth centuries there culminated a long-developing discussion of agricultural problems, and at the centre of this lay the situation of the English agricultural labourers. It was at this time, for instance, that Rider Haggard set down the story of his rural perambulations. Haggard surveyed and discussed the farming scene with members of every class of rural society, and among his accounts of farm practices, rents, and prices, the labour problem loomed large. In a typical encounter Lord Coventry told him that skilled men, always scarce in Worcestershire, "had grown still scarcer, as the young able-bodied men were leaving for the towns, whither they were attracted by the higher wages and the seductions of city life." And again in Essex Haggard met an old labourer whose memories went back to the Crimean war and beyond. In those days he lived on bread and onions, washed down with small beer, and his wife produced in lieu of tea a beverage made by soaking a burnt crust of bread in boiling water. With such a record it was not surprising, said Haggard, that "resentment against past sufferings, at any rate as yet, is deeper than gratitude for present benefits."[1]

Other writers also attempted to provide systematic factual material for the discussion of the problem. In 1911 F. G. Heath followed up his account of the labourers' conditions of 1873, when the first widely-organized agricultural labourers' unions were appearing, with a new and more detailed analysis that covered wages, allowances in kind, hours of work, and housing, in Wales, Scotland and Ireland, as well as England.[2] And between his two volumes appeared the first *Report* by the Board of Trade on the *Wages and Earnings of Agricultural Labourers in the United Kingdom.*[3]

Books which dealt with the social problems of rural life were not lacking. Among them were F. E. Green's *Tyranny of the Countryside* (1913), and Georges Bourne's *Change in the Village* (1912), a sympathetic study of Surrey country life which found the labourer hanging "between two civilizations", emerging from the reeking poverty of the old days, but not yet integrated into twentieth-century society. William Savage's *Rural Housing* (1915) lit up an aspect of

[1] H. Rider Haggard, *Rural England* (1902), pp. 363, 458–9. Haggard's interest in the land question continued, and in 1905 he published his pamphlet *Back to the Land*, and a report on the Salvation Army land colonies, *The Poor and the Land*. In 1913 appeared his study of a successful peasant agriculture: *Rural Denmark and its Lessons*.

[2] F. G. Heath, *The English Peasantry* (1874); *British Rural Life and Labour* (1911).

[3] Cmd. 346 (1900).

the countryside which had helped to stimulate the migration and unionism of the 1870's, and Joseph Arch's autobiography put that era into its social and political context.[1] In a more romantic reaching back into the past came W. H. Hudson's picturesque tales,[2] and for a superficially attractive picture of the countryside at the onset of the great depression one might turn to the limpid prose of Richard Jeffries.[3]

In parliament and the press, radicals presented the case for land reform, and the vans of the political parties decked in their appropriate distinguishing colours quartered the countryside, as Hudson said, and might be found in the remotest villages. "Their words—wild and whirling words they may be—are sinking into the hearts of the agricultural labourers of the new generation."[4] The flight from the land, the rural migration to towns and overseas, had reached a peak in the 1870's and 1880's, and still created much alarm. Belated improvements in wages, housing, schools, and allotments could do little to stem the tide, and when it eventually subsided at the end of the century this was merely because most of the unfettered and enterprising had already gone. "Fewer potential migrants were being born, because the parents who might have reared them had already migrated." [5]

The basic factor in the labourer's poverty and unrest, it was widely argued, was his landlessness. The labourer had become divorced from the soil on which he worked, and while it was true that at this time most labourers had a vegetable garden or access as a tenant to an allotment or potato patch, this was a mere supplement to his inadequate wages, an amelioration of his lot and not a share, by right, in the land itself. It gave him no great measure of independence or security. The labourer could only be

[1] *Joseph Arch: The Story of his Life, Told by Himself*, ed. the Countess of Warwick (1898).
[2] See for example his *A Shepherd's Life* (1910).
[3] See R. Jeffries, *Field and Farm*, ed. S. J. Looker (1957).
[4] Hudson, *op. cit.* (14th ed. 1933), p. 77.
[5] A. Cairncross, "Internal Migration in Victorian England", in Cairncross, *Home and Foreign Investment 1870–1913* (1953), p. 75.

kept on the land by giving him a true share in it, so it was argued, by giving him the opportunity of becoming a small farmer or cultivator. Thus sprang up the interest in land reform, in the provision of larger allotments and market gardens, and the consequent legislation of 1887, 1892 and 1907. But these measures achieved much less than the more ardent land reformers hoped and desired. William Booth in his *In Darkest England and the Way Out* (1891), and Christopher Turnor's *Land Problems and National Welfare* (1911), connected the farm labour problem with the need to colonise the Empire, and hardly more realistic was Jesse Collings's *Land Reform: Occupying Ownership, Peasant Proprietary and Rural Education* (1906). More reasonable and dispassionate was the 1913 *Report* of the Land Enquiry Committee, chaired by A. L. Dyke Acland, a systematic survey of the now familiar ground of agricultural wages, working conditions, allotments, housing, land tenures, rents and rates, which concluded with a discussion of the single tax remedy and proposals for nationalisation of the land.

In practice it proved difficult to restore even a small part of the soil to a peasantry of whom the great majority had been landless for at least a century. The technical reasons for this were examined by, among others, A. W. Ashby,[1] whose own father had experienced the labourer's life of the nineteenth-century village and had rebelled against it.[2] To succeed, the smallholder needed land certainly, enough but not too much, but he also needed capital, a fertile and easily-worked soil, with near access to a railway and profitable markets; yet all this would not suffice unless he possessed also a degree of enterprise, adaptability, and endurance, above that commonly found in many walks of life, let alone among the poverty-stricken, poorly educated and inarticulate agricultural labourers.

[1] A. W. Ashby, *Allotments and Smallholdings in Oxfordshire: a Survey* (Oxford, 1917).

[2] M. K. Ashby, *Joseph Ashby of Tysoe, 1859–1919: a study of English Village Life* (1961).

It was against this background, an agricultural industry meeting difficult times, declining in economic and social importance, and losing its labour force to other industries and other lands, that the first generation of agricultural historians took up their pens. The problem which most interested an important group of them was when and how the labourer had lost his land: the process by which a peasantry was turned into a proletariat. For the starting point of their enquiries they could turn to Marx, who after all had distilled into his analysis material from an impressive assortment of ancient and modern authorities, stretching from Aristotle through Bentham and Joseph Chamberlain to Locke, Montesquieu, Plato, Smith and Turgot. Indeed, it was Marx who showed the historical value of the writers of the age of parliamentary enclosure—Addington, Cobbett, Eden, Price and Young, as well as the classical economists. And it was Marx who set the tone and provided the framework, with his chapters so tendentiously headed: *Expropriation of the Agricultural Population from the Land*, *Bloody Legislation against the Expropriated*, and *Genesis of the Capitalist Farmer*. These titles referred to a process which, he said, began in the fifteenth century, was accelerated by the Reformation, and was completed by the enclosures of the eighteenth century and the Highland clearances of the nineteenth century.[1]

The historians of the late nineteenth and early twentieth centuries were of course more radical than Marxist, but they were concerned with the same problem: they began, as Marx did, with the presumption that the countryside was in the past populated by a settled peasantry of small owner-cultivators, while in their own time, as it was only too obvious, all but a little over a tenth of the land was in the hands of absentee landowners. The remnant of the former independent peasantry was now mainly represented by some half-million or so agricultural labourers, poor and landless. And this was in sharp contrast to most of

[1] K. Marx, *Capital* (English ed. 1886), pp. 458–468.

Europe, where in the process of historical development the peasant had managed to retain a title to at least a substantial share of the land.

There resulted a series of comprehensive and detailed histories. The earliest were J. E. Thorold Rogers' *History of Agriculture and Prices* (1866) and G. C. Brodrick's *English Land and English Landlords* (1881), the latter including a discussion of the current proposals for land reform. Then after an interval came works specifically concerned with the labourer: the German scholar W. Hasbach's *History of the English Agricultural Labourer* (English edition 1908, but first published in German in 1894), a carefully detailed work clearly influenced by the Marxist interpretation of the role of enclosure; Russell M. Garnier's *Annals of the British Peasantry* (1908), a painstaking discussion which ended topically with the findings of the Royal Commission of 1891 and the Parish Council Acts of 1894; and O. Jocelyn Dunlop's *The Farm Labourer: the History of a Modern Problem* (1913), which like Hasbach and Garnier came up to date with the "back to the land" movement. Finally appeared another and more durable general study, Ernle's *English Farming* of 1912.

At this point, in the years before the first world war, historical interest turned more closely towards the enclosure movement. Enclosure, of course, had entered largely into the histories of Hasbach, Ernle and others, but now it came to attract more detailed examination in specialised monographs. Its historical significance was studied for the sixteenth century by Tawney and by Gay,[1] and for the eighteenth century, more particularly, by Slater, Johnson, Levy, the Hammonds, and Gonner. What these scholars were concerned to explore was the validity and factual detail of what was now the traditional story of the peasantry, a story which in its fundamentals went back to the bitter generalisation of Marx. "About 1750 the

[1] Tawney, *op. cit.*; E. F. Gay, "Inquisitions of Depopulation in 1517", *Trans. R. H. S.* n.s. XIV (1900); "The Midland Revolt and the Inquisition of Depopulation of 1607", *ibid.* XVIII (1904); "Inclosures in England", *Quar. Journal of Economics* XVII (1903).

yeomanry had disappeared", Marx said, quoting from contemporary pamphlets, "and so had, in the last decade of the eighteenth century, the last trace of the common land of the agricultural labourer." After the restoration the landed proprietors abolished feudal tenures and adopted the modern rights of private property, and the glorious revolution brought into power "the landlord and capitalist appropriators of surplus-value. They inaugurated the new era by practising on a colossal scale thefts of State lands. . . ." In the eighteenth century the law itself became "the instrument of the theft of the people's land . . . The parliamentary form of the robbery is that of Acts for enclosures of commons—in other words, decrees by which the landlords grant themselves the people's land as private property, decrees of expropriation of the people. . . . While the place of the independent yeoman was taken by the tenants at will, small farmers on yearly leases, a servile rabble dependent on the pleasure of the landlords, the systematic robbery of the communal lands helped especially, next to the theft of the State domains, to swell those large farms, that were called in the eighteenth century capital farms or merchant farms, and to 'set free' the agricultural population as proletarians for manufacturing industry."[1]

In these intemperate words Marx indicated the central role played by enclosure in the emergence of the great landlord and the capitalist farmer, and the forcing of the labourer off the land into the hell of the early factories. Enclosure, it appeared, was the key to agrarian change, and it happened that for the eighteenth and nineteenth centuries it was a subject that offered much scope for historical research, since many of the enclosure Acts and Awards had survived and could readily be studied. Furthermore, the pros and cons of enclosure had been extensively debated in eighteenth-century pamphlets and in the works of the agricultural writers such as Marshall, Stone and Young, as well as in the *Reports* to the Board of Agricul-

[1] Marx, *op. cit.* pp. 461–3.

ture. Here, therefore, was an almost untilled field which in the course of five years produced as many major studies.

Gilbert Slater's *The English Peasantry and the Enclosure of Common Fields* appeared in 1907. It was hardly a systematic or exhaustive treatment of the subject, including as it did rather brief and cursory surveys of such complex matters as types of village communities and field systems, but it did provide the statistical summaries of the areas of land enclosed by Act of Parliament in the eighteeth and first half of the nineteenth centuries which formed the factual groundwork of many later books. There was also a county by county analysis of the progress of enclosure, and a map illustrating the concentration of parliamentary enclosure in the midlands which was reproduced in many a subsequent textbook. Slater's general position on the effects of enclosure departed little from Marx. Enclosure, he said, raised total agricultural output and rents, but "tended to ruin small owners and to eliminate small farmers, so that these had to join the ranks of agricultural labourers." Destitution, recklessness, and early marriage followed, and through local depopulation "enclosure tended to assist urban industry therefore by an increased labour supply", as well as by "an increased market, and perhaps also, an increased supply of capital."[1]

A. H. Johnson devoted his Ford lectures of 1909 to a discussion of the particular question of the disappearance of the small landowner.[2] He started from the fact that in his own day the number of occupying landowners in England was much smaller than in France; and discounting the influence in this of the English law of inheritance and entail, he began a historical survey, going back as far as the Black Death, to establish when and how the small landowner had disappeared.

After discussing briefly the enclosures and other developments of the sixteenth and seventeenth centuries, Johnson

[1] G. Slater, *The English Peasantry and the Enclosure of Common Fields* (1907), pp. 265–6.

[2] A. H. Johnson, *The Disappearance of the Small Landowner* (Oxford, 1909).

concentrated on the eighteenth and nineteenth centuries as the critical period. The great and novel feature of his work was the use he made of the Land Tax assessments. These records showed that in very many parishes small owners had disappeared before the later eighteenth century, although it was this period, the heyday of parliamentary enclosure, that had seen according to Hasbach, Slater, Levy and Mantoux "the agony of the yeomanry". On the contrary, Johnson found, the Land Tax evidence showed that the years between 1780 and 1802 were ones in which the numbers of the surviving small owners actually rose. Subsequently they declined again, but the weight of the evidence led him to conclude that "by far the most serious period for the small owner was at the close of the seventeenth and during the first half of the eighteenth century; in short, the period of the final transition from medieval to modern agricultural conditions; and secondly, that the changes since the middle of the eighteenth century have not been nearly so radical as they have been generally supposed to be."[1] And this expresses substantially the modern opinion.[2]

Hermann Levy's *Large and Small Holdings* was published in German in 1904, but the revised English edition did not appear until 1911, four years after Slater's *English Peasantry* and two years after the publication of Johnson's lectures. Most of Levy's book was taken up by a discussion of "The Economics of Large and Small Holdings at the Present Day", and was concerned with the viability of small farms and their efficacy as a means of checking the rural exodus. Part I of the book, however, consisted of a historical survey which began with "The Agricultural Revolution of the Eighteenth Century". To Levy the central force in the "Agricultural Revolution" of 1760–

[1] *Ibid.* pp. 139, 144–7. A similar study for the county of Oxfordshire only was carried out by H. L. Gray: "Yeoman Farming in Oxfordshire from the Sixteenth Century to the Nineteenth", *Quar. Jour. of Economics* XXIV (1909–10).

[2] See H. J. Habakkuk, "English Landownership, 1680–1740", *Econ. Hist. Rev.* X (1940); G. E. Mingay, *English Landed Society in the Eighteenth Century* (1963), pp. 94–9.

1815 was not enclosure, but the rising price of corn, which made large-scale arable farming profitable and encouraged landlords and large farmers to carry out a far-reaching reorganisation of the farming structure—"the old agricultural system had to be broken down before the new could be built up. The small farmers and peasant proprietors, and the little holdings of the cottager and labourer had to be sacrificed." Enclosure was here not the initial cause but a principal means by which the change was brought about.

Taking his evidence mainly from the contemporary pamphleteers, Levy stated that" the passion for large farms" reached its height in the early nineteenth century, "when the small holdings disappeared in hundreds to be replaced by large ones . . . The small plots of the cottagers and little farmers . . . practically vanished altogether in the course of the Napoleonic Wars.[1]" The engrossing of small farms was greatly facilitated by enclosure, and as a result "such farms, whose families had in many cases occupied the open-field holding for centuries, disappeared in hundreds." Levy was careful, however, to distinguish between the "small yeoman", whose disappearance he believed was brought about by the technical and economic superiority of the large farm, and the larger owner-occupier who already held a medium or large holding, and who prospered between 1765 and 1815. It was on the rather inadequate ground of this distinction that Levy expressly disregarded the Land Tax evidence of Johnson and H. L. Gray, claiming that very little of their material could be definitely related to the small yeoman or small freeholder.[1]

Of all these works undoubtedly the widest readership, and the most pervasive and permanent influence, were achieved by J. L. and Barbara Hammond's *The Village Labourer, 1760–1832.* This classic study appeared along with the English edition of Levy in 1911, and provided the

[1] H. Levy, *Large and Small Holdings* (Oxford, 1911), pp. 16–17, 26, 32–3, 44.

most exhaustive treatment of the period of parliamentary enclosure and the first detailed account of the procedure by which enclosure Acts were obtained and executed. Although the discussion of parliamentary enclosure made up the core of the work, there were also extended accounts of the working of the poor laws and game laws, and a heartrendingly dramatic treatment of the Labourers' Revolt of 1830. The book was of course a masterpiece, most movingly written, yet lucid, scholarly, and apparently definitive. It displayed a wide acquaintance with contemporary sources and drew on documentary material for details from a number of actual enclosures. It was, consequently, widely accepted, and established what is still for all but the specialist the accepted view of enclosure.

The Hammond's view was basically the Marxist one of expropriation and expulsion, but expanded, modified, and qualified, of course, by the detailed knowledge which they commanded. As the one very well-known work in the field, the book ran into new editions in 1913, 1920, and 1927, and has appeared in paperback form in more recent years. In the later editions the authors made some rather minor alterations in the text, and in new prefaces they also took the opportunity of dealing with some of the criticisms that had been received. But what they signally failed to do was to make any attempt to incorporate into their treatment the highly relevant findings of Johnson and Gonner, or later those of Clapham.[1] The reason for this is plain: that to have done so would inevitably have meant a very great modification of the argument and a virtual admission that their book as it stood was very far from being historically accurate.

Thus, although there was in the preface to the fourth edition a reference to Tawney's work and the early dissolution of the medieval organisation of agriculture, and although there was in the text of even the first edition a reference to Johnson in connexion with the area of land affected by enclosure, there was not in any of the editions

[1] J. H. Clapham, *Economic History of Modern Britain* I (1926), Ch. iv.

the slightest mention of Johnson's conclusions from the Land Tax evidence, and not the least acknowledgement of the balanced arguments and great sobering mass of material provided by Gonner. And no doubt it is still the case that for every reader who takes the trouble to open *Common Land and Inclosure* there are a hundred who will avidly devour *The Village Labourer*.

Yet if there is any one book which deserves to be called the standard work on enclosure by reason of the comprehensive scope of its treatment, its orderly analysis of the problem, and its sound and impartial discussion, this can only be *Common Land and Inclosure*. Indeed, so thorough was Gonner's work that it would not be too great a compliment to it to say that, in the main, the research of the fifty years since he wrote has only confirmed the soundness of his approach, filled in his framework, and amplified his conclusions.

The neglect of Gonner, perhaps, springs mainly from the very weight of his material and his refusal to formulate simple generalisations on a subject which, in truth, allows simplification only to the ignorant and unwary. In direct contrast to the Hammonds' method, he "purposely abstained from dwelling at length on the incidents of a few cases. Such a method, while it may make things more picturesque, is misleading when the instances are few out of many thousands, and not necessarily typical."[1]

Gonner, unfortunately, did not wear his learning lightly: he had neither Tawney's majestic elegance nor the Hammonds' passion and flair for the dramatic; he is as a recent writer has commented, "remarkably dull".[2] Dullness was perhaps inherent in his approach to the subject: he saw the necessity of examining enclosure in the context "of a wider economic movement, and so often a consequence rather than a cause", and Tawney agreed with his view that enclosure should be regarded as a long-term,

[1] Preface, p. vii.

[2] R. A. C. Parker, *Enclosures in the Eighteenth Century* (Historical Association Aids for Teachers series No. 7, 1960), p. 14.

continuous historical process, rather than a sudden, revolutionary change. Moreover, unlike most other writers of the period, Gonner refused to approach the subject from a one-sided or doctrinaire point of view. "To set out its results as wholly bad or wholly good seems to me quite impossible", he wrote in his preface. "Some results, indeed, are fairly clear, but they do not point uniformly in the same direction."[1]

Gonner's treatment was essentially systematic and comprehensive, but perhaps not one that made for easy comprehension on the part of the layman. Beginning with the nature of common land and how it fitted into the system of cultivation, he went on to examine the ways in which common rights were extinguished, and studied in detail the method of enclosure by Act of Parliament. On this aspect of the subject Gonner varied greatly from the Hammonds. He considered that the securing of an Act of Parliament of landowners' was by no means a foregone conclusion, and that the great landowners' influence in the appointment of commissioners to carry out the Act did not result "in substantial injustice to those possessed of legal rights . . . When the gravity and delicacy of the task undertaken by the commissioners is considered, the existence of complaint against them is not astonishing. It is rather a matter for wonder that the complaints were not far louder and universal." Provision was sometimes made for the poor, and "in a large number of awards . . . the commissioners . . . were guided by equitable as distinct from purely legal considerations. Taken as a whole the work of division and apportionment appears to have been discharged conscientiously and fairly."[2] This view has indeed been confirmed by the comprehensive work of the most thorough recent investigator, Mr. W. E. Tate.[3]

[1] P. vi.
[2] Pp. 72, 73, 82, 94–5.
[3] W. E. Tate, "Parliamentary Counter Petitions during Enclosures of the Eighteenth and Nineteenth Centuries", *Eng. Hist. Rev.* LIX (1944); "Opposition to Parliamentary Enclosure in Eighteenth-Century England", *Agricultural History* XIX (1948).

Next, in Book II, Gonner went on to discuss the complex nature of enclosure itself and the factors controlling and influencing it. He emphasised the significance of the geographical factor, the nature of the soil and the character of local topography, and he elaborated this theme in considerable regional detail for the enclosures of the eighteenth century.[1] Probably, indeed, he over-emphasised the purely physical influence of the environment, but it is certainly a factor of significance, and one whose importance has frequently been rediscovered and stressed since. Gonner pointed out that the nature of the soil, the climate, and topography, together with transport facilities and access to markets, evidently affected the date at which enclosure occurred and the type of farming which developed and in all this he recognised the key role of light soils in the spread of convertible husbandry: "Roots indeed invest light soils with a wholly new value. They seem to have become a prime feature in the movement towards the end of the seventeenth and in the early years of the eighteenth century."[2]

In dealing with the detailed course of enclosure through the centuries, Gonner noted the shifts in area and land use that were produced by changing market forces, growth of industry, and improvements in farming, but he was careful to give a balanced picture. He pointed out that the increase in sheep farming in the period 1550 to 1650 had beneficial effects as well as adverse ones, and that even in this period "there was much demand for arable products and . . . many of the inclosures, especially on the western side of the country, were 'plentiful of corn'."[3] In the seventeenth century, he contended that enclosure "proceeded steadily and over a wide area, and that a very large amount of land from being open passed into several ownership and was enclosed." In the midlands, particularly, conversion to pasture took place, but "speaking generally, the notion

[1] Pp. 115, 203–37.
[2] P. 122; see also pp. 138–40.
[3] Pp. 132–3.

that the sole aim and result of inclosure during this period was the conversion of arable to pasture must be abandoned."[1] His extended discussion of the soil influences governing the period at which land was enclosed in the eighteenth century may be thus summarised: some areas, he found, such as the red soil regions of the midlands, the fens, and dairying districts of the west, were considerably enclosed before the eighteenth century; areas of light, dry and stony soils underwent much enclosure in the eighteenth century for convertible husbandry; land lying on the water bearing strata of the lias, mainly in the west and north midlands, was much enclosed between 1760 and 1790 for pasture; and lastly the chalk uplands, ploughed up for arable, became mainly enclosed after 1790.[2]

In Book III on the effects of enclosure, the major part of the work, Gonner made his most important original contribution. He began with the elementary but essential point that whatever were the effects of enclosure of open fields, the enclosure of commons and waste could not lead to "depopulation by reducing employment, nor could it occasion a decrease in the grain supply.[3]" This distinction is of course of the first importance, and has been emphasised in recent discussions of the question of effects on population and labour supply.[4] On enclosure of open fields Gonner stressed again the relevance of soil characteristics, and particularly the possibility of introducing roots and grasses on thin loams and sandy soils.[5] He noted that some enclosures were mismanaged, so that the fields were made too small, or unsuitable methods of cultivation were followed, and he emphasised the significance for rural employment of the availability of alternative work outside agriculture.[6]

[1] Pp. 184–6.
[2] Pp. 233–7.
[3] P. 295.
[4] See, for example, J. D. Chambers, "Enclosure and Labour Supply in the Industrial Revolution", *Econ. Hist. Rev.* 2nd ser. V (1952–3), p. 333; Joan Thirsk, *English Peasant Farming* (1957), p. 263.
[5] P. 297.
[6] Pp. 298–9.

The discussion of the defects of open-field farming, which enclosure could overcome, now appears a little too unqualified in the light of recent documentary studies of seventeenth and early eighteenth-century farming.[1] But Gonner had made an exceptionally close study of contemporary authorities, and he appreciated that open-field farming was not entirely moribund: it could be improved by exchanges and consolidation of holdings, he noted, and there was some evidence of the introduction of turnips and more progressive rotations.[2] He pointed out, too, that exoneration of land from tithes was a valuable by-product of enclosure.[3]

After the careful discussion of the effects of enclosure on the quality and quantity of farm products, Gonner turned to a consideration of changes in rural society. He began with the commons and the implications for the poor of their enclosure. He had no difficulty in showing from contemporary evidence that the right to use the common was often of dubious advantage, and that in any case the legal claims to common right were compensated, if not always adequately, and that sometimes the merely customary claims were met as well.[4] He went on to make the point that, in fact, the compensation of poor men's rights under the enclosure Acts marked a definite advance over the treatment of the poor in earlier periods. "Taking the awards, the Commissioners, as a rule, seem to have given very careful consideration to the claims of the poor owners; and it seems true that the compensation given was equal in value to the rights of which they were deprived."[5] Gonner admitted that the allotments given were often too small to merit the cost of enclosure, but

[1] See, for example, W. G. Hoskins, "The Leicestershire Farmer in the Seventeenth Century", *Agricultural History* XXV (1951); Thirsk, *op. cit.* pp. 99–101; M. A. Havinden, "Agricultural Progress in Open-field Oxfordshire", *Ag. Hist. Rev.* IX (1961).

[2] Pp. 310, 319.

[3] Pp. 315–18.

[4] Pp. 360–6.

[5] P. 367.

nevertheless his interpretation was very different from that of the Hammonds.[1]

In dealing with the small farmers, Gonner neglected Johnson's Land Tax evidence and believed that there was a "steady and widespread disappearance of the small farmer, and especially of the small owner cultivating his own little farm," a view which is not nowadays accepted. Like Levy, he was impressed by the contemporary opinion on the subject, and particularly by the arguments that the landowners preferred large farms, and that the loss of commons and the heavy capital costs of enclosure proved fatal handicaps for the very small owners. Nevertheless, he appreciated that enclosure was not the only factor working in the direction of larger farms, and that there was a variety of economic and technical forces which combined to establish a secular trend in their favour. Larger farms, he noted, were appearing even "where no open field inclosure was in progress or had been in progress for a long time."[2]

Lastly, Gonner came to a detailed consideration of the effects of enclosure on employment and population. He devoted a number of pages to the question of how far there was conversion of arable to pasture in the sixteenth and seventeenth centuries, and the effects of this on employment, at that time. For the eighteenth century he argued that although there may have been some decline in arable in the midland counties, the increase in stock, especially for dairying, and the use of extra labour in cultivating grasses and turnips, suggested there could have been but little overall fall in employment.[3] He thus disagreed radically with the view of his contemporaries, Slater, Levy and the Hammonds. Testing this conclusion in the best way he could with the necessarily imprecise statistical

[1] J. L. and B. Hammond, *The Village Labourer* (4th ed. 1927), pp. 76–78.

[2] Pp. 368–74. For a discussion of this aspect see G. E. Mingay, "The Size of Farms in the Eighteenth Century", *Econ, Hist. Rev.* 2nd ser. XIV (1961–2).

[3] Pp. 396–402.

material available, he showed that there was little, if any, correspondence between the extent of enclosure and the rate of change in the population;[1] and a comparison of the extent of enclosure with poor rate expenditure showed again no close correspondence, although there was some ground for thinking that a considerable degree of enclosure tended to produce some increase in the expenditure on relief.[2] This was the cold analytical approach, the careful testing of generalised arguments by the available facts and figures, so foreign to the methods of the Hammonds, and had they taken the results into consideration, so fatal to their interpretation.

To a remarkable extent, Gonner's conclusions on population and employment have been confirmed by recent researches. Professor J. D. Chambers, in his well-known study of enclosure and labour supply, has developed further Gonner's argument that rural employment was, on balance, little affected by enclosure, and has shown the over-riding significance for rural employment of a rising population and a growing labour supply. After discussing the evidence for the survival of small owners and tenants after enclosure, and the various factors that made for increased rural employment—the improved methods of farming and increase of output, the extension of the cultivated area and the stimulus provided to country trades and industries—Chambers concludes that "the cottage-owning population continued to grow in the newly-enclosed villages, though in character and personnel it may have been very different from the cottagers of the pre-enclosure village. . . ." It was the growth of population, rather than enclosure and the agrarian changes, which created rural unemployment, increased the poor rates, and fed the migration to the expanding industries: "Since the rural population in general was unmistakably on the increase during this time, the contribution which the dispossessed made to the industrial labour force came, in the majority

[1] Pp. 411–415.
[2] P. 417.

of cases, from the unabsorbed surplus, not from the main body."[1]

Gonner's use of statistical tests, it must be said, has met with some technical objections. In particular, it has been suggested that his methods were seriously defective because the estimate of the extent of land affected by enclosure was taken mainly from the estimates in the Acts, rather than from the more reliable figures given in the awards. Further, Gonner's figures do not distinguish between open fields and common and waste land enclosed by the same Act. This means that where large areas of waste were so enclosed, the extent to which open fields disappeared may appear misleadingly large, while in counties where there was much unenclosed waste a figure for the percentage of the area of the county enclosed may under-estimate the impact on the limited districts of open-field cultivation. There is also the objection that a number of the Acts merely legalised or ratified changes previously carried out by agreement and introduced no further changes of importance.[2]

All this is true, although it should be mentioned that Gonner recognised most of these objections and pointed out that his figures should be taken only as approximations.[3] Given the immensity of the task of obtaining really accurate figures of the area enclosed by Act, and the impossibility of allowing accurately for the acreages enclosed by private agreement,[4] it is difficult to see what else he could have done, and he certainly used his admittedly imperfect figures with restraint. In any case, as Gonner fully appreciated, the local environment in which enclosure was carried out, the local circumstances of soil, markets, communications and the availability of alternative

[1] Chambers, *op. cit.* pp. 334–6.
[2] Parker, *op. cit.*, pp. 9–10.
[3] Pp. 193–5.
[4] W. E. Tate's valuable county handlists provide the most reliable information available and can be used to correct Gonner's figures, but even these are not entirely complete or accurate. See his "Parliamentary land enclosures in the county of Nottingham", *Thoroton Society Record Series* V (1935), and other references listed by W. H. Chaloner, "Recent Work on enclosure, the open fields, and related topics", *Ag. Hist. Rev.* II (1954).

employment, all greatly affected the consequences of enclosure for any particular parish. County percentages of land enclosed, he realised, must therefore be abstractions, estimates of areas enclosed under varying circumstances and with varying results, which could not really be added up. Gonner used his figures only to put against impressionistic generalisations which rested on even less secure foundations. He never supposed that his tests were absolutely conclusive,[1] and he was careful to put his figures into regional groups in order to allow for some of the more important variables. But it seems significant that, despite these weaknesses, his conclusions have stood the test of time, and that there has never been any attempt to use the more accurate acreage figures now available to challenge his findings.

Common Land and Inclosure was of course a pioneer study. It concentrated heavily on the extent, chronology, and geographical aspect of enclosure, and on its effects on population and employment. It gave relatively little attention to open-field farming and its gradual adaptation, or to the more purely social and political aspects of enclosure. In this respect the Hammonds' book, which after all was subtitled *A Study in the Government of England before the Reform Bill*, was a complementary rather than a competitive work. Gonner's analysis of the influence of markets, prices, and changes in communications was perceptive but also highly tentative, as were some other of his conclusions. None the less, it is remarkable how little of Gonner's picture needs to be changed to bring it up to date. Modern researches, for the most part, have touched in the details and made his findings more positive.[2]

[1] P. 445.

[2] The main exceptions to this are: the important recent work on open-field farming, based largely on testamentary inventories (see the works already cited by W. G. Hoskins, Joan Thirsk, and M. A. Havinden); J. D. Chambers' authoritative discussion of the relation between enclosure, population growth and labour supply, *op. cit.*; and work on the scale of the farm unit and survival of small owners, for which see J. H. Clapham, *op. cit.* ch. iv, G. E. Mingay, "The Size of Farms in the

Common Land and Inclosure thus remains a work of the first importance in its field, and still the only comprehensive general study. This reprint, it is hoped, will give a new and more numerous generation of students the opportunity of benefitting from its balanced judgment and scholarly approach to the problems of agrarian change.

October 1964 G. E. M.

Eighteenth Century", *Econ. Hist. Rev.* 2nd ser. XIV (1961–2), E. Davies, "The Small Landowner, 1780–1832, in the Light of the Land Tax Assessments", *Econ. Hist. Rev.* I (1927), and G. E. Mingay, "The Land Tax Assessments and the Small Landowner", *Econ. Hist. Rev.* XVII (1964–5).

BOOK I

COMMON AND INCLOSURE

I

COMMON

COMMON, which now is present by way of exception from the system under which land is held and worked, was once, so far as a large part of England was concerned, an essential part of agriculture and inseparable from the life of the time. It is not too much to say that its early position was in almost every way in entire contrast to the ideas associated with it in the present day. The common is comparatively rare now, but then the common and the equally important rights of common were among the usual, and in most places the necessary, circumstances of a village or a manor. Its existence now is taken as denoting the claims, somewhat vague and precarious, of the public as against those holding the land and engaged in its cultivation. But this finds no sanction in a time when over very many, if not most, cultivated districts common was a result of a claim to land, and formed a necessary condition of its proper management. The popular disuse of the term rights of common, and the circumstances of the large open tracts termed commons in the neighbourhood of towns and of the small open village greens, mark the distinction. The early rights of common were anything but vague, and were invariably vested in those employed in cultivation, or their representatives; they were anything rather than a general claim on the part of the public. The use of a common now is regarded mainly from the point of view of recreation, and when any more directly utilitarian considerations creep in they relate only to the small chance gains or casual profits which accrue to those living round the common or green, mainly to the cottagers and the poor. But in early times the common right was an essential part of agriculture, and it was only as owing to changes in circumstances this became less apparent that casual profits and gains and the so-called rights of the poor, these latter being in many instances a trespass and not a right, came to be important. Common rights, it may be repeated, were a necessary element in the agricultural system, they were involved in the ownership and cultivation of the land, and they were largely the source of the profits obtained from the land and the means of rendering its cultivation effective.

It is possible to go further and, in respect of much of the cultivated country, to treat the common as necessary to the general life as well as to the agriculture of the village or manor, since from it were obtained many of the things required both to make the home habitable and for the general purposes of living.

The common, then, so far from being an incidental or occasional feature, or a separate and auxiliary means of small gains, was an integral part of a system. What that system was has often been described. The unit of the agricultural manor was the yardland, that is, the strip or strips in the arable fields of the manor or community, but that strip was associated with the ownership of a tenement in the village, for it is only in later times that these agricultural tenements were in many instances dissociated from the necessary holding of land.

The tenants of the manor lived in houses built for the most part along the road which was the one means of connection between the village and the outer world. On each side of this, and extending in some cases for a considerable distance, were the dwellings of the tenants or cultivators destined ultimately to develop into the freeholders and copyholders. These houses, which became known to later ages as ancient tenements and in some cases as houses of husbandry, stood within or had in close contiguity, a curtilage or small courtyard, "a little croft or court or place of easement to put in cattle for a time or to lay in wood, cole, or timber." Here cattle might be secured during the winter, and here the stores, the implements, and the moveable property of the owners could be placed, and his smaller stock inclosed under his eye and kept safe from depredation of man and inclemency of weather.

Connected with the tenement was the occupation of the yardland in the arable fields, which lay near to the village. These, in later times as a rule three, were devoted to different crops in successive years, according to the course of cultivation of the manor, so that each year the crops grown on the manor were all represented, one field, however, being in fallow. In cases where there were but two fields, fallow and crop followed one another.

The possession, however, of the tenement and the yardland, that is, of the arable strips in the fields carried with it certain other definite rights. Of these the first was the occupation of a corresponding strip in the meadows or hayfield of the community. In general, these fields would lie very near to the arable fields, but as time went on and as the pressing need for such contiguity diminished or altogether passed away, the nature of the soil and the presence of water became powerful factors in determining their situation. Thus meadows, and especially water meadows, might be at some little distance. Again there was the right to a share in the inclosed pasture of the manor, where such existed. Inclosed pasture,[1] however, is a later rather than an early feature of the agricultural manor. But closely allied in their main purport to the occupation of the meadows and the share in inclosed pasture lands were the rights of common over the waste and on the lands of the manor, likewise attached to the yardland and the tenement. To understand them it is necessary to consider the circumstances both of cultivation and of the cultivator. The manor as it is

[1] Inclosed pasture in this sense must be distinguished from private pastures.

presented to us in early history is a group of houses and a small area of cultivated land surrounded on all sides by long stretches of land under little or no cultivation. The early agricultural community, no doubt, was a little band of settlers who built themselves houses and took a little land into cultivation from amidst the great wastes, marshes and forests; and though their isolation is modified by time and the growth of population with its natural increase in the number of villages or settlements, the cultivated area of the manor evidently remained for a long time partially surrounded, if not surrounded on every side, by bare commons and heaths, and by marsh and forest. This uncultivated land, whether in plain or wood, constitutes the waste. Again, by the simple agricultural methods then pursued a part of the cultivated lands lay every year in fallow, while after the crops and hay were gathered in the fields and meadows were for the rest of the year without any specific use. In the arable fields themselves the distinction between what belonged to one man and what to another was marked by lines of turf left uncultivated, and variously called meers or hades or balks or even mire-balks. On the other hand the cultivators in pursuing their arable tasks were under sundry necessities. They had to provide for their cattle required to plough and to carry, as also for the animals needed to manure their land. This need was imperative, and its satisfaction at a time when inclosed pasture was scant could only be obtained in one way. Common rights or other like rights of pasture over the land not in use for grain or hay offered the required feed. In one way such rights furnish a counterpart to the share in the hayfields, since from these latter was largely derived the means of maintaining during the winter the beasts thus required for agriculture. They came in later years to be supplemented, though at first to but a small extent, by pasture used in common and temporarily inclosed. In another way they correspond to certain other forms of common as common of estover and common of turbary, required, the one for wood to repair implements, hedges and even houses and for the supply of fuel, the other solely for the supply of fuel in the homestead.

Viewed thus the purport of common, while mainly connected with the needs of agriculture, is in general adapted to the wider and more general needs of the cultivator living from and on the land. It provides the necessary means of carrying on arable cultivation and makes this provision from the use of lands other than those immediately under crop. It enables the supply of fuel and of wood for this and other purposes, and must have undergone important extension on account of the sheep which yielded the wool wanted for clothing.

The nature of common rights and the mode in which they were exercised, require description. Closely resembling the strict common rights were other rights, often reciprocal and joint rather than common, originating in the same or like necessities, employed under like conditions, and ultimately treated as these in ordinary practice if not in law. For the sake of convenience the one word common is often used to include these.

Common is "a right which one or more persons have to take or use some portion of that which another's soil produces." It is a right to part of the profits of the soil, and to part only, the right to the soil lying with another and not with the person who claims common. But this definition, while no doubt accurate in respect of common at the time when it became the subject of legal discussion and decision in the later middle ages and in more modern times, needs careful explanation so far as its original conditions are concerned. The position of early common is best seen by its treatment in the pages of Bracton, where it is regarded as a servitude imposed upon certain land. Its particular character as a servitude, as has been pointed out by later writers, enables it to be broadly distinguished from other servitudes as rights of way and the like by the feature present in its case of the enjoyment by those in whose favour it is, of part of the profits. But as it is a servitude imposed on land so it seems to be at this time a servitude attached almost invariably, if not invariably, to land. In other words it is the feature attached to the possession of certain lands of having rights over some part of the yield of other lands, in most cases over the lord's waste.

Common may be distinguished according to its kind into Common of Pasture, Common of Estover, Common of Turbary, Common of Piscary, and other miscellaneous rights of common.

Matters falling under the last two headings, while often of considerable interest, are not of much importance from a practical point of view. Their existence, however, throws some light upon the origin or early history of common. Far more attention is due to the rights of Estover and Turbary, as these serve to indicate the place of common as essential to the general life and well-being of a manorial community. Still even these sink into practical insignificance beside common rights of Pasture.

In common rights of pasture can be traced best the varying development of common from the early days when its place in the agricultural system and its relation to the occupation of arable land was generally accepted to the time when in response to the need of change it became a right severed from arable farming, and so a source of separate and incidental gain. Between these extremes occur many stages leading by slow gradations from the former into the latter. The prevalence of common pasture of the first type in the early manor is put beyond doubt by the particular form which it assumes in *Common Appendant*, one of the forms adopted in the legal classification of common rights. Such common appendant was the right in the freehold tenants of the manor, existing independent of grant or of proof by usage, of feeding their beasts used in agriculture upon the lord's waste. This right was universally assumed in the case of all original manors, existing, that is, before the statute of *Quia Emptores*, and was held to be a necessary part of their tenure. The claim to it was in virtue of their position as freeholders of the ancient manor and did not require to be proved either by deed or by prescriptive usage. It was thus regarded as a universal element in their tenure. It originates clearly in the early stage of the agricultural society, when, owing to the scarcity of inclosed pasture, a tenant would otherwise have found himself without sufficient pasture for his beasts when the crops were in the ground. Its strict relation to agriculture is without doubt. It was held to attach to arable land only, and it was only for beasts required in its cultivation. When claimed, as it subsequently was, as appendant to a cottage or other tenement, the claim if allowed was allowed on the presumption that the possession of such betokened or had betokened the possession of a yardland. The separation was the incident of time and the mark of the decadence of the early and strict common field system. Even when the ancient arable came, as in some cases, to be converted into pasture, the common appendant still remained attached to the land on account of its original character. Thus in theory at any rate it could not be detached from the ancient arable or from the sign of such as a cottage. Again, it is restricted to beasts used in agriculture, that is, oxen and horses to plough, and sheep and cows to manure the soil in conjunction with these. A further point is as to the number of beasts for which such common right existed. In theory, and doubtless in ancient practice, it was limited to those required for the purpose, and it would seem probable that in any suits for its recovery or assurance, such were to be ascertained by comparison and admeasurement both of the arable lands entitled to such common in the waste and latterly of the waste or lands over which the rights were claimed as such diminished. But when further definition was required, the test used was that of the beasts *levant and couchant* on the inclosed land, or to put the matter still more simply, the number which that inclosed land and its product would maintain during the winter. Lastly, it was right of common in only the lord's waste or lands.

The historical importance of this kind of common rests rather in its more general existence in connection with the freehold arable tenure than in any superior antiquity which it may possess as compared with other kinds of common necessarily connected with or appertaining to landed possession. These may possibly have been in certain cases of very early origin, but they were not so universal as to be assumed without proof by way of grant or prescriptive usage. They were thus not involved to the same extent in the origin of the agricultural society.

Such other rights of pasture which attached to land are legally known as *Common Appurtenant.* Such common affects large classes whose common rights cannot be deemed so ancient or so universal or so exclusively agricultural as those which have been described. It originates, it may be pointed out, by grant or by peaceful, uninterrupted and known usage, and could be proved either by deed or by prescription. Thus it occurs in the case of freehold tenures on manors created subsequently to the statute *Quia Emptores*, and includes agricultural beasts. But it extends much further. It includes common held by copyhold tenants of the manor or by others to whom it may be granted. Again it extends to beasts other than those necessarily used in agriculture, forming a marked contrast in this respect to the former kind of common. For whilst that was for beasts to plough and compester the land, this extends to others, and is largely for sheep, swine, goats, and even geese. This difference is a natural one, inasmuch as it is a matter of grant made to the tenant or another for his advantage, and so it may vary according to his circumstances. But in respect of number for which the right is enjoyed there are interesting points of resemblance and contrast. It was either for a number limited by those levant and couchant or actually fixed, and it is said " ought not to be enjoyed by any proprietor with more cattle than are proportionate to each piece of land." When made without number (*sans nombre*) it was usually assumed that this left the number not unlimited, but unlimited save in so far as a limit was held to be naturally imposed by the presumption of winter maintenance or of those *levant and couchant.* But this was not invariable, as in some cases this rule was definitely set aside so far as maintenance from the land to which the grant was attached was concerned. In any case it would seem that in contrast to the rule in the case of common appendant when the needs of the holding were interpreted in this particular way, here the terms *levant and couchant* rather imply the extreme advantage which might be made of the grant. Even this lost much of its importance in the case of grantees holding other lands or when the usage grew of killing and salting down stock before winter. When the grant was made for a definite number it could be attached to a dwelling-house or cottage without land. But the origin in grant or specific and acknowledged permission as shown by undisturbed usage, the greater latitude as to numbers, the partial severance from the land and from any definite agricultural purpose open the way to the more complete severance of later times, to the grant to strangers wholly without land in the manor and to the emergence of *Common in Gross.* The fixing of the number leads to yet another consequence wholly alien to the original purport of common, namely, the use of the common for sheep and beasts not belonging to those who possessed the right of common. This which might sometimes occur for the sake of preventing a right of common from falling into disuse, however temporary, could hardly be gainsaid when the grant was for a specified number. Under such circumstances it could not be to the detriment of the other proprietors or of the lord, whilst it was to the obvious advantage of the tenants on whose behalf the grant was made.

Common rights thus made might be limited in respect of time as well as place and quantity. They might be restricted whilst land was temporarily inclosed on the demesne for hay, or even it would seem while it was used by the lord for other purposes. Thus on the lord's lands tenants might have their right of common on hay inclosures after such time as the hay was carried during the autumn and winter. Common granted in general terms on the manor was further limited by reasonable assumption even if not in actual words. It could not be exercised, for instance, in orchards or on the gardens or curtilages, or in the recognised arable under crop.

With the foregoing must be placed the common which arose from the reciprocal action of the tenants. This was of different kinds. After the hay harvest the fences were thrown down, and the proprietors were entitled to drive in their commonable beasts to feed till in the spring it became necessary once more to fence for hay. When a proprietor had strips of meadow definitely assigned, such a common was due to mutual agreement extending to very early times. Similarly common of shack, as it was called, or the right of letting the beasts of the proprietors go at liberty or go shack in the arable fields after the corn was harvested, arose from a mutual agreement. The nature of the common right thus created has been the subject of much discussion. Its probable origin lay in the impossibility of each proprietor in the common arable field restricting his own beasts to his own unfenced strip. Hence arose a common almost, as it would seem, of vicinage,[1] where there is a mutual agreement to disregard trespass. By custom such a common became very similar in nature to the other common necessarily attaching to the possession of such land.[2]

[1] There were certain differences, since while common by vicinage might be and often was over waste, common of shack is held to be limited to arable or to arable and meadow. Elton, *Commons*, p. 72, Woodrych, p. 59. That certain claims of common might be over arable is clear from Britton, Book II., xxvi. 4, according to which a tenant resisting claim might say, "the soil is his several, which he may plough or enclose at his pleasure and at all times keep enclosed."

[2] In Corbet's case it was held that common of shack might become by custom common appurtenant. Coke's *Reports*, vii. 5a. (Ed. 1826, iv. p. 57.)

Closely connected with such common rights were other rights which, though differing in origin and legal aspect, were akin to them in their general economic result. Like them they enforce the necessity of common action, and bar by their existence the assertion of separate and diverse individual interests. Like them, too, they take their rise in a state of society when and where arable was the important interest, and when provision was made for adequate pasture by claims, servitudes and reserved rights. Among such must be ranked the rights of pasture existing on Lammas or half-year lands, where the possession of the herbage was really separate from the possession of the crops.[1] Here, there is considerable diversity of usage; the land, after the crop was gathered, being given in some cases to certain persons as well strangers as those who have a right to the crop, while in other cases these latter are specifically excluded. Again the cattle gaits or stints existing in a pasture, not in the waste, served a similar purpose to the rights of common. The herbage was owned[2] by a certain number of persons having stints or limited rights, the lord of the manor, if amongst them, being equally stinted with his tenants or any others. But these rights, so far from appertaining to the land or being common are really freehold or copyhold property and capable of being transferred as such. With the growth of inclosed pasture they became of increasing importance, and the agricultural villages of later centuries had, in very many cases, their separate pasture or closes or leys appropriated to different beasts, as cows, horses, and sheep, and held by the tenant cultivators in their various stints. They are, however, of importance rather in later than in early times. Lastly, there were in sundry

[1] This is the view laid down in law and in legal text-books. Lammas fields recognised 2 and 3 Vict., c. 62 § 13. They were so-called because generally open from Lammas Day (1st August) till Lady Day next (Elton, p. 36). "The Lammas Lands of Middlesex are generally laid up to be mowed on the 5th of April, and are common again on August 12th"; *Agric. Survey Middlesex* (by Peter Foot, 1794).

[2] Elton, *Commons*, p. 64.

cases certain and by no means valueless rights reserved to the lords or gradually acquired by them. Two are sufficiently important to require particular mention. On the one hand there is the right of sheep walk, which gave the lord of the manor the sole right of feeding sheep over the lands, or certain lands, of the tenants during certain seasons of the year, as from Michaelmas to Lady Day. This right was sometimes farmed out to flock-masters. On the other hand, in certain districts, chiefly in Norfolk and Suffolk, there existed the right of foldage, or freefold, or the privilege of having the flocks of the tenants folded in the demesne fields for the sake of their manure.[1]

In addition to the pasturage rights for cattle and other animals, there were some rights, of herbage, as it were, which might be granted to and enjoyed by the tenants of the manor in respect of other products to be used, often for the food of beasts, as nuts, acorns, mast and even flowers. Of these pannage and the right of mast were obviously the most frequent and the most valuable. By means of these swine could be kept. In some other cases litter, it may be surmised, was provided. But rights of these kinds were not assumed as usual, and in Fitz Herbert's time, at any rate, had to be proved either by direct grant or by usage implying such, "for there is no man that can claim to have the mast, which is a fruit, save the lord, except his free tenants have it by special words in his deed."[2]

Common of estover was a right of common to take wood from the waste or forests of the manor for sundry purposes, some directly connected with agriculture, others with the general mode of life of the tenant or other person enjoying the privilege. It was of the following kinds. Plough bote was the privilege of taking timber and other wood for the repair of carts, ploughs, and other instruments of husbandry. Hedge bote or hay bote related to the

[1] Importance of fold courses was great. It is emphasised and its method described. *Book of Husbandry*, Sloane MSS., 3815, f. 127.

[2] Fitz Herbert, *Surveying*, p. 19.

wood needed for the repair of gates, or for erecting and mending the fences of the curtilage or required for the temporary inclosures needed in the hay meadows or even in the open arable fields in some instances. Lastly, there was the house bote, which was of two kinds, the greater, which gave the right to timber for repairs or even for rebuilding of a tenement, provided that the new building was the mere reproduction of that previously existing, and not by way of general extension; and the less for taking sticks, tops, and clippings for fuel. Of the antiquity of this right to share in the wood of the manor there is no doubt, even though a lack of universality be held to deprive it of the character assigned to it by some, as an inherent or appendant right of common in the case of the freehold tenants of the ancient manor. It was, however, obviously exercised under considerable restrictions as to time, and as a matter of course as to the parts of the waste whence it might be taken. But it was further restricted as to amount, in early times, to "reasonable estovers," that is, in proportion either to the requirements of the tenant for his agricultural purposes or to the size of his house and the repairs reasonably required to make it habitable. It is only with the progress of time that it becomes defined as consisting of a certain quantity, till when it is obviously a right of common pertaining to an agricultural tenement as a common appurtenant, and incapable of separation from it.

Common of turbary was the right of cutting peat or turf for fuel; and is similar in its incidents to those occurring with regard to common of estover. Like it, it is restricted as to place; like it, too, it was to be exercised to an extent corresponding to the needs of the house; and, like it, it comes to be a right of common for an actual amount, and so able to be separated from a tenement, and to be held as a common in gross.

The other and miscellaneous rights of common to which reference has been made, whilst like those already described in many of their characteristics, and especially in their legal tenure, are different in other respects, and more particularly by reason of their occasional nature. They correspond to particular circumstances, and so cannot be taken as entering into the necessary system of life, or as being an inseparable element from the main occupation upon which depends the life of the people. Even common of piscary, important though it was under certain circumstances, and finding its origin in the needs of the tenants for the sustenance of the family, was rather the source of additional gain than a part of the chief means of livelihood. It added to the comfort of life, but it was no condition of living. The like may be said of common of fowling, common of warren, and of such other common rights as those to take or dig sand, gravel, stones and clay, or even to mine in certain parts of the manor. Rights such as these grew up where special circumstances pointed to them as of particular advantage, and on the analogy of the main common rights which existed, they too came to be enjoyed in common. They do not form part of the general system of common in the country.

The main common rights, that is of pasture, estover and turbary, the incidents resulting from or associated with common, and even in some instances the miscellaneous rights of common, are alike in two important economic respects. Taken together they supply the means whereby the system of cultivation was maintained, the wants of the tenants other than those met by the product of the arable and the meadow were supplied, and full use made both of the waste and of the land in cultivation at such time as the crops were not in the ground. Again they compose an intricate mesh of mutual privileges and obligations, which at once gave permanence and stability to the system of cultivation and rendered its alteration and improvement difficult. They affect, as has been said, the village society both in its work and in its life. Altogether in the case of common appendant and to a large extent in the case of other common, they supply the means or the conditions whereby the ploughing, manuring, and other agricultural acts are carried on. Further, they furnish in large measure the meat which is eaten, the wool which is woven, the wood required, and the fuel for heat and cooking in the homestead.

Nor are we left without indication of the method in which they were enjoyed. Thus we hear[1] of the cattle going before the herdsman in numbers proportioned to their holdings or subsequently stinted, the herdsman receiving 2d. a quarter for each beast and the swineherd 1d., to feed upon the waste or fields lying open. When the crops are cut, even in cases where some tenants have enclosed their strips or plots, the beasts entitled to common are driven over the fields and into the parts inclosed, the bars or gates being opened for this purpose.[2] It is an advantage, it is said, to plough with horses rather than oxen, since the former can be tethered on the balks or meers to get their feed.[3] Some proprietors indeed are accused of lengthening the ropes or tethers so that the scant grass might be augmented by mouthfuls of the grain belonging to neighbours in the open fields. In the lord's outwoods the tenants have bite of mouth, in return for which it is urged the lord, unlike the tenants, should not be stinted in the number of beasts which he might send in.[4] Again, some land might be rented for common, or rather joint, use; thus in Elizabeth's reign the inhabitants of Lowestoft kept their sheep on the Deans, evidently lying open, by their private shepherd, for which they paid an acknowledgement of 6s. 8d.[5]

[1] Fitz Herbert, *Book of Husbandry*, c. 123. (Engl. Dialect Soc., 1882, p. 77.)

[2] This is the point raised in Corbet's case, *v.* supra. It is clear that an ancient inclosure might be free of shack.

[3] This noted as desirable where there is no several pasture (Fitz Herbert, *Husbandry*, p. 15).

[4] Fitz Herbert (*Surveying*, p. 11) enumerates three kinds of common: (1) where there is a common close where each man is stinted, (2) a tended common open to the common field where the cattle go before the herdsman, also stinted, (3) the lord's outwoods. *History of Witney*, by A. J. Giles, gives an instance of a common at Gold Clift, etc., where, in 1647, after 22 Sept., the lord is to put in his cattle in the morning if he pleases and the tenants in the afternoon.

[5] Suckling, *History of Suffolk*, ii. p. 5.

While the above description applies, at any rate in its main outlines, to a great part of the country, there were not only large regions, but also considerable tracts scattered through the land, where an early open field system was little in evidence. Thus in the so-called forest districts, whether woodland or moor, common when it came to exist was very different, being in the main somewhat general pasture and other rights participated in by the various neighbouring townships. Again on the west the open field system is of comparatively infrequent occurrence; and much the same may be said of large parts of the north.[1]

But even apart from such districts there is evidence as to the great diversity of usage characterising the position of commons during the late years of the middle ages; with the beginning of more modern times, with inclosure and in some cases no doubt on account of the growing unsuitability of the system to the altered needs and in others from ignorance of the real purport of the common, diversity from the original type and variation increased.

Despite this, however, so deeply was this feature ingrained in the method of cultivation and in the daily habits of life that it continued as the system under which much of the country was farmed in the eighteenth century. Though a large portion of the land was withdrawn by inclosure and though much land taken from the waste or from a wild state was added to the cultivated area, this method of agriculture was of remarkable permanence and fully recognised.

The description of the township of Pickering[2] in Yorkshire as it was in the early part of the eighteenth century supplies a sketch of a parish which was thoroughly typical

[1] As to such districts; Marshall, *On the Appropriation and Inclosure of commonable and intermixed lands*; also Book II., Appendix E. "Inclosure from the wild state," and in general Book II., Chapter I.

[2] Marshall, *Yorkshire*, i. 48, etc. After this description some account is given of the progress of inclosure in this parish and district prior to date, *i.e.* 1783-87. According to this, inclosure occurred in three ways: (1) by exchanges and transfers in some common fields and common meadows, (2) by private agreements or commissions in case of stinted meadows, (3) by Act.

of the open field system as it existed at that time. In Pickering there were two hundred and sixty common right houses or sites of houses, which retained some rights, though in the process of time they had become separate from any necessary connection with a share in the arable open fields. These, which comprised in all 2,376 acres, lay in two lots, one on each side of the brook which divided the township. Each lot consisted of three fields for the unvarying round of wheat or other grain, beans or some like product, and fallow. They were divided into oxgangs, distributed in such a way that every occupier might have similar shares. The oxgangs on one side of the brook comprised 24 acres, those on the other only 12. Each division had its common meadow laid up for hay, of which each occupier of an ox gang had his due share. Then there were stinted pastures which appertained wholly to those holding common field land, each having in proportion to his oxgang a limited number of cattle *gaits* for cows and working oxen. Further, each had a right of common for sheep or cattle.

At the end of that century, or rather in the early years of the nineteenth century, we have a good picture of the same system in Rothwell in Northampton.[1] "The parish of Rothwell is supposed to contain about 3,000 acres, of which 600 acres may be inclosures near the town; and 2,400 acres open land in three district fields of about 800 acres each; these fields contain a considerable breadth of grass land never in tillage; for the sake of round numbers I will suppose 600 acres of arable land in each field and 200 acres of grass land. The nature of the soil varies from a brown or snuff-coloured to a reddish brown light loam, more or less tenacious; some inclined to sandy and others more loamy. About one-third of the whole is also a grey or darker coloured loam, stronger or more tenacious than the red land; in the familiar dialect the former is called the red land, the other the black land. . . . The course of the cropping is thus: of the fields one is always in fallow or turnips and two in crops. The fallow

[1] *Agric. Report, Northampton* (1809), pp. 64-68.

field is thus conducted: about one-half of the red land is annually surrounded with a temporary fence of coppice underwood and fallowed for turnips, the other half of the red land being fallowed for wheat, and this alternately, the course upon the red land being,—1, turnips; 2, barley; 3, promiscuous crops at the pleasure of the occupier, beans, peas, barley, rye, oats, or vetches; 4, fallow for wheat; 5, wheat; 6, promiscuous crops as before and then turnips again.

"The black land is invariable in the course, (1) fallow, (2) wheat, (3) beans or other pulse or grain....

"Grain is sometimes grown in the inclosed land, but in no great quantity: no clover or grass seeds sown in the open field. A large live stock is kept as follows....

"The common field is occupied in what are called yard-lands.... The parish consists of about eighty yardlands, each comprehending about thirty acres of the common field with a right of pasturage for four heads and a half of cattle and twenty-four sheep to every yardland. The cattle are kept in distinct herds, of about a hundred and eighty in each, and pastured on different sides of the parish, attended each by a herdsman and assistant.... They are driven home at night through the summer, separated to each one his own, confined in yards or home closes during the night and sent out again in the morning to pasture in the grass lands of the common field. After harvest they are left at large in the common field till wheat seed time. Notwithstanding the attendance of the herdsman, depredations upon the skirts of the corn are sometimes committed.... The sheep attached to the common field consist of one thousand nine hundred and twenty, or twenty-four to every yardland. These graze promiscuously in the grass plots of the fallow fields."

Like pictures might be furnished from many districts, as for instance from the country surrounding Royston[1] where we hear of villages as "being groups of a few inclosures and wood, with houses and a steeple and surrounded by the

[1] *Annals of Agriculture*, iv. p. 145.

common fields"; or from Stewkley[1] in Buckinghamshire, where the three field system held sway, "with roads very difficult for a stranger to distinguish, having no characteristical mark, distinct from drift ways to the different properties in the field"; or from Wilts[2] where the yardlands vary in amount in different parts of the district; or to choose a later instance from Cambridgeshire, where of the fields one was in a uniform crop, another cultivated according to the owner's wish, and the last lay "a vast open pasture."[3]

In each of the above descriptions, while the general outline of the ancient system is preserved, certain later features, by no means uniform in every case, present themselves. Thus we find attempts at separate cultivation according to the individual desire of the tenant, and the use of turnip husbandry as at Rothwell. But more important and more common is the disassociation between the ancient houses and the arable strips which is seen very clearly in many cases. Though by no means invariable, and though in practice often counteracted by the two being separately held by the same occupier, this severance was important in divers ways. It led, as we know, in some

[1] "Stewkley is a village of farmers and labourers, upon an eminence, surrounding one of the completest and best specimens of a Saxon church to be seen in this island, environed by three extended fields, the one fallow, the second wheat, and the third beans, etc." *Agric. Report, Buckingham* (1810), p. 358.

[2] *Agric. Report, Wiltshire* (1813), p. 15, etc. This refers to South or South-East Wilts.

[3] *Notes and Queries*, Third Series, vol. iii. p. 28 (1863). Within the memory of the writer of the passage "The parish or manor mainly consisted of three large tracts, all uninclosed. The first, arable, was required by custom to be cultivated in each year in one stated kind of crop. The second, also arable, might be cropped according to the various owners' pleasure. The third, a vast open pasture, owned in various and rather small portions, which were cut yearly by each owner for hay; but the whole grazed in common of pasture by the cattle of all the commoners between appointed days.

"There were besides ancient homesteads or sites of such, each conferring a right of common. The number I forget, it was some multiple of 4—say 48; and there were also just as many ancient enclosures, four acres each, of old pasture as there were common rights."

cases to legal disputes as to the common rights respectively enjoyed by the ancient tenements and the lands; it marks the dissolution of the necessary connection between the common and arable; and it stands in no distant relation to the general claim to common rights raised by those who dwelt near a common or even by the general public. It was part of the attempt to adapt the common right system to a time when agriculture and rural life was no longer uniform or necessarily based on arable cultivation.

This is not the place to discuss the extent to which the open field system, with its concomitant rights of common, predominated or existed in different parts of the country but the illustrations selected come from such different counties as Yorkshire, South Wilts, Cambridge, Bucks Northampton, and Hertford, and could easily be supplemented[1] to show that (whether widely practised or not) this system was at any rate in its general features a recognised system in the country at large, and not merely a local survival in a particular district.

Its leading features, often indeed marked by some variation, either by way of adaptation or by reason of ignorance of their original import, find frequent mention in contemporary records.

The farmhouses, barns, and curtilages[2] occupied by the cultivators of open fields still lie close together in villages. At Naseby, we are told, "these open fields are very inconvenient farms on account of distance as well as want of contiguity. The farmhouses and barns are all in the village, which is two miles from a great part of the

[1] *Agric. Report, East Riding* (1812), p. 92, of the villages of the wolds. Stone, *Suggestions*, p. 7, dealing with open field cultivation on clay and good lands.

[2] Stone, *Suggestions*, p. 5. "There are but very few parishes (generally speaking) considered as totally uninclosed, or in an open field state, which have not a cluster of small pieces of inclosure near or adjoining to the farmhouses in their respective parishes, by way of homestead, or stowages, for cattle employed in the cultivation of the land; or which are not applied to the purposes of shelter and for the convenience of foddering cattle and sheep in inclement seasons."

field."[1] In Gloucester a distinction was drawn between the manor or "court" farms,[2] which "are very entire and lie well round the homesteads. But farmhouses in general stand in villages." This fact is noted elsewhere as indicating their early erection;[3] as being a necessary consequence of common cultivation;[4] and as not taking place in new inclosures.[5] A like distance separated the meadows from the village farmhouses.[6]

The arable fields were large, sometimes very large indeed, as between Wantage and Wallingford, where Arthur Young saw "a sandy field, an open one, more than two miles across" with such crops,[7] and often marked with very high ridges, the result of immemorial ploughing and of common cultivation;[8] the strips in them being freehold, copyhold, or let out in leases[9] of varying length, or even let without lease for a time determined by custom.[10] These strips were in some few cases interchangeable,[11] but

[1] *Annals of Agriculture*, vi. 464.

[2] Marshall, *Rural Economy of Gloucestershire*, i. 49.

[3] *Agric. Report*, *Worcester*, p. 19.

[4] *Agric. Report*, *Middlesex* (1798), p. 40.

[5] *Agric. Report*, *Nottingham* (1798), p. 9.

[6] *Agric. Report*, *Oxford* (1813), p. 205.

[7] *Annals of Agriculture*, vi. 139.

[8] This most noticeable in strong soils and attributed to a belief that by such means land was rendered drier. *Agric. Report*, *Leicester* (1809), p. 89: On strong lands in Leicester, and particularly in ancient common fields, ridges much broader and higher, *i.e.* one to three feet deep in hollows. *Oxford* (1813), p. 103: Very high ridges in some of the old open fields. *East Riding* (1812), p. 109: "Formerly the arable land in the open common fields, where each occupier seldom possessed more than one or two contiguous lands or ridges, was raised remarkably high by continually ploughing towards the middle either with the view of keeping the soil and manure from the neighbouring ridges or from the mistaken motive, that the land would in moist situations be thus rendered drier." *Gloucester* (1807), 103.

[9] Marshall, *Rural Economy of Gloucester*, i. 20-21; *Agric. Report*, *Wilts* (1813), pp. 31, 167; *Agric. Report*, *Worcester*, p. 38.

[10] As to custom, *A. R.*, *Worcester*, p. 38.

[11] *Agric. Report*, *Lincoln* (1799), p. 21; *Oxford* (1813), p. 205; *Notes and Queries*, Third Series, iii. 28, at Over.

this probably was not frequent at so late a period. The course of cultivation, which depended on the number of fields, was usually a rotation of either three or four years. When four field the course as a rule was fallow, wheat, beans or pease or oats, barley. When three field it consisted of two crops and a fallow, the crops as a rule being wheat and barley or beans. In many counties the eighteenth century records the transition from the three to the four field system. Thus in Nottingham,[1] "The old way in Oxton fields was the usual one of two crops and a fallow, there being only three fields. In consequence of the act for the cultivation of common fields of 1773, they have now sown broad or red clover with their wheat or barley (except a few who chose to have their old crop of pease and beans the next year)." To admit of this one of the old fields was divided into two. The attempt to introduce turnips led sometimes to a more extended and varied course, as may be seen from the instance of Rothwell.[2]

The meadow and pasture were, in some districts at any rate, duly proportioned to the arable;[3] a relation ordinarily observed in the possession of common rights where such were attached to land at all. Thus in Yorkshire we are told of the right of pasture and of common associated with arable for the stock necessary to the land. But, of course, with the growth of inclosed pasture and the severance of ancient houses from the arable, the observance of this through the right of commonage for as many beasts as could be maintained through the winter was no longer possible. Still, in general, this measure was understood to exist,[4] the difficulty in its application arising in cases where the summer rights of pasture were such that each owner

[1] *Agric. Report, Nottingham*, (1798), p. 37.

[2] Cf. *Agric. Report, Rutland* (1808), p. 49, as to courses in open fields at North Luffenham.

[3] Thus in Worcestershire: "In our unenclosed hamlets the meadow and pasture are fairly proportioned to the arable." *Agric. Report*, p. 56. Cf. *Observations on a pamphlet entitled an Enquiry into the advantages and disadvantages resulting from Bills of Enclosure*, 1781, pp. 9-10.

[4] See *Observations*, pp. 9-10.

strove to obtain in some way or other as much winter fodder as could be procured from any source. In the laws and orders of the Mendip miners it was provided "that the commoners of Mendip should turn out their cattle at their outlets as much the summer as they be able to winter," a right which in Westmorland made it "a principal object" with every occupier "to provide for them plenty of winter food."[1] Some, after putting cattle on the common in summer, sold them before winter.[2] In other cases, we are told, they managed as best they could in the winter.[3] This difficulty, which it may be surmised was the original cause of stinted commons, is here seen in operation: As many beasts are put on the common as possible and winter food procured in all possible ways, with the result that the common is overstocked. The reasonable conclusion, which was affirmed in a case tried at the York Assizes in 1795, was that the number, in addition to its relation to summer feed, must also be proportioned according to the size and power of the common,[4] a decision carrying out the proposition laid down by Bracton. At Beccles in Suffolk[5] both stinted and unstinted commons existed "and even the rated are overstocked." Speaking broadly, it may be said that where the open field system was maintained in good order a definite restriction on numbers had been introduced, and all the rights of herbage were duly attached to arable lands. A yardland in some parts included, as it were, a number of what were called cattle gaits; in other parts they were stinted to what was called a *lease*,[6] but the rule of limitation by number was observed. Where, however, no such method had come to be adopted the common was actually unlimited, since the ancient methods once employed of

[1] *Agric. Report, Somerset* (1798), p. 23.; *Westmoreland*, p. 314.

[2] *Agric. Report, Bedford* (1808), p. 224.

[3] *Agric. Report, Bedford* (1808), p. 224; *Essex* (1807), i. p. 166.

[4] *Agric. Report, North Riding* (1800), p. 200.

[5] *Agric. Report, Suffolk*, p. 149.

[6] *Agric. Report, Dorset* (1815), p. 171.

restriction according to beasts levant or couchant or to winter feed had become inapplicable under the new conditions.[1] In many parts of the country land in great quantities still lay in sheep walk, as in Norfolk at the beginning of the eighteenth century,[2] a condition which gave way as improvements progressed. Connected with it, as indeed with common in general, were curious and particular individual privileges. In one parish in Suffolk the chief proprietor, who had two-thirds of the whole property, had "a right of sheep walk over the whole parish, except about 40 acres."[3] At Ferraby in Lincoln Sir John Nelthorpe had the right to turn in horses in the common meadows saved for hay.[4] But in general the rights were reciprocal, and regulated in cases where custom admitted of change, by common agreement.[5]

[1] Young, *Eastern Counties*, i. 469, etc.; *Agric. Report, Gloucester* (1807), 104-5; *Suffolk*, p. 149; *Westmoreland*, p. 321.

[2] Young, *Eastern Tour*, ii. 150, etc.

[3] *Annals of Agriculture*, ii. 449.

[4] *Agric. Report, Lincoln* (1799), p. 21. Cf. Marshall, *Rural Economy of the West of England*, ii. 135, as to commons where the lord and his tenants have rights over commons, the other freehold lands being without rights. Cf. *Agric. Report, Suffolk*, p. 9. Rights of foldage often a matter of special grant: good instances given, Cullum, *History of Hawsted*, p. 92; *Notes and Queries*, Seventh Series, x. 250. Some curious and interesting rights had been the subject of grant in early times. Cullum, *History of Hawsted*, mentions right *apri et verris*, sometimes *tauri et apri*; Thoroton, *Notts*, right of bull and boar at Keyworth "free to go and eat in the corn, meadows, or any other place in the said town." Probably a reference to the common ownership of such animals; thus Googe, *Four Books of Husbandry*, p. 122, "In some places they have common bulls and common boares in every town."

[5] Thus privilege or permission to make temporary inclosures. Elton, *Commons*, 277. *Agric. Report, Cornwall* (1794), 56: Tenants allowed to break up furze crops for a crop or two of agriculture. *Nottingham* (1794), as to similar action in Forest of Sherwood. Collins' *History of Somerset*, iii. 586, gives an interesting account of the lot or dole meadows at Congresbury. In Congresbury were two large pieces of common land, called dole-moors, divided into single acres, each bearing a peculiar and different mark cut in the turf, as a horse, a hare, etc. On a certain day in the year, the proprietors and their tenants assembled on the common; a number of apples were marked in the same way as the acres aforesaid, and then distributed to the commoners

Of incidents closely connected in practice with the exercise of common right of pasture there were many. Meers and balks were still in grass, sometimes fed off by cattle but often of little value.[1] The beasts, either as to kind and number or ownership, could be determined by a majority of the occupiers or proprietors, or by the lord of the manor with consent of his tenants or homage.[2] Curious cases of usage occur, as at Kidlington where "the cow common is a horse common, after harvest till 5th November, then the sheep and cows go in common meadows and stubbles."[3] At Charnwood, the small commoners and cottages enjoyed a common of fern, "they had their fern harvest, at which the fern was gathered and burnt to make ash balls."[4] The parish flockmaster acted in places as of old.[5]

Turbary was still a well recognised common right, as may be seen from the provision made in its place by the

from a bag. After the distribution, each repaired to his allotment and took possession for the ensuing year. Cf. somewhat similar custom, *History of Brampton*, by Rev. J. A. Giles, 1848, pp. 79-80. Dole meadows frequently occur in Awards, etc.

[1] In some cases, land might be in common field without balks: thus round Toringhoe in Bucks, "no rein," *i.e.* acre rein, "between the lands." They were separated by water furrow: Kahn's *Account of his Visit to England*, tr. by J. Lucas, 1892, p. 266. According to the author of *An Inquiry into the connection between the present price of provisions and the size of farms, etc.* (1773), p. 87, land in balk was largely wasted: "balks are of different widths, from two to sixteen feet; they are never ploughed, but are kept in grass under pretence of their being common field pasture. They are literally of no benefit to either the occupier or the Poor; for they are too narrow either to mow, or to graze without a boy to attend to each beast with a halter; and when the corn is off them, their grass is too old to feed; nor ought the common field to be kept open till it is consumed, for that must prevent putting in wheat in the proper season and is a total prohibition of turnips and cabbages."

[2] *History of Tottenham*, by William Robinson, i. 139-141, vestry determines rights of common, etc. Cf. T. Faulkner, *Chelsea*, i. 74; *History of Hertford*, by Lewis Turner; *History oj Hampstead*, pp. 130, 131; *Agric. Report, Leicester*, 283.

[3] *Agric. Report, Oxford* (1813), 231-2.

[4] *Charnwood Forest*, by T. R. Potter, p. 23.

[5] *Agric. Report, Hertford* (1804), 75.

Inclosure awards.[1] On the other hand the general rights of Estover, once of such great importance, find little mention[2] except so far as connected with fuel. Miscellaneous and other minor rights find place in accounts and records, but they play an unimportant part; even the right of fishing or piscary, formerly so highly prized in view of fast days, and especially by religious houses, is obviously an interesting survival of small practical importance. It is probable that the right to take clay and gravel from pits on the estate is of greater value.

Instances of divided ownership, and of other incidents connected with a system of cultivation carried on under common direction, and within a network of closely interwoven rights and duties are not rare. The mentions made of Lammas lands and half-year lands show the many kinds of divided ownerships which existed.[3] Again, foldage or the right of having the flocks of others folded in the land of any individual for the sake of manure was so much valued that at times it was reckoned as an equivalent for their feed, "a farmer keeping his sheep on the common land in return folding a certain number of acres for the other tenants."[4] In some cases it was the privilege of the lord of the manor. Joist or so-called ley cattle are taken in to meet the wants of those who have insufficient pasture,[5]

[1] *Agric. Report, Norfolk*, 176. As to abuse of this right. *Agric. Report, Middlesex* (1793), by Baird.

[2] Inclosure Award of Forest of Salcy in Northampton makes allotments to commoners for "sere and broken wood." Incl. Awards, *Com. Pleas Recovery Rolls*, 10 Geo., iv. Easter, f. 7. Marshall, *Rural Economy of Gloucester*, p. 44, gives a good instance of a common wood appropriated to the messuages of the township it belongs to, but not divided. He adds, "this is a species of property I have not met with elsewhere." It is not merely the waste, but apparently an appropriated common.

[3] See above p. 13, note 1. Cf. as to divided ownership or divided rights. *Agric. Reports, Oxford*, 205, 231-2, *Somerset* (1798), 273; *Dorset* (1815), 307.

[4] *Agric. Report, Suffolk*, 2nd edition, p. 15. Cf. *Annals of Agriculture*, iv. 149.

[5] *Annals*, as above; also *Agric. Report, Derbyshire* (1811), p. 197. A good instance of this as an admitted practice in earlier times is shown by the mention in a will of 1493 of a legacy of 'all such sheep as I have at geyst' cited by Cullum, *History of Hawsted*, p. 140.

though it is difficult to say if the practice had increased.

There are certain significant changes noticeable in the comparison of village economy in the eighteenth century with that existing at the end of the middle ages. The severance of the ancient tenements from their connection with the land has already been mentioned. Equally important was the substitution, when the right of pasture had not become unlimited, of stints or definite numbers of beasts for those formerly entitled to common according to some assumed connection between the necessities of the soil and the beasts which could most wisely be kept. The way was opened to the creation of common ingress, or rights of common which might belong to anyone, wholly irrespective of his occupation of either land or tenement, or even the possession of a toftstead signifying hypothetical possession. Such rights could be bought and sold or even let. Two other changes rank with these in importance and combine with them in effect. On the one hand there is the great increase in permanent or inclosed pasture lying in common ; on the other there are the claims to common raised on behalf of those who live near the waste, especially in respect of small gains which might accrue to cottages.

In Fitz Herbert's time pasture in common was of three kinds : the common close where each man is stinted, the tended common where the cattle go before the herdsman and where stints prevail, and lastly the lord's outwoods where, in that writer's view, the lord should not be stinted though the tenants should.[1] But this threefold division, with the importance attached to the first two kinds, marks an advance from early village economy. Inclosed pasture, as distinct from the hay meadow, increased as time passed. Nothing indeed is more striking than the great disproportion in early manors between the amount of land in arable and that lying in either meadow or pasture.[2] The growth

[1] Fitz Herbert, *Surveying*, p. 12.

[2] See Cullum, *Hawsted*, pp. 105, 205. The same author cites (p. 236) from a lease of 1593 the prohibition of a tenant from breaking up pasture land.

of meadow and pasture may be due in part to the reclamation, as it were, of some part of the waste from its wild condition, though in some cases it seems to have taken place side by side with a reduction in the arable acreage. Be the cause what it may, it all tends to substantiate the importance of inclosed permanent pasture, the common closes of Fitz Herbert. By the eighteenth century these had become an ordinary feature of the villages lying in common, and from all appearance features not novel but of long standing. Inclosure records give many instances of ley pastures and of fields which, as betokened by name, are allotted to the use of particular beasts as Cow Down, Sheep Down, Pig Marsh, and the like: it is evident that by mutual agreement such common pastures could be fairly well utilised. Such fencing for common pasture did not necessarily imply severalty, but the division into smaller fields, and especially the assignment of such fields to different classes of animals, mark the importance attached to live stock as a source of wealth wholly apart from the arable. The untended common becomes more scarce with the advance of time. It appears, moreover, that in certain cases temporary inclosures were allotted to individuals for their sole use.[1]

[1] Pasture under inclosure was of three kinds. Firstly, there were in many open field villages common closes such as these to which Fitz Herbert alludes. These existed in the sixteenth century; the need for them increases with the use made of stock in places where inclosure to severalty did not occur. As is said in the text they are often of importance in the eighteenth century. Cf. *Agric. Report, Wilts* (1813), p. 4. Secondly, there were temporary intakes sometimes definitely for pasture and held for this in severalty, see p. 26, note 5. Probably the so-called shifting severalty in lot meadows was of this nature, but cf. Elton, *Copyholds*, p. 15. Compare also stocking closes, though these were less temporary; thus the writer of a letter from Leicester (*Bibliotheca Topographica Brit.* vii. p. 620) desires to get "my stocking closes inclosed upon the same considerations my father had." Thirdly, there were private pastures which might originate in different ways. There were inclosures for winter feed; thus at Wandesley the owners of these were to make "reasonable hedges and fences about their winter feed in their assarts." Thoroton, *Nottingham*, ii. 261. Possibly, however, these were not always fenced in. With the development of sheep farming and inclosure they necessarily increase. It seems that private pastures, in conjunction with common, existed in the sixteenth century. In the

Claims of common on the part of those dwelling near ensue almost inevitably as the connection between these rights and arable agriculture becomes obscured. One such claim in Hertfordshire, advanced by the dwellers in new tenements, met with the decision that whilst allowed for the life of those concerned it should cease afterwards. In Tottenham the inhabitants, *bonâ fide* residents, appear to have obtained a declaration from the vestry supporting their claim. But it is in the case of the cottagers and the poor living round the open commons that these privileges were most often asserted. Throughout the country it may be said that often the poor living near the commons, wholly without question of the occupation of ancient cottages, came by usage to enjoy the minor rights of common.[1] They turned out their pigs and geese, they

time of Henry VIII. among the lands of the Abbey of Selby there were closes subject to common, and closes not so subject. Dugdale, *Mon.* iii. 505. In the seventeenth century this was also true (M. Stevenson, *The Twelve Months* (1661), p. 47: in October "you may spare your private pastures and feed up your cornfields and commons").

Of the temporary inclosures some were for arable, see above p. 26, note 5; also *Annals of Agriculture*, viii. 438; *Agric. Reports*, *Cornwall*, p. 46; *Lincoln* (1799), p. 21; *Nottingham* (1798), p. 21.

Either use may have been made of the intakes from the common or common field which were more permanent. In Tusser's day, these would appear to be well known from the lines—

> Now sow and go harrow, where ridge ye did draw,
> The seed of the bramble with kernal and haw
> Which covered overlie, soon to shut out,
> Go see it be ditched and fenced about.

On this passage the editor, apparently D. Hillman, writes (*Tusser Redivivus*, 1710, February, p. 9): "This, I take it, to be meant of a way of quick setting or fencing enclosures out of the common field they had in the days of our author; they ploughed or drew round the ground they intended to inclose, a very large ridge, commonly a rod wide and sometimes much more; this they sowed with hips or the fruit of the bramble, with hazel nuts, haws, and such like to produce their kind; they carefully harrowed it and weeded it for two years, and in a few years time they had a pretty coppice, and are what we call shaws and in some places springs. This is an excellent way to improve bleak grounds, and it is a pity it is not continued."

[1] See *Agric. Report*, *Bedford* (1808), p. 224; *Cambridge* (1813), p. 76, etc.; *Norfolk*, p. 107, etc.; *Worcester*, pp. 52-53; *General Report*, Appendix iv.

gathered fuel, and in some instances found pasture for a cow. In some cases they acted as though possessing common shackage,[1] that is, pastured geese and pigs in the stubbles of the open fields after harvests. These privileges, though in the main by sufferance rather than of legal origin, were, whatever their ultimate effects, often of a substantial character, and their loss by inclosure occasioned much complaint and were met sometimes by special allotments. They were in reality a trespass and an encroachment.

If we turn from matters affecting pasturage to the circumstances of arable cultivation we find there, too, attempts to adapt a system of cultivation complicated by rights of common and mixed ownerships to the changes in need and opportunities. The temporary inclosures from waste and forest are probably due, at any rate in part, to the need of supplementing arable too hardly worked, by supplies of fresh soil. Where these intakes were cultivated in severalty, as seems to have been the custom, an opportunity is offered for new developments, of which the better farmers would willingly take advantage. Still more important were the agreements made in places to enable the introduction of clover, turnips, and other crops. Thus, in South Wiltshire tenants in many common fields came to an agreement to introduce clover, or ray grass, in place of fallow, and in some cases carried this out by making four fields instead of three; this when unaccompanied by a good sheep down made a four field system desirable, as follows: 1, wheat; 2, barley with clover; 3, clover, mown; 4, clover fed till time to plough for wheat. "But in the course of this some farmers have thought some land too good to lie for two years, and so in place of sowing the whole barley field with clover, they have reserved one-third or one-fourth of it for veitches, pease, beans, to keep under these for two years, but to come in again for wheat. This part of the land is called a hookland or hitchland field, and

[1] This is mentioned in the *General Report*. The poor enjoyed the privilege of feeding in the stubbles. Compensation was sometimes given for this.

where thus applied it is discharged from commonage."[1] Likewise in open fields, as at Brampton, in Oxfordshire, "hitching the field" was often adapted, and variations in the ordinary course were introduced by consent. Efforts were made to introduce turnips in the open field, but without general success. The difficulties of turnip cultivation in the open field are dwelt upon by many writers; and both agreements and the Act passed to facilitate the practice met, speaking broadly, with but little success.

Between the system of cultivation and common thus sketched in the eighteenth century and that existing under the manorial system prior to or even at the time of the changes taking place in the fifteenth and early sixteenth centuries there is much resemblance, and there are also many differences. These latter are due indeed in many instances to local circumstances, to the alterations sure to occur when the original purport of an institution is obscured, and lastly to the selfish advantage taken by individual members of those jointly, but not always, similarly interested in the land; but putting differences such as these aside, the remainder, and they form by far the larger part, are to be accounted for on two grounds. On the one hand, there was the growing lack of suitability between the system and the circumstances; on the other there were fresh efforts to accommodate the system to these new circumstances, efforts which, if successful at the moment, usually ended in producing a condition lacking the old stability, and inadequately realising the new need for elasticity and individual management. Underlying these differences, however, the system in its main broad outlines continues. The reasons for its permanence as also those which tended to produce change, call alike for attention.

The origin of the manorial system itself has been the subject of much controversy, but this controversy rather concerns tenure than the subject of interest here, namely the system of cultivation. That system may be held to be reconcilable with the different theories of early tenure,

[1] *Agric. Report*, *Wilts* (1813), p. 59; cf. *Oxford* (1813), 122.

which have been propounded, though certain of its incidents may lend their weight to arguments adduced on different sides. The cultivating village, whether originating in a free community or in servitude, was alike subject to the pressure of the necessities and dangers attending settlement in a country largely uncultivated and sparsely populated, amid forest and morass, and exposed to depredation and attack. The concentration of the houses with closes and barns in villages marks the force of external circumstances. So, too, the contiguity of the arable fields and the meadows to the little settlement. While these facts have been frequently emphasised, sufficient attention has not been given to the advantages presented by the open field system of cultivation in respect of the internal circumstances of the village. These probably were of equal, and in later years, of even greater weight. It has been surmised that the frequent absences of the men on warlike expeditions must have made concentration a necessary condition of cultivation. The lands were only too liable to be deserted by their occupiers and left to the care of women and of the aged and the young. Under these circumstances, with the whole village or township in one common system, management and cultivation were rendered easier. Again, as was noticed even at later times, a common system of cultivation, though possibly an obstacle to the improvements which the more energetic might wish to introduce, was equally a safeguard against bad husbandry and extreme negligence. Carelessness and bad practices could be more easily detected by the steward of the manor under a system of uniformity. Mere uniformity of practice, indeed, tended to preserve a certain though not necessarily a very high level of agriculture. Again, under the circumstances which then existed, common rights of pasture, of estovers and the remaining incidents enabled the community to get the most that was possible out of or from the soil. It must be remembered likewise that the village was, of necessity, substantially self-subsistent, that conditions of cultivation were almost invariable, and that little opportunity existed for the exercise of skill, either on the part of the cultivators or by the use of better appliances. But these facts, while amply sufficient to account for the early cultivating village, are not by themselves adequate reasons for its permanence. In many particulars change creeps in and becomes considerable. Four things, however, must be noted. Such changes were apt to be local. Throughout a long period the dependence of a community for its main necessities on local supplies continues little impaired, at times being reinforced by political turmoil. Again, the scarcity of population left large tracts of land available for herds and flocks. Lastly, the rights of common once introduced formed a complex of intermixed and mutual rights which, consecrated by immemorial usage, made conscious change well nigh impossible, save under the pressure of strong forces.

Yet the seeds of decay and the causes of change early and widely manifested themselves.

The basis of the system as a permanent system was its suitability, and that suitability rested in its turn on the presence of certain fairly well defined conditions. But these conditions were sweeping. The pursuance of the open field and common right system could be reasonably expected, provided, firstly, that arable was the necessary basis of English agriculture and the chief source of profit; secondly, that the methods of cultivation were fairly uniform, and not such as to admit of great differences by reason of skill and capital; thirdly, that the relation between stock and the arable was fairly stable in different districts, and given to but gradual alteration with the lapse of time; lastly, that there was a supply of land as yet outside the area under strict cultivation. Granted these conditions, and, on the whole, they held good in early manorial days, the system was admirably adapted to the wants of the time. As they weakened its suitability grew less, a fact strongly accentuated when any great current of change set in in any one direction. However adapted to early circumstances, a system dependent on conditions such as those enumerated above, could not afford permanent satisfaction in a changing and progressive country, particularly when that country differed, as England differed, so greatly in the special advantages offered by various districts for particular branches of agriculture, and above all when history combined with climatic considerations to make pursuits other than arable pursuits a substantial and, in some localities, a chief source of gain. By the beginning of the eighteenth century altered circumstances had achieved many changes, the particular features of which will require some account. Much land had been inclosed, and that which remained in open field or liable to the incidents of common did so under modified conditions, which by their very nature witnessed to the tendencies at work. To some extent the causes of inclosure may be judged from the character of the changes effected in the open field system. What these were has already been indicated so far as their general aspect is concerned. It remains to point out their significance with reference to the conditions which have been laid down as determining the suitability of the system in question.

With the growth of means of communication arable culture had ceased to be necessary in all villages alike whether the land was suited or unsuited to it. That it was no longer the one recognised basis of agriculture is shown both by the accounts we have of the agriculture and of the results of inclosure in different districts. In some farms we find that farmers are beginning to turn to other sources of profit and require inclosure for that reason.[1] When the land was inclosed, in some districts there was a positive increase in the corn area, while in others, as in Leicester and Northampton, a large amount of land was converted almost at once to pasture.[2] But both these tendencies, and especially the latter, were of old standing. They were after all but part of the

[1] As, for instance, in time of *Considerations*, cattle are a source of profit, etc.

[2] *Agric. Report, Leicester* (1807), pp. 67, 70, etc. On the other hand, new inclosures in Essex, *Agric. Report, Essex*, i., p. 123; *Worcester*, p. 55.

general progress towards differentiation of employment which becomes possible as one result of improved locomotion and transport. It is worthy of notice that where the soil was not particularly suited to pasture, even the advocates of inclosure admit that in such cases inclosure is less profitable and open field less unprofitable to the owner than elsewhere.[1] It was pointed out that under the open field land will be put to other uses[2] than would be the case if its owners were free to choose; and in the eyes of some this was clearly undesirable. In some districts the advantages sought by inclosure were, others contended, attained by the laying together of intermixed lands coupled no doubt with their relief from some of the incidents of common.[3]

It is equally clear that the early uniformity of cultivation had vanished. The general complaints that skill was impeded and new courses rendered impossible are the commonplaces of controversial literature during the sixteenth and seventeenth centuries, and those urging them did not attach corresponding importance to certain counteracting allegations which were probably true. Some who were by no means opponents of inclosure gave it as their opinion that the open field system, while disadvantageous to the skilful treatment of the soil, had at least the advantage of restraining extreme negligence. "Although the common field husbandry," writes one from experience, "does not make the land better, it keeps it from becoming much worse." Quite apart, however, from the evidence of controversial writers, or from a knowledge of the extent to which invention had affected the implements and methods of agriculture, the recorded condition of the open field land bears testimony to the need felt of

[1] *Agric. Report, East Riding* (1812), 93-4; *Worcester*, 53-4; Addington, *An Inquiry*, 38-39.

[2] "The fields of the unenclosed parishes have a certain proportion always in tillage; but the enclosed farms are employed sometimes in tillage and sometimes in pasture." *Agric. Report, Worcester*, p. 26.

[3] *Agric. Report, Cambridge* (1813), p. 92; *Oxford* (1813), p. 96.

doing something to enable progress to be made. Illustrative of this were the temporary inclosures held in severalty for a time, and also the so-called ancient inclosures which were often found scattered throughout the open fields. These inclosures, which often lay intermixed with the strips of the tenantry or village freeholders, and were the property frequently of the lord of the manor or the holder of glebe, are a very frequent feature of inclosures. They are to be noticed in the plans attached to Awards, and are referred to there, as elsewhere, as ancient inclosures. Some of these originated in the action of the individual who had taken his way and made it good. It does not follow, however, that land even when so inclosed would escape all incidents of common; indeed, the contrary must have been true in many cases, as where shack beasts being turned on to the arable after harvest had a right of entry into the inclosed plots through the bars or by the gates. Of equal moment are the instances of agreements to introduce new crops which but for these could not be taken from the land. Some of these have been cited already. They refer to the use of the land for clover, for vetches, and for other crops of one kind or another; but in the great majority of instances for the introduction of the turnip. They were fairly common; but despite the hesitating verdict given in their favour by some, their success in general seems to have been small. More was anticipated from the Act (13 G. III., c. 81) passed for a like purpose; but it too was without adequate result. According to some accounts it was "too generally neglected," according to others much improvement was impossible without inclosures, since, as one writer says, the agreement necessary to the adoption of the Act was difficult to procure.[1] It is possible, as has been suggested before, that an Act passed when opinion was running strongly in favour of inclosure did not receive a fair trial. But even had it been a remedy for this one inconvenience, others, it must be remembered, remained.

[1] Stone, *Suggestions*, pp. 11, 13.

The increase of sheep and cattle over a very large part of England and in particular in some districts, which began even in early times, had disturbed the proportion between the land in grass and that in tillage This movement was greatly assisted, on the one hand, by the severance between ancient tenements and lands; on the other, by the supersession of the law proportioning beasts according to levancy and couchancy or winter fodder by either definite stints or unlimited rights. By the first, rights of herbage were in some cases separated from land and attached to houses; by the other, so far as the introduction of stints was concerned, the way was opened both to the creation of common in gross, and to the letting of common rights. Of course, this was not the intention with which the practice of stinting was introduced. It was in the main an attempt to give reality to means of admeasurement, which were very difficult of application. But once the number for which common was due was defined, it was possible to claim that any exercise of common right was permissible, which, while benefiting the proprietor, was without injury either to his fellows or the lord of the manor. By the creation of common in gross, coupled with the right of taking in the beasts of others at hire, some of the difficulties inherent in the original system of common were overcome. It became possible to maintain large herds and flocks irrespective of the amount of land cultivated; and so a variable proportion between stock and land is attained.[1] The demand for additional pasture, too, was met to some extent by the unlimited rights which were claimed over commons which were not stinted or rated greatly to their injury; as also by the extensive rights of sheep walk, though these probably were of early origin. The growth of inclosed pastures lying in common and stinted,

[1] Thus Horner, speaking of rights of pasture on the commons, and property in the open field, says, "It is now no uncommon thing to find the former without the latter and the latter without the former and neither in any proportion to each other." (*Essay*, etc., p. 68.)

was undoubtedly beneficial both as regards the quantity, if not the quality, of sheep and cattle. The increase in sheep, and the increased demand for pasture for them, was an early source of weakness in the strict system of common right. It began to display itself at a very early date, and probably originated in the greater multiplicity of clothing and the consequent greater need for wool. Food, fuel, house, manure, repairs, and the service of the plough, were provided for; but by the original common right only an inadequate provision was made for clothing. Hence the early modification in rural economy and the increase of pasture, even by grants which expressly disregarded the recognised limitations imposed by manorial custom. Probably the growth of the clothing districts and the large foreign demand for English wool but accentuated a tendency already in existence. Further, the gradual utilisation of land well fitted for stock but unsuited for arable, and especially open field arable, played a part in the change.[1]

With the lapse of time efforts were naturally made to increase the cultivated area. The arable must often have been enlarged, and land, as we learn, while remaining in common, became inclosed pasture. Another mark of the demand for more land under strict cultivation has been seen in the privilege enjoyed in many places of taking up temporary inclosures on the waste or in the forest.

In every particular, then, the open field system in the eighteenth century bears testimony to the strength of the forces which had led, and which were leading, to its disintegration. Yet it must not be supposed that weakness had exhibited itself in every direction at the same time, or that its development took place with necessary uniformity. At one time one cause was most prominent, at another a different one; but the pressure was constant, and it is probable that, from the fifteenth to the middle of the nineteenth century, with some few intervals, the conversion of commonalty into severalty was in active progress.

[1] Bk. II., Appendix E. Inclosure from the Wild State.

Sometimes the movement was faster, sometimes more slow. This, however, will require investigation and further discussion.

Apart from these causes which were operative in the case of land already within the area of cultivation, or at any rate in its contiguity, there were others of equal importance arising from the essential differences in the soil of different districts and counties, and due to the extension of cultivation over the country. Some districts, either by reason of soil alone or by reason of soil in conjunction with position, were obviously unsuited to agricultural communities. They offered opportunities for sheep and, to some extent, for cattle farming, but not for much arable development. This is a matter to be dealt with elsewhere, but here it may be pointed out that in these regions there are but slight traces of any extensive settlement or growth of villages and communities dependent in the main on an arable basis. Some arable, no doubt, there was. Common fields for crops existed in some measure, but rather by way of addition to than as the basis of occupation and life. Again, in many regions the existence of forest or fen or marsh rendered land unsuited for arable, till previous changes had been effected. Woodland and forest yielded but slowly, and a large expenditure was required before much rich land could be drained and fitted rather than reclaimed for cultivation. When this takes place, it does not follow that they pass into cultivation under the same intricate conditions as to common right, and in particular as to common of shack, as existed elsewhere. Common, no doubt, was often annexed, but intercommoning was a custom and not a grant. Of course, the extent to which such land was subject to common, as also the nature of the common, depends very much on the date at which such additions were made. The utilisation of land of such kinds had an influence hostile to the maintenance of the regular common right system. New opportunities of profit were offered, and new conditions of advantageous cultivation exhibited. Where new arable was added the effects were the more considerable, since not only did the addition of new rich arable areas tend to restrict the use of old arable, often little suited for its purpose, but the greater advantage of farming under less onerous conditions rendered the lot of other farmers less easy as soon as the development of transport brought about farming for distant sale, and so a new degree of competition.

As will be pointed out further on the existence of such non-arable areas and the gradual extension of cultivation place limits on the common field system and do much to explain the lack of uniformity of various regions and counties in respect of subsequent inclosures.

The sketch given above of the common field system, and of the causes occasioning and the incidents associated with its decay, exhibits common right in three stages. In early times it was an integral part of the rural economy, necessary, that is, to its completeness and the means of its effective practice. Later on differences manifest themselves between different districts and in different cases and whilst common rights are still associated with arable agriculture, the inevitable feature in their relation has gone and they exist in large measure as a source of special profit. Moreover arable comes into use without intercommoning and with common attached, as it were as a means of additional gain. During this period, too, arable common right and open field cultivation begin to be regarded, at any rate by some, as an obstacle to improvements and good farming. These features are emphasised as time passes till by some the system of common is valued only as a means of chance gains. Others treat it as a mischievous and cumbrous survival. In the nineteenth century, if not in the eighteenth, the idea of a public interest or right manifests itself. The common is a cause of profit to those dwelling in its vicinity ; but the local public has a further claim over it, for purposes of recreation and exercise.

II

EXTINCTION OF COMMON AND COMMON RIGHTS

THE most effectual means of meeting the defects alleged against the system of common field cultivation and common was found, however, not in any modification of that system but by the inclosure of land. Inclosure was the recognised mode of supplanting champion or common by several, and so entailed in general the closing of the land inclosed against all rights save those of the individual owner. But there was a further advantage, in addition to that thus achieved, which might lead to inclosing. Economy of labour in the case of pasture led in some cases to the hedging and fencing of land under the common field system without any real destruction of common rights, despite their more rigid regulation; it was often the real end sought by inclosures which were carried out in such a way as to bring in individual or several ownership.

The ways in which this change might be accomplished were various and where important must have been of varying importance at different epochs. They may be classified under the following heads: (1) Extinction of common in the ordinary process of law. (2) Withdrawal from common by sufferance. (3) Approvement. (4) Inclosure by agreement either voluntary or under compulsion. (5) Private Acts and other parliamentary powers.

(1) *Extinction of common in the ordinary process of law.* A large variety of ways exist whereby rights of common once existing might be extinguished and cease in the

ordinary course of law and without any exceptional action on the side of any of the parties involved. They have been enumerated as follows: (*a*) Unity of possession where the land over which common was exercised and the privilege of common came into the same hands and where in consequence common would necessarily cease. (*b*) Severance of the rights of common necessarily attached to and determined by a tenement or holding from that tenement or holding. This, though ordinarily occurring in the case of common for a number of beasts undetermined save by the needs real or assumed of the holding, might take place in cases where common for a definite number was specifically attached to the holding. (*c*) Release by the commoner. (*d*) Disuse. (*e*) Destruction of the commoner's estate. (*f*) Alteration of the commoner's tenement in such manner as to severely impair the conditions under which and the purpose for which common was acquired. (*g*) Destruction of the product which was the subject of common.

Of these ways in which common might be extinguished, few are of importance save in their purely legal aspect, and it may well be doubted if any occurred at any time in sufficient amount to seriously affect the conditions of life or cultivation over a considerable area. They affected individual commoners or occasionally the tenants of a particular manor rather than the inhabitants of any district or districts. It must also be remembered that in early times at least, they were in part or wholly counterbalanced by the new grants of common which occurred under certain circumstances. There are two, however, which may be thought of some little general importance at periods of civil disorder, or where the forfeiture of manors and their regrant, as during the Civil Wars of the fifteenth century or at the dissolution of the monasteries, offered opportunity for a rapacious new lord of the manor to turn to his own advantage any legal defect. Disuse of common is one of these. It seems highly probable that such disuse might occur not infrequently and, however slight, it might offer an easy pretext to a new owner anxious to obtain the full benefit of his possession. On the other hand it is quite possible that at a time of disorder considerable encroachments might take place, and that the rights thus acquired by what is, strictly speaking, illegal use might outweigh those falling into desuetude or extinguished on that pretext; further, any sudden inclosures on this ground would certainly startle those with rights of common out of any negligence as to their use. In any case, however, the extent to which this cause operated must be a matter for surmise. The other of the two causes referred to is of a very different kind. Unity of possession would almost certainly have been of great consequence had it not been subject, so far as law was concerned, to many exceptions which went far to deprive it of importance. The only question is, if these exceptions, which are the outcome of careful legal decision, were adequately enforced in such centuries as the fifteenth and sixteenth. Extinction owing to unity of possession did not occur in the case of common appendant, where the ancient necessity of common remained, save when the commoner acquired the whole waste, or of common of shack where the acquisition by one commoner of the whole land could not debar other commoners from their rights over his own portion of land or of copyhold estates since these, even if they came into the hands of the lord, would if granted out to another tenant by the court roll necessarily have the customary rights of common. This latter exception was held to extend to rights of common over the lord's demesne. But it may well be doubted if these exceptions were sufficiently recognised at times earlier than the seventeenth century, or indeed even then, to effectually preclude inclosure when by such unity of possession the land claiming common came into the personal possession of the lord of the manor or the owner of the soil.[1]

[1] Instances of inclosure on unity of possession occur at times in the eighteenth century. *The National Debt no material grievance* (1768), p. 61: "Most of the small tenements and farms having fallen into the lord of the

Opportunities of this kind were not of infrequent occurrence, but it is difficult or impossible to ascertain how far they were taken advantage of. That would probably depend on the advantage anticipated and on the weakening of the strict manorial system. To cases under conditions such as these may be attributed some of the sporadic inclosures of ancient origin lying among the open fields of the seventeenth and eighteenth century.

(2) *Withdrawal from common by sufferance.* There were certain kinds of common far less strictly ascertained and much more open to interruption than those which have chiefly occupied our attention. A large part of the lord's demesne, so far as that was under arable, lay in the common field of the village. Here, too, were the lands of the tenants hopelessly intermixed and in contiguous strips. Over these, as has been said, a custom of common after harvest or when the crops were carried obtained in many parts of the country. Such common use of each other's herbage, which as has been said, arose rather out of convenience and of a mutual disregard of trespass than from any grant, was in one sense a common by vicinage and in any case a common the guarantee of which was usage. Its early existence has indeed been called in question, but though it is proved by early manorial accounts, as well as by the words of early law books,[1] it is far from clear how far such common could prove a barrier to inclosure. The fact that late in the sixteenth century the judges before whom a case of common of shack came

manor's hands, he has let the whole to one or two substantial farmers." Marshall, *East Norfolk*, ii. 365-71, gives history of Felbrigg inclosure, where the chief landowner, being sole proprietor of the land with exception of one small man, bought him out and made inclosures, reserving some land for common for the poor. The rest was parcelled out among his tenants and inclosed. *Agric. Report*, *Oxford* (1813), p. 91: "The parish of Clifton, thirty-nine years ago, was allotted by Mr. Hucks, being a private arrangement of his own."

[1] In answer to a claim of common rights the tenant resisting the claim might say—the soil is his several, which he may plough, sow, or inclose at his pleasure, and at all times keep inclosed.

seemed dubious as to the nature of such common, and that Lord Coke from his comments shows considerable lack of knowledge as to its extent, is evidence at any rate that cases were not frequent in the courts and that common of shack was not a universal legal incident. The real matter of importance to determine is the power of such mutual rights to bar inclosure. The issue raised before the court was whether freeholders having land in common field and intercommoning could inclose against each other.[1] This was held to be a matter of custom. It was further stated that common of shack, arising, as we may suppose, out of mere convenience, and so being of temporary sufferance, might by usage become attached to the land and appendant or appurtenant to it. In the very case in question there were several inclosures in the field into which, after the crops were taken, the neighbours claimed right of entry with their beasts for pasturage. While this was stated to be good, it was, however, held that an ancient inclosure out of arable field can be free of shack. These words throw considerable light on a phenomenon which presents itself from the sixteenth century onward, namely, the presence in the open fields of inclosures known as a rule, to distinguish them from any inclosing taking place at the time in question, as "ancient inclouseres." These are mentioned here[2] and by other writers of the century, references to them occur in the seventeenth century, while in the eighteenth century, alike in the account of the villages and districts and in the Awards of the inclosure commissions, they are very familiar objects. Such inclosures find their origin in different ways. In some cases they may be due to

[1] Corbet's case, Coke's *Report*, (ed. 1826), iv. 57. Coke adds, the like intercommoning is in Lincolnshire, Yorkshire, and other counties, as well as Norfolk.

[2] In the comment on the same case, it is said an ancient enclosure can be free of shack. Tusser's reference to the fact that in Norfolk, where Ket's rebellion was, "to this day they take the liberty of throwing open all enclosures out of the common field," relates, it is probable, to the same class of inclosure. Tusser, July 9.

extinction of commons, in others again, as we shall see, to approvements of waste, but in many instances, especially when contiguous to or amidst arable, to the inclosing of land under conditions fairly plainly indicated by the above case. The arable of the lord, if lying separated from the tenantry land, was undoubtedly easy to inclose. If tenants held land which they might plough or sow or inclose at pleasure, so certainly did he. The case was different, it is true, when his demesne lay in open strip intermixed with the lands of his tenants. Here, indeed, difficulties from a custom of common might arise, but that he could inclose, at least partially, seems almost certain. Those cases are the most doubtful where his action would injuriously affect those to whom he might have made actually grants of common over his demesne. Still it may be said that without violation of law he could hedge and ditch much of his arable land. His action might be supported on the analogy of the legal right of approvement. But the case commented on raises the further question as to the possession of like powers by the freehold tenants in the common fields. Theoretically they were held to have such power save when bound by long custom. But this power, even if it could be employed to any large extent owing to the prevalence of custom, only touched freehold and not copyhold tenants. That during the fifteenth and sixteenth centuries the lords often inclosed demesne lands once in arable is beyond doubt, that their lands often lay intermixed is equally clear, and that inclosures exist bordering on the open fields or breaking into their continuity is also certain. The case already cited shows that their example was being followed, though to what extent it is difficult to say, by freehold tenants. The movement among these latter was checked probably owing to the attention thus directed to what was already occurring, though very probably in no great amount.

(3) *Approvement.* Approvement is the right of the owner of the soil of making such use of his property as he

may think fit, provided that his action does not interfere with the legitimate claims of others to share in any part of its profits. In most cases of importance the owner was the lord of the manor, and thus it was in their interest, as well as in the interest of effective cultivation, that the Statute of Merton, and the second Statute of Westminster operated. The view which has been supported by many authorities, that approvement was a right by common law antecedent to these statutes, is certainly strengthened by the fundamental conception of property and common right in the manorial system. The land was burdened by certain servitudes in the case of common, implying a claim to certain parts of the herbage and other products, and granted that sufficient was left to satisfy these claims, the power of the owner either to grant rights of common to others or to make what use he could of the soil yielding such product seems indefeasible. By the statutes mentioned it is specifically attached to the waste, a fact which certainly seems to indicate an original difference between the position of the lord with regard to this and that which he occupied in the case of his own demesne. It seems difficult to doubt that he had power to approve when he could certainly make new grants of common, except on the theory that the waste was set apart and, as it were, permanently dedicated to common use.

The approvement of common was of direct importance where the growth of population and its requirements rendered the fuller utilisation of the land desirable. It afforded a means for the formation of new arable and meadow, and these thus formed were liable to inclosure at the will of the lord. That use was made of the power is shown by its rapid extension by the second statute. The Statute of Merton either created or confirmed the right to approve as against the tenants of the manor, but this was found to be insufficient, and to meet the needs of the time approvement was further empowered by the Statute of Westminster, II., against neighbours, that is, against the rights of common acquired by vicinage, and probably reciprocal on the part of the lord and tenants of adjacent manors. But inclosure by means of approvement was hindered in certain ways. In the first place, as specifically determined, sufficient common had to be left to satisfy the legitimate claims of commoners. In the second place, the growth of common in gross offered a more definite barrier than that existing in cases where the right of common was attached to and determined by the general extent of the land; in many cases it amounted to common for a definite number, in some it was in practice, however, only limited by the beasts which the commoner could maintain.[1] Overstocking of commons is a complaint in the sixteenth century, and from the language of Fitz Herbert, a widespread habit. Lastly, rights of estover and turbary must have impeded its easy use. Though the statement made by some to the effect that approvement was impossible when a common of turbary or estover existed was inaccurate, it is obvious that they might hinder the process. In face of these facts it is not surprising to find the authoritative statement at the end of the eighteenth century, that the statutes of approvement were little used.[2] "It was seldom," we are told, "that any common was sufficiently extensive to afford a surplus of any moment after the claims of those who had rights of common in it were satisfied. It was hardly possible, in many cases, to ascertain what was a sufficiency of pasture." There is no doubt as to the general truth of this assertion at the time it was made. It was approximately if not equally true of the condition of things for some time previous to that date. Throughout the copious literature dealing with commons and inclosure, approvement, if referred to at all, is never mentioned as a means whereby inclosures are being effected or could be effected to any considerable amount; and the repeated demands on the

[1] *Agric. Report, North Riding* (1800), p. 200, case tried at York Assizes, mentioned where this limitation was laid down.

[2] Appendix to Report of Committee of 1795 gives Sinclair's address in which this is stated.

part of those favouring them for easier parliamentary means of effecting them in the case of wastes, no less than over open fields, supports this view of its inoperative character throughout that century. Somewhat the same may be said of the seventeenth century, as far as actual literary mention is concerned, though during that period there are more indications of arbitrary inclosure, which may have been a kind of unlicensed and quite indefensible imitation of what was a strict legal operation. The text-book on the Law of Commons and Commoners does not treat of approvement at any length or as though it had been a power of importance or greatly exercised. The reverse may be gathered from its pages. Evidence in the sixteenth is different, since we hear that "the lords have enclosed a great part of their waste grounds and straitened their tenants of their commons therein."[1] In connection with this the re-enactment of the Statute of Merton must be read. In ordinary circumstances the re-enactment of a statute frequently points to its small effect; but in this instance the new statute reads like the definite reassertion of a right, which otherwise might have been deemed in suspense owing to Somerset's proclamation. Should this be correct, corroboration is afforded that approvement had been taking place, while, in addition, there is clear evidence that further occasion for its exercise is thought desirable.

(4) *Agreement.* Inclosure by agreement was of very many kinds, varying from genuine voluntary agreements to agreements where consent was obtained by hard pressure, or even to agreements concluded by Chancery suits, in which the consenting parties by collusive action sought to enforce inclosure upon those who dissented, or to distribute the land in severalty among the consentient

[1] Fitz Herbert, *Surveying*, p. 20: "And then was their tenements much better cheap than they be now, for the most part of the lords have inclosed their demesne lands and meadows and keep them in severalty, so that their tenants have no common with them therein. And also the lords have inclosed a great part of the waste grounds," etc.

parties, to the exclusion of others. The menace of such suits was at one time a powerful instrument to procure voluntary consent. With regard to agreements in general, the assertion that private agreements were practically impossible, must be treated as only applicable, if applicable then, to the time after the great inclosures, that is, to the later eighteenth century.

Earlier in that century, when inclosing by act was a recognised procedure, and when in consequence there must have been a rather general tendency to resort to that method as having greater finality, inclosure by consent with, in some cases, subsequent resort to parliament, was well known. Both Arthur Young and Marshall refer to it as within their knowledge and of importance, the former writing that entire townships and many stinted pastures have been laid out by agreement, or proprietors possessing large interests, have inclosed land after procuring the necessary assents on the parts of those interested, while the latter refers to it as a general means in more places than one. Both agree in eulogising such proceedings as being cheaper, and so more beneficial, and Marshall adds that it takes place without the hazard and inconvenience attending application to Parliament. But as a rule some legal intervention was required, particularly in the case of unstinted commons. These general statements are corroborated by particular facts recorded in particular districts. Several took place in Leicester, Nottingham, and Durham, and are duly recorded by writers who give something like a full list of all the lands inclosed, distinguishing in two of the counties those dealt with by act from those dealt with by agreement, while in other cases allusions by contemporary authors point to a like existence in other districts, as Yorkshire and Norfolk, to single out two counties. Though no close estimate as to the amount of land thus inclosed is possible, the facts referred to above, especially when corroborated, as they are, by the incidental agreements which find their way into the various lists of inclosures, and even among the awards, justify the statement that it forms an appreciable addition to that dealt with by act.[1]

During the seventeenth century agreements were even more important. The testimony as to their prevalence is strong, and spread throughout the period. They find mention in the record of the action of the Privy Council, between 1630 and 1640, which illustrate the difficulties which beset those anxious to agree, and also the methods whereby a reluctant consent was often wrung from those

[1] With regard to agreements to inclose, the following references are important. As to general facts, *General Report*, p. 70, etc.; Marshall, *Yorkshire*, i. 99; *On the Appropriation and Inclosure of Commonable and Intermixed Lands* (1801), p. 11.

As to Midlands, *i.e.* Marshall's central district, Marshall, ii. 204, the parts of Warwick, Stafford, Derbyshire, and Leicester, which border on each other, stand low in inclosure by act during the whole period of acts; thus Leicester, Ashby-de-la-Zouch district, 10 p.c.; Warwick, Atherstone, 2 p.c.; Meriden, 12 p.c.; Nuneaton, however, 22 p.c. Both Stafford and Derby exhibit extremely small amount of inclosure, prior to Marshall, who writes, "Half a century ago the district was principally open, now it is mostly inclosed."

Leicester, a list of inclosures in Leicester (*Agric. Rep.*) gives several that are not by act.

Nottingham, here again lists are given, and this time good lists with details, *Agric. Report*, *Nottingham*, p. 23, and Appendix iv. p. 180. Reckoning from these, inclosure by agreement form about 10 p.c. of total inclosures before 1798.

In Durham, according to list given in the *Agricultural Report*, about 2 or 3 p.c. of the inclosed land during period prior to 1813 inclosed by agreement.

In Yorkshire, see Marshall, *Yorkshire*, i. 48-105, and references in Young, *Northern Tour*, ii. 179. For Norfolk, *Agric. Report*, *Norfolk*, p. 31, etc., gives date of north-west inclosure, 1730-60, before much took place by act; see also *Eastern Tour*, ii. 150-163; *Southern Tour*, i. 22-23. In Berks *Agric. Report*, Wallingford is in severalty by agreement if not fully inclosed, p. 150. In Worcester, agreements also occur, *Agric. Report*, *Worcester*, p. 58; also in Bedford, *Agric. Report*, 225.

To this evidence as to existence of inclosure by agreement during the period of active parliamentary means, there should be added the testimony of the early acts which are often confirmatory of agreements already concluded and sometimes executed.

While any estimate must be conjectural, some such addition as 3 to 5 p.c. of the area inclosed, after 1750, might be made to allow for private inclosures, or inclosure by agreement.

who were unwilling.[1] Again, in the controversy which raged a little later as to the effect of the inclosures in the Midlands, and particularly in Leicester, we are told of the lords of the manors and others anxious to inclose that if they cannot persuade, they commence a suit in law; and Mr. John Moore writes bitterly of the persecution occasioned, and the pressure brought to bear upon those who refuse to join in inclosures, by long suits in Chancery. This is amply borne out by the very large number of Chancery suits duly enrolled. In some cases these are rather by way of record and so public confirmation; in other instances the proceedings may have acted as a menace. That these cases were frequent is obvious from the reference to them in the legal text-book published at the end of the century. Again, according to Houghton, writing in 1681, many inclosures had been made of late, or were in process. He adds, "the more, I dare say, would quickly follow, would they that are concerned and understand it, daily persuade their neighbours." This though a little indefinite, seems to point to action by general agreement, since application to Parliament had not yet begun.

It may indeed be urged that these inclosures by Chancery suit require separate treatment. This is true in a sense, as they obviously introduce an element of constraint alien to the idea of general consent or free agreement. They are mentioned here for three reasons. Firstly, as has been already pointed out, lengthy legal proceedings were held out as a menace to procure the voluntary assent

[1] *P.C. Register*, vii., Charles I., pp. 506-7: A case, where the petitioners, being the inhabitants and landlords of Croft in Leicester, had made some division of lands, setting aside lands for a general cow pasture and sheep pasture. Against them were two who wished for a general inclosure, and to procure this ploughed up the common closes thus set aside, and threatened to turn their cattle into the corn in the division for tillage, etc. Cf. *P.C. Reg.*, x. 197 (1634, 31 October). Hallhead, *Inclosure thrown open* (p. 8), "if they who wish to inclose cannot persuade they commence a suit in law"; they ditch in their own land to make others go round (p. 9), or breed rabbits (p. 9). Also Moore, *The Crying Sin of England* (p. 13), as to long suits in Chancery.

of commoners to an inclosure. Secondly, in some cases they were resorted to in order to obtain an authoritative record of agreements entered into without any legal compulsion. Thirdly, the proceedings were often collusive, hence indicative of assent on the part, at any rate, of some of those concerned. They form a stage in a process which in the main was in the direction of agreement, though they obviously are in one aspect a means of compulsion, and resulted incidentally in depriving some of their rights to common. The extent to which they are recorded shows how frequent was the resort to them, and how constant the process to which they gave certainty.

Many of them were of the nature of collusive suits, whereby two or more parties having concluded an agreement to inclose, other parties applied to the court to restrain the agreement until their rights were duly satisfied. This brought out declarations as to the nature of the common which existed, and as to those entitled to share in it, and further gave the opportunity for requiring other parties besides those thus acting in concert to put in an appearance and make their claim. By itself the method would almost inevitably occasion some to consent and some to withdraw from their rights, since the trouble and expense would prove a great obstacle in the way of the poorer commoners. There was an attempt to push things further, and to consider the decision of the suit a legal bar to claims of common on the side of those who were not parties to it, since the author of the text-book referred to, mentions this view only to refute it. He points out that the decree would not affect rights which were claimed by others than the parties to the case; in other words, apart from its coercive nature, and the general effect it might produce on people not prone to legal proceedings, it would be a mere registration of an agreement between certain parties. In some instances it was such avowedly. It may be suggested that it was the recognition of this limitation which led to the disuse of this particular method. Its inability to procure anything like a binding or universal consent, together with the difficulty attending purely voluntary, and even registered agreements, led to the open and steady demand for powers to prevent obstruction which could be obtained only by application to Parliament.

No doubt the constitutional development which was bringing into clear view the difference between the royal power, whether exercised in the council or in chancery, and that of actual sovereignty, increased the tendency to consider Parliamentary sanction necessary. This feeling found expression in the bill introduced into the House of Lords, in 1666, "for confirming of inclosures made by decrees in Courts of Equity." After being read a second time, this bill was sent to a committee and was dropped. Had it passed into an Act, it is possible that the most active period of inclosure, would have been anticipated by nearly a century, while on the other hand it may be doubted if resort would have been had to private acts for this particular purpose. Another mark of the growing parliamentary spirit as also of the importance of the question of inclosure, was the abortive attempt in the Commons, in 1664, to pass a bill "to inclose and improve commons and waste lands."

(5) *Private Acts and Parliamentary Enactments.* So far as the mere reference to Parliament was concerned, inclosure under Act of Parliament was not a novel idea when it came into constant use in the eighteenth century. From the time of the Statute of Merton the regulation of inclosure, sometimes in the direction of extension, sometimes by way of curtailment, finds not infrequent place in the statute book. This was more particularly the case after the accession of Henry VII., when, owing to the large forfeitures, many manorial properties came into the hands of new owners, and much inclosure took place, which resulted, or was expected to result, in depopulation. Hence the attention of Parliament to its regulation. It would be a mistake to assume that the invariable object of legislation was the mere preservation of commons or even

of the common field system. This view is impossible in the face of such statutes as that which re-enacted and enforced the power of approvement or those which especially empower small inclosures to be made near agricultural houses or for other minor purposes. On the whole, certain kinds of inclosure, especially inclosure from waste, were distinctly encouraged. But statutes such as these were of general importance. More closely akin to the private acts of the eighteenth century were acts such as that whereby all having rights of common in the waste within Bedford level might improve, divide, and sever their respective proportions.[1] Elsewhere grants were made permitting inclosures of lands reclaimed from the sea where such otherwise might have been held subject to some common rights.[2] But these, it may be argued, were of a particular nature. They were certainly rather by way of exception than of rule.

After the middle of the same century the need obviously felt on the part of many for inclosure or some restriction on the system of common found expression in various parliamentary efforts. During the Commonwealth a bill "for improvement of waste grounds and regulating of commons and commonable lands and preventing depopulation" was brought forward in the Commons, but rejected after being read a first time (1656). In 1661 a bill was introduced into the Commons "for making orders and bye laws for well ordering and governing of common fields." It was read a third time, 1662, but seems to have proceeded no further. In this latter year another dealing with commons was read twice, and another which aimed at their improvement was read once. In 1664 the bill already referred to, which permitted inclosure, was introduced and negatived, though only by a majority of 105 to 94. In 1666 the bill to confirm decrees of inclosures in

[1] The permission thus given by 15 C. II., c. 17 § 38, was revoked by 1 J. II., c. 21 § 4, on the ground that such severance had led to diminution of stock and decay of houses.

[2] Such a grant asserted in case of Hulcey Common. *P.C. Reg.* xii., 455, 27 Nov., 1636.

Chancery was read in the House of Lords. The idea of a general act dealing with inclosure was advocated in 1681 by Houghton, this time taking the form of a general permissive act to inclose, a suggestion pressed by the same writer in 1700 and also advocated by others. Two bills brought forward in the Commons during the last decade of the seventeenth century went some distance in the same direction. In 1696 a bill was introduced "to explain the Statute of Merton and other statutes in regard to the improvement of common," but on a division it was rejected. In the following year, 1697, leave was obtained to bring in a bill for making the statutes of Edward I. and Edward VI. against burning and destroying inclosures more effectual. After it was read a first time, a petition was presented against it which alleged that it was being promoted in the interests of a party to a particular dispute, and either on this or on general grounds no further steps were taken. A long time was to elapse before any general change in the law was made; and it was not till 1801 that a general-act for inclosure was passed. Even then the act, it must be observed, was very different from that suggested by Houghton, being nothing more than a general and uniform enactment of certain clauses which a long experience of private acts had shown to be necessary, thus facilitating inclosure by private act and not obviating the need for them.

Inclosure by private act begins systematically with the Acts of Anne, as for instance the one confirming the agreement for enclosing Ropley Commons in the county of Hampshire. There had, it is true, been an early precedent, dating so far back as 4 James I., when an act was passed for the inclosure in severalty of one-third of the land at Marden and Bodenham; but this act remained an isolated instance of this particular method of dealing with the difficulties of common field cultivation for more than a century. With the enactment of the acts for inclosure in the early years of Anne a new epoch begins. These acts were followed by several in the reign of

George I. With the next reign the acts increase till at the close they swell into a very large number in each year.

The intervention of Parliament in this sphere coincides with the general extension of its activities which marks the end of the personal rule of the crown. Here, as elsewhere, as for instance in the case of monopoly and other companies, parliamentary sanction is sought where formerly the authority of the crown exercised through the council or otherwise, as in the specific instance of inclosures, was deemed sufficient. The decree in Chancery and the private act have this element in common, that they both record the action of the crown in regard to a petition brought forward by certain parties desiring relief from the difficulties in which they find themselves. Hence, indeed, the growth of private acts and their substitution for other forms whereby assent is announced to the humble petition of the subjects of the crown marks no sudden change save so far as the form of the procedure changes whereby redress is sought. Constitutionally, of course, the change is of the utmost moment, for it signifies the recognition of the Houses of Parliament as an integral element in the sovereign's assent; but so far as action in a particular sphere is concerned, it is not of great importance. In both cases some sort of agreement among some, at least, of the parties concerned usually preceded the application.

This new stage on which inclosure enters under parliamentary authority admits of division into three periods. During the first, which extends through the eighteenth century to the general act of 1801, the growth of the private acts may be traced from the very rudimentary form of the earlier acts to that high degree of development where, by reason of the very uniformity and complexity of the provisions included on each occasion, a general act was rendered not only feasible and useful but essential. The second period is from 1801 to 1842-5,[1] and includes the private acts which were passed in accordance

[1] That is, to the general act of 1845.

with the provisions of the general act. After 1845 the powers hitherto exercised directly by parliament, and through commissioners specially appointed by act, were delegated to different permanent bodies established by act, and subject to parliamentary control inasmuch as their decisions or orders had to remain on the table of the Houses before becoming operative.

The gradual development of the private inclosure act during the first period is interesting from many points of view. In the first place light is thrown on the ends sought by inclosure, and in particular on the reasons which instigated the applications to Parliament. In the second place, with time and experience the need of particular safeguards and of particular methods is revealed; while, thirdly and lastly, we find the various local efforts and experiments growing into a uniform method and well recognised procedure.

With regard to the first point, the close connection between the inclosure by agreement and that now sought by private act is clear even in detail. Not only from the earliest time is there a reference to some agreement on the part of the petitioners, a feature which of course continues throughout, but in some instances during the earlier part of the eighteenth century the act is often little more than a recital and a re-enactment of an agreement already made, and of a scheme of inclosure adopted and partly carried out. Though in most cases the act includes the appointment of commissioners who are to do something in the way of inclosure, there are cases when it is so purely confirmatory that further action even of this kind is not provided for. In the earlier years the inclosure of Ropley, Overton Longville,[1] and Thurnscoe,[2] are of this kind, the last named indeed reciting an agreement of 1717 and confirming it. Later in the reign of George II. we have good instances of such confirmatory acts in the case of Culceth[3] and Yatton.[4] In the former

[1] 1 G. I.

[2] 2 and 3 G. II. York.

[3] 23 G. II. Lancaster.

[4] 24 G. II. Somerset.

instance the articles of agreement indented in 23 George II. having been recited, the act proceeds: "and whereas the executing and effecting the said agreement would be for the mutual benefit of all persons interested in the said commons and waste lands and be of public utility; yet the same cannot be established and rendered effectual to answer the intention of the parties without the aid and authority of an Act of Parliament." Confirmation of the agreement then follows. Such confirmatory acts occur in sufficient number[1] to warrant the assertion that in its early stages the private act was often a form of recognising agreements which formerly had been registered in the Court of Chancery or carried out without dispute. In most cases certain safeguards are taken to give some security to the rights of those who are not petitioners, that is, where a unanimous assent is not shown. Somewhat akin to such acts are those where agreement is announced on the part of some, but where the dissent or opposition of some few is alleged as a reason for coming to Parliament. This is shown in the instance of Little Rissington, where it is announced that there have been letters of agreement, "but for want of the consent of some few people . . . the same cannot be done effectually without the authority of Parliament."[2] Even in the early decades, however, there are instances of the form of act which becomes predominant with the progress of the century, that is, instances where, after the announcement

[1] In addition to the number as shown by words of act, the following passage may be cited from *Agric. Report, Derby* (1811), p. 78: "In Duckmanton, Temple-Normanton, and some other places, the division was made by consent and acts obtained, for confirming the same."

In the case of Ridley, 25 G. II., the act required for Confirming the Articles of Agreement. It recites the agreement and process, and then enacts and confirms it. Cf. Compton Bassett.

The Award at Oaksey in Wilts, 1802-3, where there is only one commissioner, accepts survey made before the passing of the act (*Close Rolls*, 1802-3, Pt. 10, No. 10).

[2] Cf. Claughton, 2 and 3 G. II., where an agreement by deed poll, 1729, is recited, and then it is stated that owing to the execution of this being obstructed by some, the authority of Parliament is invoked.

of a desire on the part of some of those interested, steps are taken to proceed by the appointment of commissioners. These, which become the normal type, are at first among the least usual. Their growth may be taken as indicative of the change whereby inclosure by act becomes an ordinary method of agricultural improvement. One particular reason for inclosure remains to be noticed. Cases occur of inclosure of commons or rather of parts of commons which are separated into individual property and handed over to the lord of the manor or a wealthy proprietor in return for a yearly payment to be applied for the relief of the poor and in reduction of the poor rate.[1] Such inclosures of commons or waste land are undertaken on account of the burden incurred in relieving the poor.

On turning to the actual development of these acts, as shown in the nature of the different clauses, it is remarkable to notice how speedily the attention of the committees to which the bills were sent was directed to the main features of importance, with the result that the work of legislation in the latter part of the century is mainly confined to elaborating and supplementing leading provisions laid down in outline in the early years. To some extent this supports the view taken above that private acts were largely by way of formal embodiment of agreements which had come into fairly frequent use, and which consequently provided a usage and a series of precedents for the legislature to follow.

The points of importance in the acts as finally shown by the provisions incorporated in the general act of 1801 relate to the appointment of commissioners, the method of procedure and work of the commission thus appointed, the laying out of roads, the mode of division, provisions as to hedging and ditching, the apportionment of the expenses, and the enrolment and custody of the award.

[1] As at Chipping Barnet, 2 G. II., an act to inclose 135 acres of common by Duke of Chandos. A rent to be paid in relief of charges for the poor; Hadleigh, 2 G. II.; East Wellow, 2 and 3 G. II.

The first few acts, while mentioning some of these matters, are very general in character; but with their exception, careful provisions are early introduced for effective security in the various directions. Such progress can be sketched under the separate headings. Speaking broadly, by the end of the decade, 1761-1770, the insertion in the acts of the requisite safeguards had been secured by experience, while in many respects an even earlier date may be taken.

With regard to the appointment of commissioners, the bill naturally follows the agreement when such is recited, but they are bidden to act with impartiality, an exhortation which is finally embodied in the oath which is prescribed. The oath was generally adopted about 1760,[1] and after that date is usually stated in the provisions of the act.

The method of procedure and work is more intricate in its development. In the first place, there is a gradual growth of prescription as to the publicity to be given to the application for inclosure and of the times and places of the meetings to be held for its determination. This need manifests itself at an early date, and in the Sunningwell inclosure elaborate care is taken to secure public notice.[2] From the beginning of the reign of George II., clauses as to the notice to be given and other like matters are common. There was another point of importance which is determined by much the same date. The commissioners are to take notice of the quality of the lands held as well as of the quantity;[3] and to enable their inquiry to be as complete as possible, in certain acts, as at Crofton, they are bidden to examine lands already held in separate ownership—that is, the so-called "old inclosed" land. A regular survey is soon enjoined, and at a comparatively early date the commissioners are empowered to appoint a surveyor. This practice appears to have been very general, and is treated by Horner as essential. On the

[1] Horner, p. 60. [2] Cf. Chenington, 1 G. II.
[3] See above, Chenington.

other hand, the early acts themselves do not contain any very definite instructions as to the way in which claimants are to make their claims. By the end of George II. it has been found necessary to state a limitation on the powers of the commissioners. These are not to extend to any decision as to the actual titles of the claimants, such titles being transferred to the new allotments.[1]

The laying out of roads is very early designated as a first duty of the commission, and instructions to this effect, though at first confined to public roads, are soon extended to meet the case of private roads.[2] The width of the roads and conditions as to fencing form part of many acts.

The actual allotment occupies considerable attention, and is fully dealt with in many early acts, with some one or two minor exceptions. Thus, they are to be made without any undue preferences, they are to be accepted in full compensation, their acceptance is to be signified within a certain limit of time, and the consent of guardians may be taken on behalf of minors, or those incapable of managing their own affairs. On this latter point, a reservation is finally made so far as such acceptance is concerned, since in the case of minors a power of acceptance comes to be reserved.

Again, the provisions as to hedging and ditching of allotments soon acquire a fairly regular form, though here a number of small points both as to time and manner occasion a certain amount of variation as they present themselves through experience. Thus the ownership of trees and hedges in land transferred claims attention. For some time the original owners have the right of removal, but by the general act (1801) they are to be transferred and paid for. Temporary fences for the protection of newly planted boundary hedges are allowed for a limited period of time, ultimately fixed at seven years.

The division of expenses and the financial responsibility

[1] See Farthingstone (Northampton), 24 G. II. Cf. p. 75.

[2] This finds place in the case of Chenington.

of the commissioners become more important features as time goes on.

So far as the general structure of these private acts are concerned, a fairly constant form seems to have been attained by the end of the reign of George II., by which time a considerable number of acts had been passed, many during the active inclosure years beginning with 1751. Horner's treatise amply confirms in this respect what may be gathered from an inspection of the acts themselves. No doubt the method adopted from the first of sending the bill to a committee led to this uniformity in usage.[1] The experience thus gained soon shows itself in this way. It is also manifest in certain standing orders passed by the House of Commons towards the close of what may be called the first section of the first period of inclosure acts—that is, the years from 1751 to 1780. Three such standing orders are important. In 1774 all bills are to include a clause compelling the commissioners to account in full for all monies laid out and assessed by them. In 1781 it is laid down that there are to be provisions as to the fencing of the carriage roads which must include a regulation as to the distance within which trees must not be planted ; and also as to the appointment of a surveyor, whose first work shall include the fencing of such roads. His salary is to be provided either by the sale of some part of the lands, or by a rate levied on those interested in the inclosure.

The approach to uniformity, together with the differences in many points, mainly, it is true small points, served to bring into prominence the need for a general act which should contain general regulations. But a general act was urged on other grounds than this. It was advocated with fervour in the interests of inclosure and in order to secure its greater rapidity. The warmest advocates of any

[1] The procedure in the case of Ropley can be traced in the Journals. The bill was received from the Lords, and referred to a Committee who heard the petitions for and against it. (*C. Journals*, xvi. 385.) It was passed by the Commons, 27 March 1710.

such measure supported it as a means of securing that which they desired, universal inclosure of the lands that lay open throughout the country. It was in this spirit that the project of a general act was put forward by Houghton in 1681, though the form of enactment as suggested by him was permissive. Similarly, the more continued support given to any such measure towards the end of the eighteenth century was largely inspired by a like desire. Thus one writer,[1] just one century later than Houghton, urges on this ground a general act to be administered by permanent commissioners. His suggestions largely confine themselves to the commons, thus ignoring the open fields. In respect of the commons he advises the appointment of commissioners for each county who shall proceed to apportion and inclose the commons. Their action might be directed first to cases where special requests were made, but otherwise it should be exerted generally throughout the county, though he admits that, on opposition by a majority of five-sixths of those concerned, their powers should lapse and the commons be allowed to remain. The attitude of such well-known reformers and expert writers as Arthur Young and Marshall was in favour of some general measure, and a like aim can be traced in the parliamentary efforts in the closing decade of the century. But the effect of a general act in procuring uniformity in inclosure receives much notice both by these as well as by other writers. Thus it is pointed out that a general act with general provisions would do much to lessen the complaints due to the bad methods adopted in certain instances.[2] Furthermore, it would be a means of decreasing expense.

With the year 1795 began a serious parliamentary struggle to introduce changes into the law which might facilitate inclosure, on the one hand by the reduction of

[1] *Observations on a pamphlet entitled an Enquiry into the advantages and disadvantages resulting from Bills of Inclosure, etc.*, 1781, pp. 56-7.

[2] *An Enquiry into the advantages and disadvantages resulting from Bills of Inclosure*, 1780, p. 27.

the attendant expenses, and on the other hand by the provision of means whereby the obstinate opponents of the improvement should be deprived wholly or in part of their powers of resistance. The attempt was keenly contested, though the weight of the new Board of Agriculture and of its president, Sir John Sinclair, was exerted in favour of the proposed change. The course of events may be traced.

On 11th December, 1795, a committee, including the indefatigable Sir John, was appointed "to take into consideration the cultivation and improvement of the waste, uninclosed, and unproductive lands of the Kingdom." Its report, presented 23rd December in the same year, treats of the general position of common and common right, and of the difficulties and expenses attending inclosure. On 2nd February, 1796, it was read and a bill brought "for facilitating the division and inclosure of waste lands and commons, by agreement among the parties concerned, or a certain proportion thereof, and for removing certain legal disabilities that might otherwise stand in the way of such agreement." On 22nd February it was read a second time and sent to a select committee. It was brought into the House on March 18th and again sent to a select committee. The report stage was reached on April 22nd, when the consideration was deferred till May 4th. When the Speaker took the chair on that day the House was counted out, the bill consequently falling through. As may be judged from this rather remarkable record the bill met with steady opposition, due, it may be, to its failure to meet the considerable difficulties of the position. The most controversial clauses were those empowering a majority to decide and compel inclosure and appointing commissioners. Together with these there were proposals of a much less disputed nature, and it was no doubt with the aim of drawing a line of separation between these very different proposals that a motion was made (March 21st) to allow the committee to cut the bill into two. This, however, was negatived.

A new attempt was made in 1797, when on March 27th another committee, with a like reference and including Sinclair, was appointed. Its report was followed by resolutions which were moved and then embodied in two bills; both of which were brought in on 5th May. This to some extent shows an attempt to carry out the idea of separating the less from the more controversial aims of those anxious to forward inclosure. One bill met with a fair amount of support. It sought to facilitate the power of agreement, and especially provides that in cases coming under it all those interested should be agreed; in other words, it furnishes a uniform method of formal agreement.[1] This bill passed the House of Commons, being read a third time 7th July, and was read a first time in the Lords; a motion, however, to commit the bill (14th July) was negatived, and the bill itself rejected. The other measure was far more extreme. Its aim and its methods may be judged from its title. It enabled any person or persons entitled to any waste, uninclosed, and unproductive lands, common arable fields, common meadows, or common of pasture, in that part of Great Britain called England, to divide, inclose, and hold the same in severalty." But this fails to represent adequately the very drastic nature of its proposals. It almost gratuitously emphasises points on which controversy was sure to arise, going in this respect far beyond the bill of the preceding year. By that a majority could compel inclosure; by this a minority, however small, could require a separation and allotment in severalty of that which was determined to be theirs. The rest of the land would remain in common. The clause as to the appointment of the commissioner also deserves a word. A commissioner was to be appointed by both assenters and dissentients. These two might agree,

[1] "For dividing, allotting, and inclosing the waste lands, commons, common fields, and the commonable lands in that part of Great Britain called England, by agreement amongst the parties interested therein, and for removing any legal disabilities that may stand in the way of such agreement."

From the body of the bill it applies to England and Wales.

if they could, upon a third. If they failed to agree, they were to draw lots, and the one who was successful was to have the right of appointment. It is surprising to find that this measure received a second reading (15th May) and went so far as to be sent to a committee. On May 24th its further consideration was deferred for three months.

The account of these two attempts brings into clear relief the different motives instigating the parliamentary campaign. On the one hand was the desire to introduce a much needed administrative reform ; on the other a desire to force inclosure in all directions and on all lands. The unstatesmanlike pertinacity of those who clung to the more extreme hindered for some time the practical relief which could be obtained by an alteration in the legislative method of dealing with inclosure.

A new campaign opens in 1800, but this time the more moderate party was obviously in the ascendant. On 8th March in that year a third committee was appointed. Its report, which was presented to the House of Commons on 17th April, dealt mainly with the difficulties and expense attending inclosures. In view of these certain resolutions were agreed to, and with more caution than on previous occasions sent up to the Lords. After consideration the Lords passed resolutions in much the same sense, which were duly sent down to the Commons (9th July). The main point thus dealt with was the desirability of incorporating in one measure the general provisions requisite on inclosure. A bill for this purpose was brought into the Commons, 16th July, and read a third time, 23rd July. It was read a first time in Lords on the same day, but there it stopped, its further progress being cut short by the prorogation on 29th July.

Next year a bill "for consolidating in one act certain provisions usually inserted in Acts of Inclosure" passed both Houses,[1] and received the royal assent on 2nd July.

[1] Its passage was rapid: thus in the Lords, First Reading, 25th June; Second Reading, 27th June; Third Reading, 30th June.

The circumstances occasioning the demand for the general act relate to the marked increase in inclosure taking place during the last decade (1791-1800) of the century. A steady growth, largely to be attributed to the rising price of provisions, was manifesting itself, and with this growth the desire for a more uniform and less expensive method gathered strength. On the other hand, to the enactment itself may be attributed much of the continued activity manifested in the early years of the nineteenth century. So this measure, while originating in the prominence given to the need for better machinery, by the improvement it introduces in this respect lends new force to the movement. Private acts were simplified, though, unfortunately, there is little ground for believing that the heavy expenses were diminished greatly, if at all.

In another sense an important result was achieved. The passage of the act, aided by the results of the first census, really marks the defeat as a party that counted of those who had been opposing inclosure and denouncing its results.

III

THE METHOD OF INCLOSURE IN THE EIGHTEENTH AND NINETEENTH CENTURIES

PRIOR to the eighteenth century the method of inclosure was so much a matter of voluntary assent or arbitrary action that little uniformity or principle could be expected in the division of the land concerned. Land was allotted and the fields were inclosed in a manner which was agreeable to those acting together or in such fashion as the stronger might determine. But with the systematic development which took place in that century a fixed method and certain principles of apportionment manifested themselves. As the years passed, and as the acts multiplied, these became stereotyped in practice to such an extent that on the one hand the method followed in inclosures conformed to certain definite and almost invariable principles, while on the other hand the administration of the law grew to be nearly as important as the law itself. So large was the discretion of the commissioners entrusted with the actual determination and carrying out of the inclosure that a sketch of the way in which they proceeded is a necessary basis to any attempt to estimate the fairness of the division and the general effect of the great change. Fortunately the materials for such a sketch are not wanting. On the one hand we have the statements of able contemporaries, especially Horner and Marshall;[1] on the other hand the awards

[1] The best account of the process of inclosure is undoubtedly to be found in Horner's treatise, *An Essay upon the nature and method of ascertaining the*

drawn up by the commissioners furnish interesting information as to the way in which their functions were performed.

In the main the matters requiring attention relate to the steps whereby the acts were carried out, but in one or two aspects the process of obtaining an act is of at any rate equal importance.

The application for an act involved expense, and though this may for one purpose be regarded as part of the general expense, from another point of view it requires separate notice by reason of certain particular effects. Some one or more people had to be found prepared to undertake this initial expenditure, in case of failure to obtain an act and to carry out the project. In such case this expense would fall upon the promoters of the scheme. When the application was successful, it, together with other expenses, was defrayed out of a fund raised in the course of the inclosure. No doubt, as time went on, the matter became largely one of routine, but though the probability of failure was comparatively small, it could not be overlooked. Even in the latter half of the eighteenth century failure was a possibility to be taken into account. Sometimes the attempt to promote a petition broke down, sometimes the private bill failed at some point in the proceedings prescribed by the standing orders, and had in consequence to be withdrawn.[1]

specific shares of proprietors upon the inclosure of common fields, 1761. Next to this may be placed Marshall's *Appropriation and Inclosure of Commonable Lands*, 1801. This, however, is less systematic and complete for this particular purpose. The process itself is illustrated in the awards. These, taken together with the acts in pursuance of which they are made, give an authoritative picture, but one which needs some interpretation.

[1] In the case of Sancton, an antagonistic petition was presented and referred to the committee with instructions to hear counsel (*Com. Journals*, xxxii. 2, xxxii. 182). Cf. case of Ryslip, 1768-9. In the case of North Littleton the petition was ordered to lie on the table (8th Feb. 1770, *Com. Journals*, xxxii. 674). The bill for Ereswell was not brought in (10th Feb. 1770, *Com. Journals*, xxxii. 688). Petitions might be opposed; thus the attempt at Weston Zovland was opposed and defeated by Bishop of Bath and Wells. *Agric. Report, Somerset* (1798), p. 199. Cf. *North Riding*, 201, bill dropped on opposition of lord of manor.

This need for preliminary outlay combined with other causes to give the large proprietors of land a very dominant interest in the case of any application. Their assent was necessary, and their wishes and interests largely determined the particular form of the application. The part played by the small proprietor was, at any rate at first, insignificant. During the controversy in the latter part of the century, mainly indeed from those opposed [1] to inclosure, comes complaint as to the power placed in the hands of the great proprietors. In one case a bill is dropped on the opposition of the lord of the manor; in others we are told that the application is determined by the wishes of a few great proprietors. These instances might seem to confine their influence to determining whether or not there should be inclosure; but it went further. The petition might be drafted to suit their interests. After drafting it had to be submitted undoubtedly to a meeting of those interested, but in that case the meeting often could do little but either accept the proposal without alteration or reject it entirely. Often, we are told, the small owners were practically unable to resist,[2] even though opposed altogether to inclosure. With regard to this matter it should be remembered that the part thus played by the large proprietors and lords of the manor was less dominant than in earlier days when the action of the lord of the manor, either alone or in concert with some few large owners, was unchecked by the consideration of the rights of others. It was subject in theory to some assent of a certain proportion of those interested, and as time passed this assent became a more real factor. Further, the question of expenses must be borne in mind. From another point of view, that is with regard to the general interest of the country and the

[1] Thus Addington, *An Enquiry into the reasons, etc.*, p. 21; *An Enquiry into the advantages and disadvantages resulting from Bills of Inclosure*, p. 18. Among those favouring inclosure Young bears testimony to much the same effect (*Northern Tour*, i. 222-233).

Agric. Report, Lincoln (1799) p. 85.

improvement of cultivation, the enterprise of the large proprietors was required. They were more alive to what was taking place in other districts, and keener to share in the advantages offered by new methods. But for them and their interest, inspired though the latter might be by the hope of personal advantage, the progress of inclosure would have been much slower. Still, it is no doubt true that in the first two-thirds, and to a considerable extent throughout the whole eighteenth century, the real power in determining on inclosure and in devising the particular form and detail of the petition lay with the few and not with the many. One matter was held to be of great importance. In most cases the commissioner or commissioners were named in the preliminary agreement or petition, and the appointment merely ratified by act. In others the choice was to be made at a public meeting to be held subsequently. In practice, however, it does not seem correct to assert that this appointment of the commissioners, in which the promoters undoubtedly exercised great influence, resulted in substantial injustice to those possessed of legal rights. Their duties were defined by practice, while in many districts the office became almost professional in its character, the same individuals proceeding from one inclosure to another.

As has been said the commissioners were appointed in different ways. They were in most cases named in the petition or draft bill, but sometimes they were elected at a public meeting held under conditions laid down by the act. In the case of vacancies caused by retirement or death the surviving commissioners often had power to appoint a successor after due public notice. Their number varied. In most instances three were appointed, but sometimes one man was chosen to act alone, largely, no doubt, on ground of expense.[1] Nor are instances

[1] Only one commissioner was appointed in the following, for instance: Oaksey, Wilts (*Close Rolls*, 1802-3, Pt. 10, No. 10); Iken, Suffolk (*Close Rolls*, 1804-5, Pt. 15, No. 14); Damerham, Wilts (*Close Rolls*, 1841, Pt. 69, No. 1). At Goring (*Close Rolls*, 1812-13, Pt. 26, No. 3), there were two com-

wanting where a neighbouring gentleman acted without payment.[1] This, however, was not usual, and it may be doubted if it was desirable, since, as will be seen, the task was one of considerable intricacy and such that both time and experience were required for its equitable performance. Probably the best commissioners were practical men with knowledge of farming and surveying, who gained experience from being employed in inclosure after inclosure. The commissioner was bound by oath to administer the work with justice.

The powers of the commissioners were very considerable; and against this excessive power considerable complaints were raised. Except so far as the actual decision of the title to property was concerned the award of the commissioners was final. It determined at once the claim to common, the amount of that claim, and the allotment to be made in respect of it; and from this decision, provided all forms were complied with, there was no appeal. Against this unrestricted but inevitable power it was protested that the decision of the commissioners ought to be subject to appeal to a court of law, that there was frequent mismanagement,[2] and that the powers thus entrusted were, at any rate in some cases, exercised in an arbitrary manner. With regard to the complaint, it is of course clear that any attempt to supplement the inquiry and decision of the commissioners

missioners. These occasional instances taken from the *Close Rolls* show that at times in small or rather small inclosures less than three were chosen. One commissioner instead of three at Staverton and Boddington in Gloucester, and consequent saving in expense (*Agric. Report, Gloucester*, p. 92).

The usual number was three, and the author of *An Enquiry into the advantages and disadvantages, etc.*, argued that there should be more than three (pp. 46-7), that they should be legally qualified (p. 48), and that an appeal (p. 36) should be allowed from their decision. Such a system, had it been adopted, would have made proceedings almost impossible by reason of delay and expense.

[1] *General Report*, p. 98. *Agric. Report, Hertford*, p. 44.

[2] Stone, *Suggestions for rendering the inclosure of common fields and waste lands a source of population and riches*, 1787, is very emphatic as to frequent mismanagement, p. 81.

by a subsequent legal appeal would have proved a grave obstacle to the reform which it was desired to promote. In this instance, as so often, protest against special powers was with many a mere veil for the desire to obstruct the very purpose for which those powers were conferred. But whilst this was true of many it was not of all. There was mismanagement in many cases, and there was much that was arbitrary in the action of some of the commissioners. One strong advocate of inclosures accounts for the undoubted disfavour attending them in some parts on the ground of mismanagement. Nor was he alone. Again, as to the charge of arbitrary conduct, some confirmation can be found in the statement of some of the commissioners themselves. One, for instance, said that it was his custom when he found that additional expenses had been incurred by what he deemed unreasonable opposition, to take that into account in apportioning allotments to those guilty of such conduct.[1] Another, with an equally rough attempt at equity, made it his business to consider the allotments to the smaller proprietors first and favourably because they, as he said, had little power to decide on the inclosure or to control its course.[2] But instances such as these show a desire to act with fairness. Again, the claims of the poor were very differently dealt with by different commissioners, principles admitted in some cases being ignored in others. Still, taking the conduct of the inclosures and the awards as a whole, there seems to be no ground for alleging a general partiality on behalf of any particular class. The work appears to have been honestly, if not always well, done, and to have been marked by a rough and ready fairness. The defects lay not so much in the commissioners as in the absence of any general body of rules to guide them or of uniformity in the acts they had to carry out, a defect more noticeable in the earlier years and cured by the growth of precedent; and, further, in

[1] *An Enquiry into the advantages and disadvantages, etc.*, p. 40.

[2] *Agric. Report, Lincoln* (1799), p. 85.

the want by some of an adequate appreciation of certain almost inevitable though unintentional consequences. But these will concern us more elsewhere.

The local proceedings were obviously arranged with a view to publicity, a feature more marked with time and distinctly emphasised in Parliament. As a rule they opened with a public meeting called by advertisement, which either considered a petition, in many cases already prepared, or empowered such to be drawn up. After that notices of the intended application had, by the standing orders of the House of Commons, to be affixed to the church door in each parish affected for three Sundays, these falling as a rule in August or September. The draft was then prepared, and signatures obtained, showing consent or degree of consent. With regard to this point the committee demanded proof by witness. The bill then was brought in and passed through its various stages.

But the act obtained, and the commissioners thus appointed, the real work began. As a rule the commissioners held a public meeting in the district and then appointec the officials required to assist them. Apart from a clerk these consisted of a surveyor and a valuer, both of whom had work of considerable importance. Before anything could be effected two things were necessary, the survey and the valuation. The survey, of course, was the simpler of the two. It was a measured plan of the lands and fields to be inclosed, and of the separate parcels belonging to the various proprietors. As a rule existing or ancient inclosures were also measured. If a general exoneration of tithe was involved, a money payment would have to be made on their behalf. The valuation required to be made by some one possessed of good farming knowledge and judgment, who could estimate the real value and capacity of the different acres and parcels of land according to the crops they could bear. "There should be," we are told, "a critical examination of the soil, as well as of the herbage which it produces, an enquiry into its latent qualities, whether it contains anything noxious to any species of profitable cattle? Whether particular seasons are not adapted to it, and how far it is affected by the present? What management it has been under for a course of years past, and the like? To these should be added a due regard to its situation for convenience; and a consideration of the different expense of inclosing according to its greater or less intrinsick value."[1] The object was to ascertain the value of all the land and each part of the land when put to its proper use, that is, after inclosure. With the survey, the valuation, and the present rent roll before them, the commissioners had the materials necessary for the serious work of allotment. The difference between the present value of the land as shown by the existing rents and by the valuation was the *improvement of the field* and the sum of the advantages to be expected from inclosure.

The problem which then presented itself was the fair division of this advantage between the different parties concerned. This may be treated under three headings. First of all rank the expenses of the inclosure and other payments due rather out of a common fund than in any proportion to a right or claim. Secondly, the general, or as they were sometimes termed the abstract, rights of the lord of the manor and the owner of tithe had to be met. Thirdly, the respective claims of those possessing rights required satisfaction.

The general expenses were heavy; but their estimation presented little difficulty. Land had to be set aside for roads, and means provided for their making. In some cases common drainage works were undertaken,[2] and in one celebrated case an irrigation system[3] was provided for. Very often land for a gravel pit might be put aside for road repairs. Again in many inclosures a fund is provided for the poor, though in other instances these receive

[1] Horner, *Essay*, pp. 48-49.

[2] Thus special drainage scheme in Maulden (*Agric. Report, Derbyshire* (1813), ii. 485, etc.).

[3] At Ridgemount (*General Report*, 93-5).

a common, apportioned, it would seem, as a matter of grace. Finally a deduction was to be made for the expenses entailed by the passage of the act and its administration. But these various forms of expenditure are interesting rather from other points of view than in respect of the work of apportionment.

The abstract rights,[1] such as those of the lord of the manor, or it may be the forest ranger, or of the tithe owner,[2] ranked next. With the exception of the last mentioned their determination presented little trouble. Certain deductions were made on a rather arbitrary basis. In the case of tithe there was difficulty. The burden of tithe was heavily felt, and there is little doubt that exoneration from tithe was in some cases a sufficient ground by itself for inclosure.[3] Under these circumstances the claim of tithe to share in the improvement of the field was naturally debated. On the whole this claim was conceded; but the way of giving it effect was by no means uniform. In many instances the share of tithe was reckoned at one-seventh of the land to be allotted, a proportion, Horner contends, sometimes too great and sometimes too small. The other way, and that which was commended both by him and others, was to allot to tithe an amount equal to its former value together with an increase proportionate to the general increase over the whole inclosure, subject to deduction of its equivalent share in the expenses.[4]

It was after these deductions had been made that the real difficulty presented itself. Allowing for expenses and other matters, the rest of the improved value, together with the unknown land or commons, remained for distribution

[1] Marshall, *Appropriation and Inclosure of Commonable Lands.*

[2] As to position of tithe holder see *Argumentative Appeal addressed to the Right Rev. the Bishop*, by the Rev. Baptist Noel Turner (1788).

[3] This seems undoubted. Unfortunately allotments in lieu were not always made, and land not always exonerated. See *Agric. Report*, *Hampshire*, 121-2. *Gen. Report*, p. 20, as to neglect of this in Norfolk.

[4] Horner, *An Essay, etc.*, pp. 82-83: Marshall, *Appropriation and Inclosure, etc.*, pp. 22-25.

among all those who had common rights.[1] Further, inasmuch as they were not to retain their original holdings, one object of inclosure being the consolidation of property and the separation of what belonged to one individual from that belonging to others, an entire redistribution had to take place. At first sight the method of apportionment might seem simple, since the share of each in the estate as it now stood might have been assumed to be the same as that previously enjoyed. The one could be ascertained from the value of each prior to consideration of inclosure values, taken together with that of the whole under like conditions ; a like proportion of the estate at its improved estimate would seem the amount due. But this assumes that the relations between yardland and yardland on the one hand, and yardland and pasture rights on the other, remained in their original state, or, to put the matter from another point of view, that the property of each individual had risen in value in the same ratio as the entire parish or area. This was far from being the case. Some land, such as meadow, was prior to inclosure more nearly rated at its real possible value than other land ; and the various holdings did not consist of uniformly proportioned amounts of meadow and arable. Again, small holdings were more highly rented as a rule than large holdings. Lastly, in the pre-inclosure values or rents a quite inadequate difference was made between lands with large common rights and lands with small common rights. As a result, holdings or yardlands might differ not only in value and amount, but also in the rights of pasture attached to them or in its effective use.[2] In the earlier inclosures in the eighteenth century this difference was largely disregarded, and the proprietors of

[1] Such common rights did not necessarily attach to, and if attached to, did not necessarily correspond to, holdings in the open field.

[2] It is pointed out in *Agric. Report*, *Norfolk*, p. 440, that the proprietors living close by a common make the most of the profit from it, and that hence their interest may be against that of those further off. In one case this led to the refusal to give a lease of common land by joint agreement, those living near objecting. Cf. Marshall, *Appropriation*, *etc.*, p. 31.

the yardlands shared in the improved value and had allotments made in proportion to the value of their holdings. No deductions were made save in the case of land which for some reason or other had no right of common. The lack of justice in this method is obvious, and was soon perceived. To remedy it a modification was introduced. The average value of the lands was taken, and in the case of yardlands or arable holdings in excess of this a deduction of four or five shillings in the pound was made from their real value, that amount carrying with it a diminution of the allotment made to them. This was given to those proprietors whose yardlands fell below the average. By this means it was sought to correct the injustice involved in the assumption that pasture rights corresponded to the value of the arable; whereas, as a matter of fact, the more valuable arable did not necessarily carry with it larger common rights than existed in the case of poorer lands. This modification, however, clearly only served for this one purpose. Even with it the system of apportionment assumed that the yardland had something like a uniform pasture right. Another and very different system was introduced, and was approved by Horner. In the case of each holding subject to common rights a deduction is made from the value in proportion to the nature of the right in question; in other words, an attempt is made to arrive at the real value of the individual property apart from the rights which, before inclosure, were shared in common by the body of the commoners. The value of these deductions was added to that of the commons and like common property, and the fund thus formed was, after needs and claims coming under the two previous headings had been satisfied, divided among the proprietors, either according to the yardland as a unit where each yardland possessed equal stock, or according to the actual number of different beasts[1] for which common right was enjoyed. The

[1] As to differences between rights of common for horses, cows, and sheep, see Horner, *Essay*, pp. 70-2.

allotment to each was made according to the total composed of (*a*) the value of his *several* property, and (*b*) the amount thus ascertained.[1]

When the gravity and delicacy of the task undertaken by the commissioners is considered, the existence of complaint against them is not astonishing. It is rather a matter for wonder that the complaints were not far louder and universal. Apart from the mere matter of quantity and the situation of the respective allotments, the change entailed in the new arrangement of the fields and the consequent alteration of old customs must often have led to dissatisfaction. The commissioners had, as it were, to lay out the village anew. In place of the old fields, cultivated in strips and according to a common order, each man was allotted now a small or large several piece. The new inclosures were as a rule regular and compact, thus differing from the ancient inclosures.[2] They lay, in the case of

[1] The question of title to common, especially as between ancient houses and sites and lands, was sometimes raised as a legal issue.

[2] *Agric. Report, Cumberland* (1805), p. 214, observes that the ancient fields are small and irregular, and those divided within the last thirty years are laid out in straight lines; Marshall, *Rural Economy of West of England*, ii. 169-70, states of the Vale of Taunton that the fields are "of various form and size." In some places fields differ; thus about Little Gaddesden, in Hertford, an observer in 1748 says the arable fields are nearly all in small inclosures, most of which are quadrilateral, some square, some oblong, a few curved, and the meadows likewise (Kahn's *Account of his Visit, etc.*, pp. 215-6). The curved shape of hedges is said by some to arise from the sweep of the plough, and it has been pointed out that it was the custom to plough round the field in which the strips lay. It has also been attributed to the line of division following water-courses, etc. (*Notes and Queries*, Second Series, vii. 373-4, viii. 19, 32, 440). If we take Tusser's account of the way in which fields were formed out of the waste or common, another reason for a curvilinear shape and an irregularity of size is given; above, p. 30, note 1, giving account from *Tusser Redivivus*.

A considerable difference is to be expected between inclosures according as these occur sporadically and in early times, or by way of uniform treatment of a township and in later times. The inclosures of later date often involve the treatment of a considerable area, even the old inclosures within that area being sometimes brought into the division.

There are certain tests, though not necessarily invariable tests, of early inclosure.

some, at a considerable distance from the little village of farmhouses, while others had the advantage of having their holdings conveniently near. Roads had to be made, hedging and ditching done; while in some instances little or no increase in value could be perceived for many years. Some of the allotments might be unprofitably small. Some land as meadow highly valued before the inclosure might even undergo some diminution through having to contribute to the expenses. No doubt the individual proprietor was indemnified by a rise in the value of other land, but the absence of immediate and invariable advantage was enough to try his faith. That discontent was so small and satisfaction so general is the greatest testimony which can be adduced as to the advantage of the change.

One of the most important duties imposed on the commissioners from a public point of view was the laying out of roads. Though inclosure did not escape criticism in this respect, which alleged that existing roads were interfered

Firstly, there is the irregularity in the form of the fields, alluded to above. The fields often small.

Secondly, in old inclosed country the hedges were often more thickly filled with trees. Marshall points to the old coppice hedges in Devon, Dorset, and Somerset. *Rural Economy of West of England*, i. 65, large mounds topped with coppice wood. The age of these fences is great beyond memory. ii. 108, in vale of Exeter even older than in other districts, as shown by smallness of fields, and the mounds topped by hedges, in general furnished with trees. Leland, *Itinerary*, ii. 65, as to elms in hedge rows of Somerset. These trees, elms and oaks, as in Kent and other districts. Cf. ii. 136, 169-170; *Agric. Report*, *Kent*, citing from Halsted's *Kent*: "The inclosures in the hills are small, and furnished with thick hedgerows of elms." See also as to fruit trees in hedges, Nourse, *Campania Felix*, p. 28; England's *Remarques*, as to Worcester, p. 211, etc.

Thirdly, inclosures of villages formerly in arable common field usually preserve some trace of the early village of farmhouses and of the high ridge and furrow, whereas those lacking in cases of inclosure from the forest state (Marshall, *Rural Economy of West*, ii. 137-8, as to houses; also see notes on chapter i.).

Probably much land marked by these features was inclosed from the wild state. (Marshall, *Gloucester*, ii. 190; *On the Appropriation and Incl., etc.*, pp. 9, 10.) High banks are regarded by some as an indication of this.

with, complaint of this kind was rare;[1] and the general effect of the movement was undoubtedly to develop and improve the means of locomotion. The roads mentioned in the act were of two kinds, public and private; a distinction which accurately describes the twofold object which had to be borne in mind. On the one hand, thoroughfares were to be maintained, regulated, and, if need be, provided. On the other hand, access to the various buildings or allotments was required. From the public standpoint, the former were undoubtedly the more important. The increasing attention paid to them may be traced through the acts of the eighteenth century. This work precedes the division of the land. It appears as a duty and first charge, as it were, in early acts; forms the subject of a standing order in 1781; while by the general act of 1801 it was the first duty of the commissioners to lay out public roads and prepare a map which should be open to inspection. These roads were to be constructed at the common charge of the inclosure. In some cases their fencing is provided for, but that might be part of the charge of the allotments. In addition, in many cases, as has already been noted, provision was made of gravel pits or quarries[2] to be at the disposal of

[1] Addington (*An Inquiry*, 1767, pp. 17-18) complains that roads were often interfered with in inclosure. Cf. *Agric. Report*, *Rutland*, 155-156, as to bad methods of making roads in some cases; *Agric. Report*, *Hunts*, pp. 277-8, as to bad methods of maintaining roads when made. The writer of the last says roads sometimes good and sometimes bad. Speaking of the private roads, he says that many of them were bad; but where concave he deems that this occurs not by intention, but by subsequent neglect.

In early times, inclosure and hedging may have been harmful, since many roads then were little other than tracks unmade and without foundation. In such cases openness was a safeguard; and if the word "lane" be rightly interpreted as a road the following passage from Fitz Herbert indicates some apprehension: "Also it may fortune men wyl say, that if all should be inclosed, that there would be many foul lanes as there be in Essex" (*Bk. of Surveying*, p. 98.) But when roads were made this danger becomes less real. As inclosures ordered and provided means for the laying out of roads, they ensured many roads where otherwise there would have been fewer.

[2] Thus Award at Chilton Foliat (*Close Rolls*, 54 G. III., Pt. 8, No. 1).

the local surveyor for their maintenance. The case of private roads was somewhat different. As these were for the benefit of individuals, though their course was to be determined and they were to be laid out by the commissioners, the expenses were to be apportioned by the individuals among the interested parties. The herbage along their sides belonged to the adjoining proprietors. There is no doubt that the roadmaking performed under the inclosure acts co-operated with the increase in and improvement of roads under the Turnpike Acts[1] in effecting the great change in the means of locomotion which marks the end of the eighteenth century. The complaints of Arthur Young and of others as to the condition of the roads are familiar: if not the cause of, inclosures often accompany improvement. Not the least evidence as to this development is the curious and active discussion as to the form of roads. The form was important, because many roads were in the process of construction. As against the arguments of those who urged that roads should be made concave in shape, with a gutter, as it were, down the centre, the slightly convex form was generally adopted. Of even greater importance than the uniform adoption of this method, which appears to have been general where roads were made at all, and something more than mere tracks worn by traffic and occasionally repaired, was the system of roadmaking introduced by Macadam. Prior to him, stones of unequal size, together with gravel and soil, were thrown down. They seldom welded together into a uniform surface.

[1] Turnpike Trusts originated in the desire to maintain and improve roads. In many cases, however, they are directed to the provision of new roads (see *P. P.* 1851, xlviii. *County Report*, *Kent*). While the first act was in the seventeenth century, such acts are scarce till Anne, and not really plentiful till towards the end of G. II., thenceforward they are very numerous. The Trusts were usually for limited periods, but these were open to renewal. By the beginning of the eighteenth century, the length of road under Turnpike Trusts was about 17,000 miles (in 1818, 17,601, *Parl. Papers* xvi.; in 1821, 17,329, *Parl. Papers*, 1821, iv.), of course the majority of roads were not under such Trusts, other roads being given in 1818 at 86,116 miles.

Frost destroyed cohesion, and heavy rain washed away the gravel or sand till too often the roadway consisted of a bed of uneven boulders set in mire, clay and gravel. The introduction by Macadam of stones broken small and into like sizes, and then spread evenly over the surface, was an invention of the greatest utility.[1]

Another respect in which the public interest is manifestly sought is in the provision made for the poor in many of the awards. Without discussing the general effect of inclosure upon either the small owners or the poor, it may be pointed out here that in a large number of cases special action is taken to obviate the hardship which might be felt by the poor where strict legal rights alone were taken into account. From that point of view they had little to expect when the common lands were inclosed, though custom had enabled them to participate to no small degree in the profits of the common, or even in those of the open field. The loss of these chance gains would have been a grave blow to them, and in a real sense a public injury. Provision for the poor was frequently made, sometimes by the reservation of a common, sometimes by letting some land—the proceeds going to a common fund to provide coal.[2] It is difficult to say how far this provision was made out of a sense of fairness to the individuals otherwise injured, or in view of the public interest. Probably the first motive was there, but the circumstances of many of the inclosures and the motives which underlay them make it probable

[1] Macadam's evidence before the Commons Select Committee in 1819 (*Report*, 1819, pp. 17-34, *Parl. Papers*, 1819, v.), contains his own description, which is fully corroborated by other experts. His contention was that by this means a road was made solid, consistent and yet flexible.

[2] At Shernbourne, allotment was made for the poor; *Close Rolls*, 1769-70, Pt. 17, No. 15; cf. *Agric. Report*, *Norfolk*, p. 169, at Stokesby. As to a common, *ib.* p. 162, 176; *Agric. Report*, *Oxford*, 27-9. As to land let for a fund for coals, *Agric. Report*, *Norfolk*, 94-5; in several cases also (*Agric. Report*, p. 92) a case of payment of a sum for turbary, probably turbary customs, not for turbary attached to land, cf. *General Report*; and as to need of compensation to poor without rights, Horner, *Essay*, p. 25.

that the latter was not without force. From an early time the dangers of depopulation and popular distress had been the most cogent arguments alleged against inclosure. They were treated as deserving serious consideration by the crown, the privy council, or the parliament as the case might be. Again, at a later time, opportunity was taken of the occasion of an inclosure to reserve a portion of the land for public purposes and for recreation. Care for the poor ranks with these as a matter of public interest.

Another matter relating to the conduct of an inclosure requires some notice.

Fencing or hedging[1] was required to be done, and regulations were made as to the time when such work had to be complete. In one way it complicated the work of apportionment, since, as was obvious, some allotments involved more expense in this direction than did others. As was pointed out by one writer, the expense of fencing small allotments was proportionately greater than that incurred in the case of large allotments. Hence, he argues, their share of the general expenses should be diminished.[2] This was one of the matters which the commissioners had to bear in mind when determining the respective allotments awarded to the various proprietors. Horner emphasises this point with particular relation to the case where the size of the allotment is large, because of the inferior nature of the soil.[3] Again, the expense of fencing land invested the whole question of the best and cheapest methods with much importance. Several technical treatises and reports bear witness to this.

Finally expense was an unfortunate and an inevitable

[1] *General Report*, section v., treats of fences, etc., which are said to be very expensive, p. 81 ; in an average inclosure this came to something like seven or eight shillings an acre. *Annals of Agric.*, viii. 103, the expense of fencing one of the great obstacles. This sometimes unnecessary, quicksets being cheaper than posts and rails, " when wood is scarce."

[2] *Agric. Report, Gloucester*, p. 92.

[3] Horner, *Essay*, pp. 90-98.

feature of inclosure.[1] Quite apart from any cost incurred in the improved[2] management which became possible when once properties were separated into several ownership, itself no light matter to small proprietors if they were to enter into competition with large owners or their tenants with large capital, there were the expenses involved in procuring and administering the acts. Of these, the expenses required for fencing or hedging and ditching, and for general drainages, where such were carried out in pursuance of, or in conjunction with inclosing, rank as charges for improvement, and are analogous to those mentioned above, except in so far as the performance of the work under the auspices of the commissioners enacts a difference. In all probability this did not lessen the expense, though it may have ensured better methods. In addition, however, there was a large body of general expenses. The cost of obtaining the act was heavy, Again, the work of the commissioners in laying out roads and performing the incidental work, caused a considerable deduction from the anticipated value of the improvement. The commissioners and their officials required payment, and public liabilities involved had to be met.

These latter expenses must be distinguished from those more immediately concerned with improvement. They are equally inevitable, but the work in respect of which they are incurred, is not in itself beneficial or, at any rate, directly remunerative to the individual proprietor.

[1] It was, however, no novel incident nor confined to inclosures by private act. At the beginning of the century, before these were in use, reference is made to "the great quantities of lands which in our own time have laid open in common, and of little value; yet when enclosed have proved excellent good and suddenly repaid the present great expense incident to enclosures" (*Dictionarium Urbanicum Rusticum et Botanicum*, under Enclosures). The probability is that by the system of agreement then in operation, the cost was much the same as under the earlier acts, except in respect of parliamentary expenses. E. Lawrence gives a form of agreement which he recommends (*Duty of a Steward to his Lord*, 1727, p. 37).

[2] *General Report*, pp. 32-3, states that inclosure is sometimes opposed by farmers because it will cost more in cultivation, especially in outlay of capital at the beginning.

Hence it was that against these expenses a natural outcry arose. In many cases the prospect of them led to the defeat, or at any rate the postponement of the projects, where otherwise such would have been favourably considered. The general burden indeed was admitted on all hands, even by those most desirous of urging on the change.[1]

The more practical minded of these turned their attention to the consideration of the best way of lessening them. Passing over the local and occasional economies effected, as for instance where the number of commissioners was lessened, or where the free services of local gentlemen were obtained, this requires some attention. First of all it is necessary to realise both the magnitude and the nature of the expense. The Board of Agriculture, taking the average of a considerable number of acts, calculated that the average number of acres involved in each act was 1162, and that the average expense of each act was as follows. In connection with obtaining the act, £497; the survey and valuation, £259; commissioners, etc., £344; fences, £550 7s. 6d. Of these items, the latter three would obviously vary very greatly with the size, and further with the nature of the questions involved. An inclosure of a common was less intricate than where open fields as well as commons were concerned. The estimate is quoted, not as showing the average cost proportioned to the size of the inclosure, but to afford some idea of the amount, and of the items comprised. An examination of the cost affixed to many of the awards, shows that this so-called average does not exaggerate the burden, and that the complaints of expense were not unnatural.[2] Where was reduction possible? It does not seem that the cost of

[1] As to this *Agric. Report, Oxford* (1798), by R. Davis, p. 28; *Somerset* (1798), pp. 55-62; *General Report*, p. 98, etc. An instance given of a case at Haltwhistle, where expense has proved the only, but a sufficient deterrent. But there is no difference of opinion among writers as to the great expense.

[2] The Ashton Keynes inclosure (*Recovery Rolls*, 19 G. III., Hilary, 115), in which there was little charge for fences or roads, and where the acreage was 1980, cost £721. This was executed very cheaply, the cost of the act being only £320.

fencing was too great, if that was to be done in a satisfactory and permanent manner. Again, the expenses and payment of the commissioners, though heavy, were not successfully impugned in the complaints made. On the whole, the indignant repudiation by Mr. Davis of the charge of extravagance on the part of the commissioners was probably justified.[1] Certainly the accusation occurs rather as a general complaint against expense. Again, the legal expenses in connection with procuring the act were high, but this was common to the system of private acts, and was not peculiar to the case of inclosure acts. These indeed appear to have been promoted and obtained at the lowest cost, owing to the uniformity of treatment secured by the standing orders passed with regard to them. It was, however, urged that economy might be achieved by a General Inclosure Act. Granted the feasibility of such, this was probable. But in this case the real economy would have lain in an act, compulsory at least on the assent of a majority, and administered uniformly by special local officials. This was suggested more than once. Against it was ranged the feeling of those who disapproved of compulsion, and also the opinion of those who urged that a general act would not take account of local circumstances. Another suggestion was more successful. The general act of 1801 contained the various clauses necessary and common to all the private acts ; but though it may have lightened the expenses in some measure, the parliamentary cost continued high, while the administrative cost remained undiminished. The expense was met in different ways. In a great many cases part of the land was sold ; in other cases a rate was levied on the land of all those interested. Sometimes other expedients of meeting part at any rate of the cost were attempted. Thus some of the land might be temporarily let, or during

[1] *General Report*, 331-3. From the constant repetition of the same names in awards, it is clear that the office of commissioners was professionally discharged in many cases. Thus Mr. Davis was at one time engaged in sixteen inclosures (*General Report*, 332).

the period of inclosure ley or joist cattle might be taken in at so much a head.[1]

Some other duties presented to the commissioners. When all the land was not the subject of apportionment, exchanges of land had to be arranged and authorised in order to make holdings compact; mineral rights had to be dealt with; while in some cases the herbage along the roads was specially awarded. It belonged, as a rule, to the neighbouring lands.

The commissioners having laid out the land and effected the division, embodied their decision in what is known as an Award, to which a map was often appended. Of these Awards a copy had to be deposited with the clerk to the county. In addition copies were often enrolled, these latter finding a place most often in the Recovery Rolls. There are some in the Close Rolls and the Plea Rolls.

After the passage of the act of 1801, while the private acts were simplified and the process made more uniform, the actual business of the inclosure proceeded in much the same way; and when by 8 and 9 Victoria, c. 118, Inclosure Commissioners were appointed, the former procedure was obviously copied. The method under this may be briefly summarised.[2] An application on a particular form has to be made to the commission and signed by the owners of one-third in value of the interests in the land. Unless the project is manifestly objectionable an assistant commissioner is then sent down to inspect the land, to inquire into the accuracy of the statements, and to hold a meeting to hear any objections to the proposals. On his report a provisional order for inclosure would be issued setting out certain conditions as to allotments of land for exercise or

[1] At Knowle, in Warwick, 307 acres sold to defray expenses (*Recovery Rolls*, 1 and 2 G. IV., Hilary 61). *Agric. Report*, *Derby*, ii. 79-80: At Ashby Wolds, in Leicester, the commissioners after declaring extinction of common rights, let the fields for the next two years, and the rent went to expenses. ii. 197: At Brassington, the commissioners during inclosure took in ley or joist cattle at so much a head. Elsewhere some of the land was sold, or a rate levied.

[2] The machinery is sketched by Cooke (*Inclosure*, pp. 85-88).

recreation and for the labouring poor, specifying the proportion due to the lord of the manor and the means to be taken for the protection of public rights, and determining the ownership of minerals. By the first act active steps could then be taken in certain cases, some, however, requiring parliamentary sanction, but by the fifth amendment act the need of such sanction was applied to all cases. The provisional act or order was then deposited in the parish, and an assistant commissioner sent down to hold a meeting for obtaining assents and dissents. On the assent of two-thirds a special act was obtained. A valuer was then elected, who had to value, to determine claims, and to lay out allotments, his decisions being subject to the commissioners, and, in the case of claims, to the courts by way of appeal. After this, a meeting was held by the assistant commissioner to hear objections in general to the report, and these being disposed of, the report was embodied in an award signed by the valuer, which, on confirmation by the commissioners, became final.

Apart from other matters this act is of interest as illustrating the development of central control, shown in the Appointment of Commissioners, whose powers ultimately pass to the Board of Agriculture. But there is another point deserving notice. Allotments for public exercise and recreation are recognised, as also those for the labouring poor; these latter might indeed be subject to a rent charge not exceeding the value of the land so allotted prior to inclosure. The former recognition of public interests was in fulfilment of the policy embodied in a resolution of the House of Commons of 1837 (March 9), "that in all Inclosure Bills provision be made for leaving an open space sufficient for purposes of exercise and recreation of the neighbouring population." In the discussion on this resolution it was fully recognised that such allotments were in view, not of legal, but of what might be termed moral, rights.[1] It was also urged by one member that a distinction must be made between

[1] *Hansard, Third Series*, xxxii., pp. 162-4.

commons with open fields and stints, and those dealing only with wastes, a distinction embodied in the act. By a return made in 1841, it was shown that this order had been complied with in all but 9 cases out of 63.[1] In 1869, a select committee of the Commons reported[2] that since the act of 1845, 618,800 acres had been inclosed of which 368,000 could be assumed to be waste of manors, not subject to stints, and so falling under sections 30 and 31 of the said act; out of this 368,000 acres, the allotments to the labouring poor amounted to 2223 acres and those for purposes of recreation to 1742 acres. As the committee considered these amounts inadequate, a bill was introduced to secure their extension. The discussion which took place showed an almost grotesque misunderstanding of the early nature of common.

As the system laid down under the Inclosure Commissioners grows out of that gradually formulated in the Private Acts, so this latter was very probably a development of the methods adopted in the agreements of the early eighteenth and of the seventeenth century,[3] that is of the agreements referred to by experienced men like the Lawrences. These methods probably involved some method of representative assent by the interested parties. If so, they carry into effect the interesting proposals[4] of Alderman Box with respect to the division and allotment of wastes. "And therefore your Lordship's orator desireth some good order, law or decree to be had or made between the lords and the tenants for their assurance. That every lord of any manor, where such wastes are, with four or five of the gravest tenants, appointed and chosen by the tenants of the same manor, upon a pain by a day assigned to him and them, to appoint and divide the wastes of the same manor orderly to every tenant of the same manor a portion

[1] *Parl. Papers*, 1841, xxvii. [2] *Parl. Papers*, 1869, x.

[3] In early seventeenth century D. Lupton writes (*Harl. Misc.*, vol. 9), against the landlords inclosing their villages. "The surveyor is his quarter-master which goes like a bear with a chain at his side, and his two or three parishioners who walk with him help him to undo themselves."

[4] Lansdown MSS., cxxxi., 22 (1576).

of the same waste grounds according to the rent he now payeth; and the same so appointed, divided and set out to remain and continue to the tenement for the same tenant, and the same tenant to have and occupy the same tenement with the waste ground so appointed and all the appurtenances to the same tenement belonging during the estate he hath in the same tenement, without any more rent paying for the same but only his labour and cost, to grub, cleanse and sow the same within two years following or else to lose the portion of the waste to him allotted."

The circumstances giving rise to the introduction of a commissioner are a matter for conjecture. Possibly mutual convenience may have led to the appointment of an arbitrator in agreements, and out of such an office that of commissioner may have grown. But this is surmise.

So far as the work of division and allotment is concerned there is little or no ground for any charge of unfairness. The influence of the large proprietors and of the lord of the manor, to which allusion has been made before, no doubt determined the application for inclosure and may have decided the nomination of the commissioners, but so far as the latter point is concerned, the choice was much restricted by "the necessity of peculiar qualifications as well as a reputation for experience and integrity in powers employed for this purpose,"[1] while there was ample opportunity for protest against any undue exercise of power in this respect. In the latter part of the century, at any rate, the parliamentary requirements in the case of inclosure were exacting and the procedure in committee seems to have been careful and well considered. Direct allegations of general unfairness are rare.[2]

[1] *General Report*, p. 119.

[2] The writer who emphasises this risk is the author of *An Enquiry into the advantages and disadvantages resulting from Bills of Inclosure*, 1780. Even his language is vague.

The value to be attached to his criticism in this respect is considerably discounted by his own suggestions that there should be more than three commissioners, that they should be legally qualified, and that there should be an appeal from their decision.

The most doubtful matter was the action of commissioners with regard to the claims of the neighbouring poor, that is, with regard to the recognition of claims which were not based on legal right. Some greater uniformity would have been desirable. Two things must, however, be borne in mind. Private agreements to inclose were equally free from a legal obligation to recognise them. In the second place, in a large number of awards these are given fair treatment, the commissioners, in other words, being guided by equitable as distinct from purely legal considerations. Taken as a whole, the work of division and apportionment appears to have been discharged conscientiously and fairly.

APPENDIX A

LEGAL NATURE OF COMMON

The legal distinction of common into *common appendant*, *common appurtenant*, *common of gross*, and *common by vicinage* is of great importance as marking different stages not only in the conception of common, but in respect of the part it appears to have played in the agricultural system and the life of the people. From this view *common by vicinage* perhaps should be excepted, since it arises rather by way of convenience and in imitation of common as it otherwise exists. Of the remaining forms the two first, *common appendant* and *common appurtenant*, are by way of both contrast and comparison ; they differ in form, often in matter, and largely in incident. They are alike in being attached in some way or other to the possession of a holding or a tenement. *Common appendant* is the right to common on the part of the possessor of a freehold created prior to the Act *Quia Emptores*. It is limited in respect of kind to pasture for animals necessary to plough and manure the soil, and is proved not by prescription or grant but by the mere possession of such an estate. Its extinction through unity of possession is only possible on the purchase of the whole waste. *Common appurtenant* consists of rights attached either by grant or prescription to holdings either freehold or copyhold. It includes pasture for beasts other than these mentioned above, and also estovers and turbary. Proof may be required of its existence.

With regard to these, the main difference lies in the distinction thus drawn between common necessarily and invariably involved in the ownership and cultivation of early property, and that which exists partly through need and partly as supplement. *Common appendant*, that is, points to the view early held that common of a particular kind was practically involved in the very early stages of the village or manor. Without it cultivation was impossible.

Therefore it is proportioned to the holding and equally of necessity restricted to animals whose use was essential in early agriculture. The very circumstances of its existence assume actual uniformity in cultivation. Arable is the central feature of the agriculture. With *common appurtenant* other elements come into sight. The circumstances of the time are viewed as changed. New holdings, some freehold and some copyhold, have been created, while on the other hand, variation in the methods of cultivation has made its appearance. Thus both in character and amount the common attached to cultivating tenements varies very much. The change in the nature of common reflects with much accuracy the change which necessarily occurs with agricultural progress and development. Common varies because cultivation is no longer carried on in an invariable way, and because the proportion of arable and stock is not constant. Common is not throughout to be regarded as a means of maintaining the land in efficiency, because some part of it exists for the profit it directly yields, and not for the profit which it assists the ploughland to yield. In other words, though no doubt still a part of a system, it is not solely as such that it is granted or enjoyed.

These conceptions are distinct, eminently reasonable, and their growth may be traced through legal decisions and writings. But it is difficult to point to a definite recognition of the difference thus portrayed in very early times. Even when Fitz Herbert ventured on definition his language is anything but precise. According to him, "Common appendant is when a lord of old time hath granted to a man a meseplace and certain lands, meadows and pastures, with their appurtenances to hold of him. To this meseplace, land and meadows, belongeth common, and that is called common appendant," while "common appurtenant is when a man hath had common to a certain number of beasts or without number belonging to his meseplace in the lord's waste, this is common appurtenant by prescription, because of the use time out of mind." If we go back to Bracton it is quite clear, firstly, that a marked distinction is drawn between rights of herbage which are held without a tenement and these which appertain to any such tenement, and secondly, that in the case of common without number, the *free tenant* claims according to his free holding in the vill (539). Even then, however, there were differing rights both as to kinds of pasture and kinds of cattle. Legal decisions, however, early assumed the existence of the limited agricultural common described above under *common appendant*. The conception based on this usage treats *common appendant* as an incident of socage tenure, and hence universal in the case of lands in original socage and as applicable only over the lord's waste in respect of arable holdings. Service is thus the basis of such common rights and its proof carries with it a claim to them. That service as shown by outward sign was a basis of common is obvious from the pages of Britton (II. xxviii.), which treat of the proceedings where common over a manorial waste is claimed by those who are not tenants of the manor. Here their lord is sued, and he must reply by showing on their behalf either that there is reciprocity between the manors in this respect or that they yield some sign of service. Common of this kind is in a different category to that which arises from grants. The refusal of some writers to include common of estover and turbary under *common appendant* rests on the ground that these are not, and through their nature cannot, be universal. That they were very variable in amount and that they appear to have been by no means universal is true, but on the other hand it should be observed that their treatment by early writers as Bracton and Britton gives no ground for their separation from ancient rights, as of pasture, and further that right of estover and fuel seems as essential to the early constitution of the vill, as those of pasture for beasts actually employed on the land. So far as actual grants are concerned, a greater diversity is to be observed as to amount and kind, thus marking the different conditions of cultivation adopted in different districts and in different manors.

To the historian a far more vital distinction than that between *common appendant* and *appurtenant* is that between common measurable by its relation to the holding or tenement, and that which is determined in amount by grant or by usage. It is the gradual development of this latter which marks the change in the position of common from a means of cultivation to a separate source of profit, and much of the special importance of *common appurtenant* rests on the fact that such common was increasingly of this kind. It paves the way to a further stage in the history of common.

Common in gross is a not unnatural result of the definition of common by number or amount instead of by immediate reference to the needs or capacity of the arable land. It stands in startling opposition to that early condition when common was an inalienable element in agriculture, and necessarily proportioned to the amount of the cultivated land; and yet the change whereby rights once thus held merged into common in gross, is so gradual and continuous that it is almost impossible to point to any particular stage in the development as marking the alteration. Common apportioned to land merges into common for a limited number, and that comes to be attached to dwelling houses or cottages without land, presumably because these mark the former possession of the land in respect of which the amount of common had been previously determined. It is a step further, but a great one, to sever the attenuated tie which still remains to indicate the relation between the restricted common and the arable. *Common in gross* obviously could not come into existence save in cases of stinted or numbered common; and till usage had obscured the primary nature of common, it was not to be recognised as part of common. This, at least, would seem the natural interpretation of Bracton's words, "It ought not to be considered a right of common which one person has in another's ground by paying for it or by purchase, when he has no tenement to which the right of common can appertain, but it ought rather to be called a right of herbage than of common." The legal recognition of *common in gross*, even though the actual change to this form was not frequent, is a significant sign. The essential unity of the system of cultivation, based on the relations of arable and common right, was at an end. In some instances, and in some districts, it could no doubt be argued that common right was a necessary adjunct to the plough; but in the main this contention could no longer be maintained. Common was a separate form of property, and time was to decide how far property of this kind was profitable.

The interest of *common by vicinage* lies in the evidence it affords of the extent to which convenience ruled the common. Technically speaking, such commons arose rather in a mutual agreement to disregard trespass than in any definite creation. There are two points of interest.

On the one hand, the claims to common by the tenants of one manor on the waste of another were a matter of sufficient importance to receive separate legal treatment, and are explained at some length in the handbooks of Bracton and Britton. Here the question of reciprocity plays an obvious and important part; though, as has been already said, such claims might rest on a basis of service.

On the other hand, the common of shack, which was a feature of the common field and its customary cultivation, evidently originated in a kind of common by vicinage. Britton says: "Between neighbours resident in one fee such common is more properly called vicinage than common, as where one neighbour allows another to common with him provided the other allow the same" (II. xxvii. p. 389). This and other passages seem to show that the practice was at that time far from universal. Again, as is shown elsewhere, the extent to which common of shack prevailed in the sixteenth century is doubtful; but then by that time a large quantity of new land must have been taken in from the wild state with the result that inclosed arable existed, quite apart from arable with incidents of common. It may be doubted if it prevailed uniformly in those parts where the common field was small in comparison with the commons and pasture grounds.

APPENDIX B

ADMEASUREMENT

In all early common and also in later creations, save where the common to be enjoyed was precisely determined by number of beasts or some other numerical test, the amount was held to be apportioned to the free arable holding, the tenement, or yard-land of the commoner or tenant. The method, or rather methods, whereby this was carried out are a matter of considerable interest. In Bracton's time there were, in many instances at any rate, two elements to take into account. One of course was the arable holding itself. If a man claimed more than his due, as Bracton tells us (335), either the lord of the manor might impound his surcharge, or others possessing rights which were infringed by his claims might proceed against him. The matter is put very clearly by Britton, who laid it down that a right of common was limited by that to which it was appurtenant (383). Thus, he adds, if a man possessing common appurtenant to 100 acres alienate all but one, he should retain right of common proportioned to that one acre only. The other element was the capacity of the common itself. As Bracton says, if a grant be without number enquiry must be made as to the number of cattle the pasture might suffice for at the time of feoffment. But in the earlier period the limit would be reached no doubt by the needs of the land, since the waste was large. Hence came the lord's right of approvement, which was a right of using the waste as he chose, providing only that sufficient was left to the commoners. It is only as common or waste diminishes that the limit thus imposed by the capacity of the common itself begins to be effective. The suggestion that the early rights of common necessarily consisted of the whole herbage or other yield of the common divided in due proportions among the various holdings without regard to the needs of these, does not seem tenable in the face of the circumstances under which a lord might make new grants of common over the waste, of the fact that an action against him for over-burdening the common had to allege injury to the commons and of the passages referring to the actual requirements of the land. As to this latter, Britton states that at a trial of a claim of common the jurors would determine how many beasts the commoners may common there *in respect of every acre*. This, it may be remarked, points to the actual needs of the particular land as determining the amount of common due to the individual holder. As a matter of fact, even after the general allotment of the land to common and the original feoffment of the tenants, subsequent grants and feoffments might so reduce the common available that the whole might have to be remeasured and the superfluous claims made on different sides reduced (Bracton, 539; Fleta, 263); in other words, the common rights acquired would be proportionally curtailed in the case of all commoners. But this would only occur as population and holdings alike increased. What, it may be asked, would measure the needs of the land. It is clear, as has been said, that the amount of common was proportionate to the arable land. It seems equally clear that this amount bore some relation to the general requirements of arable. But the words already cited from Britton carry us further. They suggest, though somewhat vaguely, that the requirements early taken into account were those which actually existed in the case of each holding. If this were so land would claim according to the labour really required to work it in each case. Some acres would require more, some less. It is not unreasonable to suppose that this was actually the case at first, and that in early times the beasts for which common pasturage was due were those needed on the particular acres in question. An analogy is presented in the case of common of estover, where the quantity of timber depends on the actual house (Bracton, 551). Such actual correspondence, if ever definitely recognised, could not last. When Bracton wrote, in most cases the quantity of the tenement, apart from its nature, determined the common, and Britton, when writing elsewhere of claims of common by usage, says that the pasture "then should be in hotchpot and so divided that all there might share alike in such a way that every acre might be put on equal terms."

The abandonment of the test of actual need rendered necessary some other practical means of determining the amount of common pasture due to the arable land. This was sought in the number of cattle or beasts levant and couchant on the land; that is to say the number kept habitually on the acres in question, it being apparently assumed that the number so kept were required for the general purposes of cultivation. The method thus adopted amounted to the right of common for as many beasts as could be supported from the land during the winter. In a certain sense this would depend on the particular land, but it would rest on the quality and yield of the land, and not, as formerly, on its need. In this form common of pasture, so far as it does not give way to definite numbers, continues. The test at best was a rough one, and was obviously open to a good deal of evasion. Undue claims find a particularly ready place when common of pasture in gross comes into being, and when in cases of stinted common, where the number of beasts for which common is due is stated, the practice grows of taking beasts at joist to make up the number. It is hardly too much to say that by the sixteenth century the unstinted common had become a claim of common for an unlimited number of beasts. Hence the unstinted common was almost invariably overburdened, a fact which is not surprising when we read that there are grave complaints of the overstocking of even stinted commons. This state of things was largely to the advantage of rich commoners or the lord of the manor, who got together large flocks and herds and pastured them in the common lands to the detriment of the poorer commoners, who, unlike them, could do little in the way of providing winter feed, and now found themselves ousted even from their slender privileges in the commons.

The limitation of common of pasture by the need of providing winter feed becomes wholly vague and impracticable with the breaking down of uniformity in cultivation. Rights restricted only in this way become practically unlimited, and thus stand in contrast to those where a stint is established of definite numbers. Thus it is that a curious change occurs in the meaning of common without number. Where this phrase is used in early times, as for instance in Fleta (262) "sine numero" or by Bracton, the statement of such common is to be taken as restricted by considerations of acreage and needs as given above. When it comes to be used later it reflects the actual result experienced then. Such common has become right of pasture for an unlimited number. Cases of grant, it is true, occur at earlier times when in response to the need, as it would seem, for more pasture than is required for the beasts engaged in cultivation, there is the specific statement that other than these or than those levant and couchant are included. Thus in a grant to the convent of Armethwaite the common of pasture is for their tenants with *all* their beasts. Still more unrestricted was the grant to the prior and monks of Beauvale by N. de Cantelope in 1343 to "have common for all manner of cattle whatsoever, wheresoever they couched, or from whencesoever they came, through his whole dominion or lordship" (Thoroton, *Nottingham*, ii. 242).

BOOK II

PROGRESS OF INCLOSURE

I

THE GENERAL PROGRESS OF INCLOSURE[1]

In tracing the progress of inclosure it is necessary to bear in mind the extremely complex nature of the movement. Inclosure was no simple and uniform process. Further, it arose from agricultural causes and formed part of an agricultural development, acting thus as a means of adapting the land to the needs of the time, either wisely where the interests of the community at large were served, or unwisely where individual agricultural profit, though opposed to the general interests, yet dictated the course pursued. But to say that it was part of the agricultural development necessitates the consideration both of the nature of inclosure and also of the factors determining and the conditions attending it.

So far as the character of inclosure is concerned, it is pointed out elsewhere that this differed very considerably, the term itself being applied to three very different actions. It took place sometimes as a part or adaptation of the ordinary system of common or common field; sometimes as the means whereby land wholly outside cultivation or but

[1] This chapter attempts a summary of the general progress of inclosure, and consequently includes much dealt with in the two next chapters. Detailed references are to be found in Appendix A, p. 238 *et seq.* This, as also Appendices B and C, should be consulted throughout.

It should be remembered in dealing with the amount or percentage of land inclosed, both in the text and the tables, that a certain amount of the land in any district or county was occupied by the actual villages, the public roads and the inland waters. Hence the percentage would be higher if only land open to use were taken into account.

partially affected by incidents of common was brought within the area of effective cultivation; while lastly there was the inclosure movement which superseded the common field system, and so forms a further stage in the cultivation of the particular land in question.

In the first place, as cultivation developed, some inclosure almost necessarily occurred. Not only was such not subversive of the open field system, but in some cases it was essential to its effective and practical working.

Thus closes were taken in and doubtless increased for various purposes till we find them existing to the considerable extent described and advocated by Fitz Herbert. Such or similar to these are the stocking closes occurring in different places, possibly as the necessary means of providing feed at times when common was either not available or present in insufficient amount. No doubt in certain places particular needs for some inclosed lands arose, as, for instance, in fruit districts as in Worcester, Hereford, Gloucester, and elsewhere.

Again temporary or even permanent inclosures were sometimes made out of the commons or wastes, as described by Tusser, and alluded to in different cases. These plots might be used for different purposes but often came into arable, this in particular being the object of temporary intakes. When these were permanent, they formed some of the "ancient" inclosures which often present themselves in eighteenth century awards. In some cases they are numerous, constituting a considerable amount of the land of the townships.

Another and not infrequent source of such ancient inclosures was the practice of some land in the field being inclosed forming "several in open." The extent of this practice can hardly be estimated. It was evidently not infrequent, to judge from the references of both Coke and Fitz Herbert, and from the various legal cases which arose; and equally evidently it did not imply the cessation of the open field system, though clearly tending to its modification. When practised on a small scale, such inclosure probably strengthened the existing system by making room for new or increasing needs.

Taken together, these varying forms of inclosure tended to the development of the common field system and probably did not lead to conversion of a kind which occasioned serious complaint. The last mentioned kind was inconvenient, no doubt, and owing to this formed the occasion for legal action. Two out of the three forms would seem to be more probable where the common field villages were firmly established and where an agricultural population was widely settled on the land. The same, however, cannot be said of the other, that is the second form.

The quantity of land inclosed for these various purposes was often considerable, to judge from the plans attached to the awards of the eighteenth century.

In the second place, the gradual growth of population in a sparsely peopled land led to the extension of cultivation over land either in a wholly wild state or forming part of a large waste employed to little purpose. Such waste or wild land consisted of three main kinds, hill or moor land, forest, and fen. Where these existed the opportunity for approvement, with or without new grants, and inclosure presented itself.

The first question which naturally occurs is as to the conditions under which such approvement or such use occurred. In this connection the distinction legally drawn between common appendant and common appurtenant has some significance. In the latter case the right to common had to be proved, a feature which shows that in grants made after Edward I. the common might and would vary. Still less would the common field system of cultivation with common in shack, that is, mutual rights over arable after harvest, necessarily prevail. As the Statute of Merton was of this date, approvement, when it took place, brought land under cultivation under conditions different from those prevailing in the earlier settlement. No doubt in many cases the established system was imitated and extended, but in other cases, and very likely in the majority of cases, land thus treated was free from the incidents of common which tended to frustrate and delay the assertion of individual ownership. Sometimes the land was inclosed directly, but it would seem probable that in others the actual inclosure might be delayed ; but here the land none the less lay ready to inclose. It was, that is, separated in ownership. In Marshall's view this was the case with much of the land in the west, and the high banks in the extreme west and elsewhere have been interpreted by some as the necessary means of protection adopted when land was directly inclosed from a wild state and required defence against the depredations by wild animals. In addition to land so distinctly marked as unsuited to cultivation by reason of hill, forest, and fen, there was much that was poor, and though within the range of some agricultural use, employed to comparatively little profit, as for instance the poor sands of Norfolk and Suffolk.

The locality of such land, and the date of its reclamation or inclosure are matters of very great importance. Evidence as to the first exists in the character and features of the land itself, and in the evidence of early agricultural settlement.

A view of the country shows that in general the Central Plain and its extensions into Lincoln and the East Riding, and into East Anglia, presents the greatest surface of open land. Despite the occasional elevations and ranges which break its monotony, it is a level surface as contrasted with the hill districts which surround it on the north, down the west, in the south-west, and along the line of the downs. Consequently these bordering regions offer the opportunity for inclosure from the hills and rising uplands. Speaking broadly, the record of the eighteenth century shows by far the highest percentage of inclosure in the district thus environed. The regions of broken land with hill and dale are little inclosed during this period. The generalisation is a rough one. Much inclosure took place at the end of the century in the Cotswold, which had remained in the main a rich open sheep pasture till late. Again there was considerable inclosure in the Mendips. The chalk hills came under the influence of the movement late, as is shown in the progress of inclosure during the eighteenth century; but at the very beginning of the seventeenth century a distinction is drawn between the Chiltern district of Buckingham and that which was less hilly; in the former there were many inclosures while the latter lay champaign. As a rule, hill districts show a lower percentage of inclosure than do the plains during the eighteenth century. This is curiously illustrated by counties divided between hill and plain. It is traceable in Buckingham. In Leicester the registration districts of Ashby and Market Bosworth are inclosed only to 10 and 14 per cent. respectively,[1] while the centre and east show a much higher ratio. The part of Gloucester west of the Severn is very little inclosed, that on the east very much more.

Forest regions in many cases coincide with those of the hills; but in certain cases these are the major and the hills the minor feature. In other instances there are great forests or woods on comparatively level ground. Thus there is the forest land on the west of Nottingham, the forests in Hampshire, the woodland in the north of Warwick. Where comparison is feasible, much the same features present themselves as in the case of the hill districts, that is, land where much forest remained to be broken up in the fourteenth, fifteenth and sixteenth centuries shows a less percentage of inclosure in the eighteenth than the neighbouring land. This is the case in Nottingham where the east and the west are in considerable contrast; thus, of the three registration districts on the west, Basford is inclosed to 26 per cent., Mansfield to 34,[2] and Worksop to 12, while of the four adjoining, Radford is inclosed to 30 per cent., Bingham to 40, Southwell to 26, and East Retford to 38. Again the difference between the north

[1] That is, exclusive of common or waste.

[2] 14 per cent. being of common.

of Warwick and the south is not only visible in the same way, but definitely recorded by Leland and succeeding writers. Bishop Gibson in his additions to Camden wrote of the inclosure which had occurred in the forest districts as the wood was diminished. The case of the forests is of peculiar importance, since these became accessible to cultivation from reasons apart from agriculture, that is, owing to the destruction of the woods for fuel and building. As woods vanish, the lands pass into agricultural use under conditions which evidently diminish the need of future legal action. In these cases the *number* of inclosures under act are out of all proportion to their *extent.* This can be seen from comparing the percentage of the townships in any district in which inclosure occurs with the percentage of the land affected in the same district. The disproportion is conspicuous in the particular districts concerned in the counties mentioned, Gloucester, Warwick, and Nottingham. A large number of the inclosures are of common as distinct from open field. A comparison of the neighbouring districts is all that is needed to make these features evident.

Nor are these instances alone. The same results in the eighteenth century records occur in respect of the Forest of Dean, the New Forest, Savernake, and Marlborough, in Hertfordshire, in the Weald, and in Rockingham. In all cases and localities where old forest land had gradually yielded and been cleared, inclosure by act is less than in the surrounding country, this holding true in the main of both common field and common. Of course where forest land had lingered on, even though partly denuded of wood, as in Charnwood, inclosure by act takes place in this very period. But where change occurred previously it could be achieved either by approvement or by actual inclosure from the wild where rights of common did not exist either for forest product or for pasture. This particular conversion of land, at one time inaccessible to cultivation, to active use is the more important, because in the case of much of this land the alteration was achieved only when some actual clearing, arising not because the land was sought but because the timber was wanted, had occurred. The connection of woodland and inclosure was recognised by several writers in the seventeenth century. Thus Gibson and Morton write of changes from woodland recently in progress. Trigge (1604), in the *Humble Petition of Two Sisters*, specifically exempts from condemnation "the inclosure of Essex, Hartfordshire and Devonshire and such woodland counties," while Blith (*Improver*, p. 83), in rebutting the assertion that inclosure necessarily means pasture, says "consider woodlands which now inclosed are grown as gallant cornfields as be in England," and instances the western parts of Warwick, the northern parts of Worcester, Stafford, Shropshire, Derbyshire, Yorkshire.

The position of the fens is well defined, and the history and conditions of their reclamation clearly ascertained. The great fen drainage schemes affected several counties, Lincoln, Northampton, Cambridge, Huntingdon, and Norfolk. Though on reclamation a considerable partition to individual ownership and to inclosure took place, some parts remained subject to some rights of common, a feature which led to the passing of inclosure acts in the eighteenth century even for areas already dealt with in the preceding century. In addition to these the marshlands in Somerset were evidently to some extent reclaimed before their final treatment under act, and here too a new area was introduced into cultivation under altered conditions. As a rule, both here and elsewhere, inclosure acts deal mainly with common. Here, too, a general disproportion exists between the number of the inclosures under act and their extent.

Turning next to the date of such reclamations, partitions, and inclosures, that of the fen districts is the seventeenth century. The forests, no doubt, had undergone contraction from early times, but this became very pronounced in the sixteenth and seventeenth centuries, when the increase of towns seriously threatened the existence of the supply of timber and wood. Outcry as to the future finds utterance. The encroachment on the waste hill lands is less easy to date. Probably it was more continuous.

In the third place, inclosure takes place on the agricultural lands, lands, that is, of mixed open field and commons. Here the object is either change in use or more effective use. The extent to which arable use and advantage led to common field inclosure in the early sixteenth or fifteenth centuries is open to debate. That it did so in some cases seems quite clear, not only from instances given by Mr. Leadam, and from Fitz Herbert's argument in their favour, but from the significant references of Leland to the results in many cases. As is pointed out elsewhere, Leland in his *Itinerary* makes mention of inclosed land some sixty times. In some twenty-six of these cases he adds references to the corn in these inclosures, sometimes noting that the land is abundant or fruitful of corn. On the other hand, it is true that very few of these instances affect the Central Plain, and that most lie in counties where there was hill land. But taking into account the position of these lands and their contiguity to champaign ground, it cannot be assumed that inclosure in all such cases had occurred out of the waste. In any case, however, the fruitfulness to which he calls attention indicates an advantage of inclosure. So far, indeed, as the later sixteenth century itself is concerned, not only do writers like Standish advocate change, but tenants inclosing against each other claim that their land is free from the entry of each other's cattle after crop. Whilst this no doubt can be well substantiated, it is not sufficient, of course, to make good the proposition that arable profit was the chief, or even a chief object in the changes occurring in the open fields in the early part of that century or in the preceding century. Certainly Fitz Herbert's words do not bear this interpretation. During those years arable profit would seem rather a not very infrequent result than a constant consequence and aim. On the other hand, the custom of intakes, and Tusser's references to inclosure on wastes and the like, point to a concurrent arable development on such lands.

The factors attending and the conditions influencing inclosure are varying both in their nature and their importance. Not only so, but the importance of these, and especially of some, is by no means constant; it changes from time to time according to the presence of and the correspondence between different causes and conditions, and especially by reason of changes taking place in the agricultural system.

In the first place, there are certain factors relating to the land both in respect of its soil and suitability.

Firstly, the soil itself requires attention. In dealing with the inclosures under act, this particular feature will be treated at length. During that period, in the chief regions concerned, the progress of the movement was largely dependent on the nature of the soil, inclosure being determined by it, chiefly of course because it was in consequence of some special feature that land could be utilised to greater or less profit when inclosed, or had in some instances remained uninclosed till that time. But in a wider sense there is some correspondence between the great drift belts of soil and inclosure of the last three centuries as a whole. To realise this it is only necessary to compare an inclosure map with the drift or even solid geological maps. The coincidence is rendered the more emphatic by the corroboration afforded by the map devised from Ogilby's *Book of Roads*.

Secondly, the topography of the country is of importance. As that has been already alluded to less need be said here. To some degree it stands in relation to the geological structure of the country. It is of importance in two ways. On the one hand it influenced the course of agricultural settlement, making land suitable by reason of accessibility or unsuitable owing to remoteness. On the other hand, it was the obvious reason why some land remained long unfamiliar with agricultural use owing to exposure either to the malign influence of the weather or to the no less dangerous attacks of neighbours. One very important result arises from the effect produced on land already in cultivation by the agricultural use of land previously in a more or less wild state.

Thirdly, the position of land with regard to a water supply counts for something. Early settlement was almost of necessity in the neighbourhood of water, and nearness to the village meant suitability for cultivation. It is to the abundance of water-bearing strata that the early agricultural development of Northamptonshire has been attributed. But, of course, as agriculture became more diversified, the abundance of this feature in a country like England pointed in a particular direction, namely, in the direction of rich pasture. This suitability tended, it may be suggested, to that development of closes near the settlement, which manifested itself even under the authentic open field system; but as time went on it naturally increased the growth of inclosure, and of inclosure for a particular purpose.

In the second place, with the growth of towns and industries an increased demand arose for food products side by side with an increased demand for industrial labour. Ogilby's account of the roads shows a great tendency for the development of inclosure in the neighbourhood of towns and in town areas. This, though not invariable, appears as very frequent from the map. But if we take the area within reach of the metropolis, and also the two industrial districts in the eastern counties and in the west, there are distinct signs that at the end of the seventeenth century, if not before, a considerable part of the land was already inclosed. This is strengthened by the words of Moore, who, writing in the middle of the seventeenth century, is careful to say that he does not complain of inclosure in counties where there are other occupations.

The influence of town development was felt in several ways. The new population increased the demand for food supplies, as indeed for raw material, where industries were established. A good instance of this occurs in the cloth-working district in Devonshire, where not only was wool required from other counties, as Cornwall, Dorset, Warwick, and Worcester, but food had to be imported. In other words, there was a pressure on the home supplies. The demand was not only for grain, but also for animal products. This was fully recognised in a later century; but even in the seventeenth century it is evident from the words of Gibson and Morton that cheese, butter, and flesh were needed. Land had to be utilised with the object of increasing as much as possible the *net* produce. Under these conditions the tendency to inclosure in the case of wastes and commons was naturally strengthened, a feature which might, and in some cases did, react upon the particular use made of the lands till then mainly devoted to arable. Further than this, it seems probable that the lands near the towns would be largely turned to pasture. This would be so obviously in the case of dairy products. It is more difficult to say how far the item of carriage, in respect of corn on the one hand and beasts on the other, would affect its use. Both in the sixteenth and seventeenth centuries there was a considerable trade in the carriage of grain, but then cattle were also transported. On the whole, the balance seems in favour of a new demand for pasture within easy reach of the towns or industrial districts, at least in the case of the provincial towns. London, however, was largely sustained by cattle from a distance. The demand for meat foods certainly increased, and probably out of proportion to that which took place in respect of grain.

Again, town labour tended to withdraw people from agricultural labour. This tendency, which was fully recognised in the eighteenth century, leaves some trace in writings and legislation of an earlier date, as, for instance, in the care taken in the Statute of Artificers to restrict rigidly the classes entitled to enter crafts and mysteries. The development of the domestic system of industries, with a population occupied, to some extent in manufacture, and to some extent in agriculture, had particular effects. Such a population was almost inevitably driven to resort to those branches of agriculture which made the least call on their labour, namely, to pasture, agriculture, when plied as an auxiliary and on very small holdings, being less suited to grain production.

Lastly, the very presence of the town with its novel and less stable conditions was subversive of the mere rule of custom. The traditional methods of cultivation went for less, and profit, and increased *net* profit in particular, went for more. This latter feature, indeed, requires emphasis. In districts where town populations were growing the demand on the land was great, and the capacity for absorbing labour was great. Taken together these constituted a very strong ground for inclosure, and their effect increased with every change in method which made the full utilisation of the soil more dependent on individual ownerships.

In the third place, the effect of inclosures and the agricultural utilisation of wastes and moors, of hill land, and of land once in forest and fen, on the settled agricultural land, needs consideration. Under any circumstances the extension of cultivation over a large quantity of land hitherto comparatively neglected may result in changes in the use made of land already farmed. The relative suitability of the old land for any particular use may be, and very often is, changed. But of course the extent of the alteration depends very much on the nature of the soil brought into use, and the circumstances under which this so-called reclamation—more accurately this introduction—of fresh land takes place. A gradual extension, due in the main to constant causes and to the increase of demand, would have less effect than that which occurs when a considerable amount of land previously inaccessible or unsuited is brought within the range of careful agricultural use, or of some particular agricultural use, especially when such occurs owing to reasons partly, at any rate, disconnected with agriculture. In other words, the supply is new, and not mainly evoked in response to demand. In the case of land which was hilly, broken, and at one time distant, it seems probable that extension took place from very early times and proceeded with some degree of constancy. But the effect of the Civil Wars and the Dissolution of the Monasteries, with the consequent changes in the ownership of manors, must not be ignored. Again, the deliberate re-enactment of approvement under Edward VI. is a matter of importance. Unfortunately, it is open to more than one explanation. It may mark the triumph of those against whom Somerset's anti-inclosure proclamation and actions had been levelled, and whose powers in consequence were doubted. If so, it was a re-affirmation of rights, and of rights which were of very practical importance. On the other hand, it may be due in part to a desire to introduce new arable in the place of that which had been converted to pasture. In this case it is analogous to the subsequent proposals of Alderman Box for partitioning and employing wastes as arable. Even where this was the aim, and it may have been the aim in part, the course thus proposed would lend itself to purposes outside and in excess of the particular need. The woods and forests, however, have a particular and somewhat different bearing, inasmuch as in their case it was the gradual disappearance of the woods through a demand for timber which opened up land to cultivation. Likewise, the inclosing of fens and marshes in the seventeenth century occurs when the knowledge of methods of drainage and the supply of capital render possible somewhat costly and adventurous schemes of reclamation.

It seems quite certain that arable use was often made of these various lands. Putting aside any argument from the analogy of what occurred at the end of the eighteenth century, when much inclosure took place on the Cotswolds and the Chilterns and neighbouring chalk, there is important contemporary evidence. Arable was the object put forward by Alderman Box, and although his scheme was not adopted, it clearly indicates some realisation of such possibilities. Again, the references by Leland to corn in inclosure, though, as said above, these may refer in part to previous open field, often relate to land in the outlying districts surrounding the Central Plain. They prove, at any rate, the use of inclosures for corn. In the case of woodlands in the seventeenth century, Gibson, in his additions to Camden, definitely attributes the conversion to pasture of land in the fielden or south of Warwickshire to the development of arable and the growth of corn in parts of the north as these were denuded of timber and left open to agriculture. This explanation is adopted by Morton with reference to Northampton. It is asserted by Blith. The reclaimed fen lands presented a very large tract of rich arable. In the case of the seventeenth century, some effect must have been produced by the reconversion to arable of land converted to pasture some time before, and inclosed and restored to fertility by its rest from the plough.

In addition the inclosure of open field had an effect upon the area available for cultivation, not only by reason of the more effective use of the fallow, but because when such took place over the land of a township, waste and commons might also be included. This of course was very frequent in the eighteenth century when all or most of the lands of a township are dealt with, being put together and then allocated to those variously interested.

There can be no doubt that the quantity of waste or wild land of which little use had been made, and which passed into the area of cultivation during the sixteenth and seventeenth centuries, was large. If the statements made about it in earlier years of the period are correct, it is certain that it was not dealt with after private acts became common. In other words much comes into use without specific account or legal process other than approvement or some like form of action. And of course this is obviously more frequent where such land abounds.

In the fourth place, the progress of agriculture and the condition of farming had much to do with inclosure both in relation to its object and also to the nature of the land affected. Different periods can be discerned.

Firstly, the incessant cropping of land unskilfully farmed, and varied only by wasteful fallowing, led in many places, and particularly on the less strong lands, to exhaustion. When this was accompanied by a great demand for wool, and a disturbance in the labour market due in part to the effect of the plagues and pestilences of the fourteenth, and to the civil discords of the fifteenth century, the partial abandonment of cultivated land to sheep, and even to a by no means careful system of sheep farming, was initially profitable. The change was hardly progressive. In some cases it meant slight use of the land and a corresponding degree of desolation.

Secondly, in the sixteenth century new tendencies and new possibilities manifest themselves, very different from the foregoing. Agriculture passes into a new stage. The skilful farmer wishes to be freed from his slovenly or less skilled neighbours. From Fitz Herbert on there is a constant succession of writers advocating inclosure from the farming point of view. Fitz Herbert himself, it must be remembered, lays stress on the advantages for breeding and grazing as much as for arable ; but this aspect must be carefully distinguished from that dealt with above. It implied careful use of the land, and provided occupation, if not to the same extent as arable, still to a greater extent than the earlier system of sheep farms.

Thirdly, with the seventeenth century and the development of convertible and also specialised farming, a new impulse is experienced. Not only is there a general motive for inclosure, but at different times there are special motives for the inclosure of particular soils. Dairy land is in demand in this century, as may be seen from the encomiums passed on inclosure for this purpose, by Houghton, for instance. The more inclosed state of the great dairy districts when the epoch of private acts is reached relegates their initial inclosure to much about the same time. This of course meant the inclosure of rich pasture and valley land. When grasses, clover, and particularly roots come into use, land of a different type is capable of a new use provided that it be inclosed. Roots indeed invest light soils with a wholly new value. They seem to have become a prime feature in the movement towards the end of the seventeenth and in the early years of the eighteenth century. In the middle of the latter century scientific breeding affects large areas of land, and particularly the North Midlands, whilst at its end the progress of farming and the pressure on land brings the chalk belt of the Midlands and the Cotswolds into the prevailing practice.

In the fifth place, the effect of inclosure, and to some degree its course, depended upon the facilities for transport at any given time. As long as there was very little opportunity for the carriage of goods, the things needed in a particular locality had to be produced in that locality; and while facilities were incomplete, to that extent much land was prevented from being put to the agricultural use to which it was by soil and climate best suited. Its employment depended more on its accessibility to other markets or its comparative isolation than on natural circumstances of fertility. As the means of carriage improved, this obstacle to a division of production according to the nature of the soil diminishes. But, of course, when this occurred, and when inclosure was the step whereby change was accomplished, a very considerable alteration might be occasioned in the occupation of a district, and when widespread conversion took place, the remedy to those thrown out of work lay at a distance. It is the difference between the mobility of population and the mobility of goods which at times made alterations in agricultural use a hardship, and occasioned complaint not unreasonable if based on fact. Again, if one thing could be carried and another thing could not, the one which could not, had to be produced where it was wanted.

Wool, of course, was easily carried and was a usual article of transport even in early times. Grain could be carried, though less easily; but apparently, save where means of water transport presented themselves, it was usually carried to markets within a comparatively short distance of the place of growth. With the end of the sixteenth century, it became an article for more distant markets, and supplies for these and the growing industrial districts were obtained from a considerable distance. Thus a writer in 1630 speaks of the necessary import into Devonshire of food from outside; and in the seventeenth century a corn trade was evidently fairly well established. Animals for food, and animal food products were largely of local consumption, a feature which remained on in the case of the latter till the eighteenth. Even in that century the local demand of the town and industrial populations for meat and animal products is mentioned as a reason for inclosure for their production within a reasonable distance. Probably in early times the poorer classes in a town were very badly off in this respect. The area, however, from which a town was served increased in the seventeenth century. The grazing butchers, whose occupation of inclosed pasture is complained of, marked a development.

Any attempt to apply these various considerations and to trace the general course of inclosure raises a preliminary question as to the extent to which certain parts of the country were, either in early times or late, really subject to a system of open field cultivation. The matter can be put in another way. It is quite evident that the great mass of the common field inclosures in the eighteenth century was on a belt of land narrow in the south-west and broad in the east and north-east, extending from Somerset and Dorset, through the Midlands and North Midlands to East Yorkshire, Lincoln and Norfolk at the wider end. In the main this consists of the Central Plain, the north of the East Anglian Plain, Lincolnshire and the East Riding. From the evidence of the seventeenth century much the same area is that mainly affected. There are additions, it is true. It may well be asked how it was that this region remained uninclosed and little affected so late. The search for a satisfactory answer to this question brings out one or two possibilities. The earlier inclosed condition of other districts may be due either to special local causes affecting these and occasioning alteration in the arable system and the inclosure of open fields, or to the absence, complete or partial, of the common field system of cultivation in these parts. Undoubtedly the chief technical difficulty in the way of complete individual separation and use lay in the intricate mutual rights affecting the arable. The attachment to arable lands of a right to pasture for a certain or uncertain number of beasts in the commons or the lord's waste presented, in comparison with this, little obstacle. Now with regard to this point there are certain points to be noticed.

Firstly, the counties where there is but little common field inclosure in the eighteenth century vary in respect of inclosure of common or waste. They may be placed under the following headings: North, Lancashire and Cheshire, West, South-West, South-East.

	Per Cent. inclosed.[1]		Per Cent. inclosed.[1]
NORTH—		WEST—	
Northumberland,	10·8 (1·7)	Shropshire,	5·1 (·3)
Cumberland,	23·7 (·2)	Hereford,	1·3 (3·5)
Durham,	17·7 (·1)	Somerset,	10·9 (1·8)
Westmoreland,	16·0 (·3)	SOUTH-EAST—	
NORTH-WEST—		Kent,	·5 (—)
Lancashire,	5·7 (?)	Sussex,	1·9 (1·7)
Cheshire,	3·0 (·4)	Essex,	1·2 (1·9)
SOUTH-WEST—			
Devon,	1·7 (—)		
Cornwall,	·8 (—)		

With the exception of the northern counties and of Somerset there is not much inclosure of any kind in these

[1] Per cent. inclosure: waste outside, and common field within, brackets.

counties. To study the matter more fully reference should be made to the detailed percentage list of inclosures.

Secondly, while a good deal of inclosure no doubt occurred during the seventeenth century, without record, there is no reason for assigning such disproportionately to the counties which figure hardly at all in the inclosure of the eighteenth. Perhaps it would be more correct to say that few, if any, of such counties can be said to have been *mainly* inclosed in that century. Indeed there is a good deal of reference to many of these as inclosed at its beginning or in its early years. The following are referred to as inclosed: Shropshire, Hereford, Somerset, Kent, Essex, Worcester, Devonshire, Hertford, Surrey, Sussex, Berkshire, Hampshire, Wiltshire. To this list there is good general ground for adding Cornwall, where inclosure went on at the end of the sixteenth century. The north, with exception of Durham at the end of the seventeenth century, is practically left out of count at the time. In other words, the counties given above, or most of them, if inclosed from ordinary common field, were so inclosed before the seventeenth century.

Thirdly, with regard to several regions, including many of the above counties, reasons have been adduced at different times for the belief that the agricultural system or the system of tenure was in great part, at least, responsible for the absence of perceptible inclosure. This has been the traditional view with regard to Cornwall and Devonshire, and Dr. Slater has suggested that the counties bordering on Wales owed their early appearance as inclosed, and their absence from the records of inclosure, to differences in the agricultural system, due to an assimilation of their condition in this respect to that prevailing over the border. Co-aration, which was not practised in Wales, did not, he considers, prevail in these counties. With this absence, one of the features which must have stood in the way of effective inclosure, namely, common right after crop over the various strips in the arable fields, also vanishes. There are traces, but the traces are comparatively slight. On the other hand there are other districts where a like cause cannot be alleged, as for instance Lancashire, and such counties as Kent. Cheshire has been allowed to stand as a border county. Kent was accounted for at one time on the ground that the system of common was incompatible with gavelkind, but this explanation was dismissed.

As a matter of fact the question is not as to common existing as attached to lands, but as to common rights over arable, and a custom or system of common cultivation. Shackage, or common of shack, was evidently not a uniform feature, at any rate in the sixteenth century. As has been pointed out in another chapter this is not strict common, but a species of common custom originating in a mutual forbearance as to trespasses, which, when long established, became of legal force. It is recognised as an ordinary feature by Bracton and others, though not laid down, it must be remembered, as a necessary and uniform feature. Britton, for instance, speaking of claims of common over arable, writes, "the tenant resisting it might say, the soil is his several, which he may plough, sow, or inclose at his pleasure, and at all times keep inclosed." It it quite clear that in Coke's time it was by no means invariable; the decision in Corbet's case is decisive on this point. Coke's note is also of importance; "the like intercommoning," he adds, "is in Lincolnshire, Yorkshire, and other counties, as well as Norfolk."

Taking these points into account, it is impossible to regard the system as restricted to the counties in the old kingdom of Mercia. The instance of Dorset, which falls well outside this region, and shows more than 8 per cent. of common field inclosures, is also a distinctive fact. Further than that, the somewhat startling differences between the northern counties, in respect of common inclosure, and those on the west and elsewhere requires explanation. It is also clear that open field with intercommoning was established in parts of East Anglia—probably at one time through the agricultural and early settled district. The position of Hertford is of interest here. There is no doubt that that county was, with the exception of the north on or abutting on the chalk hills and particularly the north-east, early in an inclosed condition, the amount of inclosure under act in the rest of the county being small and very like that taking place in Hereford.[1] Though some weight may be attached to the influence of Celtic customs upon the March counties and upon Cornwall, and possibly some portion of Devonshire, this explanation is insufficient by itself in their case, and is evidently inapplicable when applied to Lancashire and the neighbouring districts of Cheshire, or to East Yorkshire and the north.

Another explanation is that a difference in system was due to the different nature of the land, either by reason of hill, or because of the uncleared forests and long moors, which were unfavourable to agricultural settlements in which arable was the central feature. A large part of these districts came into effective use late from a wild or nearly wild state, either by direct inclosure or under a system of cultivation free from the more complicating forms of common, and in particular from intercommoning over arable. But mere lateness of treatment does not seem sufficient to account by itself for the curiously slight traces of the open field system. Though that was present in some places and to some extent, several influences evidently join to restrain its more general establishment. Among these the nature and circumstances of the land, reinforced on the Celtic side by the reasons alluded to, may be held to occupy a very prominent place. The case of forest by itself has been adequately dealt with; but on hill land, interspersed with forests or covered by moors, the prospects of arable were unfavourable, and, relatively, the advantages for sheep and cattle, not carefully pastured but wandering with little supervision, were great. In addition the triassic formation on which the land rests appears to

[1] Thus the percentage of land inclosed is disproportionately low compared with the number of the inclosures, see Appendix C.

have been more suited to herds and flocks under these conditions. Further, so far as the two border regions are concerned, the unsettled conditions of the country and its exposure to hostile raid made settled agriculture perilous. If it be remembered that the great early advantages and economies of inclosure were associated rather with sheep and cattle than with arable, an early inclosure from the wild or waste state in districts devoted to such use appears as probable and even normal. As soon as such advantages are realised and can be obtained, inclosure ensues, at any rate, to a large extent. Moreover, the difference between the north and the west in respect of the inclosures of common and waste under act and in the eighteenth century is in part explicable by the earlier introduction of order and security on the Welsh marches, as also by the superiority of the land and its less exposure. Inclosure, or rather partition of this kind, takes place in a different way from the inclosure due to a desire to convert the land from one use to another. It is obstructed by fewer obstacles, and in early times it occurs largely over pasture; of course the poorer lands, even if partitioned, remain open to a great extent by reason of the cost.

Evidence as to the difference in the state of the country between the more settled agricultural regions and those lying to the west and the north is to be found in the results on the comparative wealth and population. The order of the counties given by Thorold Rogers[1] shows conclusively the superiority of the counties where industrial development had progressed or where settled arable agriculture was of old standing. It shows also the very low position in respect of assessable wealth of the counties in the north and the west in 1503. Between 1341 and 1503 both Shropshire and Hereford rise in the order. Somewhat similar evidence is exhibited in the position of the parishes in the Tudor times. This can be best seen from the maps of the various dioceses prepared from the

[1] *History of Agriculture and Prices*, esp. iv. p. 89.

returns in the time of Henry VIII. It can be roughly judged by a comparison between the number of parishes in the counties, as given by Camden, and the respective acreage. This calculation is open to the criticism that the position of some counties though high is disproportionately and unduly depressed by areas of very poor land; while counties of more equable characteristics show to greater advantage. It affords, however, a rough general guide as to the distribution of population at the time, and, further, some indication as to the development of settlement in even earlier times.

The features dealt with in the preceding pages may be summarised under two headings. On the one side are those affecting and determining the course taken in the early settlement, and in particular the course of that settlement which depended on and was embodied in the arable villages. Where such were comparatively rare, the area of land lying in waste, and often, probably, in an absolutely wild state, was correspondingly great; and though incidents of common existed in differing degrees of importance, such land was liable to approvement, and was made the subject of new grants or inclosure. Nor must the influence of such inclosure and partition on the land already under the common field system be overlooked, whether exercised by direct competition through a supply of corn or by indirect competition and the force of example. On the other side are the causes affecting the desire to inclose. These, of course, varied from time to time and from place to place, being due in the main to industrial growth, the character of the land, and the state of agriculture. The progress of the movement as definitely recorded in history relates to the action of these causes, and in the main to the later stages of their action.

In comparing the condition of the land in respect of cultivation at different times one point requires emphasis. No doubt at all times land in common field or under developed common right was but a portion of the land. In early times, however, the other land was in the main waste or in forest or absolutely wild; but in later times, as for instance in the sixteenth century, much was in cultivation. This partly explains the difference between the position of common of shack in Bracton's time and in Coke's time. When Bracton wrote he was dealing with manorial arable, and though inclosure did exist, intercommoning on the lands was usual; but from Coke's account of Corbet's case, as indeed from his *Institutes*, it is evident that though rights of common of pasture and otherwise over waste and commons was well known, a great deal of arable existed unaffected by common of shack; some inclosed and some possibly in open field free from shackage.

With these features in mind, some attempt may be made to summarise the movement towards inclosure and to trace its progress through its various stages.

During the years before the fifteenth century there is little sign of anything but very gradual change and development save in districts characterised by town and industrial growth. In the country at large inclosure is a feature of the expansion of the area under cultivation and its adaptation to the ordinary needs of the district and of an agriculture undergoing no striking change. As may be concluded both from the language of legal authorities and the descriptions given by writers on agriculture towards the end of this period, many closes were inclosed for cattle, while, in some instances, intercommoning on the arable was disused; but on the old lands the early common field system continued. Further cultivation was gradually extended either by approvement of common or on land being taken in from the wild state, the most important scene of this latter movement being in the west. Moreover the settlement of the country proceeding from the east the western districts were less affected for some time. Not only so, but their very nature and formation presented obstacles to wide-spread agriculture, while the unsettled condition of the border acted as a further discouragement. But as the country developed, and as order was secured, much really good land in this region was made accessible. As a rule its use was accompanied by inclosure, and hence its early cultivation was largely unattended by incidents of common affecting the actual arable or by co-aration. Possibly, to some extent it may be true that agriculture in this part of the country was affected by the usages across the border, a possibility which might seem strengthened by a like absence of open field in Devon and Cornwall. On the other hand, the condition of counties like Lancashire and Cheshire shows that this, if an influence, was not the sole or the chief influence. The nature of the land, and the very character of much inclosure with high banks, point to concurrent introduction of cultivation and inclosure over much of its area; and where there was some common field, the addition thus made would affect its continuance. The west, in other words, seems to have been inclosed into use. Further, it seems probable that stock and sheep played a large part in farming operations in this district.

A distinction may be drawn between the circumstances of the west and the north. Insecurity continued much longer on the northern border, while the land in itself was less suited to arable agriculture.

But in certain districts a new factor was beginning to operate. The growth of towns and industrial occupation affected the use of the land by reason of the new demand for local supplies, and because of its effect on the local supply of labour. Added to the need of food, and of animal food, was the demand in textile centres for wool. It must be remembered that the advantage of inclosure on the farming side was early recognised in respect of animals; and of stock as well as sheep. The detailed considerations advanced in the account of the various counties give some ground for assigning to this period the beginning of the inclosure in the East Anglian Plain, in the clothing districts of the west, these being somewhat later, and probably in other places, as for instance the land near Newbury in Berkshire.

(*a*) *From the fifteenth century to middle of sixteenth century.*

In the fifteenth century the growth of sheep farming begins to exert a dominant influence on farming in many places. That this in some cases took the form of conversion of arable open field to pasture by means of inclosure is undoubted. The testimony of Rossus as to the actual facts within his knowledge in Warwickshire is sufficient as to that district in the early or middle of the fifteenth century, and his view is substantiated by Latimer, who refers to the early sixteenth, and by such a careful, though not contemporary, writer like Dugdale, who, it should be remembered, when he wrote in the seventeenth century, was not opposed to inclosure in general, which he regarded as one of the chief means of improvement. Writers who deal with the matter in general add their almost unanimous evidence. Nor does Fitz Herbert really contravene this view, though he considers the advantages in farming undoubted and great. The real question is as to the extent and locality in which results such as these would occur. Now, with regard to the growth of sheep farming, several points require notice. Firstly, it might well occur under circumstances where no conversion of arable and no inclosure of this order occur; in other words, there was much land not lying to arable and either wild or waste. Use of the former, whether by inclosure or not, was no disadvantage, and approvement of the latter, though doubtless a grievance to individuals, was not necessarily a cause of evil. Secondly, when sheep were multiplied in districts where there was local demand for the raw material, wool, any disturbance was compensated for in some measure. In the eastern counties there were inclosures and inclosure risings in the sixteenth century, but the risings may have been by way of resentment at private loss of common, while further it is evident that very large numbers of sheep were pastured in the open. Thirdly, much of the inclosure, as indeed Fitz Herbert tells us, occurred on demesne.

The effect, then, on the inclosure movement, was threefold. In the first place, wool was a product which could be carried, and which in many places was produced for distant and not local use. In the second place, commons, as distinct from open field, were often interfered with. In the third place, demesne was frequently inclosed while other land previously brought into cultivation from the wild was changed in its use. This latter feature needs to be borne in mind since in some counties and regions it adds considerably to the area over which change was possible. It seems doubtful if such land would be included in the returns to inclosure commissions. Certainly the figures of these do not seem very striking. Possibly this was the case in Warwick, where the gradual disappearance of forest must have brought and been bringing much new land into cultivation.

On the other hand it by no means follows that the movement implied national or widespread evil. It meant local disturbance, and local disturbance where the mobility of labour was slight, entailed individual injury; but on the other hand much land was exhausted and the rest enjoyed brought about an increase when later on it was reconverted. Further, the material was the basis of the prosperity of parts of the country. Lastly, there was much demand for arable products and, as Leland shows, many of the inclosures, especially on the western side of the country, were "plentiful of corn"; Somerset, a county with inclosure, was "good for wheat," and Suffolk was "full of styles."

As to the locality, there was no doubt considerable increase in general inclosure. Next in the fifteenth century inclosure in the textile districts probably advanced very considerably. Thirdly, in the sixteenth century parks and demesnes were often inclosed and commons or land over which people had exercised common rights of pasture and the like curtailed in many counties. Lastly, in the later fifteenth and the sixteenth centuries, a definite advance in inclosure appears in (*a*) Warwick, Northampton, Leicester;

(*b*) Buckingham, Oxford, Berkshire; (*c*) Bedford. These inclosures being the cause of disturbance, or recorded by commissions, were not, obviously, merely inclosures of land otherwise but little used or wild or sporadic.

In the first named group, evidence as to inclosure comes from various sources, Leicester and Northampton occupying a very marked place in Dr. Gay's lists for 1517 and 1607, and Warwick, though less conspicuous, still prominent. All these are mentioned by Strype. Inclosure in Northampton is also complained of by the author of *Certain Causes, etc.* It seems probable that the inclosure in Leicester was mainly in the south, and in Warwick in the north. Standish speaks, it should be added, of the inclosures existing in Warwick.

The second group are also conspicuous in the list for 1517, while Bucks ranks among the five counties dealt with in 1607. All three are mentioned by Strype, and the inclosures in Buckingham and Oxford are the subject of complaint in the tract *Certain Causes, etc.* Both Stow and Speed record risings in Buckingham. The land affected in Berkshire was apparently in the north-west, that is the Abingdon region. By the end of the sixteenth century, there was almost certainly much inclosed land in the south of Oxford and Buckingham, while in addition there were in the latter county many inclosures in the Chilterns. These may have occurred from a forest or wild state and thus be in addition to those forming a grievance. None the less they may have been connected with these latter as a cause.

A considerable amount of inclosure occurred in Bedford, as is shown by its position in the lists for 1517 and 1607, and also in Strype, and from the records of the acts there is some ground for placing such in the centre, the Ampthill district.

Inclosure was frequent in Middlesex in the earlier part of the period, as the list for 1517 proves.

In addition to the above, inclosures were evidently a factor in the growth of Somerset, some leading to risings, some occasioned by the development of the wool industry which existed in Taunton; in the districts neighbouring on Wiltshire and Gloucester; and also in all probability near North Devon, where there was industrial development by the beginning of the seventeenth century. By the end of the sixteenth century Somerset was considered inclosed. Also the development of the Great Weald district proceeded, and addition was made to the inclosed ground, leading to the appearance described by Aubrey. Of course more may have occurred in the early seventeenth century. Further, the fruit hedges and orchards of Gloucester, Worcester and Hereford must be ascribed to this period. Probably in the west border country the process continued, whereby cultivation was enlarged and the rich pasture lands of the region utilised.

During this period, that is, till past the middle of the sixteenth century, inclosure probably tended to change in occupation in some districts. It must of course be looked at from two sides. The area of possible cultivation was no doubt increased, much land being brought in both on the west and also in places where woods were being cleared. In such parts arable was increased as well as pasture, a feature affecting the neighbouring districts where agriculture had been established at an earlier date. On the other hand, within the area of cultivation lands had been inclosed. This occurred in the case of demesne; while further there seems ground for believing that wastes over which common right had been in active use were interfered with to the loss and discontent of the commoners. Even from Fitz Herbert inclosure in these cases seems to have been initiated mainly for sheep or for other stock. The aim was not better arable use or even dairy developments. In some instances a like process manifested itself on the land of the tenants. The result in some places was calamitous. Some land slipped back into what was little more than inclosed sheep walk. Sometimes the cause was the exhaustion of the soil, sometimes the competition of new land, sometimes the requirements of the neighbouring textile industries. In many cases these co-operated. The districts which suffered most were those where compensating developments were slight, that is, which produced and sent to some distance wool requiring little labour in its production; and these were chiefly to be found in counties with good agricultural settlement. Such disturbance in occupation must be carefully distinguished from the more strictly local disturbances which were compensated for by neighbouring industrial use of the wool, or associated with increase in arable in the immediate vicinity. In North Devon both features manifested themselves, the district finding it difficult to keep itself supplied both with wool and corn. In the west, much land seems to have been inclosed either from wild or from large wastes where common, if it existed, was not an integral part of an agricultural and arable settlement. In the eastern counties wool was needed locally, as also were animal products.

There are three particular features which require notice with reference to this period.

In the first place, improvements in arable farming, though they may have resulted in some cases, are not of much account as an aim of inclosure at this time. Fitz Herbert's language by itself seems to justify this as a general statement of fact. The popular literature is much more emphatic. The reconversion of inclosed land falls mostly outside the time, and is rather a consequence than a cause.

In the second place, side by side with the oft cited husbandry acts, important as evidence if not in result, which seek to regulate the supply of arable land, must be placed the clauses of the Statute of Artificers and of various Poor Law enactments which seek to maintain a supply of agricultural labour.

In the third place, the popular discontent and risings in the middle of the century were not necessarily associated with the conversion of arable. They were probably just as much due to the inclosures of commons, with the consequent deprivation of common rights.

(b) From the middle of sixteenth century to the end of the seventeenth century.

Towards the end of the sixteenth century a new period in the history of inclosure begins, marked by the steady growth of farming improvement as an active motive, by the development of locomotion and transport, and by additions from uncultivated land more definite and with more deliberate purpose than in earlier years. These features combine together to give a different character to the movement. Thus the inclosure of arable occurs for many other purposes than conversion. It is needed to allow of skill and to permit the cultivation of new crops; and these taken together with the more general advantages of individual possession and full control, render conversion from arable to pasture an occasional rather than a frequent consequence. Further than that, where such does occur, it is often caused by the desire to put land to the use for which it is best fitted, a process not necessarily leading to hardship where labour can move freely, and when the area within which exchange takes place, and men live and move, is enlarged. Local industrial growth adds force to this consideration. Both raw material and food are required by a population increasing in many districts. The very reclamation of land emphasises the demand of the time. Land is brought in from an unused condition, not as hitherto largely without cost and often owing to the diminution of woods, but with purpose to employ it in cultivation and at a large expense, as in the fens. Nor is this all; different branches of farming develop, and, as is evident from writers during the century and especially Houghton, dairy products offer a new opportunity of profit and one to which the open field system is repugnant. The result is inclosure, and inclosure for farming purposes, and, as is elsewhere emphasised, on a large scale. To this period, too, may be assigned the inclosure of a great quantity of land hitherto wholly wild or in scant use, as in Cornwall and probably along the west. The inclosure acts of the eighteenth century quite inadequately account for what was in this condition at the end of the sixteenth century. Inclosure was further occasioned by the growth of towns and industries and their influence on the agricultural land surrounding them, by reason of both the new demands of the town populations and the effect produced on labour.

The contrast with the earlier period was great. The inclosures of the seventeenth century are essentially connected with the growth of farming. This character is due not only to the change in method and in crop, both tending to augment the desire of the more skilful farmers to be freed from the harassing yoke of their more indifferent neighbours, and the latter making change necessary because undeviating custom was the great obstacle in the way of improvement, but also to the nature of the new land brought into cultivation. That was largely arable. In some cases land inclosed in the previous century was reconverted to grain, having profited greatly by a rest from tillage. In some cases, again, the land where forest had once stood was peculiarly suited to crops,[1] and the corn thus raised supplanted that of surrounding districts. This, according to Bishop Gibson in his additions to Camden, was the case in Warwickshire, an explanation which Morton applies to his own county. But the district of the new drainage areas is the most conspicuous. The reclamation of these lands added many thousands of acres of exceptionally rich corn land to the arable, and thus rendered necessary some alteration in the purpose to which other lands should be put.

Viewed from the farming standpoint, two features stand out after the middle of the period. The one is the growing importance of the dairy, the other the enormous importance of inclosure on light lands where new grasses and root crops were of the greatest value. Thus we hear from Houghton of the effects produced on the sands of Norfolk.

[1] On this in general, see Blith, *Eng. Improver*, pp. 83-4.

Of course, in districts already inclosed, these crops were introduced without difficulty, a fact which accounts for the early cultivation of the turnip in Hertford, a county early inclosed except in the north, as the normal result of its former position as a royal forest. On the other hand, in Norfolk, inclosure was undertaken to allow of such cultivation.

While the inclosure was widespread during this period, and very considerable in amount, there are three stages deserving mention. During the last years of the sixteenth and the early part of the seventeenth century the progress of the movement was a matter of great concern to the State. Thus we hear that inclosure is worse than in the time of Henry VII., and the sheep figures as a destroyer of farms and devourer of men in the pages of various writers. Further, the proceedings of the Privy Council, with letters to the Sheriffs, and the levy of compositions, emphasise the anxiety. On the other hand, the very record of these proceedings shows that, in many cases at any rate, the complaints were unfounded from the public point of view, and other writers begin to point to the actual agricultural advantages. The counties most concerned are in the North Midlands, Leicester, Lincoln, Northampton, Rutland, Nottingham, Derby, and in the west Gloucester and Somerset, to which may be added Wiltshire on Aubrey's testimony. Next come the fen and marsh reclamations, not only effecting inclosure in their own area but a cause for change in use and so for inclosure in the surrounding land. Here the most prominent counties are Lincoln, North Cambridge, West Norfolk, Huntingdon, Northampton, and in the west Somerset. Possibly the inclosures so bitterly complained of in Leicester, Northampton, and Warwick were partly due to this development, though they may in part be of an earlier date, and may be due, as has been pointed out, to the thinning out of woods owing to the growth of the iron trade. Lastly, in the latter half of the seventeenth century we have the considerable movement which it was sought to legalise by parliamentary means, and which is referred to by many, and especially by Houghton. This would seem to have been very general. Probably it was at this time that the dairy districts of Gloucester, Wiltshire, and Buckingham, no doubt affected before, underwent further inclosure. During the later years light lands are inclosed to allow of the new crops, and show a very marked increase in fertility. The cultivation of grasses, clover and roots introduces new elements into inclosure of great and growing importance. Not only is a fresh source of profit disclosed which can be attained only by inclosure, but the effects of the change are different, especially as regards the quantity of employment. Even before this, the result of inclosure often was to increase the amount of land in some form of use, owing to the disuse or decrease of fallow, a consequence to be set against the real or alleged conversion of arable to pasture. But with new crops, and especially with roots, the total yield is augmented and the total occasion for agricultural employment increased. Root crops require labour, and the labour in this direction is just as important and just as profitable as if employed in producing grain. Not only so, but the better rotation means an improvement in the permanent fertility of the soil. In some districts little advantage is taken of these new possibilities, since in the beginning of the eighteenth century, as one writer says, some of the inclosed lands of Stafford produced seven successive crops of grain. But, as is elsewhere pointed out, the results on the question of employment become of great importance. This factor, which by itself would distinguish later from early inclosure, comes into operation, even if partial operation, in the seventeenth century.

The earlier years of the eighteenth century cannot be separated from the latter part of the seventeenth century. The movement is continuous, and all testimony points to its widespread nature in the agricultural districts. There is but slight indication of its locality, though light land was undoubtedly affected, and amongst this prominently North-

West Norfolk. On the other hand, the early date of many acts in Warwick, Northampton, Leicester, and Rutland may be taken as generally indicative of much other inclosure by agreement. In these counties some land was very probably laid to grass. But it would seem that this, if it occurred, was concurrent with an increase in the general yield. To this may be attributed comparative absence of complaint during the first half of that century.

(*c*) *Eighteenth century.*

After 1750 the Midland inclosures increase rapidly. Without doubt the increased demand for animal products and the improvements in breeding and feeding combine to associate inclosure from 1750 to 1780 with frequent conversions to pasture. This tendency decreases after 1780, partly because much of the land most suited to such treatment had been turned to grass, but partly also because in the last two decades a new inclosure wave displays itself. Improved methods made it possible to cultivate more highly soil of a poorer nature, while the demand for grain made such cultivation profitable. With 1800 and the new act, this merges into inclosure for general purposes. Expense is a little decreased, and land formerly left by reason of it in open is now inclosed. Probably the great demand is for arable, but there is evidence that this did not rule in the great grazing and breeding districts.

The sketch thus given of the direction and progress of inclosure throughout the country is interesting not only in itself, but because of the explanation it offers of the geographical position of the land in open field cultivation at the commencement of the period of private acts. To follow it out necessitates a return to certain of the factors considered in the opening pages of this chapter.

Firstly, agricultural settlement based on arable was, it is contended, determined in its locality by certain very definite causes, and its easy extension in earlier centuries restricted by opposing influence. Among such causes and influences, the geological basis of the country and the soil characteristics are prominent. Water and soil assist, while hills, woods, and fens restrict and control. To this, however, must be added the effect mainly, perhaps, in Devonshire and Cornwall, but also on the Welsh border, of other systems of cultivation and tenure which allow of common but minimise the element of common involved where co-aration habitually occurs, and also the fact that the wave of incursion and immigration presses from east to west. Within the area of settlement, the woods and fens, the downs and sterile heaths, impose limits to villages and manors with arable field. Outside the area there was arable, of course, but scattered and often different in type, a common field, in some places, lying at some distance from the settlement, and forming an adjunct, however essential, rather than the basis of the whole system of cultivation and life.

Secondly, as land previously inaccessible or for some other reason unused comes into the area of cultivation, open field does not, after a certain time, necessarily present itself. There was much inclosure from the wild state, especially on the west, where abundant soil for arable existed amid much other land unsuitable for any such purpose. In this connection the circumstances of the neighbourhood were important, owing to the influence of custom. The presence or absence of much land under the open field system affected the system of cultivation applied to that coming into use. But the time was still more important. As the inconveniences of the open field system manifested themselves and came to outweigh the early necessities leading to it, the application of any such system to land brought in became increasingly improbable. In other words, inclosed cultivation was adopted. Grants of common in the remaining waste and outwoods were attached often to grants of land made by approvement or in other ways, but these did not necessitate an open field system. As to date; there is no means of fixing date. But it certainly seems improbable that land taken in after the practice of approvement would be subject to open field incidents as a rule. This, however is a conjecture.

Moreover, the introduction of new land into cultivation, particularly when the quantity is great, affects the land already under cultivation, especially as population grows and moves and production takes place for sale and not for home use.

Thirdly, the growth of population and of towns and industries affects the use of land in their vicinity ; and from early times, the advantages of inclosure where animals were in question was recognised ; but this was even truer in the case of cattle than of sheep.

These factors have been given their place in the foregoing sketch as also in the attempt made to interpret the inclosure movement in the various counties.[1] When both accounts are reviewed some general, even though tentative, conclusions are possible.

The West Midlands pass into inclosure silently and early ; its inclosure was largely of land in a wild state or of waste subject to little use; but there was cultivated land, some indeed little affected by the complicating common rights involved in the ordinary open field system, and some forced into inclosure owing to the competition and example of land directly inclosed. Some little open field lingers on. An equally noteworthy feature is the comparative absence in these counties of commons when the eighteenth century opens. This also points to inclosure from the wild state.

In the extreme west (Cornwall and Devonshire) both custom and the character of the land are potent. There is much wild, there is little or no cultivation in open field. Here a movement to inclosure is recorded in the end of the sixteenth and the beginning of the seventeenth century.

The other western counties, Somerset, Gloucester, Wilt-

[1] Appendix A.

shire, and Dorset, have a large amount of infertile waste or wild land, while in the central districts, as indeed in the Vale of Taunton, industrial forces are at work from the fourteenth and fifteenth centuries.

The southern counties and the south-east are largely under down or dominated by the great forest. As the weald is exposed to cultivation inclosure develops normally from the wild. Kent on the coast is possibly affected by industry. On the other hand, the absolute absence of common field and the nearly complète absence of common in Kent excites attention in the sixteenth century, and it is possible that gavelkind tenure had some share in bringing about this result, though in a slightly different way from that alleged at the time. The power of inclosure of land under such tenure was free from the restrictions which existed elsewhere. A large part of the county remained woodland in the sixteenth century.

The condition of the East Anglian counties presents certain difficulties, the chief being the very marked difference between Norfolk on the one hand and Suffolk and Essex on the other. Excluding some districts, as for instance Flegg, there was more open field awaiting inclosure in West than in East Norfolk. Still even on the east there is more than in the main part of Suffolk and Essex. Taking the whole tract of the East Anglian plain certain features are present. On the west, especially in Essex, was forest and poor land ; on the coast there was in Essex and to some extent in Suffolk land rather unsuited to early and regular cultivation, the best tillage land being in the centre. Thus much land in Mid Suffolk is, according to Marshall, little suited for pasture. Again, the development of towns and industries affect this part of the country at a very early date, while in addition, the southern part of this district, as also the home counties, had to furnish much of the London supplies. The land undergoes a change from open to inclosure at an early date. From Reyce's account of Suffolk conversion to pasture does not follow necessarily, since, in his description of that county, the main district for tillage is Middle Suffolk, while the greatest number of flocks are in the champaign. Apparently there was good grazing in both East and Middle Suffolk. The plain is mainly inclosed, but this is less true of Norfolk than of the other counties.

The north, comprising the four northern counties, the greater part of the North Riding and the north of the West Riding and North Lancashire, has certain features in common with the West Midlands, but there are certain important differences. In the first place, unsettled conditions continue longer; in the second place, the amount of wild land permanently unsuited to arable is greater. Hence, though traces of open field in the eighteenth century are few, the amount of inclosure from common by act is great. In other words, part of the land continues wild and part remains in a nearly wild condition with some common rights of pasture till such a late period that its inclosure occurs under circumstances which give it publicity. At an earlier date a like inclosure would have escaped record.

Circumstances and influences such as those described above account in a general way for the earlier separation of lands and inclosure in districts which occupy little place in the record of the eighteenth or even in that of the seventeenth century. During the seventeenth century there is not only considerable inclosure in the great open area but a contraction in its extent and towards its confines by inclosure, for instance, in North Wilts, in Worcester, in Derby and Nottingham, in South and East Durham, in the fens, and in West Suffolk. The continuance of the open field in the region mainly affected by private acts is due, it is true, in part to the greater prevalence of arable open field in early times, but also and not less to the belated operation or appearance of forces which tended to its extinction elsewhere at an earlier date. For both there are several causes; amongst these the position and topography of the land and the nature of the soil are very prominent.

Of the regions treated above the most difficult to account for is that which comprises the greater part of the Anglian Plain and extends over Suffolk and Essex, with the exception of the western portions of these counties. In both the southern and western counties, where the detailed record of inclosure is very incomplete, certain definite features explain the absence of common and go far to make the course of development clear. Inclosure from the wild into strict individual ownership and its effects was recognised by Marshall as an important factor in the agricultural history of the west, but of course its importance is not confined to this region. It was potent elsewhere, and needs notice in the case, not only of regions but of parts of regions, as counties. Of equal importance are the later settlements on wild land and the waste, as in the fourteenth and fifteenth centuries, but this feature has received little attention, save by Hasbach. Here, though rights to common existed, the complex system of open field seems not to have been established as a general rule. But these factors cannot have greatly affected the Anglian Plain. Further, taking the record in the eighteenth century, with the exception of the extreme west, the traces of common field are very slight, and the traces of common, though more abundant, are not marked. In both Suffolk and Essex the individual inclosures in these parts are small as a rule. It is also shown by early descriptions that these counties were largely inclosed by the middle or end of the sixteenth century. It may well be asked then what signs there are that this district was ever largely affected by the open field system. With regard to this several facts may be noticed. There is evidence of inclosure of some kind, probably to a fair extent, in the sixteenth century; this may have been inclosure of commons and not of open field. Reyce's account of the west of Suffolk as "wholly champion or neer" certainly indicates a larger open extent of land than is accounted for subsequently; and he further states that Mid Suffolk was mainly in tillage. Additional information is given by his description of the demesnes of the manors as "proportioned into several farms" which are "hired and occupied by farmers for rent." The explanation offered above is that this district was early converted from open to several, owing to the very early development of industry and the growth of population with its demands and necessities. In other words it had, by the sixteenth century, passed through a stage of development which occurred in many other districts at a later date. It may be added that, though traces of open and common are scant in the eighteenth century, there are grounds for the belief that they were considerably more numerous in the sixteenth century. So far as the land along the sea was concerned this probably was little fitted for any intensive use. The validity of this explanation is, it must be frankly said, a matter of surmise. Nor is it much affected, one way or the other, by the possibility that some land was in some form of one field system and not in the three field system. The extent of this is doubtful in face of the condition of Norfolk, in the eighteenth century, when rotation was usual; and that county was singled out by Coke as a place where common of shack was frequent. Shackage, with its attendant incidents, was the great obstacle in later times to inclosure. On the other hand, the denser population of the east seems undoubted, and is shown in the great multiplicity of townships yet apparent and proved to be of old standing by the *Valor Ecclesiastica.*

As to the light thrown by a knowledge of the inclosures of the eighteenth century on the previous condition of the country in respect of this movement some few words require to be added. The percentage of the land inclosed, both in the counties and also in their districts, is evidence of a particular kind more valuable for some purposes than others. It is valuable as regards the general progress of inclosure, as showing roughly and broadly the extent of land which remained to be dealt with during the later period; but if considered as an indication of the course taken by inclosure previously, or of the earlier conditions affecting agricultural settlement, it needs to be supplemented. For these purposes it is desirable to know in what numbers the townships of any given district were touched by these later inclosures. The same percentage of inclosure in a county may be attained under widely different circumstances. A lesser number of townships and parishes may be inclosed, but mostly or wholly

TABLE showing approximate percentage of townships affected by inclosure either of open field or commons in certain registration counties. The percentage of land inclosed in the counties proper also given. Inclosures by Act to 1870.

	Percentage of townships (minimum) affected by inclosure in registration county.		Percentage of land included in counties. Round numbers.	
	Open field.	Commons.	Open field.	Commons.
Bedford - - -	54	2	44	·1
Berkshire - -	36	4	30	4
Buckingham - -	46	5	35	1
Cambridge - -	52	9	34	4
Derby - - -	19	12	16	5
Dorset - - -	15	7	8	5
Essex - - -	4	10	2	1·2
Gloucester - -	26	5	17	1
Hampshire - -	11	17	6	5
Hereford - -	9	10	3	1·3
Hertford - - -	37	3	12	3
Huntingdon - -	63	—	55	—
Leicester - -	40	3	41	6
Lincoln - - -	30	6	29	10
Middlesex - -	41	8	19	7
Norfolk - - -	28	15	19	6
Nottingham - -	33	6	27	4
Northampton - -	52	1	51	3
Oxford - - -	39	3	40	3
Rutland - - -	36	—	46	—
Shropshire - -	2	15	3	6
Somerset - -	6	18	2	10
Stafford - - -	5	13	6	6
Suffolk - - -	6	11	3	2
Surrey - - -	12	18	6	4
Sussex - - -	6	18	2	2
Warwick - -	39	9	23	2
Wiltshire - -	27	7	22	4
Worcester - -	22	5	13	5
Yorkshire, E.R. -	31	8	33	5

inclosed, or a larger number may contain small or partial inclosures. In the former case, if the distribution be fairly uniform over the area, an early well-established system of common field agriculture is indicated, interspersed with later settlements or inclosures from the waste probably by exercise of *approvement.*

On the other hand, the sporadic distribution of small open-field inclosures among a large number of parishes indicates a different state of things, namely, small settlements among wild conditions with much subsequent added inclosure without incidents of the open field system. As a matter of fact, however, the first system is almost uniformly associated with a much higher percentage of inclosure than the latter; in other words it seems to show that these areas, whether counties or districts, were at one time somewhat generally under the open field system. But this relates to inclosures in which open field is involved. Where common alone is concerned; a wide distribution of small commons, however, may indicate the last process in a course of inclosure where remaining small pieces of common are divided. So far from pointing to the earlier absence of a common field or three field system, it might result from the existence of such and their inclosure at an earlier date. It cannot be said, however, to be an evidence of such, as other causes for its presence in the eighteenth century are not excluded.

To draw up a table showing the proportion of the townships and places in a county, or any of its districts, means the acceptance of some list of villages, places, or townships. In the foregoing table, as also in those in the appendix, these as set out in the Census Enumeration have been taken. This of course involves the acceptance of the *registration* county, and this must be borne in mind when comparison is made between the percentages of villages or townships affected and the percentage of land, since the latter is given for the county proper. Comparison can only be of the most general kind.

Further, as an inclosure in some cases laps over the limits of one township into another, the number or percentage of townships given in the table shows the minimum. No doubt a fuller and more accurate table could be constructed, but that would be a very long and arduous undertaking. As a general guide the data are sufficient. The northern counties and the North and West Ridings are omitted, because the inclosures were chiefly of moors, as also Lancashire, Cheshire, Devon, Cornwall, and Kent, because of their great paucity in inclosure of any kind.

Having regard to these particulars, and especially to the differences indicated in the table between the inclosures by act of commons and of open field, certain conclusions seem tenable.

Firstly, in the great common field districts, the inclosure which takes place in the eighteenth and nineteenth centuries is mainly of the lands of the village and township, including commons and open field, and extending over the greater part of the whole area. By its side, and in other townships, there is inclosure of small or moderate sized pieces of common. This latter, when taken with the former, points to a wider extension of the open field system in earlier years. It is at any rate a concomitant of an open field system; and its occurrence in the eighteenth and nineteenth centuries indicates a probable earlier inclosure in the same district. This view is further strengthened by the many instances in which such comparatively small inclosures of commons succeed larger inclosures of open field and common by act.

Secondly, in certain other counties, the amount of open field inclosed by act is small, while the inclosures themselves are relatively small as compared with the area of the township. In other words, the land preserving traces of common field is a very small part of the respective land of the village. This, especially when accompanied by inclosures elsewhere of commons, in greater parcels though not necessarily greater in total amounts, appears to indicate small early open settlements under circumstances which are unfavourable to arable, or such as to render a large part of the land inaccessible to use at that time.

Thirdly, small and well-distributed inclosures of commons often follow on and indicate an inclosure movement in earlier times.

The inclosure of large wastes when occurring in the eighteenth century are recorded, whereas at an early date they escape notice; so, of course, their appearance is rather due to continued infertility or inaccessibility.

The application of these conclusions to the various regions under discussion points to certain differences between the eastern counties and the west. In the former, there is little appearance of the small common field inclosure, and the inclosures of common are these which might be expected to ensue on a previous general inclosure of lands in open field. On the west, with the exception of Hereford, the inclosures of commons are on the average larger, while in Somerset, Shropshire, and Hereford the open fields as compared with village areas are smaller.

Further, Middlesex and Hertford show very plainly the effect of woods and forest land on early arable settlement in open field.

The position of the south-eastern counties, Surrey and Sussex, with which must be associated Kent, is more doubtful. Surrey, indeed, shows small commons and open fields of a moderate size. These latter, however, fall mainly in the north, leaving the Weald district with bare traces. As for Sussex, open field inclosures are small and commons small. As a matter of fact, the Weald is little touched by eighteenth century inclosure of any kind, singularly void of traces of open field, and with few commons, those that there are being small. As compared with Mid and East Suffolk, this region is even less touched by inclosure by act. The statistical criteria, however, are not adequate by themselves to differentiate clearly between these districts. They point in different directions, but they require to be taken in conjunction with the positive knowledge we have that the east counties were under early cultivation of some kind, and that the great Weald district was under wood. With these facts added, the conclusions that the former was in early open field, and that the small common inclosures are an after sign of early inclosure seem probable. On the other hand the very occasional and scattered small commons in the Weald point to an inclosure of this district from the wild, at a time when common would not be created. Furthermore, this very feature indicates a difference in soil and suitability for cultivation between this district and the west, as, for instance, Shropshire or Hereford or Somerset. The land in the Weald was not so much infertile as inaccessible for cultivation. When cleared it was fertile. To all appearance it comes into use as the woodland diminishes, and at a time when common is not likely to be created. Moreover as it is fertile land, there is comparatively little to be left idle and so to be treated as common. But this is widely different from the case of the western counties.

Taken as a whole, the statistical material set out considerably strengthens the account previously given of the course of inclosure.

II

INCLOSURE DURING THE SEVENTEENTH CENTURY

THOUGH the view which regards inclosure of common and common right land as taking place mainly at two epochs, in the sixteenth and eighteenth centuries respectively, and as due to causes peculiar to these particular times, is certainly less firmly held than was formerly the case, it is nevertheless not yet realised that thus stated it gives an almost entirely false presentation of what occurred. No doubt it is true that particular circumstances or combinations of circumstances at certain times accelerated the movement or invested it with some special character, but inclosure was continuous, and a very considerable mass of evidence as to its reality and extent exists, spread over the long intervening period of a century and a half. Some part of this evidence has been indicated by different writers, and particularly by Professor Gay[1] and Miss Leonard,[2] but as yet its mass and continuity, and so the extent of the progress to which it testifies, have not been fully stated.[3] When that is done it will be seen not so

[1] "Inquisitions of Depopulation in 1517," *Transactions of the Royal Historical Society*, N.S. vol. xiv.; "The Midland Revolt and the Inquisition of Depopulation in 1607," *ibid.* vol. xviii.; "Inclosures in England," *Quarterly Journal of Economics*, 1903.

[2] "The Inclosure of Common Fields in the Seventeenth Century," *Transactions of the Royal Historical Society*, 1905, N.S. vol. xix. pp. 101-46.

[3] Possibly some additional weight is due to the conclusions of Miss Leonard and myself, when they coincide, as is often the case, because they were arrived at quite separately. This, of course, is obvious in her case. The materials

much that the earlier view was inadequate as that it was actually the very reverse of the true state of the case, that inclosure continued steadily throughout the seventeenth century, and that the inclosures of the eighteenth and nineteenth centuries were no new phenomena but the natural completion of a great continuous movement. In dealing with this movement throughout the seventeenth century attention must be directed to certain matters besides continuity and extent. The districts, the character, and the mode of inclosure require to be dealt with.

If we turn to the later years of the sixteenth century[1] the frequent statutes dealing with tillage and houses of husbandry afford considerable evidence of the efforts of the government to secure adequate attention to arable cultivation, and to prevent land suited to corn being used for pasturage. To some extent these acts were directed to remedy conversions to pasture which had taken place in earlier years, and, taken by themselves, they do not, despite their stringency and frequent re-enactment, prove much more than the difficulty of reversing by state action a movement which, whatever its consequences, had at its base great economic causes. But this would be a very imperfect view of the condition which prevailed at the time. Economic causes were still at work, and inclosure was the natural response. No doubt they were somewhat changed in character. Even if the demand for pasture was still effective, the increased population, with its growing need of corn, and the new possibilities of improved methods of cultivation added new reasons for inclosure, though obviously for inclosure with different results, against which the old reproaches of depopulation and the diminution of the

for the present paper were collected and put together before her very valuable paper was published. The chief points of difference between us are noticed, but often our views agree and the different evidence presented fits together in a very interesting way. With Dr. Gay my agreement, as will be seen, is not so great.

[1] The end of the sixteenth century and the earlier years of the eighteenth century are here treated alongside of the strictly seventeenth century.

food supply could not be alleged.[1] In respect of this tendency the evidence of writers like Tusser and Fitz-Herbert seems conclusive, and it is probable that it was due to a like perception that, despite the very obvious anxiety about inclosure, the statute was enacted[2] which so specifically repeated the power of approvement enacted in the Statute of Merton.[3]

That inclosure from which such detrimental results as those mentioned above might be and were apprehended was, however, steadily progressing is obvious from circumstances attending the later statutes of tillage, as from other evidence. The words of the statutes are very significant. Thus the preamble to 39 Eliz. c. 2 runs:—

"Whereas from the XXVII year of King Henry the Eighth of famous memory until the five-and-thirtieth year of her majesty's most happy reign there was always in force some law which did ordain a conversion and continuance of a certain quantity and proportion of land in tillage not to be altered; and that in the last parliament held in the said five-and-thirtieth year of her majesty's reign, partly by reason of the great plenty and cheapness of grain at that time within this realm, and partly by reason of the imperfection and obscurity of the law made in that case, the same was discontinued, since which time there have grown many more depopulations by turning tillage into pasture than at any time for the like number of years heretofore."

[1] In connexion with this reference may be made to *Conference between Plough man and Clothier*, by John Green, written in Wilts in the time of Henry VIII. (Royal MS. 7, C. xvi. f. 238), where it is stated that whereas landlords at one time could not find tenants, and therefore resorted to wool and sheep, now the case is altered through the increase of population, and tenants want landlords. It is suggested (f. 239) that the sheep and clothiers might be removed to Ireland and the land under pasture converted to tillage, which, as compared with clothing and sheep, is estimated to support people in the ratio of five to one. See also the proposals by Thomas Duckett (Sloane MS. 2404) for the improvements of commons, f. 15.

[2] 3 & 4 Ed. VI. c. 3.

[3] So far as I know no attempt was made during the seventeenth century to repeal the statute thus re-enacted.

Like language is to be found in 39 Eliz. c. 1, which states, "where of late years more than in time past there have sundry towns, parishes, and houses of husbandry been destroyed and become desolate." A like condition of things is stated in the tract *Certain Causes gathered together, wherein is shown the Decay of England*, if it may be assumed that this was written in the later part of the century. It relates to inclosures in Oxfordshire, Buckinghamshire, and Northamptonshire, and complains that there has been a change for the worse since the days of Henry VII.

Additional light on the time and on the aims of Elizabeth's ministers is thrown by a letter[1] from Sir Anthony Cope to Lord Burleigh concerning the framing of the new bill against the ill effects of depopulation, written with the draft of the bill before him. In this criticism the writer says, "Where every house is to be allotted twenty acres within two miles of the town I dislike the limitation of the place, fearing the poor man shall be cast into the most barren and fruitless coyle, and that so remote as altogether unnecessary for the present necessities of the husbandmane's trade." He then proceeds with other grounds of objection,[2] very pertinent to the working of the act, and important as showing the difficulties obviously experienced in certain

[1] Lansdown MS. 83, f. 68.

[2] These may be summarised. Secondly, the draft is defective, in that there is by this law no limitation of common or meadow, without which no limitation of common can be maintained. Thirdly, albeit the allowance is thus scant as before, there is no limit set down either for fine or rent. "But the poor that are to be restored are in both left to the will and hard conscience of him that hath destroyed the town or of him that hath unconscionably purchased the town so destroyed." Fourthly, that some immediate relief should be given for the pressing necessities of those who are to be ultimately restored, "who, being driven out of their habitations, are forced into the great cities, where, being very burdensome, they shut their doors against them, suffering them to die in the streets and highways." This is due partly to the fact that the law restricts the duty of maintaining the poor to the place where they are born and bred. Fifthly, that though the bill aims at restoration and not at a new condition, it should apply in cases where title is recent.

places. The very definiteness of statement is sufficient to show that inclosures were taking place, and that they were attended in some places at least with bad results. He specifically urges that recent titles ought not to hinder the immediate application of the statute.

The foregoing evidence, which bears directly on the conversion to pasture and the existence of inclosure at the time, and also on the remedy of the former by law, can be supplemented by that of the writer of 1607, whose careful comparison of inclosed and open lands, especially as illustrated by the counties of Somerset and Northampton, has often been quoted. He deals not only with the two systems but with the remedy for inclosing when that results in depopulation. Here he considers the expediency of offering a remedy at a time when, as he says, the mere offer or attempt may serve as an encouragement to violent attempts at redress. Inclosure, he writes, was made the pretended cause for the late tumults. However he overrules this scruple and suggests that, so far as inclosure is harmful, which in general he may be taken as denying or doubting, action must be taken not only with regard to that which has been but also in prevention of that to come. To prevent or to stay harmful inclosure he recommends that existing laws should be maintained and that new measures should be taken against ingrossing of lands. Briefly stated, no one is to hold more than one-fourth of the land of any manor, the remaining three-fourths to remain in tenantries none of which is to exceed one hundred acres. Side by side with this as testimony to the real existence of the movement is the inquisition of 1607.[1]

Though it is not intended to deal at this point with the nature of the inclosures, it should be added that further testimony as to inclosure of wastes is afforded by a memorial addressed in 1576 to Lord Burleigh by Alderman Box.[2] This memorial is interesting by reason of the information it gives as to the condition of the land, and its

[1] "Depopulation Returns"; see Professor Gay's article, *ubi supra*.

[2] Lansdown MS. 131, f. 22.

general breadth of treatment. The writer urges the necessity of increasing the tillage lands, a necessity arising from, firstly, the large amount of good and fruitful land "lying waste and overgrown with bushes, brambles, ling, heath, furze, and such other weeds"; secondly, the amount converted from arable to pasture, which he states has been estimated at one-fourth of that at one time agreeable to maintain the plough. That there has been decay of arable is assumed, and equally he has no doubt in stating that laws made in redress have been inefficacious. The decay and putting down of ploughs have not been stayed, "but are rather increased, and nothing amended." His own remedy is to leave the land in pasture alone and devote all efforts to the cultivation of the wastes. But here he points out a difficulty, which evidently was a real one. While the wastes existed the herbage and other profits belonged to the tenants; when divided and separated their division was at the lord's pleasure. Hence he advocates the introduction of a regular system of inclosure of wastes, the lord of the manor, together with four or five of the gravest tenants, appointed and chosen by their fellows, to be empowered to proceed to a division and allotment, each allotment to be according to the rent paid and to be granted on condition of clearing and cultivating in two years. His object was not only to supply the lack of tillage land but to prevent division taking place under conditions which placed the land at the pleasure of the lord; it became his and the tenant lost the free profit which he formerly possessed in herbage, etc. Here, however, the memorial is instanced as evidence that inclosure of waste to the lord's advantage was taking place, at any rate to some extent. Of course the writer's recommendation, had it been enforced by law, would have increased the amount inclosed, though it would have removed or modified the objection felt by the tenants and people in general and evinced in the discords referred to, as also later at the time of the Diggers.

On turning to what occurred during the seventeenth

century it will be convenient to examine the evidence as it presents itself under three headings—general references in tracts, pamphlets, and the like, official records, and lastly the evidence afforded by comparisons between the state of the country in the sixteenth and towards the end of the seventeenth century. So far as the first two bodies of evidence are concerned the century may be divided into periods of twenty-five years. One thing, however, must be remembered. Literary references frequently are to movements which have been in progress for some little time and have grown to sufficient dimensions to impress themselves as a general grievance in a district and within the knowledge of the writer, and yet not so long-standing as to have lost their aggressive character. A tract on inclosure does not merely deal with the events of the last year or so, but covers a much wider range.

So far as the first quarter of the century is concerned reference has already been made to the analysis of the relative advantages of inclosure and open which distinctly favours inclosure as conducing to (1) security from foreign invasion and domestic commotion, (2) increase of wealth and population, (3) better cultivation through land being put to its best use. In the *Geographical Description of England and Wales* (1615) complaint is made in respect of Northamptonshire that "the simple and gentle sheep, of all creatures the most harmless, are now become so ravenous that they begin to devour men, waste fields, and depopulate houses, if not whole townships, as one hath written." The passage is of course copied from the *Utopia*. *The Commons' Complaint* (1612) and *New Directions of Experience to the Commons' Complaint* (1613), both by Arthur Standish, advocate inclosure in every county of the kingdom. In the preface to the earlier tract he refers to "a grievance of late taken only for the dearth of corn in Warwickshire, Northamptonshire, and other places." Since this as well as the other tract is largely a defence, or rather advocacy, of inclosing there can be no doubt that the suggested cause was the inclosing. Of Cornwall

Carew writes in 1602, "They fall everywhere from commons to inclosure." Again, Trigge in *The Humble Petition of Two Sisters* (1604) condemns inclosure.[1]

In the second quarter the literary treatment of the subject is not very full. *Depopulation Arraigned* (1636), by R. P. (Powell), of Wells, was occasioned by the issue of the royal commission to inquire into inclosures, and deals in a hostile spirit with the subject. The author specially condemns what he describes as "a growing evil of late years"—namely, grazing butchers taking up land,—and gives some details of inclosure accompanied by depopulation.[2]

In the third quarter and at the very beginning there is much more to be referred to under this heading. *Inclosure Thrown Open; or, Depopulation Depopulated*, by H. Halhead (1650), is a vigorous attack on those desirous of inclosing, who are accused of resorting to any means to secure their object. As to the district referred to, the authorship of the preface by Joshua Sprigge, of Banbury, affords some slender ground for the conjecture that it refers to the South Midlands. That the Midlands formed a conspicuous area is clearly shown by other writings. In these a definite controversy centres round the inclosures of Leicestershire, Northamptonshire, and the adjacent Midlands, while it comprises also references to other parts of the country. The first publication in this series was *The Crying Sin of England of not Caring for the Poor, wherein Inclosure, viz. such as doth Unpeople Towns and Uncorn Fields, is Arraigned, Convicted, and Condemned by the Word of God*, by John Moore, minister of Knaptoft, in Leicestershire (1653). To this there appeared an answer, *Considerations Concerning Common Fields and Inclosures* (1653). Moore replied in a printed sheet which apparently is lost. To this the author of the *Considerations* published a

[1] The treatment in Norden's *Surveyor* and in Burton's *Anatomy* certainly suggests that inclosure was proceeding.

[2] See also D. Lupton, *London and the Country Carbonadoed*, 1632 (Harl. MS. 9); Fuller, *Holy State*, 1642.

Rejoinder, written in 1653, but not printed till 1656. In this latter year Joseph Lee, the minister of Cotesbatch, published *A Vindication of Regulated Inclosure.* A final retort to both the foregoing by Moore in *A Scripture Word against Inclosure* (1656) concludes the controversy. By its side must be placed *The Society of the Saints* and *The Christian Conflict*, both by Joseph Bentham, of Kettering. With regard to all these some few points require notice. The controversy begins with the inclosures in Leicestershire, Northamptonshire, and the counties adjacent, and then extends somewhat to other inland counties in general, one writer alluding to the inland counties "where inclosure is now so much inveighed against." References in particular are made to inclosure in Warwickshire, and to the existence of inclosed districts in Essex, Kent, Herefordshire, Devon, Shropshire, Worcestershire, and even Cornwall, though it cannot be concluded that the allusion is to recent inclosures in these latter counties. In the second place even Moore is careful to distinguish between inclosure which depopulates and that which has no such effect. When hard pushed he goes further, writing, "I complain not of inclosure in Kent or Essex, where they have other callings and trades to maintain their country by, or of places near the sea or city." Thirdly, a very important consideration as to the ultimate effect of the movement is raised by those in its favour in the assertion that very often inclosure is laid to pasture and then after a rest returned to arable use greatly enriched. This assertion is accompanied by a considerable number of instances. Probably the references to the large inclosures in North Wiltshire by John Aubrey in the *Natural History of Wiltshire* were written during this period, for his studies began in 1656, though his preface was not written until 1685. The same period saw the publication of what was one of the most important seventeenth century works dealing with the subject, Blith's *English Improver* (1652). In 1664 Forster in *England's Happiness Increased* prognosticates a rise in the price of corn from inclosure which he deplores, stating, "more and more land inclosed every year."

During the last quarter of the century we have the many definite assertions by Houghton in his valuable *Collections.* In 1681 he writes of the many inclosures which "have of late been made, and that people daily are on gog on making, and the more, I dare say, would follow would they that are concerned and understand it daily persuade their neighbours." He instances the sands of Norfolk as an example of what they may effect and urges the need of a bill of inclosure. In 1692, in arguing against the common notion that inclosure always leads to grass, he adduces instances to the contrary from Surrey, Middlesex, and Hertfordshire. In 1693 he gives some account of inclosed land in Staffordshire, and adds, "I cannot but admire that people should be so backward to inclose, which would be more worth to us than the mines of Potosi to the king of Spain." In 1700 he argues again in favour of a general act which should be permissive. Equally significant testimony is borne in 1698 by *The Law of Commons and Commoners*, which devotes a special section to the matter of legal inclosure. *Campania Felix*, by Timothy Nourse (1700), deals with the advantages of inclosure, as also does Worledge in the *Systema Agriculturae* (third edition, 1681). General references of this kind during the latter part of this century multiply as literature dealing with agricultural systems increases.

But to illustrate the condition of things during the last quarter of the seventeenth century, or even during the latter half, we must turn also to books and tracts published shortly after its termination. In *The Whole Art of Husbandry; or, the Way of Managing and Improving of Land*, by J. M., F.R.S. (John Mortimer), published in 1707, inclosure is treated as obviously beneficial, as with reference to it the writer adds, "I shall only propose two things that are matters of fact, that, I think, are sufficient to prove the advantages of inclosure, which is, first, the great quantities of ground daily inclosed, and, secondly, the increase of rent that is everywhere made by those who do inclose their lands." Again, the editor of Tusser in *Tusser Redivivus* (1710), commenting on a reference by Tusser, says, "In our author's time inclosures were not as frequent as now."[1] John Lawrence in *A New System of Agriculture* (1726) contrasts the inclosed and open fields in Staffordshire and Northamptonshire to the advantage of the former, and says as to the north that the example of Durham, the richest agricultural county, where nine parts in ten are already inclosed, is being followed by the more northern parts. He expresses surprise that so much of the kingdom is still open. Edward Lawrence in *The Duty of a Steward to his Lord* (1727) gives a form of agreement which he recommends to proprietors anxious to inclose. Equal testimony to the reality of the movement is offered by J. Cowper in *An Essay Proving that Inclosing Commons and Common Fields is Contrary to the Interests of the Nation*, in which he seeks to controvert the opinions of the Lawrences. Writing in 1732 he says: "I have been informed by an ancient surveyor that one-third of all the land of England has been inclosed within these eighty years." Within his own experience of thirty years he has seen about twenty lordships or parishes inclosed. *An Old Almanac*, which was written and printed in 1710, though it has a postscript bearing date 1734, urges the need of a general act and expresses the opinion that the consent of the lord with two-thirds of the tenants should bind the minority in any inclosure. Again, in the *Dictionarium Urbanicum* (1704) we read of "the great quantities of lands which in our own time have laid open, in common and of little value, yet when inclosed ... have proved excellent good," etc.

Turning from this kind of evidence to that of an official and legal character, it is fortunate that the comparative weakness of the testimony of tracts and pamphlets during

[1] However this be taken whether as referring to a movement in progress or as referring to the amount of inclosed land, it indicates a difference between the two periods.

the first half-century can be otherwise strengthened. The inquisition into inclosures in 1607 refers obviously to what had taken place in the latter period of the preceding century,[1] but during the reigns of the first two Stuarts the anxiety as to depopulation and scarcity which are apprehended as a probable if not a necessary result displays itself in almost undiminished force, as it may be seen from the Register of the Privy Council. In the reign of James I. there are some few references to cases of inclosure,[2] the most interesting of which deals with the case of Wickham and Colthorpe, in Oxfordshire, in respect of which a bill in chancery for inclosure had been exhibited by Sir Thomas Chamberlain.[3] Lord Say, however, had pulled the hedges down with considerable disturbance, and thus the matter came to the attention of the council. In a letter to the lord-lieutenant from the council it was pointed out that, owing to Lord Say's action being known, "there is very great doubt, as we are informed, of further mischief in that kind, the general speech being in the country that now Lord Say had begun to dig and level down hedges and ditches on behalf of commons there would be more down shortly, forasmuch as it is very expedient that all due care be taken for the preventing of any further disorder of this kind, which, as your lordship knoweth by that which happened heretofore in the county of Northampton and is yet fresh in memory, may easily spread itself into mischief and inconvenience." There are, however, but isolated instances of intervention.

More systematic attention to inclosure is shown during

[1] Though no conviction for depopulation was obtained, the evidence as to inclosure is unaffected.

[2] Vol. iv. p. 100 (9 February, 1617-8) refers to a case in Warwickshire; cf. p. 127. Vol. v. p. 700 (13 May, 1622-3), in Oxfordshire, a lord pleads that he has done no harm to the commoners, having left sufficient for their use, apparently an instance of approvement.

[3] *Privy Council Register*, vol. iii. pp. 111-5, July 1617. It is alleged, however, that Lord Say's action was not altogether due to chivalrous public spirit, and that he took this course to bring pressure to bear on Sir Thomas Chamberlain to induce him to refer a suit to him.

the second quarter of the century. The great administrative activity of the council in the fourth decade found a sphere here. On 26th November, 1630, a letter[1] was directed to be sent to the sheriffs and justices of the peace for the counties of Derby, Huntingdon, Nottingham, Leicester, and Northampton, calling for an account of inclosure or conversion during the past two years or at that time in progress. In the replies from Leicestershire and Nottinghamshire[2] many great inclosures were reported, and directions were accordingly despatched as to the course to be taken; some, as tending to depopulation or the undue diminution of arable, were to be thrown open. That this was deemed unnecessary in other cases is evident from a subsequent letter of 25th May, 1631, whereby inclosures begun might proceed on due undertakings that the houses of husbandry be not restricted injuriously or the highways interfered with.[3] That considerable care was exercised in the matter is evident from further references in the proceedings of the council.[4] On

[1] *Ibid.* vi. 199.

[2] *Ibid.* vi. 385. Letters addressed to sheriffs, etc., of Derby, Nottingham, and Huntingdon, reminding them of the letter of 26 November, and calling for a speedy return. *Ibid.* vi. 544; certain inclosures in Huntingdonshire to be laid open.

[3] *Privy Council Register*, vi. 540 (25 May, 1631). "Whereas their lordships did write themselves in November last and since to divers counties in the kingdom concerning the laying open of new inclosures and conversions of arable grounds into pasture and prohibiting the like for the time to come, forasmuch as divers noblemen," etc., "praying for the continuance and perfecting of inclosure begun in grounds," and undertaking that as much land be left in husbandry and that the highways be kept passable, and agreeing to give fitting security for the observances of such conditions, the board therefore order that their former orders be put in operation, save where owners agree in writing to conditions as the foregoing, "whereon a bill in chancery or exchequer to be exhibited by the attorney-general or other counsel charging the said owner, with his consent, to prevent depopulation or decay of husbandry or annoying the highways." Then follow provisions as to the due form of the undertaking, etc.

[4] *Ibid.* vii. 506-7, 6 April; also p. 532. At Croft, in Leicestershire, an inclosure is regarded as generally profitable, and some who have sought to destroy it are bidden and made to desist. *Ibid.* viii. 194, 31 August. Another

9th October, 1633, the judges of assize were ordered to attend the board on the 18th to give an account of their doings and proceedings in the matter of inclosures. Unfortunately in the account of the meeting on this date and of the interview with the judges no definite reference is made in the Register to what transpired in the case of inclosures. In general it is said that the justices of the peace do not meet often enough to carry out the Book of Orders and that the returns of the sheriffs are defective. Among the State Papers[1] is a copy of a warrant to the attorney-general to prepare commissions touching depopulation and conversion of arable in the counties of Lincoln, Leicester, Northampton, Somerset, Wilts, and Gloucester.[2]

While it is doubtful if much was done directly to stay inclosure, and while with the approach of the Civil War the time of the council was necessarily devoted to other matters, the existence of an inclosure movement is certain. It is equally clear that information was obtained of which some use was made, though possibly for other ends than the benefit of the agricultural interest and the people. In 1633-4 we find a proposal[3] that all inclosures made since 16 James I. should be thrown back into arable on pain of forfeiture, save such as be compounded for. The suggestion was not lost sight of, and from 1635 to 1638 compositions were levied in respect of depopulations in several counties of which an account is fortunately pre-

inclosure in the same county to be laid open, and land actually tilled. *Ibid.* viii. 351, 19 December 1632. The same course followed in a case in Nottingham. *Ibid.* ix. 301, 31 October 1633. A letter addressed to the president and council of the north calling their attention to an inclosure in Yorkshire. Cf. x. 40 and x. 50, where it is admitted that as yet the results are not so prejudicial as feared. Some few other cases dealt with in different parts of the country.

[1] *State Papers, Dom.*, ccxxix. p. 112. Cf. Miss Leonard, *ubi supra*, p. 129, note 1, where this document is more fully described.

[2] Detailed returns to the letters of the privy council are to be found in Miss Leonard's paper, pp. 130-4, so far as some of the counties, and especially Leicester, are concerned.

[3] *S.P., D.*, cclx. 106, 1633-4.

served.[1] Some 600 persons were fined during this period, the amounts in some cases being considerable. The following is a summary of the sums obtained from compositions in the several counties affected during these years:

—	1635.	1636.	1637.	1638.	Total.
	£	£	£	£	£
Lincoln, - - -	3,130	8,023	4,990	2,703	18,846
Leicester, - - -	1,700	3,560	4,080	85	9,425
Northampton, - -	3,200	2,340	2,875	263	8,678
Huntingdon, - -	—	680	1,837	230	2,747
Rutland, - - -	—	150	1,000	—	1,150
Nottingham, - -	—	—	2,010	78	2,088
Hertford, - - -	—	2,000	—	—	2,000
Gloucester, - -	—	—	—	50	50
Cambridge, - -	—	—	170	340	510
Oxford, - - -	—	—	580	153	733
Bedford, - - -	—	—	—	412	412
Buckingham, - -	—	—	—	71	71
Kent, - - -	—	—	—	100	100

Having regard to the size of the counties and the number of instances in each, this may be taken as indicating a considerable amount of inclosure in the case of the first six counties—Lincoln, Leicester, Northampton, Huntingdon, Rutland, and Nottingham. Only inclosures leading to depopulation were supposed to be included.

To the evidence thus given in official records as to inclosure during the first half of the century must be added that of the drainage inclosures.[2]

A large body of evidence as to inclosures and their distribution, mainly affecting the latter part of the century,

[1] Chancery Petty Bag, *Miscellaneous Roll* 20. During the last year it is doubtful if many of the compositions were paid.

[2] These were very considerable, that of the Bedford Level and the Holland Fen affecting parts of several counties. Of course waste still remained in the area, and by 15 Charles II., c. 17, § 38, all lords and all having rights of common in the waste within Bedford Level might improve, divide, and sever their respective proportions. This permission however was revoked by 1 James II., c. 21, on the ground that such severance had led to diminution of stock and decay of houses, a fact which accounts for the appearance among the private acts of the succeeding century of some dealing with wastes and commons in this district.

lies in the Chancery Enrolled Decrees, where cases of inclosure suits and agreements occur in large numbers.[1] These are of different kinds. In some instances agreements were enrolled to secure record and to bind the parties concerned; in other instances the object was to bind a minority who were not consenting parties to the case. For this purpose what seems to have been a collusive suit was brought against certain persons proceeding to inclose and a decree obtained giving allotments to the petitioners. This was used, though obviously illegally, to prevent third persons not parties to and probably often in ignorance of the action from disturbing the division of the ground in question. That this was illegal is clearly stated by the author of the legal text-book on the *Law of Commons and Commoners* (1698), but his language leaves no doubt as to its occurrence. Probably in the then state of the rural districts the method was efficacious. Not only so, but the threat of a suit at law was used frequently, we are told by others, to secure assent to a proposed agreement to inclose.[2] The mere menace would inevitably cause many to assent and others to withdraw from their rights. But the defect as against those who stubbornly adhered to their opposition, and who had sufficient means to give expression to their opposition, doubtless strengthened the growing desire for some parliamentary action, a full account of which has been given already.[3] By this it will be seen that no fewer than eight general bills dealing

[1] The number of these decrees is very great. There is little doubt that a careful examination would throw great light on some part of the inclosure. The most cursory survey of a few rolls is sufficient to show that the inclosures therein recorded are not confined to one part of the country, as will be seen from the following instances, taken at random: Settringham, in Yorkshire (1669); Shrivenham, Berks (1658); Great Coxwell, Berks (1658): Long Sutton, Somerset (1616); Claypoole, Lincolnshire (1614); Cradley, Worcester (1621). Miss Leonard's view as to the wide area affected coincides with mine. So far as Durham is concerned she shows conclusively that inclosure took place to a large extent, thus bearing out the statement of John Lawrence.

[2] Moore, *The Crying Sin of England*, p. 13; Halhead, *Inclosures Thrown Open*, pp. 8, 9. Cf. pp. 54-5.

[3] See above, pp. 57-8.

with commons or common land were introduced into Parliament during the last half of the century.

The allusions to tumults in Northamptonshire at the beginning of the century, a repetition of which was feared at the time of Lord Say's destruction of an inclosure, together with the movement of the Diggers, add the testimony of public disorder to the very considerable array of evidence adduced. A further supplement is to be found in the references made both by contemporary writers and by those of the earlier part of the next century to specific inclosures. Thoroton mentions some in Nottinghamshire. A list of the inclosures in Leicestershire, drawn up in the eighteenth century, notes some as effected in the previous century. A few instances in Northamptonshire beginning with 1600 are given by Bridges. The list might be further multiplied. Isolated instances are chiefly useful as filling up and strengthening the more general assertions made elsewhere. By themselves, however, they are too few to be of great value.

On turning to another kind of evidence and attempting some comparison between the state of the country, or rather of different districts, as described at approximately the beginning and approximately the end of the century, very obvious difficulties present themselves, except in one instance. The terms used are general and not precise, while further the obvious aim of the writer at any date is to compare the state of any particular district with that of adjacent districts or of the country at large at the same date. Hence the meaning of the terms "champion" or "inclosed" varies a good deal. But this feature, which renders the various descriptions so good for a comparison of the different parts at the same time, takes away from their value as a means of comparing the condition of one district at one time with its condition at another time, save when the change has been so great that the main character of the district is transformed, or when the change has been very irregular in its distribution.

In one instance, however, this difficulty does not present

itself, and a good deal as to the progress of inclosure may be learnt from a comparison of the *Itinerary* of Leland with the road maps of Ogilby. Out of the references by Leland to the condition of the land along the road traversed, counting as one each case where there is a practically continuous account of a uniform character, about one-half can fairly be identified with a route described by Ogilby.[1] Of these in twenty-seven cases the land is apparently in much the same condition. In the case of fourteen [2] the amount

[1] My attention was drawn to the importance of Ogilby's *Britannia* in this respect by the reference in Macaulay (*History*, vol. i. ch. iii., cabinet ed. p. 210, note). The landscapes to illustrate the *Travels of the Grand Duke Cosimo*, bearing date 1669, are not only interesting in themselves but afford some useful corroboration and illustration of the state of the country. In general, except in the drawings of the country near Rochester, Chelmsford, and Thorndon, and to some degree that near Exeter, there is much open country. It must, of course, be remembered that the illustrations are not very numerous and do not represent the whole country. So far as they go they illustrate three points:—(1) the villages lying closely together along the roads, as may be gathered also from Ogilby; (2) the general absence of scattered farmhouses; (3) the considerable extent of land without hedges and not divided into small separate fields. Careful study has led me to attach very great importance to Ogilby's testimony. As a rule the marking of the roads is very obvious, but in certain plates no distinction is attempted, as is stated in his preface. Some little care and discrimination is therefore required. The same method of distinguishing between inclosed and non-inclosed roads is employed elsewhere, *e.g.* in *The Historical Antiquities of Hertfordshire*, by Sir Henry Chauncey, 1700, which shows conclusively the great extent to which that county was inclosed and the small region in which open land still existed. This is also treated of in his text.

[2] The fourteen referred to are as follows:—

Cambridge to Eltesley . .	Cambridgeshire.
Wellingborough to Northampton	Northamptonshire.
Stanton to Leicester . . .	Leicestershire.
Uppingham to Harringworth .	Rutland, Northamptonshire.
Higham Ferrars to Bedford .	Northamptonshire, Bedfordshire.
Hinksey to Faringdon . .	Berkshire.
Southam to Banbury . . .	Warwickshire, Oxfordshire.
Droitwich to Bromsgrove . .	Worcestershire.
Winchester to Southampton .	Hampshire.
Alscote to Torrington . . .	Devon.
Fowey to Liskeard . . .	Cornwall.
Helegh to York	Yorkshire.
Kingston to Beverley . . .	Yorkshire.
Malton to Skirburne . . .	Yorkshire.

of inclosure however has obviously increased, sometimes very greatly increased. Some two or three other cases, though indications point in the same direction, have been put aside on the ground that the evidence is inadequate. It ought to be added that in no case does land stated to be inclosed on the earlier tour appear to have fallen back into an open condition. Taking these fourteen cases, two occur in Devon and Cornwall, and so the inclosure is of waste or open common, three in Yorkshire (E. and N. Ridings), one in Hampshire, one in Worcestershire, while the remaining seven are in the Midlands. Three of these last seven are in Northamptonshire. The route taken by Leland in South Leicestershire runs from Stanton (Stoughton) to Leicester, and the traveller adds "all by champain land." The neighbouring route described by Ogilby from Glen to Leicester runs through inclosed ground, a fact which suggests that there had been some increase of inclosure in this district.[1] Turning from the particular instances analysed above, a careful comparison of the two itineraries, to give a common name to both, certainly leaves an impression of a general and marked increase in inclosed land, though, except in the Midlands, it seems that inclosure rather tends to increase in areas and to extend along lines already affected by the movement than to break out in wholly new districts.

Turning to the general comparison of descriptions and records at different times, for reasons already given great care must be exercised. Certain instances occur, however, where a definite conclusion seems possible. Leicestershire is described as "champion" in the *Geographical Description of England and Wales* (1615), while Burton (1622) specially says that the south-east is "almost all champion." On the other hand according to Ogilby's road maps there

[1] As a matter of fact a private act in 1761 deals with Evington and Stoughton, but this confirms the fact of an earlier inclosure, as it is merely for a division of land left in common, as may be seen from the award. For reasons given further on, however, I think that this district was less inclosed than would appear from Ogilby.

was a large amount of inclosed ground in the south-east. Again, we have in Aubrey a definite comparison of North Wilts at an early date and towards the end of the century, the latter state being confirmed by Ogilby. Of Durham the east is "most champain," according to the *Geographical Description*, a condition apparently continuing in 1673, when, Blome writes in *Britannia*, the east is champain. On the other hand, according to John Lawrence in 1726 nine parts in ten are inclosed. In North Wilts, according to Leland, the route from Cirencester to Malmesbury was after the first mile all by champain, which continues to Chippenham. But by the latter part of the century much in this district was inclosed, a state of things very clearly shown in the roads passing through Malmesbury by Ogilby. Again, if Norden is accurate in describing Dorset, Wilts, Hampshire, and Berks as being champion in 1607, the state of the roads in Ogilby indicates that in Berkshire as well as in Wiltshire a considerable amount of inclosing had taken place during the seventeenth century. The same, though probably to a less extent, is true of Hampshire.

Before summarising the foregoing some account may be attempted of the condition of the country in respect of inclosure at the time of Ogilby's road book *Britannia*,[1] which bears date 1675, supplementing that with references of the same time or a little later. Such an account requires considerable additions to make it applicable to the end of the century, since there can be no doubt that the movement progressed considerably during the last two decades.

If we follow Ogilby's description of the land [2] lying at

1 With regard to the annexed map, prepared from Ogilby, certain points require notice. In the first place the map does not attempt to represent the general state of the country, *e.g.* in respect of towns. In the second place, to avoid confusion, it has been necessary to omit the roads in which distinction of open and inclosed country is not specified.

2 The following is a summary of the amount of open or uninclosed road as compared with the total amount of road described by Ogilby in each county, given in percentages. Of course the calculation is necessarily imperfect, and

the side of the routes he traversed as fairly illustrating the country, the area in which open land chiefly continued at that time forms an irregular triangle, the apex of which lies in South Wilts, somewhat south and midway between Warminster and Salisbury, and the sides extend in a north-easterly and easterly direction respectively to the east coast. Of these the north side may be roughly figured as passing through Warminster and Devizes to Highworth; thence almost direct north to Stow, whence it makes a détour in a north-westerly direction through Pershore almost to Worcester, thence by Alcester, Coventry, Kegworth, Mansfield, Blyth, Doncaster, Pontefract, York, to Gainsborough, and thence to the coast. The more southerly side runs through Salisbury, Hungerford, Oxford, Aylesbury, Newport Pagnel, thence with a

it must be remembered that the result, for reasons stated below, cannot be assumed to do more than very roughly represent the average throughout the county. Some few roads are omitted as unspecified.

Percentage of Open Road—i.e. *Road by the side of which the Country is Open or Uninclosed.*

Huntingdon	67	Leicester	38	Salop	19
Rutland	64	Gloucester	37	Cornwall	19
Lincoln	61	Yorks	36	Stafford	18
Cambridge	60	Berks	32	Cheshire	14
Oxford	58	Westmorland	31	Devon	13
Northampton	56	Suffolk	31	Worcester	13
Northumberland	56	Derby	30	Lancashire	12
Nottingham	54	Hants	29	Middlesex	11
Cumberland	54	Buckingham	28	Hertford	9
Bedford	51	Surrey	27	Hereford	8
Wilts	47	Durham	23	Kent	5
Norfolk	42	Somerset	21	Essex	3
Warwick	39				

In Dorset no trustworthy road is marked, and in Sussex the amount is too small for notice. In some cases the particular road or roads is one through particularly open or inclosed country, but this is less important when several roads enter into the calculation. It must, of course, be remembered that land by the side of the roads or within access, like land in the neighbourhood of towns and districts undergoing industrial development, was more subject to inclosure than that more remote. Also hedges and walls would often occur along the road and not *on* the land. Again, unfenced roads may in some cases run through land in individual or separate holdings. For these reasons the calculation can only be taken as an estimate. It is somewhat excessive.

southerly détour through Luton to Biggleswade, thence by Royston, Linton, Newmarket, to Bury St. Edmunds, and thence by Thetford, Hingham, Norwich, southerly to Great Yarmouth. The triangular area thus roughly delineated consists of the following counties: all or very nearly all of Cambridge, Bedford, Northampton, Huntingdon, Rutland, Lincoln, and Leicester, also S. and E. Warwick, S. Wilts, W. Norfolk, E. Yorks, a considerable part of Oxford, Buckingham, Nottingham, some part of Worcester, and small portions of Berks and Suffolk. There was, of course, open land outside, in addition to that lying in down, moor, heath, and hill,[1] but if Ogilby can be taken as indicating the average character of the land it was in this area that open field and commons constituted a widespread feature. On the other hand, it is equally clear from Ogilby that there was a very large amount of inclosed land in the area described, a feature particularly conspicuous in Northamptonshire, S. Leicestershire, W. Norfolk, S. Nottinghamshire, S. Lincolnshire, and Yorkshire. Elsewhere the inclosed land presents itself more intermixt and in less continuous amounts, as in Bedfordshire.[2] There is little doubt that by the end of the century the proportion of this had increased. The tendency for inclosure to prevail near towns of any size is marked and important.[3] But this suggests the need of some allowance in our account for a larger amount of open land more distant from roads and so less accessible to or more distant from towns.

[1] As, for instance, the Cotswolds (Nourse, *Campania Felix* (1700), p. 45).

[2] According to the author of *England's Remarques* in 1678, Bedfordshire was "generally champion."

[3] There is a good deal of evidence which generally corroborates the sketch here given. On the other hand cases of error, either by omission or commission, need correction. In South Leicestershire the impression of the country as judged by the land on the route described by Ogilby requires considerable modification. There is little doubt that a considerable amount of the land in the Market Harborough district remained open, though there were many inclosures. The large amount of land inclosed under private acts in this district seems conclusive.

Summarising the evidence which has been adduced, it is clear that inclosure had been going on with some activity in the latter part of the sixteenth century. When the seventeenth century opens inclosure is attracting considerable attention, some part of which is no doubt due to the menace of disorder, or even to actual disturbances as in Northamptonshire. Complaint, however, is not confined to that county, but extends into Warwickshire and elsewhere. At the same time in Cornwall wastes are being inclosed for the purpose, it may be assumed, of cultivation. With time the movement in the Midlands, so far from being stayed, gathers force and extends over the adjacent districts to such an extent that the fear of depopulation leads to official inquiry into what was happening in the counties of Northampton, Leicester, Derby, Huntingdon, Nottingham, Gloucester, Wilts, Somerset, and Lincoln. Redress in certain cases is attempted, but not, it would seem, often, the most systematic use of the information obtained by these or other inquiries being the exaction of compositions from offenders, a course which obviously assisted the king in his effort to avoid dependence upon parliamentary supplies, though it might not remedy the evil. The chief counties affected by such compositions were Lincoln, Leicester, Northampton, Huntingdon, Nottingham, and Rutland. They certainly do not do much to stay the movement in the Midlands, which leads to considerable local controversy as to the results occasioned. Whatever be thought of these there can be no doubt that inclosure in the Midlands was both continuous and widespread, though it probably was most severe in the border district between Warwickshire, Leicestershire, and Northamptonshire.[1] Meantime there are marks of like change elsewhere, as in North Wilts, where the inclosures extend over a considerable area; and in other districts where the mentions which survive are of separate instances. During the latter half of the century there is

[1] For this see the controversy from 1653 to 1656 (above pp. 160-1). Nearly all the townships mentioned lie in this district.

a great body of evidence as to the extensive nature of the movement, which evidently increases during the last two decades. As to this latter period, the evidence goes to show that very large quantities of land were regularly inclosed.[1] The question of inclosure is now not in any sense local, its advocates going so far as to seek to obtain parliamentary sanction to remove the difficulties which seem to have impeded though they could not check its course.

As can be seen from a comparison of this summary with the account drawn from Ogilby the chief area in which inclosure is mentioned as taking place coincides roughly with the region in which there still remained a large quantity of open. But inclosure also took place just on the borders, and the inclosures in Durham and the north must be treated as additional. But it must be remembered that inclosures which created no grievance, public or private, which, that is, did not threaten the realm with depopulation or dearth, or dispossess individuals of rights or of all opportunity of earning a living, were little likely to attract attention. What we know of the north or of Wilts, or of the sands of Norfolk, is due to rather casual notices. Even Moore, the vehement censor of the movement, writes, "I complain not of inclosure in Kent or Essex, where they have other callings and trades to maintain their country, or of places near the sea or city." By the side of this passage may be put his remark that "the great manufacture of Leicestershire and many (if not most) of the inland counties is tillage." Probably this attempt at discrimination is due to a desire to distinguish between what was occurring in his neighbourhood and what was taking place elsewhere. The reference may be restricted intentionally to Essex and Kent, in neither of which is it probable that there was inclosing during this century, but on the whole a wider application seems more probable. Towns, it must be remembered, were growing and manufacture

[1] Specific reference is made at this time to the sand district of Norfolk.

was on the increase, and, to judge from Ogilby and other sources, inclosure in the neighbourhood of the towns was of usual occurrence. Some further evidence to this effect is offered by the complaint that the poor, deprived of the chance of labour in the field, were driven into towns.[1] The material conclusion is that additional inclosure, which, far from being complained of, was regarded with favour, took place round the growing cities and towns. The growth of industries had undoubted influence in this direction. The weaving districts both in the east and in the west had been gravely affected in the early part of the sixteenth century, when the need of local supplies led to a considerable alteration in the cultivation of the land. It must not be assumed that the conversion, when it occurred, from arable to grazing was wholly in view of wool. The increase in the need for food, and especially animal products for consumption, must be taken into account.[2] In some districts no doubt both wool and corn were largely imported, as was the case in part of Devonshire at the end of the sixteenth and the beginning of the seventeenth centuries, when, as we hear in an account in 1630, the country was so full of cloth-making that food was imported.[3] The wool used was not only local, or even from the neighbouring counties of Cornwall and Dorset, but brought from elsewhere, as from Worcestershire and Warwickshire. Probably this was true also of Somerset. Though tillage was still the great interest in the Midlands in the seventeenth century, town growth and the spread of industry were beginning, and these had a necessary effect upon inclosure.

[1] This complaint is not novel in the seventeenth century; thus Cope writes of "the poor who, being driven out of their habitations, are forced into the great towns, where, being very burdensome, they shut their doors against them, suffering them to die in the streets and highways," etc.

[2] The reference in *Depopulation Arraigned*, p. 40, to grazing butchers taking up land is suggestive. It is termed a growing evil practised in recent years.

[3] In early times probably a near supply of grain was also very important, but this need would diminish with improvements in locomotion and transport.

Again, the inclosures in the north and in Cornwall have been mentioned. But these were not the only districts where wastes existed. To judge from the accounts of England towards the end of the sixteenth century there was a vast quantity of wild, uncultivated ground, of heath, moor, fen, and forest. To this Leland bears testimony in his *Itinerary*, while the already cited memorial by Alderman Box lays stress on its amount, as also on the desirability of its cultivation. Now any such quantity of waste land, as may be estimated from these and other sources, is, save in some districts in the north, quite inadequately accounted for in the inclosures by private act in the eighteenth and nineteenth centuries, or in the other recorded inclosures. Considerable ground was brought into cultivation by the drainage of the fens, and to this, it is contended, must be added the land recovered as it were from a wild condition. It is probable, indeed, that some portion was inclosed and cultivated during the earlier years of the eighteenth century. But, granting this and making allowance for the condition of the country in the late sixteenth century, the conclusion that a very considerable quantity of inclosure from a wild condition took place in the seventeenth or early eighteenth century is necessary. It may be contended that in a large number of cases such a course did not imply *technical* inclosure, inasmuch as the land may not have been under any common right servitude, and further that in such an event there would be nothing to tell of its inclosure, if the term be employed, even during the period of private acts. This may be true or partially true in the more outlying regions, but so far as much wild land is concerned the testimony of Box is in the opposite direction, since one object of the particular method suggested by him is to prevent tenants having rights from being deprived of them, as they evidently were being deprived on inclosure. But even in the case of land where rights either had not existed or had fallen into desuetude, from the early middle of the eighteenth century our knowledge of the movement is sufficiently complete to preclude its inclosure in large quantities without some notice. The enlargement of the whole region of or near cultivation after the middle of the sixteenth century seems to justify the conclusion that much inclosure of this kind must have taken place during the seventeenth century, possibly during the latter years.

During the long period dealt with, extending from the later years of the sixteenth to the beginning of the eighteenth century, there seems abundant evidence as to the progress of inclosure in the following counties:—

Warwick	Derby	Norfolk
Leicester	Nottingham	Durham
Northampton	Rutland	Cornwall (early)
Hunts	Wilts	

There is also testimony as to some inclosure in certain other counties, though not of so definite a character or in such great amount—

Buckingham	Hampshire	Gloucester
Berkshire	Somerset	Yorkshire (part of)

—to which might possibly be added other counties in the north to which inclosure had spread from Durham. In addition both from the Decree Rolls as also from scattered instances occasional inclosure was taking place throughout the country generally. But as to this it should be remembered that some counties were in a highly inclosed state when the period opened. Among these were Suffolk, Essex, Hertford, Kent, Devon, Herefordshire, Shropshire, Cheshire. Both Cornwall and Somerset, different in character as their inclosures are, were probably highly inclosed. Whether much inclosure went on during this period in Bedfordshire is difficult to decide. According to Ogilby a good deal of inclosure had been achieved by that time.[1] It seems probable that the northern

[1] The omission of any mention of inclosed land by Celia Fiennes in Bedfordshire and Northamptonshire is very far from being conclusive. Her references are very uncertain, as may be seen in the case of Hertfordshire, most of which was certainly highly inclosed. Against it we have a large variety of evidence in the case of Northamptonshire. According to Ogilby, whose

part of Cambridgeshire was inclosed at the end of the century.[1]

Leaving, however, the more special cases on one side the general outlines of the seventeenth-century inclosure seem clear and sufficiently distinctive to permit of certain conclusions. Firstly, there is evidence of inclosure continuing from earlier times through the Thames district. The Norfolk inclosures probably arose from new causes and at the end of the period. In Durham and the north the movement rises and develops. Probably much the same may be said of the whole district round the Wash. In the Midlands we have a movement which, though not new, since the north of Warwickshire was already inclosed to a great extent, increases very rapidly. Secondly, the country in the regions of early industrial and town growth was already largely inclosed. Thirdly, a considerable amount of land was reclaimed from an uncultivated state by fen or draining inclosures, and in some cases from encroachment by the sea.[2] Fourthly, the development of inclosure

observations are systematic and careful, there was much inclosed land in both counties. Miss Leonard's view that Northamptonshire, at the close of the century, was "comparatively" open may be interpreted in various ways according to the meaning of the word "comparatively." As compared with many other counties this was no doubt the case. Even allowing for an over-estimate in respect of inclosure of a district on the basis of that along the road Ogilby's evidence is very strong, and so far as Northamptonshire is concerned it is amply supported by abundant positive evidence, thus *inter alia* *Geographical Description, England and Wales* (1615) under Northampton; *Certain Cases Gathered Together* (end of 16th century), complaint of inclosure in Oxford, Buckingham, and Northampton; Aubrey's *North Wiltshire*, p. 104; *New System of Agriculture*, by John Lawrence (1726), p. 45; Bentham's *Christian Conflict*, p. 40; *A Scripture Word against Inclosure*, p. 10; *Agric. Report* refers to ancient inclosures (ii., pp. 36-37, 111, 129); Morton's *Northampton*, pp. 13, 14. As to earlier inclosures there are references for the 16th century.

[1] This is inferred, firstly, from the very marked difference between the percentage of land inclosed under private act in the north as compared with the south of Cambridgeshire; secondly, from the general character of the land and its neighbourhood to the fens.

[2] While drainage schemes and other reclamations did not necessarily involve the division and inclosure of all the ground affected, commons being left in

in the northern Midlands attacks a region, little affected hitherto, under very particular conditions. The soil of a large part of the district under the old common field system could not be devoted to the use for which it was best adapted—namely, grazing. Again, during that century a considerable quantity of land was reclaimed, thus adding to the area of cultivation much new and good corn land. Transport was developing and security of locomotion was greater. On the other hand towns were beginning to develop, and to some extent at any rate it would seem probable that inclosure took place owing to their development, and it may have been to supply their needs.

The method and nature of the inclosures during this period now call for some notice. The mode whereby these were effected at once follows in due sequence on that pursued in earlier times, and prepares the way for that which was employed in the next century. In the first place approvement was still in force, and there is evidence that the powers thus at the disposal of the lord of the manor[1] were in use. Among the answers to the inquiries set on foot by the privy council are references to sufficient land being left to others, in one case the lord alleging that he has left as much "as by law he ought to do."[2] That this means became of less use as time passed and with the decrease of the land in waste seems evident both from the nature of the case and also from the attempts in

many cases, and in others common rights continuing to exist, as a general rule there would be a large amount inclosed. Land liable to be overflowed by the sea or reclaimed from the encroachment of the sea and subject to common right received special treatment by statute. An attempt by Lady Wainsford to inclose Hulcey Common, in Suffolk, on the ground of a grant to inclose lands overflowed by the sea, is ordered to be not pursued till the case be determined either by the commissioners or at law (*Privy Council Register*, xii. 455, 27 November, 1636). Cf. reference to such land in *Humble Petition*.

[1] Approvement, it must be remembered, was a power belonging only to the lord of the manor. It is also limited to inclosures from waste.

[2] *Privy Council Register*, v. 700, 13 May, 1623, at Garsington, in Oxfordshire.

1696 and 1697 to revive or even extend old powers. In the second place, while arbitrary inclosures no doubt took place, they seem, so far as their direct character is concerned, to have yielded to the development in the administration of the law. Agreements take their place, though not necessarily to the prevention of arbitrary action. That is removed one stage further off, and manifests itself in the kind of pressure exerted to secure assent to these agreements. Unwilling commoners are threatened with the risks of long and expensive lawsuits;[1] in other cases they are subject to persecution by the great proprietors, who ditch in their own demesne and force them to go a long way round to their own land, or maliciously breed rabbits and keep geese on adjoining ground, to the detriment of their crops.[2] In addition, to some extent, though until the records of the decrees in chancery have been fully examined it will be impossible to say to what extent, advantage was taken of the ignorance of the small commoners to make an illegal use of judgments obtained in their absence against their right of common. Thus agreements real or fictitious were secured. Probably where but few were concerned it was not difficult to bring people to a voluntary assent, and in other cases by mingled cajolery and pressure dissent could be prevented. But the complexity of rights which existed in the larger number of open fields and the growing knowledge that decrees obtained in chancery did not bind a dissentient minority rendered resort to parliamentary sanction desirable.

Hence arose the movement which began in the promotion of a bill to make such decrees valid, and ended in the resort to private acts. These must not be regarded as involving a novel system of inclosure. They became necessary in order to carry out the system of agreements on a large and uniform scale, supplying both a means of

[1] Moore, *Crying Sin, etc.*, p. 13; Halhead, *Inclosures Thrown Open*, p. 8; cf. *Considerations, etc.*, p. 25.

[2] Halhead, *Inclosures Thrown Open*, p. 9. Cf. pp. 53-4.

registering them, where unanimous, more convenient than that previously employed, and further a legal method of enforcing agreements arrived at by a large majority upon a small and very often an ignorant minority. In many cases the early acts do little more than give legal assent and force to a division and inclosure already agreed upon and apparently in the process of execution. Nor were they without precedent. In addition to the acts passed for the inclosure and division of lands under particular conditions, as, for instance, those reclaimed by drainage or needing protection from encroachments by the sea, there is at least one early act[1] of this very nature. The precedent was not, indeed, followed at the time, owing, at any rate in part, to the other means which presented themselves for the ready accomplishment of the end in view. At the close of the period matters had changed. These means had been exhausted or found ineffective for further use. So gradually recourse was had to the system of private acts.[2] Their use, however, coincides in an interesting way with the growing assertion of parliamentary methods as contrasted with the action of the crown by ordinance or decree. A private act is the answer by the king in parliament to the petition by a subject. But the decree in chancery is the answer by the king to such a petition in his court of chancery. In this sense continuity is exhibited in form as well as in substance.

Though it is not possible here to attempt a discussion

[1] 4 James I., c. 11, "Act for the Inclosure of One-Third of the Land in Marden and Bodenham," really an act for the separation of certain parts of the land.

[2] Their introduction into use was very gradual before about 1750. Till then private acts are employed somewhat sporadically and taken all together in but few cases. There is little doubt that during this time inclosure was going on steadily. Evidence of this is elsewhere adduced and can be supplemented in the case of different localities. A very good instance occurs in the case of Norfolk. Much inclosure took place in the north-west angle in the first half of the eighteenth century, as we know from different sources. It is dated by Young as occurring from 1730 to 1760. But it did not take place by private act. From references elsewhere cited it began much earlier than the date assigned by Young, though continuing on into that time.

of the nature of the inclosures of this period or of their consequences, one or two remarks may be added. Taking the century as a whole the grave apprehensions expressed as to depopulation or diminution of arable were not fulfilled. In large measure inclosure was promoted in view of agricultural or even arable necessities. The relief of these inspired the support of the movement by its strongest advocates, as Standish, Lee, the author of the *Considerations*, and Houghton. The opportunities which were offering for skilful farming made some alteration imperative. Again, at the very close of the century there is the positive assertion that less land is devoted to stock than was recently the case, while the Records of the Privy Council show that these results were often absent in the very cases selected for inquiry. It will be remembered that writers like Moore admit that a good deal of inclosure might occur without such consequences. On the other hand it is clear that at certain times and in certain districts, particularly in the Midlands, conversion from arable to pasture took place. Diverse influences were at work. Of these the most important are the growth of towns, which, while making better farming imperative, tended towards inclosure in the neighbourhood and the local increase of stock; the improvement in farming methods, which made the difference greater between the good and the bad farmer; and, lastly, the growth of locomotion. The skilful farmer required freedom for the exercise of his skill, and it was to the benefit of the nation that land should be put to the use for which it was fitted.

Speaking generally, the notion that the sole aim and result of inclosure during this period was the conversion of arable to pasture must be abandoned. No doubt this took place in many cases. No doubt, too, that in the earliest stage of the movement conversion was an important though possibly an exaggerated feature. But the description does not apply to the later sixteenth and seventeenth centuries as a whole. In Leland's *Itinerary*, as has been already pointed out, there is mention of inclosed land in some sixty instances. In twenty-six of these notice is definitely made of corn. Sometimes the land is termed "goodly corn land"; sometimes it is said to be fruitful and plentiful of grass and corn, and at other times fruitful of grass and corn. But in each case the corn is sufficiently obvious to be noted.[1] Again, in the *Properties of the Shires*, printed with the *Itinerary*, we hear of Somerset, a much inclosed county, that it is "good for whete." If we turn to Suffolk, also a very early inclosed county, we learn from Reyce that in Mid Suffolk there is both pasture and tillage, but mainly the latter, and this is not the district which he treats as champion. On the contrary, the greater number of flocks are in the champion district, the west. There is, of course, much other evidence so far as many cases are concerned. Lee, in *Regulated Inclosure*, while claiming that hedges provide shelter for cattle also argues that they are good for crops, an opinion which, though probably erroneous, shows that the inclosure movement was definitely viewed as acting favourably on arable cultivation. Reconversion after a rest is evidence as to result, if not intention.[2] If at the end of the century we turn to Celia Fiennes's record of her journeys, despite the sporadic

[1] A good deal of contemporary evidence in writers like Tusser and Blith points in the same direction.

[2] Inclosure from waste is of course always exempt from the charge of occasioning depopulation. It must however be remembered that such inclosure, when accompanied by tillage, as was often the case, almost necessarily led to the withdrawal of some other land from arable. The law that the most suitable land comes first into cultivation, as laid down by Ricardo, received severe criticism at the hands of writers like Carey and Rodbertus, who pointed out that in the course of historical development land at one time waste, fen, undrained, or distant from a centre often becomes the chief arable—that is, after reclamation. The truth of this is obvious, but it hardly affects the substantial meaning underlying Ricardo's words. As it becomes more suitable other land loses its superiority and becomes by comparison less suitable. This is important in estimating the results of inclosure, and particularly in the seventeenth century, when, as has been stated, much inclosure took place which added to the land under cultivation, either because waste was reclaimed and fens drained or because poor land could be subjected to treatment which changed its position in the scale of fertility. Such a result was further enforced by the loss of fertility through too frequent ploughing and too little manure in the old arable.

character of her references, which invalidates her testimony with regard to the condition of the land, whether open or inclosed, her mention of inclosures makes it clear that these had not necessarily resulted in the substitution of pasture for arable. Her distinct references to inclosure are some thirty in number. In about half these instances there is nothing said to indicate the use made of the land. Of the remainder in some six instances she specifically mentions the corn, while in the rest the ground is styled fruitful, or good, or the like.

It will not be out of place to conclude with a brief statement of the chief matters dealt with and the conclusions reached, or at any rate indicated. In the first place it has been contended that during this century inclosure proceeded steadily and over a wide area, and that a very large amount of land from being open passed into several ownership and was inclosed. In the second place, these inclosures form part of a general movement which during this period of a century and a half extends into and then becomes very marked in a particular area, while doubtless still continuing, though to a much less extent, outside that area. In some districts it would appear that for the time it had reached its limits. In the third place, the movement was continuous not only in itself but in the means adopted to give it effect. These means follow each other in natural and explicable sequence. Lastly, the condition of the Midlands attracted particular attention. This area was affected for different reasons, and especially because, firstly, towns and industries were beginning to develop, secondly, in certain districts the old common field system had kept under grain land peculiarly suited for pasture, and thirdly, better land for grain had been added by means of drained and reclaimed or improved land.

III

INCLOSURE IN THE EIGHTEENTH CENTURY

ON turning to the eighteenth century, when inclosure was rendered conspicuous not only by its general prevalence but also by the new form which it took, that of private acts, it is necessary to avoid the assumption that this form in any sense marks the beginning of the movement, and that therefore inclosures were infrequent in the earlier half of the century. On the contrary there is abundant reason to believe that inclosures, so far from being few in the earlier period, were many.

In the first place, the testimony of writers already cited to show the activity at the close of the seventeenth can be referred to as evidence that this activity was undiminished. In this connection the words of the editor of *Tusser Redivivus* and of John Mortimer are emphatic so far as the opening years are concerned. According to the one, inclosures seemed, in his opinion, to be more frequent than was the case in the time of Tusser, while the other writes of the great quantities of land inclosed *daily*. A little later J. Cowper writes of what had happened in his own experience of some thirty years, while the Lawrences add their very valuable testimony. To one of them it was a matter of astonishment that even more did not take place, while the other, turning to the question of practice, adds the draft of a form of agreement which he recommends proprietors anxious to inclose to adopt. He also refers to partial inclosure, which, in his view, was bad, for the lord of the manor at any rate, since the tenant would seek to use all the manure from the beasts feeding on the common for his inclosure. Again, Arthur Young, writing later of the inclosures in Norfolk, divides these into two periods, the one, that of the celebrated sand district, taking place, according to him, between 1730 and 1760. Though he was apparently mistaken in the earlier of these dates, as is seen from Houghton's reference to the inclosure of the "sands of Norfolk," his testimony is quite sufficient to prove the existence of very considerable activity in this district during the first half of the century. But this is not recorded in the private acts.

In the second place, the very nature of the earlier acts is evidence of agreements. Thus the act for inclosure of Overton Longville confirms an inclosure made by consent, as also that of Thurnscoe, which recites the agreement made in 1717. In the case of Claughton the act, after reciting the agreement made by deed poll in 1729, goes on to state that this being objected to by some, recourse was had to parliamentary sanction. The same may be said of acts later in that reign, as for instance that of Yatton, in Somerset; but they are less frequent. On the other hand, even in the earliest years some acts are evidently obtained in the very first stages, as for instance in the case of Chenington, which resemble in much of the detail the form finally adopted when private acts became common. Instances need not be multiplied. In general, the acts show a gradual development from acts confirmatory to acts which are obtained to direct the method and as a necessary preliminary to action. In other words, acts obtained after a fairly general agreement had settled the division, and often because of subsequent difficulties, give place to acts which embody the agreement and seek means to carry it out. Possibly they became the normal course because the cases of difficulty remained over; but it is possible, too, that their convenience and certainty recommended them to those who knew of the troubles experienced when voluntary and general consent had to be sought.

In the third place, the sporadic distribution of these early acts, which are far from being confined to one area or one county or even one group of counties, points to the same conclusion. The following table shows broadly the percentage of land inclosed under act in the eighteenth century before 1760:

Counties where percentage of area inclosed under act before 1760 *is* 1 *per cent. or over.*

Leicester	7·9	Lincoln	1·6
Warwick	7·4	Oxford	1·5
Rutland	6	Durham	1·5
Northampton	6	Berkshire	1·4
Northumberland	2	Yorkshire	1·3
Gloucester	1·7	Hampshire	1·1
Hunts	1·6		

Other counties where there is some sporadic inclosure under act perceptible before 1760.

Wiltshire	·9	Dorset	·3
Stafford	·9	Hertford	·3
Nottingham	·9	Worcester	·3
Derbyshire	·8	Somerset	·3
Bedford	·6	Norfolk	·2
Buckingham	·5	Suffolk	·2
Lancashire	·4		

It will be seen by comparison with the chapter on the seventeenth century that nearly all the counties in the first group were subject to inclosure in that period, and much the same may be said, though to a less degree, of the counties heading the second group. The cases of Bedford and Oxford are exceptional. In this respect the two pieces of evidence are mutually corroborative. But the wide distribution of these early inclosures under act, which is emphasised by the fact that they are scattered within the separate counties themselves, must be taken as strengthening the view that they are but instances of inclosure, growing in number with the advance of time, and especially after 1750, when the former method of agreement came to be embodied in private acts. After the middle of the century the private act as the rule supersedes the agreement, and by its certainty and definitely ascertained method opens the way to the great increase which follows.

Inclosures without act, either by agreement or by sole possession, evidently still occur from time to time, as may be seen from the comparison of lists given in some of the *Agricultural Reports* issued at the end of the century, with the inclosures under act, but naturally their number decreases, since parishes and land which could be inclosed without an act would be treated earlier. As against the difficulties, such as uncertainty and so forth, *some* of the legal expenses involved in inclosure under act were escaped. That inclosure even under these conditions was expensive is seen from the *Dictionarium Urbanicum*, where in the article on Enclosures and their value, the following passage occurs, "The differences also and profits thereof are plainly to be discerned by the Severals or enclosed Parcels of Land that have formerly been taken out of the Field Land or Common, and how much they excel the others in every respect, though of the same soil and only an Hedge between, and what a yearly value they bear above them, as also by the great quantities of lands which in our own time have laid open, in common and of little value, yet when enclosed, tilled and well ordered have proved excellent good, and suddenly repaid the present great expense incident to Enclosure."

But with the general adoption and recognition of the method of inclosure by private act the movement received an enormous impetus. After making all due allowance for the acreage inclosed by agreement or in any other way during the earlier part of the century, the quantity affected by act after 1750, and especially after 1760, when such became much more widespread, affords very strong evidence as to this. As will be seen from the table given later, not only does the acreage thus treated increase greatly in most of the counties placed in the first group above, but other counties, as Bedford, Cambridge, Cumberland, Derby, Dorset, Norfolk, hitherto little touched, if touched at all, so far as private act inclosures are concerned, become prominent. Corroboration is afforded by the inclosures of the next decade. Further, the discussions arising at this period as to the effects of the movement emphasise the conclusion. Broadly speaking, this was the period (1760-90) of the great controversy to which frequent allusion has been made, and the prominence of which has done so much to colour opinion as to the time of inclosure, and also as to its nature.

The controversy, which called forth several books of real merit, assumes its true proportion in the *Essay* by Horner, thus like its precursor originating in the Midlands, since both Horner and Addington, his immediate opponent, were Warwickshire clergymen. Among other writers of importance were Lamport, Stone, Pennington, Arthur Young, and Howlett, as well as others who veil their personality under such titles as "A Country Gentleman," "A Farmer," and the like. In the beginning concerned mainly with the general nature and results of the movement, it soon assumes a particular aspect through the assertions by Dr. Price and others of a consequent decline in the population. As both aspects are dealt with elsewhere, they require little detailed notice here. But apart from these there are points deserving attention. Over and above their differences on definite points and their recriminations in matters of detail, the two parties of advocate and opponent are obviously divided in attitude. On the one side are the writers who, while often admitting though usually minimising the hardships involved, look on these as incidental, if indeed incidental, and as but temporary drawbacks to a course attended by certain particular advantages and an inevitable condition of progress. This attitude is seen clearly in Horner, who distinguishes between the conditions of the past and the present, and points out as to the former that "undertakings in husbandry were then generally small, calculated rather to be a means of subsistence to particular families than a source of wealth to the public," and in

Howlett, who throughout insists on the need of adapting the agriculture of the country to the supply of its needs. On the other side are those like Addington and the author of the *Political Enquiry into the consequences of enclosing waste lands and the causes of the present high price of butcher's meat*, to add an extreme opponent, in whose eyes present grievances loom large, and who do not see any adequate reason for interference with the past. The concessions made by Addington, for instance, are yielded in the spirit of one who altogether fails to see any alteration in conditions, and so regards the change as not only accompanied by injury but really unnecessary.

The best examination of the whole question at this time is to be found, not in any of the foregoing, but in the *Suggestions for rendering the inclosure of common fields and waste lands a source of population and riches*, by Thomas Stone, a pamphlet which, though distinctly in favour of inclosures, is less partisan in tone than was the case with the more brilliant productions of Howlett, and is moreover marked by strong common sense and wide practical knowledge.

Despite differences, it is possible to arrive at some points of fairly general agreement, and to indicate certain other matters with regard to which the divergence is due to opposing views as to fact rather than to any difference of opinion as to whether certain results are bad in principle.

Thus it is generally agreed, though not without reservation on the part of some, firstly, that the inclosure of waste and commons is, on the whole, advantageous ; and secondly, that advantages are to be gained by inclosing common fields where the soil is light and sandy ; and, thirdly, that rapid conversion from arable to pasture, if not safe-guarded, may be attended by a diminution of employment so far as the district is concerned. But more doubtful questions arise when the main difficulty is to determine the extent to which a particular danger is realised in practice or to weigh opposing considerations. Thus there is great divergence of view as to the extent to which conversion to pasture is met by additions elsewhere to the arable area, and again as to the compensation for a lack of agricultural employment by increased local industries in the district. Both Young and Stone take the view that the new system of agriculture provided in many respects additional work, even if diminishing some part of that previously plied. But these and other matters are treated in more detail in another chapter.

Here the main importance of the controversy is the evidence it affords of a considerable upward bound in the movement.

But now it will be necessary to turn to the actual record of the inclosures in the eighteenth and nineteenth centuries. Before taking the statistics as contained in the acts or as stated by various writers, there are certain important points requiring notice.

In the first place, in dealing with inclosure as a movement, it is necessary to take into account the waste lands and commons as well as the common fields, and this for several reasons. Firstly, even in inclosures of common fields so-called there is usually common included, a fact which certainly destroys some part of the point sought by the exclusion of commons and waste. Secondly, the inclosure of common is important because when brought into cultivation it added a considerable amount of land to the cultivated area and often displaced some part of the existing arable. Thirdly, while the conversion of arable to pasture is an important feature, the conversion of pasture to arable is no less so. Fourthly, if inclosure is a movement towards better cultivation and the production of more product with less labour, the one is no less significant than the other. On the other hand, it may be urged that the two are different in effect. To some extent and in certain aspects this is true. To meet the difficulty it will be well to take both and to indicate the difference as far, indeed, as that be possible.

In the second place, the accuracy of the acreage as given in the acts is open to some criticism. Firstly, it must be remembered that strictly speaking the area stated in the act does not constitute a final measurement. That is provided in the award which constitutes the legal record of the inclosure. In early cases, however, where the act is in the main confirmatory of an agreement which in some cases apparently was either in process of fulfilment or already carried out, the act would state the amount of land as finally measured. Again, when the act goes into great detail as to the size of the various parcels of land to be dealt with the difference is usually inconsiderable. In other cases there is frequent variation between the acreage given in the act and in the award. Taking the case of Leicester where comparison between the estimate of the act and the measurement of the award has been made in sixty-one cases, there is no case where there is not some difference. In some few cases the difference is *very* considerable, but this is the exception and not the rule. On the other hand no general conclusion is possible as to whether the quantity in the act is an over or an under-estimate. In the Leicester instances where over 80,000 acres is covered by the inclosures compared, in twenty-eight the statement in the act is an over-estimate while in thirty-three cases it is an under-estimate. As a rule over-estimate is more frequent in the earlier years and under-estimate in the later years. In Northampton, where comparison has been made in eighteen cases covering over 27,000 acres, there is over-estimate in eleven and under-estimate in seven cases. The following table gives particulars of counties where sufficient cases have been compared to enable some kind of an estimate.

	No. of inclosures compared.	Acreage in round figures of inclosures compared.	Cases in which over-estimate in act.	Percentage of over- or under-estimate in acts.
Leicester, - - - -	61	90,000	28	9 under.
Northampton, - -	18	27,000	11	2·4 over.
Derby, - - - - -	27	20,000	17	16 over.
Nottingham, - - -	14	20,000	7	9 over.
Lincoln, - - - -	42	95,000	24	—

In Lincolnshire where, one case of fen allotment and inclosure excluded, the total acreage is very nearly the same in acts and awards, it should be added that in the later years over-estimate is the rule. While it is obviously impossible to take as accurate the acreage given in the acts, it is equally impossible to make any regular or definite allowance for error. With the exception of Leicester it will be noticed that the tendency is for the acts to over-estimate the size of the inclosures.

But another possibility of error presents itself in the inclusion in some acts, of roads and existing inclosed land. Such inclusion does not appear to be of frequent occurrence, and is rarely if ever committed in the award so far as inclosed land is concerned, save in cases where such inclosed land is not permanently in separate ownership. There are cases where some roads are included in the total acreage. As far as the awards are concerned a detailed examination of the figures and in some instances of the map, would probably enable a correction to be made.

Further, it is usually difficult, if not impossible, from the act to determine the proportions of the land respectively common field and common or waste. Judging from the awards this is extremely variable, sometimes being large in proportion and sometimes small.[1] Hence the treatment of these as composed uniformly of open field is misleading, especially when the results of inclosure are under discussion.

In view of these facts two conclusions seem inevitable. In the first place any very minute determination of the quantity of land from the acreage given in the act is impossible; thus calculations even if given in terms of decimal figures must be taken as approximate only. In the second place, in many of the common field or open field inclosures, the area of cultivation undergoes extension not only by the greater use of land previously in fallow but by the addition of an amount of waste or common very variable in its proportion.

[1] On this see pp. 402-4.

Turning to the actual statistics, two matters seem of great importance: firstly, the period during the eighteenth century during which inclosure was prevalent, and secondly the distribution of the inclosures throughout what for this purpose is a wholly artificial unit, namely, the county. To meet these points two tables are appended.

In one of these,[1] which deals with the whole country, percentages are given of the land inclosed during the following periods, (1) before 1760, (2) 1761-70, (3) 1771-80, (4) 1781-90, (5) 1791-1800, (6) 1801-1810, (7) 1811-1820, (8) 1821 on.

The other[2] table includes the chief counties affected by the movement in the eighteenth and nineteenth centuries, together with some few others. In it the registration counties as given in the Census Return are adopted, and the inclosed townships are distributed according to the various registration districts. Two columns are given containing respectively the percentage borne by the townships in which inclosure took place to all townships or places in the districts, and also the percentage of the land in the districts inclosed. As the object in this instance is to discover the natural region affected, the abandonment of the ordinary county area for the registration area does not invalidate the particular result, though of course it precludes comparison between this table and others where the areas are different. No doubt it would have been better to have adhered to the ordinary county divisions, but that was impossible, since the only means of obtaining the percentages in question is the Census Return.

The basis of the lists from which the tables are prepared remains to be explained. The list is primarily drawn from the acts, but as many awards were examined the figures of these are substituted for those of the act, or inserted when the act leaves the acreage affected blank. Further, when the inclosed acreage is supplied by neither act nor award, good estimates or statements, such as those given in the county *reports*, have been accepted when

[1] Appendix D. [2] Appendix C.

forthcoming. In this way it is hoped that the inaccuracy involved by reliance on the estimates in the acts may be partially corrected. Of course, had an allowance for error been possible, it would have been better to take the figures of the acts as a basis and then to correct them; but as is stated above, such a method of correction would seem to be impracticable. It would be inexact in itself.

An examination of the first of these tables points to certain features in the inclosure movement, and raises certain questions as to their meaning. Indications present themselves of three—or, at any rate, of two—waves of inclosure. The first and least important of these appears in the years before 1760. Possibly this may be but the beginning of that which follows during the period 1760-1780. Then there occurs a very distinct falling off both in the number and extent of land inclosed in the next decade, 1781-90. The third wave follows, rising to its full height either in 1791-1800 or 1801-10, and continuing, though with declining force, through 1811-1820.

As has been previously suggested, the scattered character of the inclosures before 1760 seems to indicate that private acts were but one form at that time, a conjecture confirmed by the internal character of the act, and by other facts already dealt with; as, for instance, the occurrence in Norfolk of other inclosures in the early part of the century. The only counties largely affected by the private acts of this period were Leicester, Warwick, Northants, and Rutland.

Leaving this less conspicuous period for the two conspicuous periods, 1760-80 and 1790-1820, two very obvious questions present themselves. In the first place, what are the districts least affected by the decline in the intervening decade? In the second place, why were some districts subject to inclosure in the earlier and others in the later of the two periods?

With regard to the first matter, the counties thus unaffected were the south-western counties: Wiltshire, Somerset, Hampshire, and Dorset; though in the last two the comparative rarity of inclosure makes the fact of less moment. In addition to these, Derbyshire shows little falling off and Middlesex none. Yet it is not possible to assign any very certain reason for the exception which these two counties seem to constitute from what seems to be a general rule. There is nothing distinctive about them, and even in the four south-western counties the places are scattered and not in the parts of the counties lying contiguous to each other. Leaving Middlesex aside, as a rule the places inclosed appear to be in hilly districts and to have been inclosed under much the same conditions as those inclosed in the previous decade. In the south-western counties, owing to previous history and the character of the soil, there was little land to come under inclosure of the kind which swells the record of many other counties in the earlier years. This points to some difference between the land affected in the earlier and later decades. Speaking generally, the rule that decrease took place holds good. The reason for this was in all likelihood the very simple one, that with the land which best repaid the trouble already inclosed, the necessary cost did not warrant extension in face of the prices for produce which prevailed.

The second question is more important. In this case the number of inclosures is sufficiently large to eliminate the element of chance. Furthermore the area affected in each period is so wide that it cannot be contended that the movement represents a general spreading from a region where the intelligence of the people first led them to seek its undoubted if individual advantages. Even in the districts participating more at the later than at the earlier date, there are sufficient instances to prove that inclosure took place in the latter, though in a restricted measure. The simplest and most natural explanation is probably the correct one. Inclosure took place first in the districts or counties where its advantages were greatest. The factors which determined which these were, are not difficult to find. Lands where inclosure was profitable, owing either to a change in its use or to a considerable increase in yield, came under inclosure because the profit would compensate for the cost incurred: for it must be remembered that, as set forth in an earlier chapter, the expense of inclosing land was very considerable. The fairly unanimous testimony of contemporary observers points to two conditions under which land could be made much more profitable when inclosed. In the first place, light soils yielded more abundant crops when subject to root and clover crops in rotation with grain. In the second place, in other places the open field system retained in one use soil materially better suited to other uses, the most conspicuous instance of this being the obstacle to grass on land which was natural pasture land. The possibility of improvement in either direction was emphasised by the greater attention paid both to stock and arable during the eighteenth century. The skilful use of roots and of grass and the system of scientific breeding enhanced the gain. In some districts, too, draining which could only be carried out with difficulty on land under common right offered better results than could be obtained elsewhere, but in most cases the full advantage of this could not be secured without considerable outlay of capital.

The general advantages of having land in severalty, other than the above, were in the main uniform, and so would not affect one district more than another.

The approach of the end of the century brought changes, all tending in the same direction, namely, to render inclosure increasingly profitable, and so facilitate not only its development in the areas formerly affected, but its extension into districts and lands comparatively little touched till then. On the one hand the rise in the price of provisions which took place, and increased as the war progressed, provided the requisite margin of profit, even had things remained as they were. On the other hand, the tendency towards capitalistic farming, no doubt in part stimulated by the inclosures, received an impetus both from its newly recognised profitable character and from the blow inflicted on the small farming owners by the gradual decay of the small home industries. Lastly, in 1801 the general act was passed which both regularised inclosure and somewhat diminished its expense. No doubt, too, when the first decade or so was over, and inclosing with the new act in operation had become a general rule, habit in many cases governed its application, and less regard was paid to particular fitness; yet even then the consideration of profit must have weighed with the proprietors.

It is interesting to notice how similar is the rise and fall in the counties or districts where the land located was waste or of the nature of commons, to that taking place in the open field districts. In the northern counties, Northumberland, Durham, Cumberland, and Westmoreland, where it was nearly exclusively of waste, the falling off during the decade 1781-90 is just as conspicuous as in Northants or Oxford. In Derby and Notts the proportion between waste and open field is varied, not, as might be expected, to the greater continuance of the operation on the wastes, but in the other direction. In Norfolk, on the other hand, while both diminish, the open field inclosures diminish most. Taking the country as a whole, so far as there is any distinction between the two in this respect, the inclosure of waste falls off more than that of common field, a feature which certainly points to the conclusion that less profit was to be obtained from the former than the latter. The difference, however, is hardly great enough to furnish a basis for anything more than a rather general conclusion.

The second table merits equal if not more careful consideration. The county, as has been said, is, so far as any conclusions as to the causes determining the direction of this movement are concerned, largely an artificial unit. In other words, the distribution of inclosures by counties offers little intelligible explanation, owing, of course, to the fact that the county, as such, is not homogeneous in respect of the causes which might induce or discourage these. That is to be sought in an examination of the extent to which districts similar, so far as conditions of climate, soil, or economic situation are concerned, play a like part in the movement. Such an examination means a somewhat detailed enquiry into the circumstances attending the progress of inclosure during the eighteenth and early nineteenth centuries in certain counties.

Before, however, entering upon this investigation certain matters require notice.

In the first place, the distinctions drawn above between the chief periods of inclosure by private act must be emphasised. It is important to know the time at which any area passed under inclosure, since there was a marked difference between the various periods. Put broadly, in the enclosures before 1760, those by act represent very inadequately the extent of the movement; further, these took place, partly in view of general improvement and partly in order to obtain the benefit of the special advantages from including turnips and root crops in the rotation. But the inclosures of the next period are far more numerous. No doubt the movement had spread owing to experience, and owing to greater realisation of the benefits offered, at any rate on the technical side. The period from 1760-1780, or thereabouts, is distinguished by great increase and the extension of the area. In the next period, stretching from 1790, or shortly before, to 1810 or 1820, a new impetus manifests itself, which is responsible for the act of 1801, an event which removes one of the serious obstacles to the change. After that time the inclosure of any district, as, indeed, of the country at large, was merely a matter of time. Of course inclosure, when introduced or set going in an area, tended to spread, no doubt with the not infrequent result that land unsuited to the process might be subjected to it equally with that from which more profit might be expected and where the advantages would greatly outweigh the disadvantages, if such existed.

In the second place, inclosure as is elsewhere shown was a costly process, often reaching some £3 an acre, while in addition the parties receiving allotments were usually put to heavy capital charges in hedging and ditching their land, as well as in other ways in particular cases. Naturally enough the movement was restricted in its general direction to cases where the profit was sufficiently great to repay the expenditure. Thus land which was little capable of improvement in this way tended to be left alone. Equally naturally, good land which if inclosed would not undergo substantial change tends to be inclosed late. Whether land would or would not repay inclosure depended largely on the conditions of the time and the purport of the movement at that time. In this respect the most important thing is to ascertain if any particular inclosure took place in the second or in the third period, that is from 1760 to 1780 or thereabouts, or from 1790 to 1810 or so.

In the third place, in any such investigation it is important to ascertain whether the inclosure in any given area was well distributed over the area in question or concentrated in a small number of parishes, which were wholly or mainly inclosed. A given percentage of inclosure may clearly be achieved in different ways. With regard to this it should be noticed that the size of an inclosure before 1800 is usually greater than the size in the period 1801-1840. This general, though not invariable, feature admits of different interpretations. It might be due to inclosure occurring first in the places where more land presented itself, a course which, however, does not seem probable where the diminution is but moderate, or it may be due to private inclosures taking place of small parcels of land, in advance of the more general inclosure of the land of the village which occurs later. Whatever the solution, it is clear that the tendency exists for later township inclosures to include a somewhat smaller proportion of the area than was affected in the earlier cases. A more important difference is indicated by the appearance in some districts of comparatively small inclosures. Inclosure occurs in many townships, but in each on the average a small amount of land is inclosed. In some cases of inclosure it must be remembered that the existence of old or ancient inclosures is specifically stated. Such widespread distribution seems probably due to inclosure by act taking place in districts where the original inclosure had been very early, possibly not so much by agreement as by isolated or arbitrary action.

Turning to the consideration of the causes regulating the distribution and progress of the movement, the factors which present themselves are in the main three, namely, soil, climate, including effect of situation, and the stage of development of any given region.

Of these, as far as the chief matter under enquiry, the progress during the eighteenth and nineteenth centuries, roughly speaking up to 1840, is concerned, the one which calls for most attention is the soil. As far as climate is concerned the main thing is rather exposure to climate owing to situation than any great variation in climate itself, though, of course, some difference may be expected as between east and west. Likewise considerations as to the position of a district, whether level or hilly, co-operated with the soil. The difference in the stage of development, affected as it was by the change in means of locomotion and transport, will naturally follow later.

With regard to soil, the general coincidence between the area of the inclosure by private act and certain forms of geological structure is remarkable. It is at any rate true to say that the districts of great inclosure are with small exception on the region of the lias and oolite formations, some part of the chalk formation being added. To realise this general coincidence it is only necessary to compare a geological map of England with the maps annexed or those of Dr. Slater, or the map of the land left comparatively open at the time of Ogilby's description. The more closely these are inspected the more striking appears the resemblance, and the more deserving detailed study. From this comparison the wastes of the north must be excluded.

Such study means the determination of the various regions in which inclosure took place and their examination. To enable the comparison of the different parts of a county the percentage of land inclosed by act up to 1870 in the various registration districts of the counties most concerned has been calculated approximately, and is given in an Appendix.[1] Probably this is the most convenient method of enabling a comparison between districts of inclosure and districts in which soil varies. Of course this method involves, as has been said, the use of the registration county instead of the county proper, a change which must be borne in mind if the figures be used for any other purpose. For the present purpose it makes little difference, since neither registration county nor county proper necessarily coincides with the true region or district. As Marshall tells us in the examination "of a country like England, with a view to the existing state of its Agriculture and the other branches of its Rural Economy, the arbitrary lines of counties are to be wholly disregarded." He adds further: "A natural district is marked by a uniformity or similarity of soil and surface, whether, by such uniformity, a marsh, a vale, an extent of upland, a range of chalky heights, or a stretch of barren mountains be produced. And an Agricultural District is discriminated by a uniformity or similarity of practice; whether it be characterised by grazing, sheep farming, arable management, or mixed cultivation; or by the cultivation of some particular article, as dairy produce, fruit liquor, etc., etc. Now it is evident that the boundary lines of counties pay no regard to these circumstances." As, however, to ascertain the proportion to which land was inclosed some measured area is necessary, the best that can be done is to take the small unit of the registration district.

The regions to be examined in respect of the points referred to may be classified in the following groups.

1. The East Anglian Group—Norfolk, Suffolk, and Essex.
2. The Western Group—Wilts, Gloucester, and Somerset.

[1] Appendix C.

3. Metropolitan Group—Middlesex and Herts.
4. Cambridge.
5. The Midlands.
    (*a*) Warwick, Northants, Rutland, Leicester, Hunts.
    (*b*) Oxford, Bedford, and Buckingham.

East Anglian Group. In the case of Norfolk certain interesting features appear. The geological characteristics of the county are simple, a division from south to north separating it into two main halves, the one, the western, being on a chalk basis, that to the east lying on the Norfolk clay. In addition, along the coast line of the north, from Hunstanton to about Sheringham, was alluvial, the same being characteristic of the extreme west, a portion of Norfolk reckoned into the registration county of Cambridge. Between the alluvial and the chalk is a belt of green sand. The substratum, however, is so far as soil is concerned unimportant, being greatly modified by drifts, and the districts may be described as follows.

(1) In the north-west was a considerable area of good sand, tending to narrow as it advances south. This constituted the scene of the Norfolk husbandry, referred to by Young, and probably also by Houghton when he speaks of the sands of Norfolk. Of this soil the registration districts of Docking, Walsingham, and to some extent those of Erpingham and Aylsham, are composed.

(2) South of this, in Thetford and the south-west generally, up to the limits of the alluvial, there is, according to Young, some sand, but the subsoil is chalky and the soil is not so good and far less amenable, according to him, to cultivation. This soil may be assigned largely to the districts[1] of Thetford and parts of Swaffham and Downham.

(3) In the east, in Flegg, that is from Yarmouth northwards along the coast, are very rich loams with some alluvial, extending over the area of the district of Flegg and part of that of Tunstead.

(4) The south-east has a considerable amount of poor

[1] District here and subsequently used for registration district.

sand with much boulder clay, described by Young as difficult to work. It is not very distinctive.

On turning to the record of the inclosures of the period of private acts certain coincidences reveal themselves between these and the soil, modified in some respects by other circumstances.

In the first division the percentage of inclosure is on the whole low, Docking 29, Walsingham 22, Erpingham 15, Aylsham 13. With the exception of Docking, inclosure in all these districts occurs late, that is with little exception after 1800, and to a considerable measure after 1810. In Docking, however, while there is some late inclosure, the most is very early. Again, the inclosures in Docking almost all involve common field, as is likewise the case in Walsingham. In the other two districts there are some of each kind.

It would seem that this region was initially inclosed in the years prior to the use of private acts, when, owing to new crops and especially to the use of roots, the good sands offer considerable profits to those prepared to encounter the necessary outlay. This movement, which is known from different sources, continues into the early years of the private act record, land being inclosed, especially in Docking, a fact which goes far to explain the higher percentage of that district as shown above. The first wave subsides early, little apparent as it was in some districts and only visible in Docking till 1780. But there is land left uninclosed which comes under the movement at a much later date, when both higher prices and the diminution of cost owing to the general act increase the chance of gain. Then, indeed, as would seem initially probable, some of the inclosed land, and, in Aylsham a good proportion, is common, possibly sheep walk.

The land coming under the second division was a poorer soil. The amount inclosed by private act is greater, Thetford 26, Downham 30, Swaffham 31. The inclosure is early, that is, much is inclosed before 1790, though some remains for treatment after that date, usually remaining unaltered till after 1800. In the main the inclosures are of land with common field. Gradually, so it would seem, the husbandry with some use of roots spread downwards.

The case of Flegg and the surrounding lands grouped in the third division is the very reverse. Here the percentage inclosed is high, reaching in the case of the district of Flegg itself to 59 per cent., and in Tunstead to 38. In one sub-district of the latter, that is in the portion adjoining Flegg, there is an inclosure in every township. In both cases the inclosures are during the third period, even after 1800. But here the explanation would seem to be the very reverse of that previously offered. This region of rich loams could yield little more profit when inclosed than when open, and consequently cost was only incurred when rendered advantageous by circumstances elsewhere alluded to. These inclosures are nearly all of common field.

Taking, however, the main part of the east, that is with the omission of the district just treated, most of the inclosure is after 1790; this is the region described by Marshall. From this the south-east must be partly excluded. So far as act is concerned this is not a district of any great inclosure from common field by act. Commons are inclosed especially in the south-east. The soil which was often poor sand or poor clay yielded scant promise.

One difference between the progress in inclosing land in the west and east, especially the south-east, should be noticed. There is more common field inclosure in the west during this period, while on the east there is more inclosure from common. Possibly this may be due in part to the soil and in part to an earlier need for higher cultivation, and so to the additional profit of cultivation on land coming within reach of Norwich and the manufactures.

Turning to Suffolk, the geological resemblance to Norfolk is considerable. The north-west corner contains the alluvial with chalk. According to the description of the soil, the north-west was composed of poor soil, with fen in the very extremity. Mid Suffolk was a good loam on a boulder clay, while on the east is a narrow sandy district save in the spit running up towards Yarmouth from a line drawn from Beccles to Kessingland where the soil, according to Young, is partly loam. In the south, especially about Sudbury and Hadleigh, London clay makes its appearance.

Now as far as inclosure by private act is concerned the greater part of Suffolk presents little difference. The county was practically inclosed some time before that period opened. In nearly all districts the percentage is very low; but there is one difference just perceptible between the east and the west. In the west the occasional inclosures are often of land including common field, whereas in the east nearly all inclosures are inclosures of common. With few exceptions the period is after 1790. But there are two regions where the change is considerable. In the north-west corner after 1790 and especially after 1800 inclosure makes some impression, the percentage of land in the registration district of Mildenhall being 20 and in that of Thingoe 17. Most parcels of land affected include common field. On the other hand, in the spit of land running up to Yarmouth a percentage of 21 is attained, nearly all being from common.

Essex lies partly on the London clay, partly on boulder clay, with in the north-west some cretaceous land. Arthur Young marks as chalk, land which closely corresponds to the sub-district of Saffron Walden, one of these sub-districts in the district of that name. This is the only place where any inclosure worth speaking of occurs. The percentage of land inclosed in the whole district is 22, while of the nine townships in the sub-district no fewer than seven were subject to inclosure. In all cases there was common field and the period is that after 1790. The other inclosures are all later, nearly all from common, and scattered.

In two of the above districts, namely in the respective north-west corners of the two counties, the reason for the relative lateness in inclosure is obvious. The open field remains because of the poorness of the soil, while in both the position on the extremity of the East Anglian district may have assisted. In the Mildenhall district of Suffolk there was also some land approximating to the fen district. But in north-east of Suffolk, in the little spit of land, the reason is not so clear. The soil is described by Young as being loamy, but the inclosure is of common and is late.

Two general remarks about the whole region must be added. No doubt the date of the main period of inclosure was far prior to the phase of the movement now under consideration. From Norwich southwards and especially towards the east the area was one of early industrial growth, while in South-West Essex the needs of the metropolis were also to be felt. In the second place, in the early inclosed area sporadic inclosure of commons takes place. The chief districts showing inclosures under act in both Suffolk and Essex lie on the border and not in the central part of the county.

Western Group. This group, which also is affected by the presence of an important manufacturing district of early development, consists of the three counties of Gloucester, Wiltshire, and Somerset. Here the central region is formed by the portions of the three counties most contiguous, while in every case some portion of the county lies, as it were, outside this area, as the north-west of Gloucester, the south and east of Wilts, and the west, especially the south-west, of Somerset. Starting with the central region the geological formation presents, first of all, lias forming the great vale district of Gloucester, including the vales of Berkeley and Gloucester, and extending further into the vale of Evesham in Worcester. The soil is a rich loam, and, according to Marshall, is of singular wealth in the case of Berkeley. According to the same authority the greater part, some three-fourths of the first, is grass, while in the second vale this condition is characteristic of nearly the whole. This account is corroborated by that given in the *Agricultural Report*. South-east of this is the Cotswold land, a cornbrash of calcareous lime (oolite) which extends a little way into the western part of Wilts as far as Bradford, and includes Bradford district, the west of the Chippenham district, and nearly reaches to Melksham. This latter land, like that of the Cotswold, is largely arable. The oolitic strata extends, though in a narrowed belt, into Somerset, running through Frome and Milbourne. It should be noted that in and about Bradford and Melksham the valley of the Avon presents better and richer loam. South-east again of this is another oolitic formation of Oxford clay. This land, existing in a thin belt in Somerset, broadens as it leaves Westbury, includes Melksham, and runs north-east, thence embracing the east of Chippenham, the land between Malmesbury and Wooton Bassett, also Cricklade and Highworth.

Leaving for the time the description of the rest of these counties we may turn to the inclosures concerned.

The first area, namely that of the vales, with its rich dairies, is not affected by inclosure till comparatively late, nearly all, as far as private acts are concerned, being inclosed after 1790, and most after 1800. In no case is the amount of land inclosed very great, the percentages being as follows; Tewkesbury 25, Gloucester 29, Winchcombe 29, and Wheatenhurst 25. In the district of Dursley, where there was very little land in arable in Marshall's time, the percentage is only 3. The percentage for Thornbury, where Berkeley is, but which also includes much land outside the vales, is 5. Practically there is only chance inclosure in these two latter. This region, as we know from both Marshall and the *Agricultural Report*, had been for some time a well developed dairy country, interspersed indeed, and especially in the more northerly direction, that is, in the plain or vale of Gloucester and parts of that of Evesham, with arable fields. The inclosures seem to be chiefly of these; the dairy district having been earlier inclosed. In the Cheltenham district, which includes both vale and Cotswold land, the percentage is 13.

The Cotswold region presents very different features in date, amount, and object. Here inclosures by act are, on the whole, early, and occur to a larger extent in the north than the south. Stow is 41, Northleach 27, Cirencester 17, and Tetbury, where the Cotswolds end, and where some half of the inclosures, however, are late, is 25. The land was arable and well fit for turnips and barley. This cultivation, according to Marshall, was its object. From about Tetbury southwards is the land described as the Southwolds, and said to resemble the Cotswolds in soil, though the surface is more broken. This land falls into the Chipping Sodbury district in Gloucester, including other soil, and in Wiltshire, into the west of Chippenham and the south-west of Malmesbury, also Bradford. In these districts the tendency is for inclosure to fall after 1790, and the amount is not great. Chipping Sodbury should be reckoned at about 11 or 12 per cent., though owing to one large inclosure of over 6,000 acres, it is nominally 21, the total percentage for Chippenham 10, and Malmesbury 17, most of the latter district being on other soil. Bradford is 7, the only inclosure being of common. If we take the two north-eastern districts of Somerset, where some calcareous soil presents itself, though intermixed and under differing topographical circumstances, Bath has no inclosures during this period, and Frome only one with common field and one without. But this central district from Stroud, and including Bradford and Frome, will be dealt with later.

The part of this region bordering on Wiltshire is, however, characterised by some difference of soil, the part that is lying to the south of a line passing from Burford through Cirencester to Tetbury; this difference being continued from Tetbury through the Chipping Sodbury district to the neighbourhood of Bath. Here there is mixed loam lying further distant from the rock than is the case in the more strictly arable portion of the Cotswolds. Some part of the land is wet and some part well fitted for the dairy. With this the fringe of the west district lying in Wilts combines to form a belt of land intermediate in character between the Cotswolds and the great dairy districts of North Wiltshire. The date of inclosure seems to have been a little later than was the case with the Cotswolds, but still not late. So far as the districts of Cirencester and Tetbury are concerned, a considerable part of the inclosure taking place is on this land.

Beyond this belt is the third region, that of North-West Wilts. This is distinctly a dairy district. According to Marshall, the traces of a former arable state remain in marked evidence. In the north-east the soil is described as colder, though some is brashy in character. Beginning from this end we have the inclosures in Highworth and Cricklade taking place early, nearly all being before 1790, and their respective percentages being 32 and 22. Calne, where inclosure is both early and late, is only 15. Those of Malmesbury and Chippenham have already been mentioned. Melksham is only 3, and the inclosure is all from common. From the accounts of Marshall and of Davis, the author of the *Agricultural Report*, the dairying development in this region was undoubted, the proportion of grass to arable being very great. Rich grazing was succeeding to dairy land in some parts, according to Marshall. As to the general character and use of the land, this writer goes so far as to say that he finds it difficult to distinguish this region in its land and management from that of the vales in Gloucestershire.

The remaining districts of the various counties require separate notice.

In Gloucester, outside the regions dealt with, the greater part of the land is west from the Severn. Here the soil lies largely on a trias or a sandstone substratum. In early times it lay under forest. The inclosure in this area is almost negligible, the percentages for the two registration districts being between 2 and 3. Likewise in the south-west, where there is also land on trias and the Bristol coalfield, Thornbury, which reaches into the vales, is 5, while Clifton is 6. Chipping Sodbury is close to this district.

Wiltshire calls for more detailed attention. The southern and eastern parts of Wilts differ considerably from the north-west. Their basis is mainly chalk, and they may be described as consisting largely of chalk downs and hills with fertile valley. Through some of these run rich veins of fertile sand. The most important belt of greensand runs up through Warminster and Westbury, skirting the hills, and meets another wide vein in the vale district of Pewsey. Careful writers like Davis distinguish the cultivation of the south and south-east of Wilts as being mainly arable, the sheepfold, largely on down land, being valuable as an accessory to this end. The inclosures in these parts are late, and though this may have been due in some part to topographical circumstances, namely, the oblong length of the manors, lying on the valleys and extending up the side of the hills, which rendered inclosure more difficult, it would seem to be almost equally due to the nature of the soil which was associated with this formation. In any case, the co-operation of the two rendered the inclosures of this region far less profitable than was elsewhere the case. Hence, of course, their deferment. In the south-west, that is, in parts bordering on Dorset, there is Kimmeridge clay, as also in a patch north of Westbury, and in the vicinity of Swindon. There were dairy farms round Westbury, and also in the extensive south-west described above. Now to follow the inclosures. In this south-west area, that is, in Mere and Tisbury, part of which districts fall within it, the percentage is respectively 26 and 9. In Warminster and Westbury, proceeding northwards along the west border, it is 54 and 27. In the south-east, around Salisbury that is, we have Wilton 34, Alderbury 22, and Amesbury 28. Pewsey and Devizes, in the centre, east of Melksham, are 31 and 32, both having a considerable variety of soils. These percentages are measured on a total, it should be remembered, that includes a large quantity of land which was not, and is not, amenable to direct cultivation, its best use being for sheep in connection with an arable farm.

That the chalk of the south-east should come late under inclosure is natural enough. A more important point is the high percentage of Warminster at 54, with Westbury, to the north, at 27, and Mere, to the south, at 26. North of Westbury are Bradford and Melksham, practically inclosed before the period of private acts, and south and east of Mere is Tisbury at 9. Warminster was the centre of the arable, the town of that name being the most important corn market of a region which had to serve as the granary of the surrounding counties. In Mere and Tisbury, especially the latter, there are dairy farms, as also to some extent in Westbury. From Melksham, itself largely included, begins the north-west dairy district.

The inclosure of Somerset is less remarkable, both in contrast and features, so far as the period of private acts is concerned. In the districts adjoining Gloucestershire and Wiltshire there is very little inclosure. In Keynsham, Bath, Frome, and Clutton inclosures hardly occur at all. Only in Bedminster, towards Clevedon, do instances present themselves to any extent. Here cases both from common and common field take place all at a comparatively late date, with one exception. The districts, indeed, coming under inclosure during this period are two, namely, those of the Mendips and the Sedgmere alluvial. The Mendip inclosures are fairly early, about 1770 onwards, the others somewhat later. In both, inclosure is chiefly of common land; in Langport and part of the Bridgewater district there are inclosures of common field. In the south of the county, in the districts abutting on Dorset, some few inclosures, mainly from common, occur. The western district furnishes still fewer instances, but here the conditions resemble those of Devon. In general Somerset, in the districts where considerable development, together with cultivation, had taken place in earlier centuries, was already inclosed, and such cases as occur are by way of obvious survival. In the centre, and towards the Bristol Channel, the many numerous cases are chiefly of common, and usually small. They represent reclamations from a partially or wholly unused condition. In both regions alike the land had been unsuitable for use.

The course of inclosure in this whole area illustrates clearly the operation of two factors, as also their singular interaction : on the one hand, is the effect of soil, coupled no doubt with certain climatic and topographical features ; on the other hand, the growth of population, and particularly of a population engaged in home manufactures, or living in villages and small towns, leaves an impress no less marked. The first is visible in the difference mainly in date, though perhaps to some degree in the varying extent of the inclosures during this period between the three soil regions defined first of all—namely, the regions of the vales, the Cotswolds, and the dairy land of North Wilts. It is shown also in the clear distinction between the central division of Somerset and those respectively to the north and the west : and again in the curiously definite difference between the districts centring in Warminster and those surrounding it. The late period at which the chalk region of Wiltshire land comes under treatment is further evidence. The almost negligible amount of inclosure in Gloucester to the west of the Severn may be attributed to its early wild state, a feature apparent also in Somerset. There had been former inclosure from this condition. But the needs of the towns and of the population engaged in manufacture is not less important. To these no doubt is due the fact, too obvious to be overlooked, that the whole central region had been affected widely by inclosure before, and probably long before, the eighteenth century opened. Within the region they are responsible for the almost entire inclosure of the more central districts prior to this century, as for instance the south of Gloucester, the districts round Bradford, and the east of Somerset. A further definite result would seem to be the great dairy and cattle inclosures within reasonable reach. In the main the districts in which these are situated were inclosed before the eighteenth century. Even, however, where soil and other co-operating conditions were similar, proximity to the industrial district seems to have influenced the date at which inclosure took place. Thus the farther portions, as Highworth and Cricklade, of the North Wilts dairy district are inclosed early in this period while the inclosures in the portions nearer appear to supervene upon land where earlier inclosure had occurred. Again, in the Cotswold land the percentage of Stow is far greater than that attained in Northleach and Cirencester. A great distinction shows itself between the Cotswolds and the Southwolds. Nor were the inclosures for wool. The very contrary appears to be the case. The inclosures in the region surrounding this centre of the woollen industry are for food, and in many instances for dairy produce and for meat rather than for grain.

Middlesex and Hertford. Broadly speaking, both of these counties are comparatively little affected by the inclosures under act. The geological description is simple and the soil characteristics less complex and puzzling than in many other areas. In the case of Hertfordshire, there is a large bed of London clay in the south, while in the rest of the county the substratum is chalk, except in a narrow belt on the east where, in the valley of the Lee, the soil is alluvial. The geological formation is, however, much modified by drift, most of the soil being described by Young as loam, more or less suited to turnips. In the extreme south-west there is definite clay, as also towards the east; round North Mimms is some poor gravel, while it is only in the northern portion of the county that the chalk comes close to the surface. In the area round Hitchin there is chalk to some extent, but this feature is much more marked around Royston.

Inclosure occurs to a perceptible extent only in three

registration districts, or, to put the matter otherwise, only in two areas—one including two such districts. On the marked cretaceous land we have the relatively large inclosures of Royston and Hitchin; those of the former affecting 49 per cent. of the land of the district, and those of the latter, where the chalk was less dominant, some 21 per cent. Those of Royston are late—all after 1790, and most after 1800. Much the same is true of most of those in the Hitchin district, the main part of the inclosure being after 1790, though near Bedfordshire and the belt of greensand some occur at a much earlier date, even before 1780. Again, on the extreme east there is some little inclosure, otherwise the inclosure which takes place is sporadic and slight and of little significance, little indeed occurring on the loam.

Middlesex is a county mainly on the London clay. In this region the amount of land inclosed by act is slight, corresponding somewhat generally to what took place in Hertfordshire. But in the south-west, in a large area bounded by the Thames, the substratum was alluvial, largely valley gravel, with loam in certain places. It is described as arable, and this characteristic extends to some of the land lying upon the basis of the neighbouring London clay. From the Thames to a northern boundary, running approximately from Hounslow to Colesbrook, there is soil with much loamy sand on the so-called turnip and barley sand. Here the percentage of inclosure is high, reaching in the district of Staines (c.f.) 45, and in that of Brentford 43 (mostly commons). To these should be added the Uxbridge inclosures nearly all of which fall in the southern part of that district, and on land described as above. These inclosures are late—nearly all after 1790, and most after 1800. On the belt of alluvial in the east are several inclosures, all indeed of the Edmonton district with the exception of Hornsey. These, too, are late—after 1790.

Side by side with the inclosures of the south-west of Middlesex should be placed those of the Eton district of

Buckingham, where, with an alluvial soil, the percentage rises to 33, in remarkable contrast to that in the part of this county immediately to the north. These inclosures likewise are late.

In this region the needs of the metropolis evidently dominated the land from a comparatively early date. From it the population of the great city must have drawn such supplies as could not be carried far. Hence indeed it would seem probable that owing to the comparative portability of grain much land was early inclosed and converted often to pasture at a comparatively early time, the good arable alone remaining under grain. Again, another cause leading to early and unnoticed inclosure lay in the forest condition of the north of Middlesex and South and Central Hertford. Even if put to pasture when first inclosed, some land, and especially loamy land in Hertford, passes into arable at a comparatively early time, as is shown by the turnip husbandry which prevailed extensively in Young's time. There was further increase of arable in that county in the later decades of the eighteenth century. Increased skill in farming and increased demand also make it desirable after 1790 to inclose the good arable of the south-west of Middlesex and to press the cultivation of the chalk land in northern Hertfordshire.

Cambridge. The condition and circumstances of Cambridge make necessary its separate treatment. The formation on the whole is simple. In the south the substratum is chalk, with greensand in the west, while in the north part is fen with some patches of oolite. The agricultural suitability of the land in the west is affected by drift to some extent. There is a patch of boulder clay in the south-east corner. Now as to inclosures. These occur in a very high degree in the south, the Linton district having a percentage of 61, the central south district of Chesterton 62, and the west district of the south, namely Caxton 51. This latter, it will be noticed, is less inclosed during this period than the other two. Further, it should be added that the inclosures in the Linton district are mainly where the chalk prevails. All the inclosure is late, as is almost invariable in the case of chalk, taking place with very rare exceptions after 1790, and mainly after 1800. In Newmarket the percentage is 36. So far as these districts are concerned inclosure means land with common fields. On the other hand, in the north or in the region of the fens inclosure is almost always from common, though some common field is involved about Ely, and is comparatively small in extent, save in Witchford, where there was a good deal of pasture or meadow ground, and where the percentage reaches 32. Inclosure in this whole region occurs in far the greater number of cases on the patches which lie on Kimmeridge clay or oolite. Some is early and some late. Little inclosure it is clear took place in this region except in the neighbourhood of towns and villages rising out of the real fen land.

The land inclosed in this county was, according to the *Agricultural Report*, not suited to turnip husbandry, and little, as may be gathered from this and other sources, was during the eighteenth century converted to pasture or grazing.

The Midlands. Turning to the Midlands we may deal, first of all, with the very important group of counties in which inclosure during the eighteenth and nineteenth centuries was peculiarly prominent. These are Warwick, Leicester, Nottingham, Northampton, Rutland, and Huntingdon. The three more southern counties—Oxford, Buckingham, and Bedford—will be considered afterwards.

Despite the appearance and distribution of drift, geological formation exerted great influence, and certain general characteristics both as to it and as to the soil may be noted. On the whole these are simple. Through the greater part of Warwick, that is, through the county to the north-west of the Avon, extends a region of red soil on a triassic formation. This continues through the western part of Leicester into Nottingham, where it constitutes a wide east central district, running south to north, bordered on the west by the forest district also on trias, and on the extreme east and south-east by a belt of soil on lias. This latter is most noticeable in the south-east. The Trent valley has a considerable amount of alluvial and river gravel.

The belt of soil on lias covers Warwick to the south or south-east of the Avon, the north-west of Northampton, the bigger and eastern half of Leicester, the smaller western half of Rutland, together with the land already described in Nottingham. There is a fair amount of drift boulder clay. According to Young it was very capable of improvement and was good soil on gritstone. Its range includes the north of Oxford, that is the Banbury district.

South-east of this lies the land on oolitic formation. First of all comes the soil, often cornbrash, in East Rutland, the remainder of Northampton, and in a belt at the north of Buckingham, and across Oxford. It was on the lower oolite and in general suited to wheat and turnips. Directly south-east, tending more to heavier clays, is another belt of land, comprising the greater part of Huntingdon and the north of Bedford and running through Buckingham and Oxford. There is a large amount of drift.

One important feature of the land on the lias and the oolites is the water-bearing character of the strata.

Taking these various regions in order, attention must be given to the two important points, namely, the extent of inclosure relative to area and the date at which such inclosure took place.

Now, with regard to the first matter, inclosure in the first region, that is on the red soil, embraces a smaller percentage of the area than in the other regions. The difference between inclosure here and on the land immediately to the south-east is marked. In Warwick the percentage of land inclosed in the north-west is distinctly lower, in Atherstone 2. Aston 10, Meriden 18, Solihull 6, in Alcester 20; in the central district, where the red soil ends and the other begins, the percentage is higher, that is, in Warwick 27, and Stratford 31; while in the three districts of the south-east it is as follows, Shipston 41, Southam 42, and Rugby 34. The two small districts of Nuneaton and Foleshill, where there is a sudden great mixture of formations, some verging to coal, show 22 and 38 respectively. This county, moreover, from the sixteenth century was notably different in respect of inclosure on the two sides of the Avon. The difference was observed by Leland and is also remarked by others, though whether from independent observation or not, is difficult to say. Now, taking the inclosures by act to 1840, a comparison between the districts to the north and north-west of the Avon and to the south and south-east may be attempted. These districts correspond approximately to the districts of red soil and soil in lias, the latter, a southern district, according to Leland, being largely champion. Of the total Warwick inclosures of the period there lie

South-east of Avon, - -	97,000 acres.
North-west of Avon, - -	49,000 acres.

There are, however, some cases with regard to which the exact position is not ascertained. Of the five thus undetermined, two with an acreage of 3200 certainly seem to lie to the south. If these be added the southern total is say 100,000 acres. Thus, speaking roughly, there are inclosed some 100,000 acres on the south-east, and some 50,000 or less on the north-west. But the county is very unequally divided by the river, the portion to the south being much the smaller. If we take it at two-fifths, the total acreage to the south may be taken at 225,000, and that of the north at say 338,000. Taking these figures the percentage inclosed to the south may be put at 40, while that to the north is not 15.

In Leicester, though the distinction between the two sides of the county is not so marked in the record of inclosure by act as in Warwick, it still is apparent. In

Ashby and Market Bosworth it is low, and the same may be said of the west of Loughborough, where, however, the percentage for the total district reaches 50, including 19 of commons and land near the alluvial valleys. Hinckley, in the south-east, is 31. In the central districts, where there is much alluvial and boulder clay drift, that is, Barrow and Blaby, the respective percentages are 52 and 49. On the east, Melton Mowbray is 33, Billesden 25, Market Harborough 40, and Lutterworth 29. The record on the west is possibly rendered less low than it otherwise would have been from inclosures in the neighbourhood of Charnwood, the actual great forest inclosure, being included in the reckoning.[1] Here, too, early writers as Leland and Burton remark, the south and east is largely or almost all in champion. It must be remembered that considerable inclosure took place in Leicester in the seventeenth century.

In Nottingham inclosure in the west is low; in the centre higher, East Retford 38 and Southwell 26; and in the east high, Bingham 40 and Newark also very high.

Turning now to the date of the inclosures, in Warwick those in the more northern parts are distinctly later, and in general there is a tendency for those in the north-west to occur later than in the south-east. In the case of Leicester all the inclosures, which seem to develop outward from the junction line between Warwick and Leicester, are early. There is no great difference between the east and the west, though the few late inclosures occur as a rule in the latter. In Nottingham no distinction can be drawn. Speaking generally the inclosures are later than in the two preceding counties.

As between the land on the lias and that on the oolitic formations, the chief distinction in the inclosures of this period is in respect of date. On the whole the

[1] The large Charnwood inclosure has been apportioned among the registration districts concerned by a rough general estimate. The figures for inclosure of commons in these districts must be regarded as conjectural (Appendix C.).

percentage of inclosure is higher in the former, a feature more marked when comparison is made with the land which is of Oxford clay, or rather when there is a considerable amount of Oxford clay. The drift substratum and the large areas of boulder clay tend to modify the effect of the geological features. But this much may be said. In general the extent of act inclosure is greatest in North-West Northampton, and in the Banbury district of Oxford, as compared with the remainder of these counties, just as it is heavy in south and east Leicester and south-east Warwick relatively to the other parts of these counties. The same region was the earliest in date, a distinction which prevails in the west as compared with the east of Rutland. In this whole area, that is, roughly speaking, in the area characterised to some extent by the lias, the great balance of inclosure is early, mainly before 1780, and to a not inconsiderable extent before 1760. The inclosures to the south-east are more widely distributed in date, inclining to the years after 1780.

In the south midland counties of Oxford, Buckingham, and Bedford, despite the great intermixture of soil, there are features, sufficiently visible, of a relationship between soil and inclosure. In Oxford where as in the southern districts some cretaceous soil is present, the inclosures are low in percentage, and late. This is the case in both Henley, where the percentage is 10, and in Thame where it reaches 21. In the latter case some deduction must be made for the more mixed land. These districts correspond fairly closely with similar land in the neighbouring county of Buckingham. Again in the north the district of Banbury consists of good soil, described as good red land, lying on lias. The percentage of inclosure is very high, and the date very early, as indeed on the like soil in Daventry and Brackley in Northampton. On the stonebrash to the south of this, capable of improvement and suited to grain and turnips, as in the north of Buckingham, the percentage is not so great as in Banbury, being for Bicester 49, Woodstock 39. Witney and

Chipping Norton are more mixed. The date of inclosure is early on the whole, but not so early as in Banbury where nearly all is prior to 1780. The most part of Buckingham north of Watling Street is described by Young as good for turnips, and corresponds to the district of Newport Pagnell which is of stonebrash on oolite, and shows a very high percentage of inclosure, namely 64. Most of it, as indeed of Winslow, with its percentage of 59, was in pasture, according to the *Agricultural Report*, though some was arable. Winslow was partly stonebrash and partly Oxford clay. In the south of the county was clay and lime, in Amersham inclosure was low, only 6. Likewise that part of Wycombe furthest from the Chilterns was less inclosed. But where the Chiltern chalk prevailed, that is mainly in Wycombe, the percentage of land inclosed was high. The rate for the *whole* of the Wycombe district was 25; a rate which must be considerably increased for the cretaceous soil in that district, on which most, indeed nearly all, of the inclosures occur. There is considerable inclosure also in the southern part of the Aylesbury district, subject to the same influences of soil. In both cases inclosure is late, after 1790. In the valley district of Aylesbury marked by the Kimmeridge clay and singularly fertile for the dairy, inclosure is also considerable, but very early. Returning to the south, in the extreme south below the clay district, which is so singularly void of inclosure, is land largely of alluvial with a gravelly loam where the rate, in the Eton district, rises to 33. Here inclosure takes place mostly between 1790 and 1810. It corresponds to the neighbouring districts of Middlesex. The character of the land in Bedford is so complex, both by reason of the geological features and the drift that little that is specific can be concluded. This much, however, is clear that the inclosures in the north where clays, either boulder clay or Oxford and oolitic clays, prevail, is greater and earlier than in the southern part where there is chalk.

A comparison of Worcester with the neighbouring

counties of Warwick and Gloucester emphasises the features observed. In the south-east of Worcester, that is in the portion bordered by a line running from Tewkesbury just east of Worcester city to Droitwich, and thence continued east with a slight depression to the south to the confines of the county, the lias clay prevails. According to the *Agricultural Report* the soil is of loamy clay and rich, more particularly in the vale of Evesham. The vale of the Severn with its alluvial meadows is to the west. Outside of this area comes soil on a triassic basis with Devonian and old red sandstone formations in the extreme west. The south is more mixed. Nearly all the inclosures of common field are in the south-east, the lias district, as in Warwick. Taking all inclosures the percentage of land inclosed by act is 42 in the district of Pershore, and 25 in that of Evesham. In both these, inclosure is generally of land which includes common field. In both Droitwich with 8 and Upton with 12 per cent. there are common field and commons inclosures. Nearly all other inclosures are of common, and the percentage is not high save in Kidderminster with 17 where a large number of commons were affected. Otherwise the rate of inclosure during this period is exceedingly low.

From the foregoing description and account some general tendencies may be deduced:

(i) It seems evident that many inclosures had occurred in early times on the red soils in Central and North-West Warwick, West Leicester, and West and Central Nottingham. Lists of such are extant as far as the district at or about the juncture of these counties is concerned. To the above may be added the central district of Worcester. In these regions Marshall notes townships of old inclosure. As to the general result there is said to be more grain in the west than in the east of Leicester, and the same appears to be true of Warwick. As to the cause, the connection between soil and woodland, dealt with elsewhere, must be remembered.[1] In the more eastern district

[1] Pp. 111-2. Cf. 231.

it would appear as though comparatively little change from open field occurred until circumstances altered and a pressure took place for stock breeding and higher grazing. Then inclosure occurs and extends rapidly and with marked results. It occurs early in the period of private acts, chiefly before 1780. The inclosure taking place on the red soil during this period is secondary, that is, occurring on land already subjected to the process, and is later in the century in consequence. It is somewhat significant that the counties indicated as experiencing decrease in wheat during the latter part of the eighteenth century possess a considerable amount of the land on a lias substratum, affected though that be by drift. They are Warwick (2180 acres), Leicester (3793 acres), Northampton (5587 acres), Rutland (498 acres), Bedford (1157 acres), Buckingham (3297 acres), and Nottingham (984 acres). Of these the first four are certainly largely concerned with this land. Buckingham may be affected by the inclosure of oolitic clays, and also by the large dairy district of Aylesbury. In the case of Bedford it is stated that the clays in the north were often badly mismanaged in inclosure.

This latter land was the great grazing district and one where careful breeding was practised.

(ii) The stonebrash soil is continually stated to be suited to turnips and wheat. Both here and on the Oxford and other clays, the inclosures were rather later in date, and there is little evidence, if Bedford be excepted, of any diminution in arable.

(iii) Inclosures on cretaceous soil are invariably late. Almost equally invariably they are said to take place for arable use. Their late occurrence is easily explained. Owing to the great toil and care required to make their soil successful, their inclosure and cultivation were deferred until the demand for wheat increased prices, and until skilled farming and capital were available.

The foregoing sketch of certain of the chief districts of England, though necessarily but partial and incomplete, is sufficient to indicate the connection between the physical features of the various regions and lands and the progress of the inclosure movement. It would be difficult to carry it out in close detail, partly because as yet full knowledge of the soil characteristics is wanting. The solid geological maps, while helpful in certain places, are in others rendered comparatively or wholly useless by the prevalence of drift. As yet drift maps have only been prepared for some districts. But even drift surveys do not adequately disclose the soil. For information as to this the surveys and maps attempted by the early Board of Agriculture and the researches of Young and Marshall still retain their value. On the other hand, other influences, sometimes conflicting and always uncertain in extent, require to be taken into account. Even with like soil, the position of the district with regard to markets, for instance, precludes a like result. Despite the difficulties, however, in the way of any precise determination the connection is clearly visible. Conspicuous differences between the soils of the districts noticed are accompanied almost invariably by a difference in inclosure, either in the proportion of land inclosed during these centuries or in the date of the period in which the inclosure occurred. Some few examples may be picked out for the sake of illustration. There is the difference between the sands of Norfolk and the district of Flegg, between the north-west corner of Suffolk and the rest of the county, between the districts of Hitchin and Royston and the remainder of Hertford, or again between the vales in Gloucester and the Cotswold districts. Again, contrast Warwick, north-west of the Avon, and Warwick on the other bank, or to turn to a small though equally conspicuous case, the inclosure, as to quantity and date, of the Staines and Uxbridge districts in Middlesex and that prevailing in general in that county. Of course there are many cases where intervening causes preclude the result experienced in their absence; but in general a marked difference in soil is reflected in the inclosure. As a matter of fact inclosure is a stage in the progress of cultivation, and the causes affecting cultivation necessarily influence it. Another point. The introduction of inclosure into a district seems to have led in some cases to its extension even to land not particularly suited to it at the time, owing no doubt partly to the simple desire to imitate a process taking place in the neighbourhood, and partly to the divergence between private and public interests.

The connection thus indicated in general becomes of importance in so far as it is possible to isolate cause and its corresponding effect in the case of various soils. The more important conclusions are the following:

(1) There were certain lands inclosed with a view to their whole or partial use as arable. First amongst these are the sands, as in Norfolk, where, till the introduction of the turnips chiefly as a crop to be eaten off by the flocks, the soil was too light for continuous arable use. The most conspicuous instances are in the districts of Norfolk, but elsewhere examples occur. In those cases where inclosure was absolutely essential and where the profit under rotation was great, inclosure occurs early, often before the period of private acts. Secondly, we have brashy lands suited to arable use but still of value before. Amongst such are the Cotswolds where enclosure was required, but its progress depended a great deal on the demand for arable products. Again, there is some part of the brashy lands in the Midlands evidently similarly affected. Turnips and root crops generally are of great value on these brashy lands, but partly, it must be remembered, to be used as winter food for cattle. Both in the Cotswolds and in these districts inclosure reaches a fair percentage under the acts and is usually late in the second period, that is, not long before, but still before, 1790. Somewhat different are the inclosures occurring on chalk soils, where inclosure is late and evidently due to high prices and skilled farming which make the cultivation of these lands with profit a possibility. The movement is always late, that is, in general well after 1790. The range of inclosure is very considerable, including, as it

does, much of the south of Cambridge, North Hertford, parts of Buckingham and Oxford, and indeed of Berkshire and the south of Wilts.

(2) The next feature to note is the inclosure of the dairy districts. In many cases these have evidently taken place before the period of private act, small secondary and late inclosures only occurring during such time. Here we have the Gloucester vales, the dairy vales of Wiltshire, Aylesbury, and to them might be added part of the vale of the White Horse in Berkshire and others. Inclosure by act is late and usually slight save in Aylesbury. It seems probable that such dairy districts passed under real inclosure in the seventeenth century, possibly in the early eighteenth. Of course inclosure was essential to their full use.

(3) In the region where red soil has come under observation, there is ground for assuming the occurrence of considerable inclosure, often from a wild or woodland state, at a time prior to this period. Some further inclosure takes place, though to a less extent and at a later date in the period, than on other land under like conditions. More arable use appears to have been made of this red soil than of other neighbouring land.

(4) In certain cases very rich loams or very good mixed lands remain unaffected till a late date apparently because inclosure would produce little change, and so would be a source of loss rather than of profit in view of its inevitable expense. Under this heading comes the Flegg area, with its high percentage and very late date. Possibly some like reason accounts for the late and extensive inclosures in the south-west corner of Middlesex and the southern point of Buckingham.

(5) The great wide belt of grazing land, with its extremely high rate of inclosure, comes under inclosure early in the period. Indeed it marks the beginning, some occurring before 1760, though the full change takes place mainly between 1760 and 1780. With regard to it two features require attention. It was of heavy land on water-

bearing strata, features only partially shared by the belt of land to its south-west where both elevation and drift make the soil suitable for wheat. Again, as compared with other large regions, it appears to have been less affected by earlier inclosure. Not only is the percentage of land inclosed exceptionally high, but the percentage of parishes in which inclosure took place is also high, pointing to a uniform high distribution. The matter at issue then is the reason why it long remained so little disturbed. To some extent the belt of land on the south-west is also concerned, though to a less degree. Possibly in part the geographical position of the area, lying as it did well removed from the districts where early manufacture prevailed, may account for much. But there were other districts, as on the west, also remote. On the other hand, it was almost certainly more settled than these in agricultural occupation; but this seems an inadequate explanation. It is impossible to escape the conclusion that the character of the soil was an influential feature. This may have prevented its earlier inclosure with profit, and certainly would have made it unsuitable for the less careful sheep farming. Stock in its heavy pastures needed care, and under inclosure the land could be drained. As to the result there is little doubt that the change issued in much conversion of land. The land was used for careful grazing and breeding. But grazing lands, needed for the meat supply, other than those in the immediate neighbourhood of towns, became important first in the seventeenth century; while it is only in the eighteenth century that systems of breeding develop. Further, the gradual growth of industrial occupation in the Midland districts creates a new need for the utilisation of the soil to the best advantage.

(6) The district of the fen drainages shows as might be expected comparatively little inclosure in this period. Portions of Norfolk, Cambridge, Huntingdon, and Lincoln are included, as also the north-east of Northampton, where, as may be seen, a considerable diminution occurs

in the percentage of the land inclosed as compared with other parts of that county. The fen and drainage inclosures were of seventeenth century origin. Land thus treated might, and in many cases did, fall under subsequent inclosures, since in some of the original measures land was divided rather between the different villages than between the inhabitants in these villages. Still, as can be seen, the extent of later inclosure is slight.

(7) In like manner districts in early times covered with wood show less marks of eighteenth century inclosure than the lands which surround them. Nor must the connection between woodland and soil be ignored, a connection which may account in part for the coincidences to be observed between the inclosure map and the drift or soil maps. To some extent much the same may be said of the technical forests, even when these were but little in wood. There is, however, one difference. While in both much early inclosure would occur from a wild state, woods had to be removed before cultivation or other use was possible. They were thinned out as the need for timber grew.

Whilst in these respects the influence of the soil and of physical characteristics, some directly due to the soil, is distinct and obvious, it is equally clear that in different places there were in operation differing conditions or intervening causes. Of these two are of peculiar importance.

The first and most important is the position of a region or district in respect of industrial occupation, and the urban or semi-urban conditions associated with early industries. Both in East Anglia and in the western area described above, that is, in country near the manufacturing districts, often very wide districts with industries lying scattered over their face, the land is evidently much inclosed before the opening of the eighteenth century. The same appears to have been the case in the parts of the home counties surrounding the metropolis, as also in the district near Birmingham. In addition, near many of the older and yet growing towns, the land lying open at the beginning of this period is often comparatively small in amount. This feature may be corroborated from evidence outside that contained in the inclosure returns. It is evident, for instance, in the description of the country in Ogilby's *Britannia.* Nor is the explanation difficult. Old systems prevailing largely by virtue of custom hold their place with increasing difficulty in the presence of the industrial or town spirit. Again, the increased needs of the population make high and economical cultivation essential, while further, the nature of these needs brings about the devotion of the neighbouring lands, in part at any rate, to the production of supplies which could not be easily carried under the existing conditions of locomotion and transport. Except to some extent in respect of grain, most towns had to be fed, in the main, from supplies produced in the neighbourhood, and as towns grew the need of land in the vicinity for grazing and dairy purposes increased. Arable may be discouraged by the drift of labourers into the towns. Doubtless with the improvement of locomotion during the eighteenth century, the distinction thus indicated between grain and other supplies tends to be modified. This particular need affected inclosure in another way. Turnips and other roots were required as winter food for cattle and stock, and these were grown with difficulty except in inclosed fields.

Secondly, as has been pointed out elsewhere, the enlargement of the area of land under cultivation, either by the greater use made of the fallows or by reclamation of waste or fen, or by the inclusion of commons in open field inclosure, which often took place to a large extent, would affect the use to which land already under arable cultivation could be profitably put, since, in these instances, land formerly debarred was now available for arable use. In many cases, as in reclaimed or drained land, the new land was far more fertile than that previously under crops.

In any attempt to apply the various conclusions stated above to the progress of inclosure during this period, a distinction must be observed between inclosures which are advantageous by reason of the general economy achieved in working the land and those which are advantageous because of special facilities or opportunities afforded by particular soils or other conditions affecting particular districts.

From the evidence contained both in the statistics derived from the acts and awards and treated above, and also offered by the literature of the subject, some fairly definite indications are afforded of the special causes promoting inclosure both during and before the eighteenth century.

In the first place, on certain lands inclosure evidently occurred before the eighteenth century.

On the red soil belt lying north of the lias, the movement during the eighteenth century is so markedly distinct as to preclude the inference that it was casual or unaffected by the nature of the land, and its previous availability for cultivation. In Warwick, there is a very obvious difference between the amount of inclosure under act on this land and that taking place in the rest of the county. The same is true in the case of Worcester, and on the whole, though less distinctly apparent, in Leicester. But not only is the percentage much less, but the date of inclosure is different. On the red soil such scattered inclosures as occur take place in most instances later, that is, usually after 1780-90. Further, in these counties inclosure from common is more apparent in this area than elsewhere. There seem to be signs of inclosure making its appearance again on land already subject to the process at an earlier date. In the case of Leicester it should be added that the cases of inclosed villages mentioned in the controversy during the seventeenth century are mostly in the south-west portion of the county. Of course it should be remembered that drift and clay deposits modify the geological structure of this land.

The fen inclosures are another instance of this earlier movement. Their area may be detected during the period of the acts by the much smaller percentage of inclosure, and also by its later date. This is true at any rate in general of Huntingdon, Northampton, and Norfolk. It is less apparent, though still apparent, in the case of Cambridge. The same may be said of forest districts.

Again, the inclosure in the dairy districts, though less completely before the eighteenth century, may be grouped with those thus characterised. Probably it was spread over a considerable period beginning with the middle of the seventeenth century, and extending on well into the eighteenth. In such districts the percentage inclosed under act is invariably comparatively less than on the neighbouring land. In respect of date, dairy inclosures fall into two divisions. In the case of the Gloucestershire vales and of the West Wiltshire district lying mostly in Mere and Tisbury, the date is late, inclosure taking place mainly after 1790, and often in the early nineteenth century. Here the main inclosure appears to have been early, probably well back in the seventeenth century. On the other hand, in North-East Wiltshire, in the sub-districts of Highworth and Cricklade, and in the vale of Aylesbury, inclosure though low in percentage is very early. Here it would seem we have inclosure under act co-operating with and completing inclosure of recent occurrence.

In the second place, under certain conditions particular soils tend to be inclosed over a considerable period, and mainly in the eighteenth century.

Thus there is a movement towards inclosure of land, where such is necessary to allow the introduction of turnips, or to facilitate the use of grass-seeds and clover; in other words, in view of a desired change in the crop rotation. The light soils of North-West Norfolk apparently underwent inclosure with this object, and in Hertford, though here new inclosure was not required, it was considered by some that turnip culture had been introduced at an even earlier date. The demand for inclosure of suitable land was widespread, and from different references it is evident that this motive produced some effect in different parts of the country. By the Act of 13 George III., the attempt was made to facilitate the introduction of turnips even in the absence of inclosure; but this act, though possibly utilised in a few cases, was in general inoperative, partly, it may be conjectured, by reason of the difficulty of procuring the necessary consents.

In general, moreover, on light, dry, and stony soils inclosure was practised, and with more or less general approbation. When attempted under such conditions it led in very many cases to more careful arable or mixed cultivation, and not to any conversion from arable to pasture. Thus Addington, no favourable critic, writes "as to heaths and light, sandy, or stony soil, there inclosing facilitates such improvements in tillage as will do real service both to individuals and the public," and in his recommendations he advises that in these cases it might well be allowed. His attitude, as well as that of other writers soon after the middle of the century, is sufficient evidence in itself as to the occurrence of inclosure on such soils.

As is pointed out by Stone, the constant wheat crops taken from the land under the open field system tend to exhaust both light loams and sandy soils, which cannot bear so much plough, and need to be laid down to grass now and again. This feature is of considerable importance. With the new alternatives offered both by grass-seeds and roots, inclosure on such soils meant improved arable agriculture. Hence the profit from the change. In some instances conversion to pasture might occur owing to particular reasons; but in general such was not the case.

But while this was the result after the introduction of new crops, the issue of inclosure when undertaken at an earlier date was not necessarily the same. Indeed it seems highly probable that light loams and good sandy soil in particular, might well be inclosed for pasture because of the decreased yield of grain after many years of the open field courses. If this be so, some light is thrown on the course of inclosure in the years prior to the seventeenth, and possibly in the early seventeenth century. It may partly explain the priority of the red soils in inclosure over that other soil lying in its immediate neighbourhood.

In the third place, we come to the inclosures which attracted most attention in the eighteenth century, and which, with their results, still continue to be considered typical of the movement, to the obscuring of other inclosures, such as those dealt with in this and other chapters.

The land which comes under inclosure during the period 1760-1790 and is subject in large measure to conversion from arable to pasture, lies in general on the water-bearing strata of the lias. With this may be associated some of the soil marked by oolitic clays, which are inclosed rather later, though partially in the same period, and are less marked by conversion. This matter has already been treated in certain areas, and certain general conclusions as to it have been stated. But something more may be said. If a line be drawn between inclosures before and after 1780, and ranging from the early acts to 1840, the following counties are those having the largest percentage inclosure during the earlier period:

	—1780.	1780—1840.
Leicester, - - - -	32 p.c.	16 p.c.
Warwick, - - - -	17	9
Northampton, - - -	29	25
Nottingham, - - -	15	16
Rutland, - - - -	20	27
Worcester, - - - -	7	11

In all these counties there is land of the kind first named, that is, land on the lias formation. If, further, the inclosures be investigated in detail, it will be seen that it is the districts on this soil which are most characterised by these early inclosures, that is, the private act inclosures before 1780. Thus in Northampton the registration districts thus affected are those in the north-west, namely, Brackley, Daventry, Brixworth, and Northampton, in Warwick, the region south of the Avon is conspicuously under inclosure all the time, and so too the east in the case of Leicester. The same marked prominence of such inclosure is to be seen in the south-east of Nottingham, in Persham and Evesham in Worcester, and also, though to a less degree, in the east of Rutland. Again, if we take both Oxford and Buckingham, the districts in lias in the north fall very much under inclosure at the same time. The complaints of conversion mainly affect these counties.

In the fourth place, with the new influences affecting agriculture and demand for produce, from 1790, the movement, though apparent in other land becomes most conspicuous on land hitherto little affected. The chalk lands, and especially the chalk uplands, are inclosed very little before 1790, and in large measure rather after than before 1800. Again, the brashy uplands, like the Cotswolds, come under the movement. In both cases the result is the increase of arable. There is an extension of the movement in hilly country generally.

But there are other inclosures equally late. In some districts the rich lands, as in Flegg in Norfolk, are also inclosed, probably with but little change in the nature of their crops. Also there are other instances, as the south-east of Middlesex and the southern land of Buckingham, both in the Thames valley.

APPENDIX A

PROGRESS IN THE COUNTIES

SURREY, SUSSEX AND KENT.

The position of these counties with regard to inclosure cannot be understood without knowledge of their physical conditions, and especially apart from their difference in respect of availability for agriculture in early times from that presented now. In the first place, the great stretches of chalk downs must be taken into account, and in the second place, it must be remembered that the weald which occupies so much of the area was a great forest and heavily wooded. The extent of this was very large, and the woodland characteristic continued for a long time. Even in

Kent, Lambarde remarks "that wood occupyeth the greatest portion," and adds "except it be towards the east which coast is more champion than the residue." It is, of course, probable that the woods though still considerable had been diminished even by that date. In the middle of the seventeenth century this process had greatly changed the aspect of the whole region. Thus Aubrey (*Nat. Hist. and Antiquities*) writes: "From Dorking to Northdown Hills in Sussex is a large prospect of several miles off, over a spacious vale, very broad, full of inclosed pastures" (iv. 172), and of the weald in Surrey says "which like the wealds of Sussex and Kent is a rich, deep inclosed country" (iii. 48). These inclosures took place from the wild state and would doubtless affect by their example contiguous land under common right or even in common field. In the main the land went into pasture. This forest area probably constituted the largest portion of the three counties. Of the remaining land a very considerable part was absorbed by the downs. This is described as more champain. Thus Lambarde speaks of the east of Kent, and Blome writes of the same county, "the East where it is more champain," and again referring to Sussex says "that part called the Downs is a very pleasant and champain country." This refers to its open condition, and must not be taken to imply that it was in arable open or even subject to common rights of pasture. It was not inclosed or hedged. Of course some part may have been separated by early approvement; such part as lay open, as described in the seventeenth century, was probably already in separate ownership as there is very slight trace in the eighteenth of any recourse to acts or even agreements to separate the land. Another factor of importance may have affected some of the land nearer to the coast, especially in Kent, namely, the growth of towns and industries. Yet with all this, common field is not absent. This at least is true of Surrey and Sussex. As to the former, Blome says "where it beareth upon the Thames, and lyeth as a plain and champion country it is grateful to the husbandman." In the acts, common field inclosure reaches 9 per cent. in Chertsey, 10 per cent. in Kingston, 17 per cent. in Epsom, despite the quantity of common, and in Croydon it is high, owing, however, largely to one or two particular cases, Much of Croydon being mainly pasture was inclosed in Aubrey's time (ii. 3). Again, in Sussex, in the rich land behind Worthing and near, arable open field passes under act (16 per cent.), while it exists still more to the west to about 10 per cent. In these counties there is also inclosure under act from common, mainly towards the same districts. Kent, however, is singularly void of common. According to Lambarde, it is stated that no man ought to have common in lands of gavelkind, but he adds "howbeit the contrary is well known at this day and that at many places" (p. 567). According to Elton, *Tenures of Kent*, it was an ancient usage respecting common in gavelkind lands that the lord could inclose at his discretion. The inclosed condition of Kent was fully recognised. Thus Burton in the *Anatomy of Melancholy*, Moore in *The Scripture Word*. Common field was absent and common very infrequent. It should, however, be remembered that inclosure as a cause of complaint or disturbance is mentioned by Strype, Stow, and Speed. It may be concluded that this referred to commons.

The facts stated and the features emphasised above point to a region which in respect of much land was unsuited to husbandry and in respect of other, the greater part, only open to use as the woods were cleared and the land inclosed from a wild state. This took place gradually, mainly in early times; and its progress, together with the existence of town demands, tended to the inclosure of open field even in the districts where natural conditions had facilitated its establishment. Some inclosure of common occurs in the sixteenth century: and possibly in the seventeenth, in Surrey and Sussex, inclosure both of common and of open field occurs. The acts of the eighteenth century represent the final phase.

The average size of inclosures in Surrey and Sussex, and in Kent also for the few commons, is low, that is, for Surrey 680 acres and for Sussex, say 760, and even this size misrepresents the case owing to the occurrence of two or three very large inclosures with some open field. The true average is even less and thus differs considerably from that in counties where inclosure occurred over uniformly settled agricultural land. It points either to a secondary inclosure, or to the open field as an element in the cultivation rather than as its basis.

BERKS.

Berkshire presents very different characteristics in different parts. It was evidently affected by inclosure in the fifteenth century, appearing in the list for 1517 with inclosures amounting to 1·39 per cent., and being mentioned by Strype. It is equally clear that in the north-west considerable inclosure went on between the surveys of Leland and Ogilby, this being shown conspicuously in the case of the road from Hinksey to Faringdon. At Ogilby's time this road was partly in open arable; thus from Oxford to Abingdon, from Abingdon to East Ilsley, and from Abingdon to Faringdon.

According to the record of inclosure by act, this north-west was most affected by common field inclosure, Faringdon 31 per cent., Abingdon 43 per cent., Wallingford 50 per cent., and Wantage 28 per cent. The inclosure from common was slight. The inclosures are mainly parish inclosures and of good size. The country to the south, different, of course, in its physical characteristics, differs also in its record. Its western portion, Hungerford and Newbury, has open field inclosure, high in Newbury, 33 per cent., but much lower in Hungerford, where probably the influence of some early direct inclosure from forest, as in the adjacent district of Wiltshire, is partly responsible for the alteration. Relatively to the area these inclosures are smaller. Certainly the road from East Ilsley to Newbury was more inclosed in Ogilby's time and the country more in sheep pasture. The central part of the country has open field, but on the whole much less than in the north-west. In Bradfield there is inclosure from common. In the east there is much heath and much common inclosure by act.

Probably in Hungerford and the vale of Newbury there was even before the sixteenth century direct inclosure from wild, and this reacting brought about a more inclosed condition, resulting in the wool needed in the local industries. The north-west remained practically open at the sixteenth century; but this district was considerably affected by inclosure in that century and also in the seventeenth, much, however, remaining in open arable, as was also the case round Newbury. The east was, it would appear, the subject of gradual reclamation from a waste heath, some remaining to be dealt with by act and possibly in some cases without, as about Windsor.

Part of the central district resembles the neighbouring districts of Oxford and Buckingham in the absence of common inclosure by act. On the whole the course of the movement is well indicated.

HANTS.

Hampshire was in its larger part unsuited for agricultural use in early times. On the east the downs enter and the ancient forest extends, the downs dominating in the north. In the south-west was the New Forest. In both these districts there is comparatively little trace of inclosure by act, and little sign that open field ever existed, save by way of exception. On the other hand, in Leland's time, there was much champion about Stockbridge and from thence to Winchester. Following the same authority, on the other hand, Winchester to Southampton was much inclosed ("apter for cattle than corn"). In general, the south-east below the line of Winchester was considerably inclosed (the isle of Portsmouth partly inclosed and fruitful of corn).

Hampshire appears in Dr. Gay's list for 1517 (·46) and is mentioned by Strype. By Ogilby's time there is more appearance of inclosure in the south-east district mentioned above, and some more inclosure seems probable in the west. But with new land coming into use this could only be expected.

Probably before the fifteenth century there was little land in general agricultural use, save in the districts named, the reason for the early inclosed district not being clear. With the fifteenth and sixteenth century, fresh land comes in from the more wild state and some inclosure of common field occurs. This apparently continues in the seventeenth century. But its original position is clearly traceable in the inclosures under act.

DORSET.

Specific information about inclosure in Dorset is lacking. The most important feature is the broad distinction between the north and the south, the two parts being separated by the high ridge of hills. The north was more flat and once all forest, and in Coker's time, that is, beginning of the eighteenth century, "abounding in very good pastures and feeding for cattle" (Coker, *Dorset*, p. 3.) The south was hilly, with downs for sheep, and in the valleys good fields of corn. He calls it inferior to the north in profit; and mentions its comparative freedom from inclosure. Under act inclosure is much more conspicuous in the south, and especially so in the areas of Weymouth, Dorchester, Blandford. The part near Poole, and extending into Wareham, was heath land, and the common inclosures in this district are mentioned as extensive in the *Agricultural Report* (1815), p. 93. The common field inclosures in the above districts run earlier than elsewhere.

It must also be remembered that the ports of Dorset were of early importance, and that there were early industries. The wool of the down sheep was locally used, according to Coker, while corn was exported by ship, and cattle sent to London by graziers in his time.

A large portion of the north came directly into inclosed use from the wild state before the end of the seventeenth century. In the south common field was more extensive, but probably contracts with the addition of new land. Much of the down land and heath would seem to be separated by agreement, if this took place in the eighteenth century. In a county like this the need of local supplies and the presence of land once wild would exert great influence.

WILTS.

Wilts must be divided into two parts, the north and the south-east.

From Aubrey's Wilts (*Nat. Hist. of Wilts*, p. 104) considerable inclosures took place during the first half of the seventeenth century in the north-west, the extreme fringe abutting on the Cotswold still remaining open in his time. He suggests some inclosure in latter part of sixteenth. Large part "old grass land" (Marshall, *R.E.*, *Gloucester*, *etc.*, ii. 142).

By the Cotswold there is still open ground (Aubrey; Nourse, *Campania Felix*, 1700, p. 45; Marshall, *R.E.*, *Gloucester*, *etc.*, ii. 9).

The south obviously remains open (as to this, *Agricultural Report*, 1813, pp. 32, 39, also edition 1794, p. 78), though there are some few old severalty farms.

SOMERSET.

As compared with midland counties, Somerset was early and distinctively inclosed, and yet it presented a considerable agricultural area. Its hedgerows of elm are mentioned by Leland, "elm wood, wherewith most part of all Somersetshire is in hedgerow inclosed" (p. 65). Its comparison with Northamptonshire is well known (Lansdown MS., 1607; also Hayward, *Life of Edward VI.*). On the other hand we hear of Somersetshire "good for wheat." But this obviously does not refer to all parts of the county. It does not refer, for instance, to moors on the west, nor to the Mendips, nor to the undrained marsh land. In Ogilby some references to common fields occur in the south; on the other hand good corn was raised in inclosed land in Leland's time. Probably there was much early inclosure from a wild state. On the other hand the town development played a part. Thus round Taunton, in the rich vale, there is a conspicuous absence of common field inclosure by act. That common fields existed in some districts, at any rate, is clear, not only from references by Leland but from their traces in the acts.

The references to actual inclosure consist of mentions by Strype and also by Stow and Speed. Collins quotes an account of the risings occasioned in 1549 by inclosures, mainly, it would seem, of parks and demesnes. The position of the county in respect of any abnormal inclosures may be judged from Dr. Gay's list, in which Somerset figures very inconspicuously.

Thus it seems probable that there were firstly, large inclosures from wild in early times, diminishing such common field as there was; and secondly, inclosures of open fields also in early times round the woollen towns, near Taunton, and also on the north-east towards the borders of Wiltshire. Inclosure occurred of demesne, and possibly also of common field, in the sixteenth century, while land may have been taken in from the wild state in this century as well. Practically the bulk of county is inclosed when the seventeenth century opens, some from wild, but some from an arable open state. Further inclosure ensues, and land is added by reclamation of marsh. The inclosure by act is a final process, and owing to the previous course includes little common field. It is most conspicuous in the Langport district.

GLOUCESTER.

Gloucestershire is greatly lacking in uniformity. There are two regions singular in the eighteenth century for their lack of inclosure acts, and two in which there is a fair amount of inclosure, mainly of open field. Indeed as a whole Gloucester has very little common inclosed by act. The two regions of very low inclosure are that across the Severn, really the old Forest of Dean, and the district extending from Bristol by the Severn and northward, taking in the clothing district. The other two regions are the vales and the hills with the Great Cotswolds sloping off east and north-east. The area representing the Forest of Dean was undoubtedly inclosed as the forest was thinned, probably before the seventeenth century. That from Bristol north by the Severn appears also to have been of ancient inclosure, owing in large measure to the development of the clothing trade and its towns. It is doubtful if much or any of the inclosure movement recorded falls within these areas. Gloucester was included in the returns of 1517 (·46). Strype refers to it, and letters were sent to the sheriff as to inclosure in the seventeenth century. The vales probably underwent considerable inclosure as the demands for food from the other districts increased. Probably it was to them, or in general to the land in the north that Standish referred when he grouped Gloucester with Worcester and Hereford in respect of fruit trees. It is in the vales that the dairy occupation grows and spreads. This must be put as far back as the seventeenth century. When the period of inclosure by acts occurs these districts are affected somewhat late, and to something like 20 per cent. East of these is the ridge of the Cotswolds, and east again the Great Cotswold slopes. This was the great wool-producing district, and remained under sheep and probably in a fairly open state in the seventeenth century. Still it would seem likely that it included much several property, even if that were but slightly inclosed in a material sense. If not, much inclosing and division must have taken place in the latter part of the seventeenth century, or by agreement. Interspersed with the sheep land was common field, since it is an important fact that nearly all the Cotswold inclosures by act include open field.

From what has been said, the development of the movement in this county seems to have been much as follows.

In early times the clearing of woods and the taking in of hill or plateau lands lead to a divided and inclosed condition in the part over the Severn, in the Cotswolds, and in many of the wooded hill districts. This had its effect on neighbouring arable. Inclosure in the more agricultural regions occurs in the sixteenth century. About this time probably occur the inclosures in the southern clothing district. In the seventeenth century there is inclosure in the vales, leading to dairy developments, and possibly in the Cotswolds. The movement finds its normal completion in the inclosure by act.

WORCESTER.

There is a very clear demarcation between the inclosure history of the land in the south-east of Worcester and the rest of the county. This corner was largely inclosed after 1760, most of the inclosures being of open field. The rest of the county is said to be ancient in inclosure, and most inclosures which occur by act are of common. The *Agricultural Report* says, "the greater part of this county is ancient inclosure," but from Pershore north are modern inclosures. As to the time of the ancient inclosures, that is evidently very early. Inclosure and hedgerows are referred to by Nourse in 1700, but the county is reckoned as wholly inclosed in *The Vindication*, 1656, while the sign and symbol, the ancient hedgerows, are referred to in *England's Remarques*, 1678, *The Geographical Description*, 1615, and by Standish in 1612, who refers to the fruit trees in hedges and fields (p. 34). The distinction between the south-east and the remaining country is clearly shown in Ogilby, while Leland notes the inclosed condition of the land north from Worcester. According to him there is much corn in this inclosed district (see also Blith, p. 83). Strype, it should be added, alludes to inclosure in Worcester.

The history of this ancient inclosed part is to be viewed in connection with that of the neighbouring western counties. While a large part of the south-east is definitely inclosed by act, even that area is imperfectly accounted for. Probably some inclosure followed as a consequence on the condition of the rest of the county.

WARWICK.

According to all descriptions from middle of sixteenth century, much difference existed between country north of Avon and country south: the south more champion, the north more inclosed, especially about Arden (Leland, *Itin.*, iv. pt. 2, p. 65, etc.); the south more champion (*Geographical Desc.*); the Fielden which lyeth southwards more champion (Blome, p. 229); county divided by Avon (*Brief Desc.*, Harl. MS. 5190, p. 21).

Inclosure early in seventeenth century, if not in sixteenth century, Diggers' Petition, J. I.; evidence of Moore, etc. The part, judging from the general tenour of controversy by Moore and others, affected is in north, towards Leicester and Stafford. In the country north of Avon the woods thinned owing to ironmaking, Speed, *Geography*, i. 53; also Gibson's additions to Camden, ii. 328 (*i.e.* 1694). But according to Gibson, this affecting the Fielden in south since more land in north being free for crops, need arose for cheese, butter, and flesh to counterbalance. Blith (*Improver*, p. 83) instances western parts of Warwick as woodland which are grown as gallant corn fields as be in England.

Marshall gives ten townships (*Rural E.*, *Midlands*, i. 80) in the old inclosed parts of his midland district. Of these nine are in the following districts: Tamworth of Staffordshire, and Atherstone of Warwick. These and other townships appeared to him to have been long in a state of inclosure (i. 8). Compare with this Morton's reference (*Northamptonshire*, 16) to the richest knot of pastures in the angle where the three counties, Leicester, Warwick, and Northampton meet.

Warwick appears in Dr. Gay's lists for 1517 (1·68) and 1607 (·93) and is mentioned by Strype. The difference in inclosures under act between the north (esp. N.-W.) and south-east is very marked.

On the evidence cited above the course of inclosure seems clear, a large amount of direct inclosure from woodland and wild in the north taking place, and creating a tendency towards inclosure in the south. The movement in north continues in the seventeenth century and is the cause of complaint, possibly because land under corn and in several is turned to pasture, and some open fields are affected.

NORFOLK, SUFFOLK, AND ESSEX.

At the end of the sixteenth century, the west of Norfolk was largely champion; thus *Geographical Description*, Speed, *Geography*, both saying Thetford to Burnham and thence west, champion or most champion. Speed adds that the rest had more wood. In the main this tract is poor, and in later times noted as sheep walk. Blome confirms the account or possibly merely repeats it. According to the *Dictionarium Urbanicum* the land near the sea champion, yielding plenty of corn. This leads to the conclusion that the district between the line thus drawn and Flegg and Tunstall had a considerable amount of inclosed land at the end of the sixteenth century. Into this region the district surveyed by Marshall falls. He describes it as an old inclosed and highly cultivated country. Commons of course existed; indeed, there is more inclosure by act in this part of Norfolk than elsewhere in the county, a possible accompaniment of very early and incomplete inclosure.

That Norfolk was affected by inclosure during sixteenth century is clear. It appears, though not very conspicuously, in list for 1517 (·71), and is mentioned by Strype, Stow, and Speed.

Less difference between the west and the main county appears from Ogilby, though it still remains more open. But it is clear from the record of inclosures under act, that if at beginning of seventeenth there was *great* difference between the two parts of the county west and east of the line, which is emphatically stated, considerable inclosure must have occurred before 1750, as the recorded inclosures show no such difference. As to the north-west, Arthur Young's account of what took place on the introduction of turnips and other root crops is adequate; there must have been a considerable change in the whole of the west. Probably the fen inclosures partly account for this, both directly and indirectly.

The existence of common of shack in Norfolk is emphasised by Coke in Corbet's case.

From these facts and descriptions it would seem that agricultural settlement may have made less way in the west in early days, that in central Norfolk it existed, but gradually yielded to inclosure partly in the sixteenth century, and possibly also before, by reason of the development going on in town life and in the demand for food, this not affecting the extreme east as Flegg, because that would have undergone little change on inclosure. It was pre-eminently corn land. Meantime the west remains largely open, coming partly into use. Such use increases in the seventeenth century largely by reason of the reclamation of the fens.

Norfolk inclosures under act are of varying size, the majority a fair size, but there are many small. Most of them are late, occurring that is after 1790 and especially after 1800. These features taken together suggest that the movement by act was of a secondary nature, following, that is, a previous and distinct period of very considerable inclosure.

It would seem probable that the inclosure movement recorded in the sixteenth century affected the middle area.

In the sixteenth century Suffolk was evidently much advanced in inclosure, the author of the *Properties of the Shires* speaking of "Suffolk full of styles" (Lel. *Itin.* V. xxx.). This almost certainly refers to High Suffolk and East Suffolk. Reyce speaks of Middle Suffolk as mainly in tillage, but with pasture; of the East as chiefly pasture and feeding, while the western parts in contradistinction he describes as either "wholly champion or neer," the fielding abounding by tillage and flocks of sheep. In the champion, that is the west, there is less wood, and the greatest number of flocks [Reyce, *Breviary*, 1618 (some written 1603), published 1902]. According to Blome, parts about Bury and north-west champaigne, except about Newmarket. The *Dict. Urbanicum* repeats this, and says it is "generally champion" and has plenty of corn.

Here as in Norfolk there were risings against inclosures, probably in High or Middle Suffolk.

Of this county the *Agric. Reports* say: "Suffolk must be reckoned among the earliest inclosed of the English counties, but there are very large tracts yet open" (*Agric. Rep.* 2nd edit. p. 30); the turnip "has been cultivated in Suffolk largely beyond the memory of the oldest man" (*Agric. Rep.* p. 83).

With regard to inclosures under act, as in Norfolk, these imperfectly account for the amount of open land described on the west, and seventeenth and eighteenth century inclosure by other means must be assumed.

Essex is uniformly treated as of very old inclosure, and this, the north-east omitted, is fully borne out by the record of inclosure under act. These show for the great part of the county little common inclosure and very little of open field. As to the inclosed condition at the end of the sixteenth, and to its traditional character even then, many writers combine; thus Burton in the *Anatomy*, the Lansdown MS. of 1607, *The Scripture Word*, *Vindication of Regulated Inclosure*; the accounts in the *Agric. Reports* speak equally confidently.

Essex is treated as affected in the sixteenth century by the movement. Thus it is mentioned at any rate in the list of 1517, and is said to have been disturbed by Strype, Stow, and Speed. There is little probability that anything of any moment occurred in the seventeenth century.

Taking the three counties together, the inclosure of the west is well accounted for. In Essex there was the forest district which came into use and inclosure concurrently and from time to time, much of it at a late date. Similarly the fen reclamation affected a large area in the seventeenth century; while the more open field land, that resembling the land of Cambridge, is inclosed by act. Much of the land near the sea in the north of Norfolk, as also in the east, can be accounted for. The real problem relates to the great Anglian Plain between the East Anglian heights and the sea, narrowing as Norfolk is approached. In the north the traces of common field and so of full early settlement are more frequent; in the south, especially in Essex and part of Suffolk, they are very few indeed. If inclosed from common field it was very completely inclosed. The coincidence between this district and the soil is striking; but it cannot be taken as an explanation. In some districts the one field system may seem a partial cause; but this is quite inadequate for the whole region, and indeed in all districts leaves much to be explained.

The only cause that seems at all adequate is the early development of these counties and their industrial growth which brought about a prior development in inclosure. This might be helped, and no doubt was helped by the inclosure from wild land on the west, but this latter is only of partial application. Its importance lies chiefly in the south. In other words, this district, owing to its earlier growth marked by industry and still traceable in the signs of a large population, appears to have passed through its stages of inclosure at a very early date. Some signs of the movement are recorded, but they are of concluding stages, whereas in certain districts the concurrent signs indicate the beginning. Further, there are scattered common fields which increase and become plentiful as we pass to the north.

MIDDLESEX.

There is considerable difference between the south-west and the rest of the county. In Leland's time the land near Staines was much champain (ii. 116), while up near Uxbridge was a tendency to more inclosure. The correspondence with the immediately neighbouring parts of Buckingham is close. The inclosures under act are high in both the Staines (45 per cent.) and Brentford (43 per cent.) districts, the latter nearly all from common, and the former all involving open field. This was on alluvial, like the Eton district in Buckingham, offering good ground for general agricultural settlement. Near Uxbridge there was considerable common field inclosure. In the Hendon and Edmonton districts these are 16 and 11 per cent. respectively, but the inclosures of the south-west are large while those in these latter districts vary, some small and secondary. Probably the north and east of Middlesex were much affected by clearing of forest, especially about Enfield, where Evelyn speaks of the Chace about 25 miles in compass and as wild with only a few inclosures (*Diary*, 2 June, 1676). In a letter of 1766 it is said "a notion prevails that a bill will be offered for inclosing Enfield Chace and Epping Forest and dividing them into small farms not exceeding 100 l. per annum, as a means of adding considerably to the supply of provisions wanting for this overgrown metropolis" (*Letters of First Earl of Malmesbury*, p. 144). There was also at Ogilby's time considerable wild or open land about Finchley. It seems probable that some land in the north was brought into the cultivable area after the time of Evelyn and Ogilby, and obvious that much division and inclosure occurred without act in the eighteenth and early nineteenth centuries.

Middlesex was affected by the movement in the fifteenth century, appearing in 1517 with 1·52 per cent. of inclosure.

HERTFORD.

All accounts coincide in regarding Hertfordshire as an old inclosed county. From this the district in the north must be excluded. As far as the rest, that is the main part of the county, is concerned there is little record of inclosure. In Leland's time the county is "full of wood" (Leland's *Itin.* V. xxx.; *Properties of the Shires*, verses out of remains left by Rawlinson, apparently of date about 1575); the same in Leland's travels from Luton by St. Albans and Barnet to London where inclosured ground and wood noted (v. 117). At end of seventeenth century Chauncey states hundreds of Odsey and Hitchin "most champion," while he notes that Hertford is inclosed, also Edmonton, except in north by Barley and Barkway.

The only inclosure in seventeenth century probably was of open chaces.

At end of eighteenth century inclosures by act widely in north, also sporadic from centre to west. The references in *Agric. Reports* (*Rept.* by Walker, 1795, p. 48) "the land is generally enclosed, though there are many small common fields or lands lying intermixed in small pieces," the larger mostly towards Cambridge. *Agric. Report*, 1804, "a county so generally inclosed of old time," p. 48, "an old inclosed county," p. 53.

The explanation of the course of inclosure in this county is not difficult. In large measure covered with royal forest, inclosure as the land came into use was fairly complete. As to time, probably much took place before the sixteenth, but judging from Leland some further clearance may have occurred in that century. But it was simple. The north, where the conditions were different, remains fairly open, more so in the north-east than the north-west. The whole county is singularly void of common inclosures. The land in early times was mainly in the possession of the crown, a feature which Chauncey emphasises.

BEDFORD.

Bedford evidently came very completely under the common field system. Most writers combine in regarding it as in the main champion. Thus Speed (*Geography*, p. 41) describes it as a plain and champion county, it was generally champion; "Bedford is a place of champion country" (Harl. M.S. 5190); generally the county is champion (*Geographical Descrip.*, 1615); this county is generally champion, but in many places intermixed with meadows and pasture grounds (*England's Remarques*, 1678). Camden (i. 323) says the north was most plentiful and wooded, a feature which is repeated more than a century after in the *Dict. Urbanicum*, which states that the south was leaner than the north, the latter being most fruitful and better wooded. The later descriptions, especially that in *England's Remarques*, suggest some extension of inclosure.

Turning to Leland and Ogilby, this general impression is both confirmed and modified, because amplified. Leland (i. 112) gives inclosures south of Ampthill and the north evidently in open field. The south abutting on Buckingham is open, but of course its soil is characteristic and distinct. Ogilby's maps show that the main and northern districts were mainly in open field, a feature very much emphasised in the road from Oxford to Cambridge (p. 159 and plate); the area of inclosed land south of Ampthill is enlarged and there are intermixed inclosures in the north as well as the south. About Biggleswade he mentions a good deal of open meadow and pasture.

The inclosures under act, which amount to 44 per cent. in the table, are uniformly of a good size, the average acreage before 1800 being 1778 acres, and after that date about 1250. They were in fact fairly large parish inclosures. The Ampthill district was rather below the main part of the county, while the district by Leighton Buzzard is greatly lower. There is but little inclosure of common by itself.

The record seems fairly clear. The county, with the exception of the south-west, came into general agricultural occupation. There was, no doubt, some inclosure in the fifteenth and sixteenth centuries (see Dr. Gay's lists, percentage of land recorded 1517, is 1·37, and in 1607, 3·32, a somewhat marked figure) which occasioned complaint. Strype also includes Bedford in his list of counties affected by inclosure. Probably some of this inclosure was in the Ampthill neighbourhood. During the seventeenth century the progress of inclosure in the county at large was of a very ordinary character and does not obtain particular mention, though it led to such notices as that in *England's Remarques* and is fairly shown in Ogilby. To this century, however, the inclosure of the south-west, which was lean and under little cultivation, may be assigned. Ogilby's plates may be taken as showing that it occurred, at any rate in large measure, before his time, and on the whole Leland's accounts, as far as they go, indicate open in the south. If this be correct, and if due allowance be made for the inclosures in the late fifteenth and the sixteenth centuries, the inclosure of the county is well indicated, though the whole area is not as fully accounted for as in some other cases.

CAMBRIDGE.

Of Cambridge the *Geog. Description* says the south champion, the north fenny; Speed, *Geography*, p. 37, writes that the south is champion with corn. The *Dict. Urbanicum* describes the county as for the most part a pleasant, fruitful and champion country. The north was fenny and very obviously affected by fen reclamations, while the south, but for sporadic inclosure, remained till late in open arable, save in the neighbourhood of Newmarket, where open grass predominated. The open arable forms a very marked feature in Ogilby's description of the roads passing through the middle and south; he, too, notes the prevalence of heath, grass and furze land in the region of Newmarket. Cambridge occupies a position very low down in the list of inclosure, 1517 (Dr. Gay, ·25).

The inclosures under acts are common field in the south and of a large size. In the north there are commons, some of which appear to have been small; some were very large indeed.

There seems little, if any, ground for assuming any considerable early inclosure in Cambridge; on the contrary, the land when at all suitable remained in large stretches of open but little intermixed with much inclosure.

During the seventeenth century, to judge from the conditions described by Ogilby, some inclosure began to appear, as contrasted with the little shown by Leland, though not in sufficient amount to alter the general description. In the north, however, the great fen inclosure occurred, possibly affecting the use of land previously in cultivation. The Cambridge inclosures are very late in the eighteenth century, the land probably not requiring or responding to the new root crops and not promising much by conversion. In other words, the motive of change was wanting.

Evidently the inclosure of the north, amounting to a reclamation, covered the greater part of that region, and if allowance be made for this, the inclosure of this county is fairly complete.

HUNTINGDON.

Information as to the progress of inclosure in Huntingdon is scarce. The county figures high in the list of compositions for inclosure (Petty Bag, *Misc. Roll* 20) in the seventeenth century, and letters were addressed to the Sheriffs in 1630-1. In the *Dict. Urbanicum*, the N.E. described as fenny but yielding plenty of grass, while the rest is fruitful of corn. According to Ogilby much of the open in the north seems to have been in grass; in the south arable predominates. The N.E. probably affected by the reclamation of the fens and consequent inclosures.

In Ogilby's time there was inclosure obviously, but only in a moderate amount. It seems to have been rather more inclosed than was Cambridge, save in the St. Ives district, which approximates to the adjacent county, coming under late inclosure in the eighteenth century. On the other hand the north-east resembles the neighbouring districts of Northampton, namely, Oundle and Peterborough. Its time of inclosure was earlier in the century.

Huntingdon would seem to have escaped any important inclosure before the seventeenth century. The north was fenny, the south in open field. During that century, however, change appears. The north and north-west were affected in the fen reclamations. On the other hand, as pointed out above, inclosure from which depopulation was apprehended took place.

At the beginning of the eighteenth century, the extreme south was largely in open field, namely, to some 58 per cent., probably under conditions resembling those of Cambridge. Though there is not much reason for estimating previous inclosure as high, this region may be said to be fairly well though not completely accounted for. Its inclosure may be placed later than that of the north.

NORTHAMPTON.

Northamptonshire was evidently a long settled and prosperous agricultural county (for populousness see maps in the *Valor Eccle-*

siastica), lying largely in common field from early times as far as the main part was concerned; but this description is less true of the north-eastern districts, namely those about Kettering, Oundle, and Peterborough; the last of these being partly touched by the fens, while over the other two there was much early forest (Pearson's Historical Maps). It is not surprising to find that these three districts were less affected by the inclosure acts than the rest of the county where the percentage of land inclosed is very much higher. It would be difficult to date the clearing of the forest district and the consequent appearance of this land in cultivation. Probably some took place before the seventeenth century, but Morton certainly suggests some as occurring in that century and so occasioning an inclosure of open arable and its conversion to pasture (Morton, *Northampton*, p. 14). There is little to be gathered from Leland, but according to Ogilby there was a large amount of inclosed road, and therefore it may be estimated a not inconsiderable amount of inclosed country in the more northerly part, less perhaps in the extreme north-east, near Peterborough. There was some forest land south-west of Northampton in Salcey and Whittlebury, and possibly the special rights of common allowed on account of injury by the deer (Morton, *Northampton*, p. 11) gives rise to some inclosure of common by act in this district. As a general rule forests when taken into cultivation are little affected by common.

The existence of inclosure in the fifteenth and sixteenth centuries occasioning difficulty and complaint is definitely shown by Dr. Gay's record of inclosure amounting to 2·21 per cent. in 1517, and of inclosure inquired into in 1607 amounting to 4·30 per cent., to which Strype in his account of the commissions, and Stow in his account of the disturbance, add important evidence. But the inclosures beginning at the end of the sixteenth and occurring in the seventeenth seem to have been of greater extent than these of an earlier date. Speed (*Geography*) and Camden, however, while considering the county mainly champion, complain of the number of sheep, a complaint which Morton at a later date considered greatly overstated. According to Hayward's *Life of Edward VI.* the country was open. There is complaint in the tract *Certain causes gathered together*. But though there is some difference as to the estimate of the inclosures early in this century, the inclosures at the close, as also those during the seventeenth century, are abundantly testified to. They lead to the tumults in Northampton (see *inter alia P.C. Records*, James I., Vol. iii. p. 111), and that they were extensive is shown by the position of Northampton in Dr. Gay's record. During the seventeenth century letters are addressed to the Sheriff of this county among others, in 1630, as to effect of inclosure; the county stands high in the list of compositions for inclosure, 1635-8 (Petty Bag, *Misc. Roll* 20); in the tract *Considerations*, 1653, a reference is made to Bentham's assertion as to the depopulation in eleven manors in this county; Brydges gives several instances of inclosure; Aubrey refers to inclosures in Northampton (*Nat. History of Wilts*, p. 104). There is further evidence as to the fact of inclosures existing at the end of the century. Morton is quite definite; Lawrence (1726) says there was some inclosure and some open; while further, in the *Agric. Report*, there is mention of 150,000 acres as estimated in ancient inclosures. Again, not only may Ogilby be cited as to the existence of inclosure, but the comparison between his routes and those of Leland assigns some part to the period intervening. The extreme north-east formed part of the fen inclosures. It was to the new use of the area added from woodland rather than of that reclaimed from the sea that Morton attributed some part of the scattered inclosures in the rest of the county.

Of course there is no doubt that the major part was still open, and mainly in open of the general common field type, during and also at the close of this century. That much soil was champion or mostly so is substantiated by the *Geographical Description*, *England's Remarques*, by the Lansdown MS. of 1607, and by the *Dictionarium Urbanicum*, the latter calling it rich fruitful champion, populous, and replenished with towns. It was probably one of the counties adjacent to Leicester alluded to in the *Vindication*, 1656, as open and being affected by the movement to inclose. Morton says the fielden was larger in extent than all the other kinds of land.

The large number of inclosures proceeding in Northampton under act, and prior to 1760, namely 7 per cent., points to a necessary allowance for inclosures by agreement in the early part of the eighteenth century. On the whole inclosure by act in the districts of Oundle, Thrapston, Kettering, and particularly Peterborough were later than elsewhere. Taken as a whole the inclosures were large, averaging 1704 acres before 1800, and afterwards 1888. The type is the same as in Bedford for instance. The total percentage is 54.3.

Making allowance for the inclosure in the fifteenth and sixteenth centuries, and for the greater movement in the seventeenth, both in the north-west and also generally, and for the probable agreements in the first part of the eighteenth, the area is very fully accounted for.

BUCKINGHAM.

According to most writers Buckingham in the sixteenth as well as the seventeenth century differed very considerably in its characteristic. Camden (i. 314) and Speed (*Geography*) both describe it as divided by the Chilterns, the former adding that the vale land to the north was "almost one continued plain, with a clayey, strong, rich soil and rich meadows feeding innumerable flocks of sheep." Much the same is said in the *Geographical Description*, though there tillage is mentioned in the vale as well as meadows and pastures. This account is echoed in *England's Remarques*. The existence of arable in open field in the seventeenth century is fully substantiated by Ogilby's descriptions. In this region there is considerable inclosure by act, though that in the district of Newport Pagnell is almost certainly outside the land alluded to. On the other hand, in the southern part there were in early times extensive woodlands sloping to the Thames valley. This land in Ogilby's time was mainly inclosed, and there is little inclosure by act recorded. This, however, does not hold good of the extreme south with its alluvial round Eton and near the Staines district of Middlesex.

In the northern and bigger half of the county the inclosure by act in the eighteenth century begins in the middle of the century, while in the southern part it is late, largely in the nineteenth century.

It is impossible to say when the woodlands in the south were cleared. Probably this inclosure from the wild state and addition to the cultivated area was early, and it may be that it was a cause leading to the inclosure mentioned in the sixteenth century.

Buckingham stands high among counties in 1517, and is mentioned in 1607 (see Dr. Gay's lists, respectively 2·08 and 1·48). The inclosures receive mention by Strype and are referred to by both Stow and Speed in their accounts of the early risings. Further, Buckingham is one of the three counties, the others being Northampton and Oxford, in respect of which inclosure is censured by the author of *Certain causes gathered together, etc.*, 98-101.

A comparison, admittedly imperfect and difficult, between Leland and Ogilby suggests a decided increase, but it is impossible to say if this was largely in the seventeenth century. As it certainly began in the sixteenth it was probably early. There are, however, some scattered inclosures in the seventeenth.

Taking the sixteenth century inclosure as considerable, and making an addition for the wild inclosure then or earlier, both from woods and from among the hills of the Chilterns, the course in Buckingham is very well indicated. A careful distinction must be observed between the south and the north. The inclosures in the larger and north part of the county on the average are much nearer to the acreage of the parishes affected than in the south, a circumstance which points to more early inclosure in the south.

OXFORD.

In certain respects there is a considerable similarity between Oxford and Buckingham, especially in the south, where like conditions prevailed and where apparently as a result a like paucity in inclosure under act in the eighteenth century occurs. In Banbury the amount 58 per cent. is unusually high. On the west in the region between Chipping Norton and Witney lay Wychwood Forest, and just here eighteenth century inclosure is slight. The percentage of land inclosed in Chipping Norton is comparatively low, 24 per cent., but in Witney 45 per cent. Comparing Ogilby and Leland, there is a distinct increase in the period. In Dr. Gay's list for 1517 the percentage returned is 2·45. Oxford is alluded to by Strype, and complaint made in the tract *Certain causes gathered together, etc.* There is little trace of the movement in the seventeenth century. Oxford occurs in the list of compositions but not conspicuously, and it may be that some of the wave affecting Northampton and Leicester touched the

Banbury district. The Preface to Halhead was contributed by Joshua Sprigge of Banbury. In this north region the comparison between Leland and Ogilby lends some corroboration.

During the fifteenth and sixteenth centuries, forest inclosure seems to have affected the south with some considerable result on neighbouring common field. At this time, too, the west was also affected partly by clearances of wood which had lingered on, but partly owing to the tendency to some inclosure in the neighbourhood of the west country wool towns.

Of any movement in the seventeenth century comparatively little trace exists, and the north at any rate was mainly in open field when the eighteenth century inclosures begin, waste and common existing chiefly round Oxford.

DERBY.

In this county several diverse factors were present, and it seems very doubtful if any part came into early agricultural settlement with the exception of the south. Blome, in 1673, speaks of the south and east parts which are generally inclosed and improved, but a distinction must be made between these. The east shared almost certainly in the forest condition of the neighbouring district of Nottingham, and in the act inclosure of the eighteenth century plays little part. There are a fair number in the south. The east, no doubt, was fruitful in the seventeenth century, but it may be doubted if there had been much, if any, inclosure of common field. The west was more hilly and not so fruitful, according to the *Dictionarium Urbanicum*, but while the north is bare of act inclosures, in and about Bakewell these are very evident. In 1517 Derby is mentioned, but only to a small extent (in Gay's list ·10). Letters as to inclosure are sent to the sheriff in 1630. Inclosure of common is fairly conspicuous in the north in the eighteenth century.

As the forest yielded, very probably in the sixteenth century, there was inclosure in the east. At the same time some inclosure, and this may have been of common field, in the south. Some inclosure goes on in the seventeenth century, probably in the south. In the north the land was probably much in waste, save in the valleys, till the eighteenth century; but a great deal was several, whether hedged and walled or not.

STAFFORD.

In this county a distinction must be drawn between the land in the south and in the north, or according to Plot, that north-east of the Trent and that to the south-west. The north or north-east was mainly heath and woodland (Plot, 107), the moorlands lying more to the north. This corresponds with Speed (*Geography*, 67) who says that there was wood to the north and some in the middle. This middle portion included Needwood Forest and Cannock Chace with its surrounding old woodland and waste. The south had more arable than the north, where it was very scant (Plot, 109). There was good feeding land in the valleys of the moorland, and the dairy country within reach of Uttoxeter was evidently rich. According to the *Dict. Urb.* the south had plenty of grass and corn. Plot tells us (and is quoted by Houghton) that the clay land in tillage was usually in open field (p. 340), and that heath land was never inclosed except when put into tillage for five years or so, after which it reverted to commons. Houghton and Blith speak of the high yield of the inclosed arable. According to an estimate from Plot one-third of the county was commons. In the *Agric. Report* the amount of common and waste is put at 141,000 acres out of 780,000 acres.

According to Lawrence in 1726 there were both inclosed and common fields in the county.

Stafford is just mentioned in the list of inclosure in 1517, but with the negligible percentage of ·06.

Two things seem clear. The great amount of rough land unavailable for mixed or arable use precluded good early agricultural settlement, and its employment for dairy use made inclosing a frequent feature. Secondly, there was more appearance of common and common field in the latter part of the seventeenth and the beginning of the eighteenth than is accounted for by the recorded inclosures under act.

Much land was, doubtless, brought in from the wild, but largely for pasture or temporary use; and probably the common fields, never very widespread, tended to be diminished. The nature of the soil and its profit under inclosure, even for arable, further encouraged such inclosure, at any rate during the seventeenth century. Probably inclosure at the junction of the seventeenth and eighteenth centuries was very considerable, and was instigated by the dairying tendency. In the more extreme south the industrial activity further accelerated inclosure before Plot's day as well as later.

But a good deal of the unused moorland in the north remains to be taken in by act, which accounts for the higher inclosure of land under some common right, *i.e.*, commons, in Leek (18 per cent.) and Cheadle (13 per cent.). In the Pottery District there was some common inclosure but no open field shown in act.

The record is that of a county with continuous additions into several from a wild or nearly wild condition. Further, the superior advantages for pasture and dairy land must be borne in mind.

NOTTINGHAM.

Many sporadic inclosures (Thoroton, *Notts*), in seventeenth and also in sixteenth century, especially E. and N.E. In seventeenth century letters sent to the sheriffs (*P.C. Reg.*), and appearance in composition. Also, to judge from Ogilby, inclosures on wolds and in forest achieved at end of this century, but date uncertain. In Vale of Belvoir some few old inclosures, but it is mostly open (*Agric. Report*).

The distinction between the west and the east, insisted on elsewhere, must be borne in mind.

RUTLAND.

Specific facts as to the early condition or inclosure of this county are few. Some small amount of land (·55 per cent.) is denoted as inclosed in the returns of 1517. Taking Leland's route, open is marked where the character of the land is specified, and a comparison between his *Itinerary* and Ogilby leads to the conclusion that progress in inclosure had taken place. This may have been occasioned in part by some clearing and inclosure of woodland near the junction with Northampton. Certainly the land does not appear to have been bare of wood as in some very old open field districts. Compositions for inclosure were paid 1635-8. The *Dictionarium Urbanicum* mentions Rutland as having plenty of wood. Inclosure under act began early, leading to the assumption of inclosure by agreement in the first part of the eighteenth century. Then the movement dies down, to revive with very great vigour after 1790. The type of inclosure is that of the large general common field as in Northampton and Bedford, and it is worth noting that the percentage of land inclosed under act is lower on the side nearer to Northampton and especially close to Rockingham. It is probable that there was a good deal of early common field with some inclosure occurring in the sixteenth century; and that forest land was inclosed, as also some more common field in the seventeenth.

Adding to the 46·4 per cent. of land inclosed under act, that coming gradually into inclosed, and that inclosed from woodland, some fair general indication is given of the progress in this county.

LEICESTER.

There is little record of inclosure during the sixteenth century, at the end that county being reckoned as open. Burton, *Leicester*, calls it "almost all champion," and the same may be inferred from the Lansdown MS. In the *Geo. Description* it is called "a champion county." Leland states that the south and east are largely in champion, and the existence of cattle beyond the Wreak suggests inclosure in the north-west (*Geographical Description*).

During the seventeenth century considerable inclosure. Letters are addressed to the sheriffs (*P.C. Register*, C. I. vi. 199). Leicester prominent in the iist of compositions (Petty Bag, *Misc. Roll* 20). In the mid-century controversy Leicester figures, mentioned by Moore and also by Lee in *Vindication.* These appear to relate to inclosures in the south. The same is true of miscellaneous inclosures (*Bibl. Topogr.* (1678), vii. 616, 620, etc.), need of bringing up people for hedge breaking. Still according to Evelyn (*Diary*), much was open in south. From Ogilby, increase of inclosed land in S.E., but that still largely open.

The N.W. inclosures were probably directly from wood land and new land. Hence no record probable.

Leicester appears in both Dr. Gay's lists with 1.09 per cent. and 2.32 per cent. respectively. The difference in respect of inclosure from open field under act between districts on the west and the rest of the county is marked; and the inclosure from commons or wood by act in the former should be noted. Total inclosure under act, 47.5 per cent.

LINCOLN.

Lincolnshire was evidently a county in early and full agricultural settlement, with the conspicuous exception of certain large regions where the practice of agriculture was obstructed in the neighbourhood of the wolds or by fen and marshy land. The latter appears in large quantities in the south-east and the north-west. The former, the Holland fens, and the latter, mainly in and about the Isle of Axholme, were both the subject of drainage reclamation in the seventeenth century, and both differ from the bulk of the county in respect of inclosure by act in the eighteenth century. In both cases the amount of open field inclosure by act falls off comparatively, this being truer of the land immediately round the Wash. In the south-east, however, there is inclosure from common owing to land being left in common by the acts empowering the draining and improvement in the seventeenth century. The county was somewhat affected by inclosure in the fifteenth and sixteenth centuries, showing a small percentage in Dr. Gay's lists for 1517 (·29 per cent.), and being mentioned as affected in 1536 both by Stow and Speed. In the seventeenth century letters as to inclosure were sent to the sheriff, and the county stands high in the list of compositions (Petty Bag, *Misc. Roll* 20). A comparison of Ogilby with Leland points to an increase by the later date of land under inclosure on the west side of the county in the neighbourhood of Sleaford and Lincoln. The indication, however, is not precise. But Ogilby's description is useful for other regions. From Croyland to Boston the road is first open but by fen, then closed but crossing dikes, without reference to arable. From Boston to Lincoln the country along the road, which is unhedged, is first described as fenny. Nearer Lincoln it is arable. About Lincoln, especially to the north, there is much heath. In the inclosures under act two features are to be noted in addition to those referred to above. The land about the wolds displays a lower percentage of inclosure, especially of open field. It would be lower still in the more southern part of this region but for one big inclosure. In the second place, the Lincolnshire common field inclosures are large, in a great many cases the lands of the parish.

Some inclosure was no doubt effected in Lincolnshire in the fifteenth and sixteenth centuries. More follows in the first part of the seventeenth century, but the important feature of that century was not this earlier general and more normal inclosure, but the great reclamations effected from the fens, whereby much land was brought within the area of cultivation, and the use made of other land affected. Some inclosure from the wild state is also suggested by the subsequent history of the wolds. In the eighteenth century regular farming inclosure ensues about the middle of the century, that in the region of the wolds occurring somewhat later. Leaving on one side the wold district and the land between the wolds and the sea, the rest of the county seems fairly well accounted for. Possibly the region round the wolds may have been considerably affected, as suggested, by inclosure from the wild state.

DURHAM.

That part of Durham was under arable cultivation in the sixteenth century, at any rate, is proved by the description of the east as richest and most champion both by Speed (*Geography*, p. 85) and the author of the *Geographical Description*. Blome in 1673 speaks of the east as most champion and the south as most fertile. Open arable is shown in Ogilby (Plate to 197) on the road from Whitby, shortly after its entry in this county, and also towards the north. According to Lawrence (1726) "nine parts in ten are already inclosed, and consequently improved in their value and rents to a degree almost incredible. Accordingly the more northern parts are following their example"; while the *Agricultural Report* of 1794 says, "the lands or common fields of townships were for the most part inclosed soon after the restoration." He adds that intercommoning persisted in ancient inclosure. It is possible, of course, that this was true only of some. The west and the north was in moor, and consequently show big inclosures from common by act. But the east and south are free from open field inclosure by act, and with little exception from inclosure from common.

Inclosure from common field, and probably from common, evidently took place in the latter half of the seventeenth century, and in the early years of the eighteenth. Gradually it spread upwards to the north. It was evidently very thorough; but on the other hand it may be doubted if the land even in the part affected, the south-east and the east, was at all uniformly under arable in open field. There were woods and hilly country. The land of the county is only partly accounted for. No doubt most land was early separated into private ownership from a wild state, and possibly some actually inclosed.

CUMBERLAND AND WESTMORELAND.

As to the condition of these counties there is little specific information. In both a considerable amount of inclosed road is shown by Ogilby, the more particularly in the case of Westmoreland. In both there are some instances of open field inclosure by act in the eighteenth century. In both, and especially in Cumberland, inclosure from common or waste by act occurs to a fair amount.

Taking into account the physical circumstances of the county and the above facts, the probable explanation is as follows. Much of the land lay in a wild state, from which inclosure took place, some after the seventeenth century, and some before; very probably in certain districts at a much earlier date. Coupled with this would be inclosure by approvement when such a method was in active force. As has been explained, this tends to bring about concurrent inclosure of land used for arable. By the eighteenth century few traces remain of the common fields which had never been great in extent; and much of the wild land was in separate individual ownership, though some to a fair extent is under common right. The few common fields are inclosed, while inclosure of common by act begins. This latter process, however, does not become important until after 1800.

In these counties, as indeed in some other regions, particularly in the north, the position of the common field was different from that which it occupied, for instance, in the Midlands, in Lincoln, in the East Riding, and in other cases. In place of being the basis of the system by which people lived and were employed, it was a special element, though of course important. In other words, the land was on the whole unsuited to arable cultivation, and what arable there was lay somewhat apart, sometimes in a common field, sometimes by reason of the scattered condition in small private inclosures.

NORTHUMBERLAND.

Facts about Northumberland are very scarce. Ogilby's map suggests a great preponderance of open land, while the inclosures under act are of small amount, only some 12·5 per cent. From this it would seem probable that much inclosure took place about the end of the seventeenth century or by agreement in the eighteenth. That the latter was taking place seems shown in the case of commons by the *Agricultural Report* in 1805, which, after stating that the greatest part of the commons capable of being converted into profitable tillage land have been enclosed within the last thirty years, estimates them at near 120,000 acres. This amount is very far in excess of that inclosed by act up to that date. A large portion of Northumberland was naturally unsuited to agriculture, and it is possible that the process of inclosure treated of under Durham extended into Northumberland. There is more common field inclosure under act in Northumberland than in any other of the four northern countries.

The clearing, which gradually occurred with its necessary addition to the cultivated land, may have furnished the example for like inclosure of land in open.

All that can be suggested is that there was more inclosure during the eighteenth century than is accounted for by that under act, and that quite possibly some inclosure occurred in the latter seventeenth century.

APPENDIX B

TABULAR STATEMENT INDICATING PROGRESS OF INCLOSURE

	Condition as to Forest, Fen, etc., etc.	List 1517 (Gay).	Sixteenth Century.	List 1607 (Gay).	Seventeenth Century.	1700–1870. Early.	1700–1870. Recorded Inclosure. p.c. Total.	1700–1870. Recorded Inclosure. p.c. Open Field.
Bedford, - -	—	1.37	Inclosure (*a*), prob. central.	3.32	—	—	44	44
Berkshire, - -	Hills S.	1.39	Incl. N.W. (*a*).	—	Inclosures (*g*), N.W.	—	34	30
Buckingham, -	Forest S., Chilterns.	2.08	Incl. (*a*),(*b*),(*d*), prob. Chilterns, etc.	1.48	Incl., probably N.	—	35.5	34.5
Cambridge, -	Fen N.	.25	—	—	Incl. fen.	—	38	34.5
Cheshire, - -	Old woods.	.01	—	—	—	—	3	Some
Cornwall, - -	—	—	—	—	Incl. early of commons.	—	5	—
Cumberland, -	Moors.	—	—	—	—	—	23.5	4
Derby, - - -	Hills and moors, some forest E.	.10	—	—	Incl. (*e*).	—	21	16
Devonshire, -	—	—	—	—	—	—	1.5	—
Dorset, - - -	Woods N. and downs S.	—	—	—	—	—	13	8
Durham, - -	Moors, esp. W.	—	—	—	Incl. (*l*), S. and E., then N.	Some N.	17.5	Some
Essex, - - -	Epping Forest.	.31	Incl. (*a*), (*b*), (*c*).	—	Probably some W.	—	3	1.5
Gloucester, - -	Forest of Dean.	.46	Incl. (*a*).	—	Incl. (*e*).	—	18.5	17.5
Hampshire, - -	New Forest, other woods.	.10	Incl. (*a*).	—	Incl. some (*g*).	—	11	6
Hereford, - -	Hills and wild land.	.22	—	—	—	—	4.5	3.5
Hertford, - -	Forest, but not N.	—	—	—	Incl. (*f*).	—	15	11.5
Huntingdon, -	Some fen N.	—	—	—	Incl. (*e*), (*f*), and fen N.E.	—	55.5	55.5
Kent, - - -	Weald and downs.	—	Incl. (*a*), (*b*), (*c*).	—	—	—	.5	—
Lancashire, - -	Moor N.E.	—	—	—	—	—	5.5	—
Leicester, - -	Some forest W.	1.09	Incl. (*a*).	2.32	Incl. (*e*), (*f*), (*g*), (*h*).	—	47.5	41.5

Lincoln, - -	Fens and wolds.	.29	Incl. (*b*), (*c*).	—	Incl. (*e*), (*f*), also fen S.E. and N.W.	Early agreement	37	29
Middlesex, - -	Chaces, etc., N.	1.52	Incl. probable.	—	—	—	26.5	19
Norfolk, - -	Fen extreme W.	.71	Incl. (*a*), (*b*), (*c*).	—	Incl. fen.	In. N.W.	26	19
Northampton, -	Some fen N.E.	2.21	Incl. (*a*), (*b*), (*d*).	4.30	Incl. (*e*), (*f*), (*g*), (*h*), also fen.	Early agreement	54	51
Northumberland,	Moors.	—	—	—	—	—	12.5	1.5
Nottingham, -	Forest W.	.83	—	—	Incl. (*e*), (*f*).	—	32	27.5
Oxford, - - -	Chilterns, some wood S.	2.45	Incl. (*a*), (*d*).	—	—	—	43.5	40.5
Rutland, - -	Some wood.	.55	—	—	Incl. (*f*).	Early agreement	46	46
Shropshire, - -	Moors and hills.	.22	—	—	—	—	6	Some
Somerset, - -	Moor, hills, and marsh.	.06	Incl. (*a*), (*b*), (*c*).	—	Incl. (*e*), some draining.	—	12.5	1.5
Stafford, - -	Hills and woods, esp. W.	.07	—	—	Some probable.	—	12	6.5
Suffolk, - - -	—	—	Incl. (*b*), (*c*).	—	Probably some W.	—	6	3.5
Surrey, - - -	Weald.	—	Some prob. (*a*).	—	Prob. some weald.	—	10	6
Sussex, - - -	Weald and downs.	—	Some prob. (*a*).	—	Prob. some weald.	—	3.5	1.5
Warwick, - -	Woods N. & N.W.	1.68	Incl. (*a*).	.93	Incl. (*h*), (*k*).	Early agreement	25	23
Westmoreland, -	Moors.	—	—	—	—	—	16	Some
Wiltshire, - -	Some forest and hills.	—	—	—	Incl. (*e*), (*g*), esp. N.W. (*j*).	—	26	22.5
Worcester, - -	Some wood N.W.	—	—	—	—	—	18	13
Yorkshire,* - -	—	—	—	—	—	—	—	—

(*a*) Strype.
(*b*) Stow.
(*c*) Speed.
(*d*) *Certain causes gathered together, etc.*
(*e*) Privy Council Letters.
(*f*) List of Compositions.
(*g*) Comparison of Leland and Ogilby.
(*h*) Controversy, mid seventeenth century.
(*j*) Aubrey.
(*k*) Standish.
(*l*) *Agric. Rep.*, 1794, p. 43.
* References too indefinite.

APPENDIX C

EIGHTEENTH CENTURY AND NINETEENTH CENTURY TO 1870.

Percentage of Inclosure by Act in various Counties according to Registration Districts, common field and common distinguished (approximate only).

* Less than 1 p.c.

County (Registration).	Registration District.	Common Field.		Common.	
		P.c. of Land.	P.c. of town-ships in which some in-closure.	P.c. of Land.	P.c. of town-ships in which some in-closure.
Bedford.	Bedford, - - -	46	59	—	—
	Biggleswade, - -	49	48	1	3
	Ampthill, - -	39	68	*	5
	Woburn, - - -	42	56	—	—
	Leighton Buzzard, -	15	43	8	7
	Luton, - - -	34	41	—	—
Berkshire.	Newbury, - -	33	44	1	11
	Hungerford, - -	17	33	—	—
	Farringdon, - -	31	36	1	2
	Abingdon, - -	43	31	3	1
	Wantage, - -	28	52	4	9
	Wallingford, - -	50	38	*	3
	Bradfield, - -	16	32	4	10
	Reading, - - -	—	—	—	—
	Wokingham, - -	18	33	—	—
	Cookham, - -	15	33	—	—
	Easthampton, - -	22	40	—	—
	Windsor, - - -	6	8	29	8
Buckingham.	Amersham, - -	4	16	2	16
	Eton, - - -	31	42	2	10
	Wycombe, - -	24	38	1	13
	Aylesbury, - -	43	50	*	2
	Winslow, - -	55	83	4	5
	Newport Pagnell, -	63	52	1	2
	Buckingham, - -	29	30	*	3

County (Registration).	Registration District.	Common Field.		Common.	
		P.c. of Land.	P.c. of town-ships in which some in-closure.	P.c. of Land.	P.c. of town-ships in which some in-closure.
Cambridge.	Caxton, - - -	51	65	—	—
	Chesterton, - -	62	78	*	3
	Cambridge, - -	—	—	—	—
	Linton, - - -	61	63	—	—
	Newmarket, - -	36	51	—	—
	Ely, - - -	10	27	2	13
	North Witchford, -	4	14	28	57
	Whittlesey, - -	—	—	6	100
	Wisbech, - -	1	10	4	35
Derby.	Shardlow, - -	32	41	4	9
	Derby, - - -	—	—	—	—
	Belper, - - -	4	8	8	20
	Ashbourne, - -	21	12	25	6
	Chesterfield, - -	13	31	11	20
	Bakewell, - -	30	17	11	12
	Chapel le Frith, -	1	5	1	5
	Hayfield, - - -	—	—	5	11
Dorset.	Shaftesbury, - -	5	14	4	24
	Sturminster, - -	—	—	2	18
	Blandford, - -	15	23	2	3
	Wimborne, - -	10	18	2	7
	Poole, - - -	—	—	40	25
	Wareham, - -	2	3	3	16
	Weymouth, - -	26	41	3	6
	Dorchester, - -	13	24	3	9
	Sherborne, - -	—	—	1	3
	Beaminster, - -	*	3	3	16
	Bridport, - - -	3	21	—	—
Essex.	Epping, - - -	1	8	3	8
	Ongar, - - -	—	—	2	11
	Romford, - -	—	—	2	30
	Orsett, - - -	—	—	*	5
	Billericay, - -	—	—	2	19
	Chelmsford, - -	—	—	1	9
	Rochford, - -	—	—	*	3
	Maldon, - - -	—	—	*	9
	Tendring, - -	—	—	*	18
	Colchester, - -	—	—	2	12
	Lexden, - - -	—	—	3	14
	Witham, - - -	—	—	*	5
	Halstead, - -	—	—	—	—
	Braintree, - -	—	—	*	7

County (Registration).	Registration District.	Common Field.		Common.	
		P.c. of Land.	P.c. of townships in which some inclosure.	P.c. of Land.	P.c. of townships in which some inclosure.
Essex (*continued*).	Dunmow,	—	—	1	11
	Saffron Walden,	22	45	—	—
Gloucester.	Bristol,	—	—	—	—
	Clifton,	2	5	4	10
	Chipping Sodbury,	20	21	1	17
	Thornbury,	1	3	4	12
	Dursley,	3	18	*	9
	Westbury-on-Severn,	2	5	*	18
	Newent,	3	13	*	9
	Gloucester,	28	17	1	7
	Wheatenhurst,	20	30	5	5
	Stroud,	1	10	*	5
	Tetbury,	25	46	—	—
	Cirencester,	17	29	*	10
	Northleach,	28	46	—	—
	Stow-on-Wold,	40	62	*	4
	Winchcombe,	27	41	2	3
	Cheltenham,	13	23	—	—
	Tewkesbury,	25	34	—	—
Hampshire.	Havant,	—	—	3	16
	Portsea Island,	2	14	2	14
	Alverstoke,	—	—	—	—
	Fareham,	4	20	10	20
	Isle of Wight,	—	—	—	—
	Lymington,	—	—	3	18
	Christchurch,	2	33	6	33
	Ringwood,	9	25	3	12
	Fordingbridge,	—	—	*	7
	New Forest,	2	4	2	10
	Southampton,	—	—	—	—
	South Stoneham,	—	—	12	46
	Romsey,	8	15	6	23
	Stockbridge,	10	35	—	—
	Winchester,	4	12	8	10
	Droxford,	*	9	24	54
	Catherington,	—	—	—	—
	Petersfield,	—	—	12	69
	Alresford,	3	10	5	5
	Alton,	4	5	3	25
	Hartley-Wintney,	2	5	6	39
	Basingstoke,	9	12	2	13
	Whitchurch,	2	12	—	—
	Andover,	16	33	2	3
	Kingsclere,	8	26	3	14

County (Registration).	Registration District.	Common Field.		Common.	
		P.c. of Land.	P.c. of townships in which some inclosure.	P.c. of Land.	P.c. of townships in which some inclosure.
HEREFORD.	Ledbury, - - -	8	31	*	5
	Ross, - - -	—	—	1	9
	Hereford, - -	4	9	1	5
	Weobley, - - -	4	18	1	15
	Bromyard, - -	1	5	*	9
	Leominster, - -	5	10	*	10
HERTFORD.	Ware, - - -	7	20	1	20
	Bishop Stortford, -	10	22	—	—
	Royston, - - -	49	55	—	—
	Hitchin, - - -	21	39	—	—
	Hertford, - -	12	38	—	—
	Hatfield, - - -	2	12	7	13
	St. Albans, - -	—	—	—	—
	Watford, - - -	1	22	1	22
	Hemel Hempstead, -	—	—	—	—
	Berkhampstead, -	14	33	4	17
HUNTINGDON.	Huntingdon, - -	40	52	*	[2]
	St. Ives, - - -	48	52	—	—
	St. Neots, - -	58	80	—	—
LEICESTER.	Lutterworth, - -	25	32	4	5
	Market Harborough,	39	47	1	3
	Billesdon, - -	25	33	—	—
	Blaby, - - -	49	48	—	—
	Hinkley, - - -	31	31	—	—
	Market Bosworth, -	14	35	17?	?
	Ashby de la Zouch, -	10	27	12?	?
	Loughborough, -	33	48	19?	?
	Barrow-upon-Soar, -	52	52	—	—
	Leicester, - -	—	—	—	—
	Melton Mowbray, -	31	41	2	1
LINCOLN.	Stamford, - -	51	45	—	—
	Bourn, - - -	34	38	13	8
	Spalding, - -	12	25	5	16
	Holbeach, - -	—	—	7	31
	Boston, - - -	25	22	9	21
	Sleaford, - - -	31	25	4	8
	Grantham, - -	42	41	1	2
	Lincoln, - - -	39	26	1	3
	Horncastle, - -	44	38	*	1
	Spilsby, - - -	21	31	20	3
	Louth, - - -	27	23	*	5

County (Registration).	Registration District.	Common Field.		Common.	
		P.c. of Land.	P.c. of townships in which some inclosure.	P.c. of Land.	P.c. of townships in which some inclosure.
Lincoln (*continued*).	Caistor, - - -	26	28	9	8
	Glanford Brigg, -	38	37	10	9
	Gainsborough, -	25	25	3	1
Middlesex.	Staines, - - -	45	76	*	?
	Uxbridge, - -	29	60	1	10
	Brentford, - -	4	18	39	18
	Hendon, - - -	16	44	*	?
	Barnet, - - -	1	10	9	20
	Edmonton, - -	11	25	1	8
Norfolk.	Flegg, - - -	55	59	4	4
	Tunstead, - -	24	35	14	22
	Erpingham, - -	4	13	12	12
	Aylsham, - -	8	18	5	11
	St. Faiths, - -	14	16	16	22
	Forehoe, - - -	32	32	4	21
	Henstead, - -	6	5	13	18
	Blofield, - - -	19	17	16	27
	Loddon, - - -	20	30	9	15
	Depwade, - -	20	30	5	17
	Guiltcross, - -	6	14	18	33
	Wayland, - -	35	60	3	16
	Mitford, - - -	30	46	3	7
	Walsingham, - -	20	26	2	7
	Docking, - - -	24	27	5	18
	Freebridge Lynn, -	14	25	*	3
	Downham, - -	25	40	5	11
	Swaffham, - -	25	29	6	6
	Thetford, - -	26	39	*	[8]
Nottingham.	East Retford, - -	35	46	3	4
	Worksop, - -	10	20	2	3
	Mansfield, - -	20	28	14	24
	Basford, - - -	20	43	6	19
	Radford, - - -	26	35	4	15
	Southwell, - -	25	25	1	5
	Newark, - - -	35	28	—	—
	Bingham, - -	33	39	7	7
Northampton.	Brackley, - -	47	55	—	—
	Towcester, - -	48	63	*	[4]
	Potterspury, - -	50	41	1	[5]
	Hardingstone, - -	42	45	8	5
	Northampton, - -	53	36	—	—

County (Registration).	Registration District.	Common Field.		Common.	
		P.c. of Land.	P.c. of town-ships in which some in-closure.	P.c. of Land.	P.c. of town-ships in which some in-closure.
Northampton (*continued*).	Daventry, - -	65	71	6	4
	Brixworth, - -	54	51	—	—
	Wellingborough, -	67	74	—	—
	Kettering, - -	39	43	—	—
	Thrapston, - -	56	84	—	—
	Oundle, - - -	40	39	3	3
	Peterborough, - -	34	39	—	—
Oxford.	Henley, - - -	9	20	1	17
	Thame, - - -	21	24	*	5
	Headington, - -	40	33	16	4
	Oxford, - - -	—	—	—	—
	Bicester, - - -	49	60	*	2
	Woodstock, - -	39	37	—	—
	Witney, - - -	39	48	6	7
	Chipping Norton, -	24	24	*	2
	Banbury, - - -	58	50	—	—
Rutland.	Oakham, - - -	39	40	—	—
	Uppingham, - -	37	31	*	3
Shropshire.	Ludlow, - - -	2	5	3	10
	Clun, - - -	—	—	14	20
	Church Stretton, -	—	—	8	14
	Cleobury Mortimer, -	—	—	1	29
	Bridgenorth, - -	—	—	9	13
	Shiffnal, - - -	1	5	*	15
	Madeley, - - -	—	—	2	8
	Atcham, - - -	—	—	2	6
	Shrewsbury, - -	—	—	—	—
	Oswestry, - -	—	—	1	11
	Ellesmere, - -	—	—	3	16
	Wem, - - -	—	—	9	30
	Market Drayton, -	—	—	5	38
	Wellington, - -	2	8	1	8
	Newport, - -	—	—	*	21
Somerset.	Williton, - - -	—	—	5	19
	Wellington, - -	—	—	2	20
	Taunton, - - -	—	—	8	18
	Bridgewater, - -	5	11	4	14
	Langport, - -	14	29	12	12
	Chard, - - -	—	—	9	21
	Yeovil, - - -	8	8	*	2
	Wincanton, - -	3	8	*	3

County (Registration).	Registration District.	Common Field.		Common.	
		P.c. of Land.	P.c. of townships in which some inclosure.	P.c. of Land.	P.c. of townships in which some inclosure.
Somerset (*continued*).	Frome, - - -	*	3	*	3
	Shepton Mallet, -	—	—	10	25
	Wells, - - -	4	5	21	50
	Axbridge, - -	6	10	14	50
	Clutton, - - -	—	—	5	10
	Bath, - - -	—	—	*	3
	Keynshaw, - -	—	—	1	10
	Bedminster, - -	6	17	7	26
Stafford.	Stafford, - - -	5	7	1	8
	Stone, - - -	2	9	8	9
	Newcastle, - -	2	5	8	11
	Wolstanton, - -	—	—	—	—
	Stoke, - - -	—	—	—	—
	Leek, - - -	6	10	18	10
	Cheadle, - - -	3	10	13	30
	Uttoxeter, - -	1	4	1	9
	Burton, - - -	1	3	12	8
	Tamworth, - -	1	6	2	9
	Lichfield, - -	3	5	12	17
	Penkridge, - -	1	8	7	9
	Wolverhampton, -	3	11	14	27
	Walsall, - - -	—	—	11	20
	West Bromwich, -	3	?	7	?
	Dudley, - - -	—	—	1	50
Suffolk.	Risbridge, - -	6	29	*	6
	Sudbury, - - -	1	2	2	2
	Cosford, - - -	*	3	1	4
	Thingoe, - - -	15	24	2	4
	Mildenhall, - -	13	56	7	12
	Stowe, - - -	—	—	1	23
	Hartsmere, - -	1	6	5	19
	Hoxne, - - -	—	—	3	20
	Bosmere, - - -	—	—	*	2
	Samford, - - -	—	—	1	7
	Ipswich, - - -	—	—	*	5
	Woodbridge, - -	—	—	1	6
	Plomesgate, - -	*	2	*	5
	Blything, - -	—	—	2	20
	Wangford, - -	1	3	2	18
	Mutford, - - -	3	12	18	32
Surrey.	Epsom, - - -	17	44	6	18
	Chertsey, - - -	9	55	—	—

County (Registration).	Registration District.	Common Field.		Common.	
		P.c. of Land.	P.c. of townships in which some inclosure.	P.c. of Land.	P.c. of townships in which some inclosure.
Surrey (*continued*).	Guildford, - -	1	7	3	11
	Farnham, - -	—	—	23	45
	Farnborough, - -	—	—	9	41
	Hambledon, - -	—	—	2	6
	Dorking, - - -	—	—	*	2
	Reigate, - - -	1	6	2	25
	Godstone, - -	—	—	3	21
	Croydon, - - -	20	9	*	18
	Kingston, - -	10	26	2	7
	Richmond, - -	*	20	*	20
Sussex.	Rye, - - -	—	—	—	—
	Hastings, - -	—	—	—	—
	Battle, - - -	—	—	—	—
	Eastbourne, - -	—	—	1	7
	Hailsham, - -	—	—	3	18
	Ticehurst, - -	—	—	—	—
	Uckfield, - - -	—	—	2	9
	East Grinstead, -	—	—	*	14
	Cuckfield, - -	—	—	1	26
	Lewes, - - -	3	2	1	7
	Brighton, - -	—	—	—	—
	Steyning, - -	—	—	1	8
	Horsham, - -	—	—	2	20
	Petworth, - -	—	—	*	40
	Thakeham, - -	2	6	5	40
	Worthing, - -	16	39	2	3
	Westhampnett, -	3	13	2	26
	Chichester, - -	2	3	—	—
	Midhurst, - -	—	—	5	23
	Westbourne, - -	10	33	1	8
Warwick.	Aston, - - -	10	21	*	7
	Meriden, - - -	11	50	·7	16
	Atherstone, - -	1	5	1	17
	Nuneaton, - -	19	28	3	27
	Foleshill, - -	38	46	—	—
	Rugby, - - -	32	41	2	2
	Solihull, - - -	2	36	4	27
	Warwick, - -	24	42	3	9
	Stratford, - -	31	52	—	—
	Alcester, - - -	15	40	5	14
	Shipston, - - -	41	50	—	—
	Southam, - - -	38	37	4	4

County (Registration).	Registration District.	Common Field.		Common.	
		P.c. of Land.	P.c. of town-ships in which some in-closure.	P.c. of Land.	P.c. of town-ships in which some in-closure.
Wiltshire.	Highworth, - -	32	36	—	—
	Cricklade, - -	22	40	—	—
	Malmesbury, - -	12	14	5	10
	Chippenham, - -	10	30	*	3
	Calne, - - -	13	27	2	9
	Marlborough, - -	19	31	5	5
	Devizes, - - -	29	27	3	6
	Melksham, - -	—	—	3	25
	Bradford, - -	—	—	7	12
	Westbury, - -	26	23	1	15
	Warminster, - -	54	56	—	—
	Pewsey, - - -	25	33	6	17
	Amesbury, - -	25	40	3	4
	Alderbury, - -	19	30	3	4
	Wilton, - - -	29	34	5	5
	Tisbury, - - -	7	20	2	5
	Mere, - - -	25	16	1	13
Worcester.	Stourbridge, - -	—	—	4	11
	Kidderminster, -	3	15	14	46
	Tenbury,- - -	—	—	1	7
	Martley, - - -	*	7	4	21
	Upton, - - -	8	20	4	13
	Evesham, - -	19	56	4	3
	Pershore, - -	41	59	1	2
	Droitwich, - -	3	12	5	13
	Bromsgrove, - -	*	6	5	47
	King's Norton, -	—	—	10	16

APPENDIX D[1]

Inclosures under Act in eighteenth and nineteenth centuries (to 1870). Percentage of land inclosed. First line, common field; second line, total common.

[c.f. = common field. T = total, *i.e.* common field and commons.]
* = a very small amount.

		1760.	'61-70.	'71-80.	'81-90.	91-00.	'01-10.	'11-20.	'21-70.	
Bedford, -	c.f.	.6	3	4	.6	16.9	11.4	2.8	4.7	44.0
	T.	.6	3	4	.6	16.9	11.5	2.8	4.7	44.1
Berkshire, -	c.f.	1.3	.8	4.3	1.1	2.6	9	8.4	2.7	30.2
	T.	1.4	.8	4.3	1.1	2.6	9.8	9.8	4.3	34.1
Bucks, -	c.f.	.5	6	6	1.5	6.9	6	2.8	5.1	34.8
	T.	.5	6	6	1.5	6.9	6 *	2.9	6	35.8
Cambridge, -	c.f.	—	.2	1.2	.4	5.5	11.9	5.5	9.8	34.5
	T.	—	2.4	1.4	.4	5.9	12	5.5*	10.8	38.4
Cheshire, -	c.f.	—	—	—	—	—	*	.4	—	.4
	T.	—	*	.3	—	1	.3	1.5	.3	3.4
Cornwall, -	c.f.	—	—	—	—	—	—	—	—	—
	T.	—	—	—	—	—	.2	.2	.4	.8
Cumberland,	c.f.	—	—	.2	—	—	—	*	*	.2
	T.	—	2.4	1.7	—	1	9.2	5.2	4.4	23.9
Derby, -	c.f.	.5	2.3	1.1	1.6	3.1	4.8	2	.8	16.2
	T.	.8	2.4	2.8	2	3.3	6	2.2	1.8	21.3
Devonshire,	c.f.	—	—	—	—	—	—	—	—	—
	T.	—	—	—	—	.1	.2	.4	1	1.7
Dorset, -	c.f.	.3	.8	.1	.7	1.8	2.2	.8	1.6	8.3
	T.	.3	1.1	.1	.7	2.1	4.4	1.5	3.1	13.3
Durham, -	c.f.	—	—	—	—	.1	—	*	—	.1
	T.	1.5	2.8	4.1	.8	5.8	1.6	.5	.7	17.8

[1] In this table the note on p. 107, calling attention to the land occupied by the actual villages, roads and inland waters, should be borne in mind.

		1760.	'61-70.	'71-80.	'81-90.	'91-00.	'01-10.	'11-20.	'21-70.	
Essex, - -	c.f	—	—	—	—	—	.7	.6	.6	1.9
	T.	—	*	*	—	*	.8	1.1	1.2	3.1
Gloucester, -	c.f.	1.7	1.7	4.2	.7	3.7	2.4	2	1.2	17.6
	T.	1.7	1.7	4.2	.7	3.7	2.5	2.3	1.9	18.7
Hampshire, -	c.f.	.8	—	.3	1.3	1.3	.8	.9	.6	6.0
	T.	1.1	—	.3	1.3	1.3	2	2	3.1	11.1
Hereford, -	c.f.	—	—	.1	—	.6	2	.8	*	3.5
	T.	—	—	.2	*	.6	2.2	1.3	.5	4.8
Hertford, -	c.f.	—	.9	.1	—	2.8	2.8	2.8	2.5	11.9
	T.	.3	.9	.4	—	3.7	3.4	2.9	3.6	15.2
Huntingdon,	c.f.	1.6	6.4	9.9	.8	11.4	15.8	5.4	4.5	55.8
	T.	1.6	6.4	9.9	.8	11.4	15.8	5.4	4.5	55.8
Kent, - -	c.f.	—	—	—	—	—	—	—	—	—
	T.	—	—	—	—	—	.1	.2	.2	.5
Lancashire, -	c.f.	—	—	—	—	*	—	—	—	
	T.	.4	.2	.2	.1	1.3	.7	1.3	1.5	5.7
Leicester, -	c.f.	7.1	13.7	10.4	3.6	4.8	1.9	*	.3	41.8
	T.	7.9	13.7	10.8	3.8	6	5.4	*	.3	47.9
Lincoln, -	c.f.	1.6	7.1	6.2	1	5.5	5.2	2.	.5	29.1
	T.	1.6	7.9	7.1	1.2	6	9.2	3.1	1	37.1
Middlesex, -	c.f.	—	—	1.2	1.2	2.3	6.3	8	.3	19.3
	T.	—	*	1.2	1.2	2.3	6.3	13.4	2.3	26.7
Norfolk, -	c.f.	.2	.7	2.5	.6	2.4	7.2	4.2	1.4	19.2
	T.	.2	.9	2.7	1.2	3.9	8.9	5.7	2.6	26.1
N'thumberland,	c.f.	.3	—	.4	.1	—	.7	.2	.1	1.7
	T.	2	.7	1.5	.4	1.2	2.4	.7	3.6	12.5
Nottingham,	c.f.	.6	5.3	8.4	2.2	6.5	3.2	.6	1.1	27.9
	T.	.9	5.3	9	2.5	7.3	4.4	1	1.6	32.0
Northampton,	c.f.	5.3	8.4	17.1	1.7	4.4	7.2	4.1	3.2	51.4
	T.	6	8.4	17.1	1.7	4.4	7.2	5.8	3.7	54.3
Oxford, -	c.f.	1.5	5.8	7.8	1.7	7.7	4.8	3.3	8.2	40.8
	T.	1.5	5.8	7.9	1.7	7.7	5	4.4	9.8	43.8

		1760.	'61-70.	'71-80.	'81-90.	'91-00.	'01-10.	'11-20.	'21-70.	
Rutland, -	c.f.	6	9.9	4.5	—	20.3	1.5	1.9	2	46.1
	T.	6	9.9	4.5	—	20.3	1.5	1.9	2.3	46.4
Shropshire, -	c.f.	—	—	.1	.1	*	—	.1	—	.3
	T.	—	*	1	.4	.9	1	.8	2.3	6.4
Somerset, -	c.f.	.2	—	—	—	.1	.5	.7	.3	1.8
	T.	.3	*	1	1.1	5.1	1.5	1.5	2.2	12.7
Stafford, -	c.f.	.4	.1	.3	.4	1.3	3.2	.6	.3	6.6
	T.	.9	1.1	1.3	.7	1.7	3.5	1.3	1.9	12.4
Suffolk, -	c.f.	.1	—	.1	—	.5	1	1.2	.6	3.5
	T.	.2	.1	.2	*	1	1.6	1.8	1.2	6.1
Surrey, -	c.f.	—	—	*	—	1.3	2.4	1.4	.9	6.0
	T.	—	*	*	—	1.7	3.4	1.5	3.5	10.1
Sussex, -	c.f.	—	—	—	—	*	.8	.5	.4	1.7
	T.	—	.2	*	*	.1	.9	1	1.4	3.6
Warwick, -	c.f.	7	3.4	5.9	1.2	2.3	1.5	1.2	.7	23.2
	T.	7.4	3.4	6.2	1.2	2.5	1.9	1.5	1.1	25.2
Westmoreland,	c.f.	—	—	—	—	—	.1	.2	—	.3
	T.	—	.1	.3	*	—	2.3	5	8.6	16.3
Wiltshire, -	c.f.	.8	.2	3.7	3.3	4	5.3	4.4	1.2	22.9
	T.	.9	.2	3.7	3.7	4.6	5.8	5	2.3	26.2
Worcester, -	c.f.	.3	1	4.6	1.1	.6	2	2.3	1.2	13.1
	T.	.3	1	6	1.5	1.2	2.3	4	1.8	18.1
Yorkshire, E.,	c.f.	1.7	8.6	9.4	.8	2.9	6.8	1.8	1.4	33.4
	T.	2.5	9.7	10.2	1	3.3	7.2	2.1	2.3	38.3
W.,	c.f.	.4	.5	1.5	.4	1.8	2.4	2.3	1.3	10.6
	T.	.8	3.5	2.8	1.5	2.7	4.3	4.3	4.3	24.2
N.,	c.f.	.3	1.7	.6	.5	.6	1.7	.6	*	6.0
	T.	1	2.5	1.2	1	1	4.6	2	3	16.3

APPENDIX E

INCLOSURE FROM THE WILD STATE

Inclosure from the wild state, taking place that is without any general intervention of common field or the meadows thereto attached, is so important both in its direct bearing and in its indirect effects on the use made of other land, that notwithstanding the treatment in the text, it will be well to summarise the chief facts relating to it. As has been pointed out, it is of three kinds, woodland, moor and hills, and fen. Of these the moors of the north fall in large measure in the eighteenth century, and find a place in the acts and awards, though not of course to their full extent. Consequently this part of the subject is roughly indicated.

With regard to the rest and possibly to some part of this, the evidence and the references to its inclosure, that is to its introduction into the area under regular cultivation, can be conveniently placed under six headings.

(*a*) Several writers in the seventeenth century refer to the inclosure of woodland counties or districts. Thus Trigge (*Humble Petition*, *Preface*) writes "not condemning the inclosure of Essex, Hartfordshire and Devonshire, and such woodland counties," which had to be inclosed to preserve the woods and afterwards so continued without harm. Also Blith points to woodlands "which now enclosed are grown as gallant cornfields as be in England" (*Improver*, p. 83), mentioning as such, the western parts of Warwick, the northern parts of Worcester, Stafford, Shropshire, Derbyshire, Yorkshire. Again Gibson tells us of the conversion to corn of woodland when cleared in North Warwick, an explanation adopted by Morton as to some part of Northampton. In the *Geographical Description*, a distinction is drawn between the woodland and champion in Warwick divided by the Avon, as also in Norfolk. We hear further of inclosures among the Chilterns, as also in the Weald. The inclosure of commons in Cornwall, *i.e.* of waste, are mentioned by Carew.

(*b*) Several authorities refer to the hedges and the fruit trees in hedges in the three western counties, Gloucester, Worcester and Hereford.

(*c*) Further notices of counties already inclosed or mainly inclosed are given by different writers of the same century, though without any statement as to their condition in respect of previous woodland. Thus Blith (pp. 83-84) adds, "consider Hartfordshire, Essex, Kent, Surrey, Sussex, Barkshire, Hampshire, Wiltshire, Somersetshire, and all the rest which not only raise corn for themselves but to supply the great city." Moore (*Scripture Word, Advt.*) says, "I complain not of inclosure in Kent or Essex . . . or of places near the sea or city." Lee (*A Vindication, etc.*, p. 31) writes: "Are there not many places in England, Essex, Hereford, Devonshire, Worcester wholly enclosed and yet no such effects follow?" The inclosed condition of Hertford is evident from Chauncey's map and account (*Ancient Antiquities of Hertfordshire*). Burton refers to Essex and Kent.

(*d*) The reclamation and draining of the fens perceptibly affected five counties: Lincoln S., Cambridge N., Northampton N.E., Huntingdon and Norfolk W.

(*e*) Of equal importance with the foregoing is the indication of forest or fen or wild regions, directly or at any rate early inclosed, to be found in the statistics of inclosure by act and award. Taking wild or forest districts as displayed in a map of early forest land as given by Pearson, these will be found to be places of low inclosure by act as compared with neighbouring districts. As a rule such districts have a low percentage of open field inclosed under act, and save where land has remained unutilised a low percentage of commons. But this latter feature is not present where forest or moor has lingered. Further common inclosure in these cases is often composed of a number of small scattered inclosures.

An inclosure of this kind is termed a secondary inclosure, though this term also includes inclosures occuring where open field inclosure has previously taken place, and usually comes late in the eighteenth century.

As details on this point appear in the annexed table, they do not require to be set out at length here.

(*f*) Marshall in many of his writings calls attention to inclosure from the wild. Thus (*Rural Economy of West of England*, ii. 136) he describes West Dorset, and attributes its condition to ancient inclosure from a wild state, like Kent and Hereford and other places; while (*Rural Economy of Gloucester*) he gives as the signs of such "crooked fences and winding narrow lanes" (ii. 190). Again (*Appropriation and Inclosure of Commonable and Intermixed lands*, p. 9) "of this description, principally, are the wealds of Kent and Essex, and many other old-inclosed lands in different parts of the kingdom, whose fields and inclosures are of irregular shapes, and their fences crooked."

In the annexed table, the chief references to counties as generally inclosed have been added in the third column for the purpose of comparison with the notes as to inclosures under act, though no mention is made as to their condition before inclosure. In many cases this can be supplied from other sources, as for instance in Hertford and the Weald districts of Surrey, Sussex and Kent. The last column giving inclosure under act from common explains the position of the northern counties, as also of the West and North Ridings, where large inclosures of moorland took place, no doubt in continuation of a process long in operation.

From the above account, as also from the table itself, the large extent of inclosure from the wild state may be judged, and hence some idea reached of its importance as a factor in the general movement. That, as has been pointed out in the text (pp. 118; 185), is twofold; it is a process whereby large quantities of land are inclosed, and its accomplishment affected the use of other lands, and often hastened their inclosure.

In this connection one matter needs emphasis, the unsuitability of large parts of the country for a system of agriculture in which arable was dominant; an unsuitability due in some instances to the character and situation of the land, and in others to existing circumstances of other kinds. In such places common fields, if any, would be greatly restricted in amount, and the rights of

INCLOSURE FROM THE WILD STATE.

County.	Wild inclosed		Inclosed by seventeenth century.	Marshall.	Inclosed by Act.	
	Woodland.	Fen.			Common field.	Commons per cent. inclosed.
Bedford, - -						.1
Berkshire, -			(*b*)		S. rather low	3.9
Buckingham, -					S. low	1.0
Cambridge, -		N. (*c*)			N. low	3.9
Cheshire, - -						3.0
Cornwall, - -	(*e*)				low	.8
Cumberland, -						23.7
Derby, - -	(*b*)				E. & N. low	5.1
Devon, - -	(*a*)		(*h*)		low	1.7
Dorset, - -				M.	N. low	5.0
Durham, - -						17.7
Essex, - -	(*a*)		(*b*)(*g*)(*h*)(*j*)			1.2
Gloucester, -			(*l*)		W. low	1.1
Hampshire, -						5.1
Hereford, - -			(*h*)(*l*)	M.	low	1.3
Hertford, - -	(*a*)		(*b*)(*k*)		S. low	3.3
Huntingdon, -		N. (*c*)				—
Kent, - -			(*b*)(*g*)(*j*)	M.	low	.5
Lancashire, -						5.7
Leicester, - -					W. lower	6.1
Lincoln, - -		S. (*c*)			S.E. low	8.0
Middlesex, -					N. low	7.4
Norfolk, - -		W. (*c*)			W. low	6.9
Northumberland,						10.8
Nottingham, -					W. lower	4.1
Northampton, -		N.E. (*c*)			N.E. lower	2.9
Oxford, - -					S. low	3.0
Rutland, - -						.3
Shropshire, -	(*b*)		(*h*)		low	6.1
Somerset, - -			(*b*)			10.9
Stafford, - -	(*b*)					5.8
Suffolk, - -						2.6
Surrey, - -			(*b*)		S. etc. low	4.1
Sussex, - -			(*b*)	M.	low	1.9
Warwick, - -	W. (*b*)				N.W. low	2.0
Westmoreland,						16.0
Wiltshire, - -			(*b*)			3.3
Worcester, -	N. (*b*)		(*h*)(*l*)		except S.E. low	5.0
Yorkshire, -	(*b*)					E. 4.9 W. 13.6 N. 10.3

(*a*) = Trigge, *Humble Petition.*
(*b*) = Blith.
(*c*) = Fen.
(*d*) = Camden.
(*e*) = Carew.
(*f*) = Morton.
(*g*) = Moore.
(*h*) = Lee.
(*j*) = Burton, *Anatomy.*
(*k*) = Chauncey.
(*l*) = Hedges with fruit trees.
M = Marshall.

NOTE. In column 5 'low' or 'lower' is often comparative to that prevailing near.

common, when such obtained, would be simple and comparatively lax. Consequently, inclosure met with little obstacle, even where the land was not wholly wild, and where some general rights of common existed. But the inclosure of this land no doubt led in many cases to the increase of arable, since, with the introduction of individual property, some of the land previously unsuited to the plough could now be used. At times, too, inclosure was caused by changes in circumstances or in farming which made land suitable which previously was unsuitable, and occasioned a demand for its use. On the effects of such an increase of the land fitted for arable enough has been said already (p. 120). Both the small common fields of the district and the wider fields in the neighbourhood, or in surrounding counties, might be affected.

But another point of interest arises in connection with the inclosure of land such as that under consideration, which was a main source of profit by its use for cattle or sheep, and equalled or sometimes quite overshadowed the arable in value. When the land was wild, or practically so, the method was simple. Probably in such cases the neighbouring lords or owners extended their rights and took the land in. But the case of land in the actual use of several parties, and yet in use largely, if not wholly, independent of arable possession, was different. The exercise of approvement under such circumstances would be difficult. In the eighteenth century, large unstinted moors presented on inclosure certain points of difficulty, which were discussed by Marshall (*Yorkshire*, i. 48-105).

The main case with which he deals is that of Pickering, where the common fields and meadows and the stinted pastures, having been exchanged or divided and inclosed without any legal process, the apportionment of the unstinted commons remained over. To obtain this, recourse was had to Parliament. A question of legal claim arose between the owners of the lands in open field and the owners of ancient common right houses. Of these there were two hundred and sixty, most quite separate from a share in the open field arable. The application for the bill was made by the tithe owner, and supported by the owners of the houses, but opposed by the owners of the lands. The bill was passed, but the question of rights between the houses and lands was left to be tried at the Assizes on a feigned issue, the reference being whether one moiety of the commons should remain with the lands of the township, which belonged to owners of ancient common-right messuages, cottages, and sites. This was negatived, and a verdict was taken in favour of the houses; that is, to the effect that all should share alike. This decision, which Marshall considers wrong, was followed in the case of Sinnington. On the other hand, at Knaresborough the houses got little, the owners of land being substantially successful, while at Middleton one half went to the houses and one half to the lands. In Marshall's opinion a division was equitable, inasmuch as ancient common-right houses had certain rights. His main contention, however, was that common field lands had the main claim to the herbage of old common pasture, because in all times, and especially in early times, when cattle were wholly dependent on grass, the possession of plough land involved the possession of common in order to secure continuous feed.

The importance attaching to such land as that under discussion in relation to the whole question of common and inclosure is evident. This is recognised, at any rate to some extent, by Marshall, particularly in his pamphlet on the *Appropriation and Inclosure of Commonable and Intermixed Lands*, when he draws a clear distinction between forest lands and the system of common associated with open field. He further calls attention to the particular position of the west. In supplement of what has been said in the text (esp. Bk. II. c. i.) certain features may be pointed out.

When it is said that such land was unsuited or little suited to arable, it does not necessarily follow that such unsuitability was permanent. Woodland, for instance, was unsuitable till cleared, and fenland till drained, but, in addition, some land was inaccessible. Further, in some instances and regions the land might be unsuited in general to a system of arable open field and yet not unsuited to a more restricted arable in parts. After inclosure particular parts, not necessarily large, and particular fields were available for such purposes.

Again, in the case of some land of this kind, some temporary arable use of the land was not uncommon, certain parts being broken up and kept under crop for a few years and then restored to common use. But such a method was also practised in connection with organised agricultural townships, and is closely allied to the outfield in some regions. Consequently, it cannot be regarded as distinctive. Nor can the time of the introduction of such practices be well determined. It is, however, important to notice that it occurred on forest and commons in different parts of the country (Bk. I. c. i., p. 26, note 5, and also p. 108; in addition, the heath lands of Staffordshire were sometimes put to arable for five years), and was not restricted to one part, as the west, though apparently more general there. Marshall (*ib.* p. 10) suggests this as a probable means whereby "the lands of that country," *i.e.* the western extremity of the island, "have been cleared and brought into a state of cultivation.

On turning to the reasons for the direct inclosure into cultivation, and the absence of anything in general like open field, the circumstances in the case of forest lands are clear. Whether in actual woodland or merely forest in the more technical sense, these were almost necessarily inclosed (Trigge, *Humble Petition*, Pref.). If in wood, they were only open to use as this was cleared; if reserved for sport, rights, usually royal rights, had to be relinquished. As a general rule they would appear to have come into possible use at a time when there was little or no likelihood of any extension of an open field system. But does this apply to the west? This has been discussed in the text, where it is pointed out that without doubt the forces mentioned above were in operation. At the same time, other influences operating in the same direction must be taken into account. The difficulty is to determine the weight to be attached to them as compared with the undoubted factor under consideration.

Some of the more important features dealt with here and elsewhere in connection with this whole question may be briefly summarised.

(1) Taken as a whole, fewer traces of common field are present in the west than in the rest of the country, the south-east being left out of count. This is true alike of the north, the centre, and the extreme south-west.

(2) There is abundant evidence as to common field in the East Riding, in Wiltshire, and in much of Dorset.

(3) The condition of Hertford (excluding the cretaceous north)

and North Middlesex as to inclosure and traces of common field is not very dissimilar from that of Hereford. The same is true of the Weald region.

(4) There is a close correspondence in a very large number of cases between differences in soil and differences in recorded inclosure by act.

(5) The record of inclosure both in the eighteenth century and before clearly reflects the influence of forest (and woodland), moor and fen.

BOOK III

EFFECTS OF INCLOSURE

I

GENERAL EFFECTS

In any attempt at an estimate of the general effects of inclosures, even of those of a particular period, certain broad considerations must be borne in mind. Thus it is necessary to distinguish between the results produced on particular classes of the community and those which affect the general well-being of the country. Change, and especially change affecting the cultivation of the land, must almost inevitably be attended with inconvenience, if not with suffering, on the part of particular classes. Again, the effect of an alteration in method during the time of transition, and by reason of the element of change, must be separated from the effect of a new system when once introduced and firmly established.[1] In a more limited sense this was equally true of particular inclosures. New and better systems supersede old systems to the advantage of the nation and of those to be employed, but the progress from worse to better involves hardship to those, and they may be a very large number, whose ideas and powers are adapted to the methods of the past, and unsuited to the new conditions imposed by improved methods. These, indeed, are principles of general validity, though their importance in this case is necessarily emphasised by the

[1] Thus Marshall states that in a conversation which he held at Tamworth in November, 1784, the idea was generally expressed that inclosure was disadvantageous to the tenant during the first six or seven years, by reason that he could not in less time bring his land to a good turf, that is, put it first into grass and then reconvert it.—*Midlands*, vol. ii., pp. 36-38.

widespread nature of the change under review, and its profound importance to the country as a whole. But there are certain considerations more pertinent to the case of inclosure. Inclosure was, as has been shown, a general movement extending over many centuries. While it may not be necessary to labour the point that its effects may have been different at different periods, it is necessary to point out that the circumstances in response to which it took place differed from time to time. Effects sometimes attributed directly and wholly to enclosure are often due to it rather as a final or particular step in a chain of events than as an isolated occurrence. Thus, if it be true, that inclosure to pasture in the fifteenth century arose by reason of the want of labour, or the want of labour at anything like previous wages, its ultimate effect in diminishing, at any rate in certain districts, the field of employment must be considered in relation to the circumstances preceding inclosure as well as to inclosures themselves. These circumstances were obviously absent at other times. In like manner the nature of the inclosure whether of demesne, or of waste, or of open field, whether by law, or by force, or by craft, largely influence the popular attitude, and so partly determine the effect, and certainly colour the representation of that effect.

Before proceeding to any such general estimate, either of inclosure or of the inclosures of any period, it is necessary to pass in review the effects attributed to it in respect of particular details. These fall under three headings, and may be respectively dealt with as affecting Cultivation, General Features, and the Condition of the People, but these considerations may be prefaced by a brief account of certain definite circumstances involving definite differences in the results of inclosing.

The first occasion of difference lies with the nature of the inclosure, whether it be of commons or waste, or, on the other hand, of open fields. Of course a large number of inclosures comprised both. It is obvious that two of the most serious charges urged against inclosure on public grounds would not be tenable as against that of commons or wastes. Inclosing these could not lead to a depopulation by reducing employment, nor could it occasion a decrease in the grain supply. Save under exceptional and temporary circumstances, fencing in these lands meant an increase in the use of, at any rate, some part of them, and probably an increase in the area under the plough. On the other hand, inclosures of this kind were equally if not more obnoxious in the eyes of those who regarded the change as dictated by the interests of the rich and as a robbery of the poor. The minor incidents of common which had fallen either by right or propinquity to the lot of the smaller holders or the poor were taken from them. Of course this view was not invariable, as is shown by the argument that on commons the rights of the small proprietors are often rendered nugatory by the virtual monopoly[1] by the rich. Again, inclosures of commons could not be supported as a means of avoiding the vexatious interference experienced in the case of open fields. It was urged as a way of utilising land which was, in point of fact, unprofitable. During the eighteenth century, when practical results occupied the mind, a clear distinction was drawn between these two kinds. Several writers point out the need of separating them in view of the different effects produced,[2] and the opinion thus expressed seems to have been the result of experience in different parts of the country. It is emphasised in the *General Report* to the Board of Agriculture on the subject of inclosure, and special reference is made to it in the case of counties so widely

[1] Thus in the seventeenth century it was pointed out that the rich man often encroaches on the poor, especially when the latter cannot keep his due number of cattle through poverty.—*Considerations*, 1653, pp. 2-3.

In the case of Cheshunt the common was not fed by the poor, but by a parcel of jobbers who hired cottages that they might eat up the whole.—*Hertford Agric. Report*, 1804, p. 45.

Stone says that cottagers are often kept out of their rights by large farmers who overstock.—*Suggestions*, 1787, pp. 74-5.

[2] As for example, Dr. Beeke.—*Agric. Report*, *Berks*, 527-8.

different as Leicester, Yorks, Berkshire, and Gloucester.[1] Indeed it is not too much to say that the advantages of inclosing wastes and commons are accepted as indubitable[2] even by those whose judgment was not otherwise favourable to the new policy.[3] One writer indeed couples with his benediction a word of caution as to the need of regard to the wants of the poor.[4] It should be noticed that particular references are to be found at this time to the benefits of this kind of inclosure in respect of the increase of grain, and also in population.[5] In these respects a contrast was sometimes drawn between these inclosures and those which were taking place in the open fields. In many places it is probable that the sheep commons were of little use. This opinion was expressed by Stone, who attributes their poverty in part to the lack of regular manure.[6] This difference in character is of great importance in treating of the inclosures taking place at this period, as counties and districts differ very largely among themselves. Thus in such counties as Northampton, Leicester and Lincoln nearly all inclosures comprised open fields, while in others, as Northumberland, Westmoreland and Yorkshire, wastes were being taken in, and in Norfolk and some others sheep commons and small remaining commons were one object of the acts.[7] It must, however, be remembered that the so-called common field inclosures included common and often wastes.

[1] General inclosure of wastes desirable and different from inclosure of open fields.—*Agric. Report, Leicester* (1815), p. 79; *Agric. Report, Berkshire*, 527-8; *Agric. Report, Gloucester*, p. 89.

[2] Compare with the foregoing writers, *General Report*, 1808, chapter i.; Darwin, *Phytologia*, 1799; A. Young, *Observations*, etc., 1773.

[3] Thus Petition cited in *Political Enquiry*, pp. 120-2, and *Advantages and Disadvantages of Inclosing Waste Lands and Common Fields*, p. 43.

[4] *Agric. Report, Worcester*, p. 53.

[5] As to grain, *Agric. Report, Berks*, 527-8; population, *Advantages and Disadvantages of Inclosing, etc.*, p. 43; Young, *Observations, etc.*, 38-39.

[6] Stone, *Suggestions, etc.*, 17-18.

[7] See *Advantages and Disadvantages, etc.*, p. 44, etc.; *Agric. Report Norfolk*, p. 168.

Another cause of difference is due to the soil. Here there is a fairly general[1] agreement as to the advantage to be gained on the light soils. This was noticed in the eighteenth century, and has reference to the effect produced on arable cultivation. The *Report* to the Board of Agriculture on Leicester remarks[2] that inclosures have done the most good in light sound soils, but more than a century before the results on such land had been observed by the writer, who pointed out the wonderful effect produced on the sands of Norfolk by inclosure and the use of clover.[3] The reasons for the particular benefit on such soils are stated by different writers. As is said in the case of Lincoln, the common saying that clay lands do not answer inclosure is partly to be accounted for by the fact that their cultivation undergoes little alteration.[4] On the other hand, particular benefit occurs in the case of light loams and sandy soils which will not bear perpetual cropping, and must sometimes be laid down to grass and otherwise used, a process remaining difficult, despite the methods prescribed by 13 G. III.[5] On such lands turnips and clover can now be introduced.[6] The feasibility of this distinction was admitted by even vigorous opponents of inclosure. Addington reluctantly admits this possible advantage, but only as it would seem to emphasise his denunciation of the practice when applied to "rich and

[1] Thus *Agric. Report, Worcester*, pp. 54-55, draws a careful distinction between effect on such lands and elsewhere. On the other hand, all poor land was not suitable. Inclosure of some of the sandy tracts in the East Riding considered a great failure.—*Agric. Report, E. Riding, Yorkshire* (1812), pp. 93-4.

[2] *Agric. Report, Leicester* (1809), p. 76.

[3] Houghton, *Collections* (1681), letter i.

[4] *Agric. Report, Lincoln* (1799), pp. 83-4. As is elsewhere pointed out, this seems to be the reason for the delay in the inclosure of certain districts, *e.g.* Flegg in Norfolk, though the soil here is different.

[5] According to Stone this act was rarely used. He says that in his own experience he has met with no instance of its use or even of a demand for its application. *Suggestions, etc.*, p. 13.

[6] Stone, *Suggestions*, p. 27.

deep soil, which is capable of bearing good crops both of grass and corn in the open field state," and "ought never to be inclosed at all."[1] The effect on cold clay soil is questioned by some.[2]

In the third place, the management of the inclosure, when such took place on a large scale, was of no small importance. According to the testimony of one of the most trustworthy writers on the subject in the latter part of the eighteenth century, mismanagement was very common.[3] What the mismanagement amounted to can be seen from a few examples. In many cases the allotments were too small to allow of adequately sized fields. The small inclosed fields were evidently condemned.[4] Again, in other cases, the wants and wishes of the small proprietors[5] were ignored, and the lot of the poor cottagers insufficiently considered, though this must not be taken as a fair general charge;[6] or bad methods of road-making might be adopted.[7] Mismanagement, how-

[1] *Inquiry into the reasons for and against inclosing the open fields*, 1767, pp. 38-39. Cf. *Agric. Report*, *Northampton* (1809), where the possible or probable conversion of rich lands on inclosure is emphasised.

[2] Inclosing does not answer to any great degree upon clay, as they cannot have seeds or turnips; and if laid down to grass it is 20 years before it comes to good pasture. *Agric. Report*, *Lincoln*, p. 83.

Again, a bad effect is said to have been experienced from the inclosure of the cold clays in the north of Bedfordshire. This was due partly to exhaustion before the inclosure and partly to the desire to convert this land to grass for which it was unfitted. *Agric. Report*, *Bedford* (1808), 244.

[3] Stone, *Suggestions*, esp. p. 81. "That inclosures have most generally been mismanaged, may evidently be seen by their present condition."

[4] Suggestion that small size of inclosed fields a cause of mildew, *Annals of Agriculture*, vol. i. p. 332. Small inclosures condemned, *Agric. Rep. Lancaster* (1815), p. 192; *West Riding* (1799), p. 71. In both these counties many fell under this censure.

[5] According to Addington plan of inclosure usually settled by a few large proprietors, the rest having little power. *Inquiry Report* (1772), p. 21. Cf. Horner, *Essay, etc.*, p. 103; Young, *Northern Tour*, i. p. 223.

[6] This is dealt with elsewhere. A very full account of the treatment of the poor is given in the *Agric. Report* on Norfolk.

[7] *Agric. Report*, *Rutland* (1808), pp. 155-6. But there is no ground for considering that this was generally true.

ever, did not necessarily result from mistakes by the commissioners. The use made by the owners now for the first time released from the bonds or guidance of custom was often injudicious. Sometimes inadequate attention was paid to the land; elsewhere the attempt was made to gain too much from it, and it was taxed beyond its capacity.[1]

Lastly, the circumstances of the district or of the time went far to invest inclosure with particular effects. A very important instance of this was the extent to which the district depended on agriculture and especially arable agriculture. Where other employments were present, the change in method produced, even should that tend towards increased pasture, was far from being as important as where agriculture was the one great stay and industry.[2] Such considerations were of peculiar pertinence in early times when locomotion and migration were more difficult and isolation greater.

In the ardour of controversy a number of minor advantages or disadvantages were alleged rather, it would seem, as adding to the main case for or against the contemplated change than as forming part of it. Thus on the one side may be mentioned the complaint that considerable injury will be inflicted on fox hunting,[3] and on the other side comes the claim that the hedges will make the country more secure against invasion, since foreign invaders would be unable to march through an inclosed country as easily

[1] An instance of this occurred in Cumberland where on inclosure the land was often exhausted by incessant cropping. *Agric. Report, Cumberland* (1805), p. 214. That such practices occurred also in earlier times would seem probable from Houghton, *Collections*, 1693, p. 66, where it is stated that inclosed land in Stafford has successive crops for seven, eight or ten years.

[2] In the seventeenth century Moore in his *Scripture word against Inclosure* (1656) draws this distinction. It becomes a commonplace, though its full importance when considered in conjunction with the change in the means of locomotion is not always seen. See also above, pp. 191-2.

[3] This complaint is alluded to in *The General Report on Inclosure* (1808), p. 306.

as through an open one.[1] More substantial than the foregoing was the question as to the effect on the means of communication. Here, as might be expected, we find some difference of opinion. It was asserted that roads were interfered with,[2] and that thus locomotion was impeded and the charges incurred on its account increased. But this charge which proceeded from Addington met with little support from others, and seems untenable in respect of the inclosures under private act in the eighteenth century, in respect of which it was advanced. It is quite clear from the acts and awards, as also from the direct testimony of commissioners that particular care was taken in laying out both public and private roads. Of course there may have been particular cases where customary roads and paths were obstructed, a feature present indeed in inclosures of a much more recent date, but the total result would seem to be the very reverse of that alleged. Considerable deductions for roads were made from the land to be inclosed in nearly every instance, and there is no reason to doubt that these inclosures, occurring at a time when the demand for more and better roads was active, as shown by the turnpike acts, resulted in a general improvement of the ways of communication. The roads over the old open fields and commons were often little more than mere tracks.[3]

During the seventeenth century the claim was advanced that the introduction of several ownership would have the incidental advantage of producing greater equality in the

[1] Lansdown MS., 487. Standish, *Commons Complaint* (1613), p. 30.

[2] The words of Fitz Herbert, "also it may fortune that men will say that if all should be inclosed there would be many foul lanes as there be in Essex." *Book of Surveying*, 98, is a very early reference to this charge.

On the other hand in *The great improvement of Commons that are Inclosed*, 1732, roads over commons and wastes are said to be miry and useless.

[3] See *Agric. Report, East Riding*, 1812, according to which, in the district where the country was open, which it was till a few years ago, the roads were chiefly of grass and carriages little used, the corn being chiefly carried to market on the backs of horses, p. 266. Of course matters varied very much from district to district.

taxation of the land, since yardlands were taxed alike irrespective of differences in size and quality.[1] But more accurate assessment was not wholly dependent on, though it might be hastened by the change.

[1] "A poor man for a small yardland and peradventure not halfe-stocked shall pay as much as a rich man doth for a great one stocked to the full." *Considerations* (1653), p. 15.

The tax of land is after the yardland; a name very deceitful by the disproportion and inequality thereof, the quantity of some one yardland being as much as one and a half or two in the same field, and yet there is an equality of taxes, but if the taxes be paid by the pound rent, then the rich man saith, shall my yardlands bear out or pay for another's barren land? So they are at variance. *A Vindication of the Considerations concerning Common Fields and Inclosures*, 1656; summary at end, pp. 42-47.

II

AGRICULTURE

If a long period be taken, the general benefit of inclosure, so far as the efficient cultivation of the ground and the conduct of farming were concerned, seems beyond reasonable doubt. It is true that on other grounds, and, also, it must be noticed, in respect of particular crops, hostile criticism of the new movement was frequent; but in relation to cultivation with due economy and in general, adverse opinion is far outweighed by the wide consensus of testimony presented from many quarters.

That testimony is not confined to one period. In this particular aspect the balance of opinion is uniform through the seventeenth and eighteenth centuries. Indeed, the advocacy of inclosure as a farming measure seems as strong in the middle of the sixteenth and the beginning of the seventeenth century as in years when Young, Howlett, and Marshall voiced the opposition to common cultivation. The favourable opinions of Tusser and Fitz Herbert are well known. Another writer in advocating inclosure in every county of the kingdom in 1613, asserts that "the barest lands inclosed do in profit far exceed the best vallies; the people much the richer and able of body to serve their prince and defend their country," and speaks of the champaign or open counties "where land is barren and fewell so scant that they are constrained to burn the straw and manure."[1] In the seventeenth century technical

[1] Standish, *New Directions of Experience to the Commons Complaint* (1613), p. 30; cf. Carew, *Survey of Cornwall*, ed. 1769 (1st ed. 1602), p. 38. They fall everywhere from Commons to Inclosure, etc.; also p. 23, testifying to improvement in sheep "since the grounds began to receive inclosure and dressing for tillage."

writers, amongst them Blith, advocate it strongly. In like manner Houghton, at the end of the century, tells of the high yield and the continuous capacity of inclosed land, adding:[1] "I cannot but admire that people should be so backward to inclose, which would be more worth to us than the mines of Potosi to the King of Spain." Another writer, a few years later, treats inclosing as obviously beneficial, adding in support of this: "I shall only propose two things that are matters of fact, that, I think, are sufficient to prove the advantages of inclosures; which is, first, the great quantities of ground daily inclosed; and, secondly, the increase of rent that is everywhere made by those that do inclose their lands."[2] The evidence of these two centuries is emphatic, as also that which follows throughout the middle and latter part of the eighteenth century. Authorities are almost too numerous to cite. They include scientific men as Linnaeus, advocates of scientific farming like Young and Marshall, and practical agriculturists.[3] Nor is the evidence as to the general farming consequences confined to one part of the country. We hear of it in the north[4] and

[1] Houghton, *Collections*, 1693, p. 66.

[2] *The Whole Art of Husbandry, etc.*, by J. M., F.R.S. (John Mortimer), 1707, p. 1; cf. *Dictionarium Urbanicum* (1704), under title "Enclosures." "The differences also and profits thereof, are plainly to be discerned by the severals in inclosed parcels of land that have formerly been taken out of the field land or common; and how much they excel the others in every respect, though of the same soil and only an hedge between, and what a yearly value they bear above them as also by the great quantities of lands which in our own time have laid open, in common and of little value; yet when inclosed, tilled, and well ordered have proved excellent good and suddenly repaid the present great expense incident to inclosure." It is also added that inclosed land "generally maintains treble the number of inhabitants or more than the champain grounds do." The chief argument as to profit used is the advantages offered for corn.

[3] J. C. von Wöllner, in the introduction to the German translation of Horne's *Principles of Agriculture*, attributes (1779) the great improvements in English agriculture mainly to two things—inclosure and the excellent use of the hay meadows. The advantages of inclosure on which he lays most stress are—freedom to make the best use of the particular land, shelter and the supply of wood. *Grundsätze des Ackerbaues*, übersetzt (1779), pp. 27-33.

[4] *Inter alia* Young, *Tour Through the North*, i. 222-233.

Yorkshire,[1] in the east as in Norfolk and Cambridge,[2] in the west[3] in Gloucester and Somerset, and, indeed, from all parts.[4] The evidence as to the Midlands in the middle of the seventeenth century was peculiarly strong.

Even those most adverse hardly venture on a broad denial. Their opposition is in part on account of the methods employed, and the general social results, often the ordinary and inevitable results due to a mere change of system, and in part a specific denial in respect of particular crops or under particular conditions. Thus, distinctions are drawn by some between the effect on sheep and on corn, or by others between that produced in the case of light soils as contrasted with heavy and rich land.

Descriptions, however, of the general condition of the champaign country, or the open fields, given by travellers and others, while they do not necessarily belie the defects which became graver with time, show that in the earlier period, and, indeed, up to the end of the sixteenth century there was greater fertility in some parts of the country than might be imagined from some of the expressions used. Leland, in his *Itinerary*, frequently comments on the rich crops to be seen in the champaign. Similar glimpses are afforded by other writers of a somewhat later date. Thus, in 1615, the Vale of Buckingham, beneath the Chilterns, is described as "plain and champion, a clay soil, stiff and rough, but withal marvellous fruitfull, naked of woods but abounding in meadows, pastures, and tillage, and maintaining an

[1] Marshall, *Yorkshire*, esp. i. 292.

[2] The *Agric. Report* on Norfolk enumerates three advantages: (1) Greater compactness of holdings and less necessary uniformity; (2) extinction of shackage in case of half-year lands in addition to foregoing; (3) utilization of commons. These treated of at considerable length. Cf. Houghton, *Collections*, as to use of clover and hay seed on inclosure. *Agric. Report, Cambridge*, gives list showing improvements. *A.R.* (1813), 56, etc.

[3] *Agric. Report, Gloucester*, 89, etc.; cf. special instance of Eastington on the Cotswold. *Agric. Report*, 379. Somerset, *Agric. Report*, esp. general discussion, pp. 49-73.

[4] Thus see *Agric. Report, Wiltshire*, esp. 104; also *Warwick*, p. 62.

infinite number of sheep,"[1] and "South Cambridgeshire as champion, which yieldeth corn in abundance, with meadowing pastures." The east[2] is at once the richest part of Durham, and also the most champion; the champion in Norfolk "aboundeth with corn, sheep, and cows," while Leicester and Northampton, both mainly champion, are rich and fruitful. Elsewhere we read of the great flocks and herds in the open lands, and of the beautiful prospects of the country.[3] In Suffolk the greatest number of flocks are in the champion.[4] Like descriptions may be drawn from writings towards the close of the seventeenth century, when, for instance, the districts of Surrey, neighbouring on the Thames, are said to be mainly open and "grateful to the husbandman."[5] References might be multiplied. They occur, also, though in much diminished number, in the literature of the eighteenth. Their importance, however, must not be over-estimated. There is little or no attempt at a comparison between open and inclosed land. Their use is to correct the exaggerated impression left by adverse critics of the existing agricultural system, who are probably perfectly accurate so far as certain districts or certain instances are concerned, but whose language too often suggests that these are uniform types of existing cultivation rather than illustrations of what such a system permitted, or of the state towards which it would tend with time. As has already been said, the

[1] This and the following quotations are from *The Geographical Description of England and Wales*, 1615. It shows very clearly the large extent of land open and under cultivation at the close of the sixteenth century. The descriptions of the various counties may be compared with the scant and brief ones in *A Brief Description of England*, Harl. MS. 5190 (? end of sixteenth), and with those in *England's Remarques*, 1678. It is difficult to avoid the suspicion that the last mentioned is a reproduction of the *Geographical Description*. Cf. also, Blome's *Britannia*, 1673.

[2] According to Blome, *Britannia*, p. 92, the south was the most fertile.

[3] Norden (John), *Speculi Britanniae Altera Pars*, 1610, pp. 24, 31-32.

[4] Reyce (R.), *The Breviary of Suffolk*, 1618, p. 38.

[5] Blome (R.), *Britannia*, 1673.

condemnation of the old system lay not in any absolute infertility, but in its growing unsuitability, in the obstacle it presented to progress, and last, but not least, in the greater total advantages, advantages which increased century by century, offered by the system which was taking its place.

The general advocacy of inclosure was often accompanied by a depreciation of the actual value of the commons and of common right to those supposed to share in their advantages. Thus it is pointed out alike in the sixteenth, seventeenth and eighteenth centuries that the poor owning rights may be largely kept out of their rights by the action of large farmers who exceed their rights and thus surcharge the common to the detriment of all,[1] or by the lack of winter feed in the absence of which summer grazing could be of little worth.[2] Again, jobbers would hire cottages in order to obtain, as it were, a right of entry to the common and then proceed to eat up the common; or new cottages would spring up near the common, and though legally without rights, would encroach in practice on those to whom the common really belonged.[3] While there is undoubted truth in the matters thus brought to notice and while further, owing to other reasons, common rights in practice were often of much less value than was supposed, it should be remembered that this absolute decline in value was typical of the declining suitability of the system. The system was falling into disuse, a new system was taking its place, and with the change the actual use made of the common or common rights declined. It might indeed have been

[1] Sixteenth century: Fitz Herbert, *Bk. of Husbandry*, p. 77. Seventeenth century: *Considerations, etc.* (1653), pp. 2, 3; cf. *Vindication*, summary. Eighteenth century: *Tusser Redivivus*, March 9; Stone, *Suggestions, etc.*, 74, 75.

[2] *Gen. Report*, p. 5. Stone, *Suggestions*, 75. *Agric. Report, Essex* (1807), i. 166.

[3] *Agric. Report, Hertford* (1804), p. 45. Again, lazy tenants may leave crops standing and so hinder common. *Duty of a Steward*, E. Lawrence, p. 38.

retorted that what was wanted was a stricter enforcement of the whole common right system.

In some, indeed in many cases, the inclosure when achieved failed to produce the advantages expected. For this there were often special reasons, quite independent of any allegations against the change as a whole. Partial inclosure was, it was pointed out, bad for the lord, as the tenant would use all the manure from the common for his own small inclosure.[1] Again, in some cases there was general mismanagement of the inclosure. The land before the inclosure was often exhausted by continuous cropping,[2] or in other instances the early enthusiasm of the proprietors of the new allotment lead to incessant cropping and so to speedy exhaustion.[3] On some new inclosures it was difficult to obtain sufficient manure or it had to be carted from a distance.[4] Elsewhere the indiscriminate conversion of land to pasture whether suited or not led to loss and disappointment. Again, on some land where conversion to pasture was taking place, a period had to elapse before the ground could be brought to a good turf, during which time there would be temporary loss. Much more important, however, than these or similar occurrences, which after all were incidental to particular inclosures and not essential to inclosure as a system, was the effect produced in the case of good meadow land, already at a high value, where such formed part of the land to be treated. It was comparatively little damaged by the existence of common right and so little benefitted by inclosure; and it had to bear its share of the expenses incurred. These, as we hear, often led to a positive decrease in its value. But even here a real diminution in the general value of the land does not take place. All that happens is a contribution levied from land, already highly cultivated, towards the cost of a

[1] E. Lawrence, *Duty of a Steward*, p. 62.

[2] *Agric. Report, Bedford* (1807), p. 244.

[3] *Agric. Report, Cumberland* (1805), p. 214.

[4] Addington, *An Inquiry, etc.* (second edit.), p. 4.

change whereby the remaining land is greatly improved and its value enhanced.

The general advantages thus claimed may be placed under the following headings: (*A*) Improved arrangement and management; (*B*) Relief from existing disadvantages; (*C*) Improvement in the system of cultivation.

(*A*) Under this heading a considerable number of matters present themselves for consideration:

Firstly, it is claimed that by inclosure and only by inclosure is reasonable security obtained that the land will be devoted to the purposes for which it is best suited; inclosure, as one writer tells us, "leaving the employment of the grounds to the discretion of the occupant." This choice, as he added, had been beneficial and without inconvenience in such counties as Essex where it had been tried and its extension was not likely to be detrimental. In its broad sense this is what is meant by the author of the *Considerations* when he says "when tillage is more profitable than pasturage, men will break up their pastures to till; and why should they not have liberty to lay down their arable land to grass, when pasturage is more profitable than tillage."[1] It is repeated, though with more attempt at detailed reasoning by later writers who urge that among other disadvantages of the common field, that which made it necessary to plough and crop all kinds of land alike ranked high.[2] After inclosure there was a better distribution of land in inclosure to its own most suitable crop.

Secondly, the greater compactness of the estate, together with the more complete ownership enabled the farmer to work his land more systematically and to exercise more thorough superintendence over his labourers. They were more under control and direction.[3]

[1] *Considerations, etc.*, p. 21. Blith, instancing the inclosed counties, argued that tillage, on account of its profit, would always hold its own (p. 83).

[2] Horner, *Essay on Nature and Method*, p. 36. *Kahn's account of his visit to England*, 1745, tr. by J. Lucas, 1892, pp. 281-2. *Agric. Reports*, *Norfolk*, 177; *Oxford*, 99-101; *Wilts*, 40; *North Riding*, 90-1.

[3] *Agric. Report*, *Oxford*, 99-101.

Thirdly, the same circumstance would lead to greater economy in working and promote convenience. Under the open field system not only were the arable lands often distant from the farmhouses, but in most cases divided up into strips lying far apart from each other. As to the disadvantage of this intermixture and dispersion there was indeed little dispute. It does not seem to have been seriously denied even in the seventeenth century, when its consequences were summed up in the following words: "Disorder appears thereby, the intermixt and dispersed lands, lying here one and there another, as 4, 6, 8, or 10 parcels of ground to an acre of land, to the great hindrance and damage to the owners, both in tilling the land and raising the fruits of the same. For example, if one day's work in 20, 30, 40 lands tilling be wholly lost, how many days' work must necessarily be lost in 1, 10 or 20 fields? how many more in 1, 10 or 20 counties? So likewise in carriage of manure and harvest stuffe, and also other carriages, the labour is lost, which might be saved, if each man's land lay together."[1] The same inconvenience with the correlative advantage accruing from inclosure was dwelt on by others both then and subsequently. One emphasises the economy in getting in the hay and corn when all land lies together;[2] another the inconvenience of shifting the plough teams from one strip to another;[3] others dwell on the expense of such a system, but all agree on the general disadvantage of detached lands and the benefit to be gained by exchange. To the inconvenience thus described must be added that occasioned by the distance between the farmhouses and the lands, strips, or fields of different kinds,[4] as at Naseby

[1] *Vindication of the Considerations*, summary. Cf. J. Lee, *A Vindication*, pp. 21-25. Also for later times, Horner, *Essay*, p. 30, etc.

[2] Lee, *Vindication*, pp. 21-25.

[3] Stone, *Suggestions*, p. 15. Cf. *Agric. Report*, *Oxford*, 99-101.

[4] See especially, *Vindication of the Considerations*, summary; *Annals of Agriculture*, vi. 464; *Address to Board of Agriculture*, by S. J. Nash, p. 12; *Agric. Report*, *Middlesex* (1798), p. 40.

where "the farmhouses and barns are all in the village, which is two miles away from a great part of the field." The manure had to be carried out, the crops brought in, and teams spent a considerable time in going backwards and forwards. One curious advantage, it was considered by some, might be achieved if the farms were compact with the houses in their centre or neighbourhood. Horses would be less used for draught and so fewer would be kept;[1] the ploughing might be done by oxen which subsequently might be eaten.[2]

While these difficulties were generally admitted it was urged indeed that exchange and consolidation of intermixt lands as the arable strips might take place without inclosure.[3] To some extent this was correct, as different instances proved, but on the other hand it cannot be doubted that the whole tendency of such exchange would be in this direction, and that if the meadows were to lie near their respective strips, and the farmhouses were to be in close proximity, common right would be left to linger on as a precarious survival.

Fourthly, the use of manure in the open fields was held by some to be wasteful, it being imperfectly spread and some part of its strength exhaled and spent by the weather.

Fifthly, ploughing in the open fields was attended by certain difficulties. The strips could not be effectively cross ploughed or harrowed.[4] Again, in the condition in which some large fields were in the eighteenth century, damage was inflicted on the owners of certain of the strips. At the top or bottom were strips lying transversely, these as a rule were kept drier by the furrows of the lands lying

[1] Stone, *Suggestions, etc.*, 19-20.

[2] Lee, *Vindication, etc.*, 21-25.

[3] "I believe there is much truth in Sir C. Willoughby's idea that open fields for corn are far superior to inclosures, supposing two circumstances: 1. That the lands be laid together; 2. that all extraneous rights be excluded," *Agric. Report, Oxford* (1813), p. 96, etc. But from what follows it seems that open field is here used mainly in the sense of unhedged.

[4] *Agric. Report, Middlesex* (1798), p. 114.

below them, and so would be earlier sown, or else they might be earlier prepared owing to the more efficient farming of their owners. When this happened, the horses and ploughs of the other farmers who were later at work, would cause much injury by turning upon them. The seed when just sprouting would be disturbed.[1] The corners, too, of the long strips would escape the plough, a loss which could not fail to be considerable if calculated upon the whole field.

Sixthly, certain special advantages were claimed for inclosure. Thus under common cultivation the fallow field was considered to be largely wasted.[2] The balks between the strips were a loss.[3] Again, there was a waste of seed in the sowing of the open fields, and great economy might be practised after enclosure. When particular strips required rest they could not be separately treated, having to submit to the common rotation practised over the whole village or hamlet.[4] The absence of rest was indeed a general defect urged against common cultivation, but this will require mention when the question of improved rotation comes under consideration.

Lastly, a great controversy arose as to the relative

[1] *Agric. Report, Gloucester* (1807), p. 91. Cf. Nourse, T., *Campania Felix* (1700), pp. 28-9. "In common fields the first plough always receives a considerable damage, especially upon his headlands."

[2] "The fallow field to the weak or unstocked husbandman is a great charge and no profit. 1. The ordure or dung of sheep is in many places of more worth to be let, than the grass on which they feed. 2. This field often rots the sheep, to as much damage as the whole lordship is valued at per annum." *Vindication of the Considerations*, 1656, pp. 42, etc. "That barbarous custom of fallows" is Young's description, see *Annals of Agriculture*, vi. 140. Cf. *Agric. Report, Gloucester*, 104-5. Again the same writer in *Political Authentic*, "Dr. Price and the other writers who assure us we should throw down our hedges and waste one third of our farms in a barren fallow by way of making beef and mutton cheap," p. 145.

[3] Blith points this out (*Improver*, p. 81). He notes the common error of speaking of common fields as though before inclosure all was invariably in tillage.

[4] This and other points dealt with in the summary appended to the *Vindication of the Considerations*.

advantages and disadvantages of the hedges or means of separating the allotments. These are claimed by some as distinctly advantageous to cultivation, and denounced with equal if not greater vigour and point by others. One thing at any rate is clear. They were expensive both to make and to maintain. Different methods of division presented themselves. Fences, walls, or hedges had been adopted in different counties. But whatever the alternative, some land was inevitably taken up. In a certain sense it may be true that fencing is not essential to the idea of separation, that is, land may be laid together and extraneous rights abolished without its use; but there is no doubt that boundary divisions are essential to its successful practice and continuance. The hedges and ditches which were generally adopted save in the north occupied a considerable amount of land. Further they were expensive to make, a point already touched upon, and their maintenance formed an additional cost, which the open fields likewise escaped. On the other hand the hedges themselves might be made a source of profit. In some places large trees were planted in them for the sake of their timber, in other places they contained fruit trees. A not inconsiderable profit was said to be obtained by their due use, in part, no doubt, from sources such as the foregoing, but in part also by their regular clipping.[1]

Their effect on cultivation needs a few words.[2] It is probably correct that the shelter afforded by them was beneficial in the case of cattle, and they may well have proved of service in protecting both grass and crops from

[1] Hedges and fences occupy space especially with ditches, *Agric. Report, Oxford* (1794), p. 24; expensive to make and maintain, *General Report*, p. 81. Nourse, *Campania Felix*, p. 26, of value in themselves; cf. *Whole Art of Husbandry*, by J. M., p. 47, *Geographical Descrip.*, Worcester.

[2] Shelter beneficial to cattle, Horner, *Essay, etc.*, 36. *Whole Art of Husbandry*, p. 47; safeguards from theft, Lee, *Vindication*, 21-25; leaves add to fertility, *Agric. Report, North Riding*, 90-1; breaking wind, *Agric. Report, Hunts*, p. 167; giving shelter, and possibly decreasing mildew. *Agric. Report, Rutland*, p. 108.

depredation. Much more, however, was claimed. Thus according to one writer their leaves added fertility to the soil, according to another they, especially if timbered, were valuable as breaking the wind and affording shade and warmth to plants growing in the inclosures, while another with more ardour than accuracy even asserts not only that the shelter they gave increased fertility, but that if anything they were serviceable by decreasing the danger of mildew. Against these latter very optimistic views must be set much condemnation of hedges, and especially of well timbered hedges in respect of the crops in the fields. Marshall, for instance, writes strongly of the "folly of high hedges to arable fields in keeping back or spoiling grain," and in the *General Report* to the Board of Agriculture as well as in several reports on the counties a like view is expressed.[1] This verdict from those who were on the whole favourable to inclosure is of even greater weight than the statements of others whose general views were adverse.[2] It should, however, be noted that as a rule it is high timbered hedges, and especially these surrounding small fields, which are condemned.

(*B*) *Relief from existing restrictions.* It is amply clear that under the common field system serious obstacles were placed in the way of improvement. This has already been indicated, but it will bear further illustration. The best husbandmen were handicapped with the worst,[3] a feature which was of more moment when it became more important to enable progressive farmers to advance beyond existing standards than to prevent those who were indolent from falling below them. While it endured there was little opportunity for experimental husbandry.[4] Again if the old customs were bad, there was not much chance of departing from them.[5] To do that with ease required the

[1] Marshall, *Midlands*, ii. 329. *General Report*, p. 86; *Agric. Reports, Derby*, ii. 259; *Leicester*, p. 80.

[2] As Addington, *Inquiry* (1772), p. 4.

[3] *Considerations*, 14, 15.

[4] *Agric. Report, Worcester*, p. 68.

[5] *Agric. Report, Gloucester*, pp. 104, 105.

general removal of restrictions enforced by custom and secure as long as their maintenance appealed to the more ignorant or the idle. By inclosure improvements became possible without general agreement. How difficult this was, was learned by experience when it was sought to bring into action legislation which like 13 George III. c. 81, made it possible for a specific majority to effect certain changes in common usage. It could be done in many cases, but if difficult with a majority it was still more difficult when the nature of the improvement required the assent of each and all.

Apart from these miscellaneous advantages to be attained by inclosures, there were certain directions in which specific and more uniform relief was sought.

In the first place, the slovenly farmer became less of a detriment to his neighbours. What this meant may be judged from the complaints made at different times and from different quarters. In the open fields the lazy farmer who left his corn standing might hinder the common use of the ground. If he ploughed late, as has already been said, he would cause incalculable damage by turning his cattle backwards and forwards on the land already sown. He might drive cattle to and fro unnecessarily, and so add to the mischief from trampling always involved in the common use of arable. Bad husbandry leading to weeds, on the part of some, inflicted its full injury on others, where lands lay intermixt and with no effectual barriers.[1] Again, one farmer who neglected to drain might render the efforts of his neighbour of little or no effect.[2] Inclosure was needed to restrict within limits the harm done to neighbouring farmers, especially to those seeking to improve their methods, by the indolence or ignorance of a few.

In the second place, it was a defence against injury of a very different character. Common cultivation offered every occasion for trespass, and even for wilful fraud. The meers and stones—that is, the boundary marks of

[1] Stone, *Suggestions, etc.*, 16. [2] *Agric. Report, Worcester*, 56.

the various properties—were moved,[1] an offence indeed of old standing, finding mention in the Mosaic law, and significantly emphasised in the Commination Service. The dishonest farmers in ploughing would plough "further than they ought to do, in balks and hades,"[2] even as we are told by one writer, ploughing "by night for the express purpose of stealing a farm from their neighbours."[3] Again, "those who have consciences large enough to do it will lengthen their ropes, or stake them down so that their horses will reach unto other men's lotts";[4] an offence which another writer of the same period says was singularly tempting, since "no man can be just in taking his own grass, and no more, though with a tether; he must either take more or leave some, for a circle cannot fill a square nor a square a circle."[5] In making hay, some would encroach upon others. Offences of this kind, which seem to have been particularly prevalent in the sixteenth and seventeenth centuries, continued on into the eighteenth century.[6] Quite apart from their bad moral effects, they were to be deprecated, because in common with other trespasses, as for instance trespass by cattle, they led to frequent quarrels and to litigation, with its heavy cost. In this sense, commons and common rights were the occasion of disorder, and their abolition tended towards harmony and economy.

Lastly, inclosure offered an excellent opportunity for ridding the land of the burden which tithes imposed upon cultivation. The effect of tithes on progressive farming, and so on improvement, was very fully considered by writers like Young. In their opinion tithes opposed a great obstacle to advance. They were peculiarly vexatious in their method of payment, and weighed unduly on the better as compared with the worse farmers. So long as

[1] "To deface the marks of other men's lands, and where they find lands not marked at all to mark them as their own." *Considerations*, 2, 3.

[2] *id.* [3] *Agric. Report, Oxford*, p. 239. [4] *Considerations*, 2, 3.

[5] Summary given in *Vindication of Considerations*.

[6] Horner, *Essay, etc.*, p. 36.

open field continued, it seemed impossible to alter the method of their collection, and it was contended by some that they were exceptionally heavy under such a system. Their levy on beasts led to the loss of manure, a feature of particular importance in such cultivation.[1] Hence it was contended that inclosure might be made the occasion of confirming great benefit on the land. Exoneration from tithe was to be achieved by allotments to the Church. The effect of inclosure in the interests of the clergy was great, owing to the method adopted of calculating the allocation of land in lieu of tithes, and the share which fell to them of the new profits gained from wastes and commons, this latter accruing whether exoneration took place or not.[2] There was general approval of allotments in lieu of tithes expressed by most observers; and the non-adoption of this as a part and consequence of inclosure—as, for instance, in many cases in Norfolk and elsewhere—was held to be a cause for regret.[3]

The policy as to exoneration from tithe was not adopted uniformly throughout the country.[4] In addition to causes

[1] Stone, *Suggestions*, p. 16.

[2] Thus the owner of tithe obtains the advantage of the land as improved in cultivation, as by the bringing into use of the arable in the fallow field which was of little or no use in the common field system. See Lee, *A Vindication*, p. 21. It is urged that when allotment was given in lieu of tithe the incumbent should be empowered to burden it with a sum of money, to be used in its improvement. *An Argumentative Appeal addressed to the Right Reverend the Bishop*, by Rev. Baptist Noel Turner, 1788.

Allotments were sometimes made for other ecclesiastical claims. See Award at Hoby, in Leicester, when an allotment made for Easter offerings. *Close Rolls*, 3 G. II. 1760-1, Pt. 19, No. 14.

[3] *Agric. Reports.* See esp. Rutland and Buckingham. Exoneration not usually in Norfolk. *Gen. Report*, p. 20; cf. *Hampshire*, *Agric. Report*, 121-2.

[4] The calculations as to the proportion to which awards contain provisions as to tithe exoneration depend on a comparison of the numbers given in the Parliamentary Return of 1867 as to such allotments or money payments (*Parliamentary Papers LIV.* 159) with the number of acts of inclosure in the various counties. Though obviously incomplete, inasmuch as it deals only, save in the case of Yorkshire, with awards deposited with the respective Clerks of the Peace, it is sufficiently accurate to indicate broadly the distinctions laid down. It would, however, not be safe to enter upon more precise calculations

purely local in character, or due in large measure to custom and initiation, two chief causes of differences existed. Exoneration did not take place in many instances where inclosure was occasional and sporadic during this period, or where it occurred in the main for the purpose of utilising large wastes and heaths or of adding to the arable lands already inclosed, the ground remaining in commons for pasture or fuel. Thus in Kent and Essex, where the acreage inclosed at this time was comparatively small, and in such counties as Cumberland, Northumberland, and Yorkshire, where the inclosures were largely of wastes, the percentage of awards containing allotments in lieu of tithe was comparatively small. With these may be grouped Chester, Cornwall, Durham, Lancashire, Norfolk, Shropshire, Somerset, Stafford, Surrey, and Sussex, in all of which commons, apart from open field land, were a chief feature. In the Midland and West Midland counties, on the other hand, where inclosure played so great a part and where large common fields predominated exoneration from tithe in whole or in part appears in a large proportion of the awards. Conspicuous among these are Northamptonshire, Rutland, Bedford, Lincoln, Oxford, Notts, Cambridge, and Huntingdon on one side of the Midlands, and Warwick, Worcester, and Gloucester on the other. In Leicester and Berks they are not so noticeable, but still fairly frequent. In the former group the percentage of awards

as to percentage of awards making allotment or money payments in lieu of tithe not only because of the omission mentioned, but because the return itself leaves room for further error. Firstly, many of the allotments to rectors, vicars, and others are in respect of common rights or of glebe brought into the inclosure, and not on account of tithe; and these are but seldom distinguished. Secondly, in many cases the exoneration is only partial, the allotment or payment being made in lieu of certain tithes only. Thirdly, the returns made by the various clerks vary greatly.

Where no exoneration occurred the inclosure might be opposed by the tithe-holders; thus an attempted inclosure at Western Zoyland was opposed and defeated by the Bishop of Bath and Wells in the fear lest the conversion of arable to pasture might be occasioned, and lead to a decrease in tithes. *Agric. Report, Somerset*, 1798, p. 199.

containing some provision as to allotment or money payment in lieu of tithe, often indeed only partial, may be set down as exceeding the half. In Leicester, Derby, and Berks, it is not so high.

(*C*) *Improvements in the System of Cultivation.*—Under this heading we come, as will be seen, to advantages which operated as motives towards inclosures only during the latter period of its history. Unlike those concerned with general farm management or connected with relief from the more oppressive customs or the tyranny of neighbours in the open field system, these are novel and involve the introduction of striking changes. They may be dealt with respectively under the heading of changes in the rotation of crops and new and more systematic drainage. Changes of this kind were not only difficult to effect while custom ruled and where substantial agreement was necessary to their introduction ; but so far as the rotation of the crops was concerned, they were largely inconsistent with the actual practice of common rights.

The need of a different or improved rotation of crops attracted little attention till comparatively late ; indeed, it is doubtful if it really affected the demand for inclosure till the eighteenth century was well advanced. Houghton, it is true, in 1681 pointed out the advantages to be gained by clover in inclosure or by the like use of hay-seeds.[1] Artificial grasses also were recognised as of value in cultivation. But it was only after the great success attending the experimental use of turnips that new rotations became so firmly established where private ownership or agreement allowed of their use as to render obstacles to their introduction a felt and definite grievance. It was, of course, urged by those opposed to inclosures that to remedy this did not necessitate the wholesale abandonment of the open field system, and that by agreements either voluntary or under conditions to be determined by law, the new crops could be introduced. This is partially true in theory ; and even in practice

[1] Houghton, *Collections*, 1681, 1.

agreements to vary the rotation were more common than the convinced advocates of the new system were willing to admit. But the real point at issue was not whether it could be done, nor even whether in some cases it was done, but rather whether the way was such that it was likely that it would be done widely and throughout the country. The actual extent to which turnips and clover were introduced by mutual consent is doubtful. Evidence as to such came from many counties at the time when the *Agricultural Reports* were written; but except in a few cases it is clear that the practice is recorded as a departure from the usual custom. In Northamptonshire there was said to be considerable use of turnips in the open fields by temporary inclosures,[1] while in Oxfordshire "hitching" the field, that is, variation from the three field course by agreement is stated to be frequent.[2] On the other hand, the words used in most Reports, or the emphasis laid on special cases, when such agreements were recorded, mark them as exceptions.[3] In some cases the small progress made with turnips, for instances, is directly attributed to the open fields.[4] Much the same may be said of the cases recorded by Young and by others. Nor does the act passed with the distinct purpose of facilitating the introduction of turnips appear to have been successful. Stone, for instance, states that he knows of no instances of its use, and his statement is not without corroboration by others.[5] Even when turnips were cultivated in the

[1] *Agric. Report, Northampton*, ii. p. 111. [2] *Agric. Report, Oxford*, p. 131.

[3] *Agric. Reports*: *Bedford*, p. 340; *Hampshire*, p. 373; *Middlesex*, p. 48; *Huntingdon*, p. 107; *Wilts*, p. 104; *Worcester*, p. 68; *North Riding*, p. 109.

[4] *Agric. Report, Camb.*, p. 145. As to agreements and instances of such, *Annals of Agric.* viii. 54, iv. 144. In *An Inquiry into the connection between the present price of provisions and the size of farms*, the author says of common fields: "They are not capable of producing half what they would otherwise do, unless indeed the whole belongs to some very few, who are sensible enough to agree among themselves on a good mode of culture; but this is rarely the case," pp. 85, 86. In vale of York only some few cases of common consent. *Agric. Report, North Riding*, 1800, p. 109.

[5] *Agric. Report, East Riding* (1812), p. 111. As to neglect of the act, see one instance of its use, p. 115.

open field, it is doubtful if they met with invariable success.[1] The great drawback consisted in the difficulty of securing anything like general agreement to a change which involved a considerable alteration in the time at which the arable was thrown open for common pasturage. To some this alteration meant loss, and they would be unwilling to postpone the time of entry. In some few cases, no doubt, temporary inclosures for turnips were maintained by leave, but this involved a loss of pasturage over them and also meant expense, and as a rule turnips, if introduced at all, had, it may be assumed, to be introduced as a crop in a general course, since temporary inclosure was difficult. Without safeguard no single farmer would of course keep turnips in the ground, with as a result a valuable present of them to his neighbour's sheep.[2] Open fields, as one writer says, cannot be sown according to the tenant's pleasure.[3]

In its relation to drainage, inclosure differs in its importance, according as the drainage concerned was a means of reclaiming the soil and bringing it under cultivation or the ordinary and improved drainage of lands already cultivated.

The large seventeenth century reclamations were made the occasion of inclosures. Partly as an inducement to the various parties interested, and partly no doubt to avoid difficulties and disputes which might otherwise arise as to the apportionment, leave was given to divide and separate their estates. When inclosure of fen land takes

[1] "I know no township in the West Riding, except that of Wath-upon-Derne, where the turnips are cultivated in any degree of perfection in the open fields." *Agric. Report, West Riding* (1799), p. 134.

[2] But common consent was insufficient, unless a common method was adopted in using turnips when grown in the open fields. The best farmer anxious to obtain the best results from this consumption often sold the crop to a butcher or grazier, who would turn in his sheep. Other farmers might pull their turnips and carry them home. The result of this difference was to the advantage of the latter, who not only had their own turnips, but shared in the manure of the sheep fed on the turnips of the former. They might, it is suggested, get even a larger share, since the sheep would prefer lying on bare land. *Agric. Report, North Riding*, p. 109, etc.

[3] *Agric. Report, Middlesex* (1798), p. 114; *Hertford* (1804), p. 48.

place during the eighteenth century, a like necessity presented itself. In certain cases some demarcation of rights, as where different hamlets and villages were interested in the same inclosure, was inevitable. The common fen or property was divided, and so assigned to the various villages, to be held by them in common as far as their inhabitants were concerned, an allotment which led to subsequent inclosure, either by act or agreement.[1]

But drainages of this kind, which were required in order to make land cultivable, were not always welcomed by the inhabitants, even by those possessed of rights. "Some, we hear, have objected on the ground that it is better for them when it is most under water, as the fodder, thatch, and the like cannot be destroyed by cattle, and there is plenty of fish."[2] As a rule, it may be assumed, the better employment of the land would outweigh such minor advantages so far as those *legally* possessed of rights were concerned, and to such employment drainage was an obvious preliminary.[3]

Quite distinct from the above was the ordinary drainage of agricultural land. Here the question was not that of bringing land into cultivation, but of cultivating it to advantage, and to this the abolition of intermixed rights was essential. In the open field system incalculable damage might be inflicted on a number of owners by the obstinacy, ignorance, or neglect of one man. The water-courses essential to the whole field might be stopped by one occupier.[4] The good of inclosure in different counties in this respect is dealt with in the *Reports* to the Board of Agriculture[5] and elsewhere. In addition to this is the

[1] Holland Fen, *Lincoln*, *Recovery Rolls*, 9 G. III. (1769), Trinity 141. Cf. King's Sedgmoor, *Somerset*, *Rec. Rolls*, 36 G. III. (1796), Hilary 29.

[2] *Reflections on the various advantages resulting from the draining, inclosing, and allotting of large commons and common fields*, by W. Pennington, 1769, p. 39.

[3] *Agric. Reports*: *Norfolk*, p. 137; *Somerset* (1798), p. 130.

[4] Stone, *Suggestions*, pp. 20, 21. *Agric. Report*, *Worcester*, p. 56.

[5] As *Oxford*, pp. 99-101, etc. In the absence of proper drainage, lands often ploughed into high ridges. *Agric. Reports*: *Gloucester* (1807), p. 103; *East Riding* (1812), p. 109. Cf. *Oxford*, p. 103.

incidental opportunity offered at the inclosure of carrying out certain works of advantage common to the district and the various lands affected, as, for instance, irrigation or large drainages.[1] The cost could be defrayed at the common expense of those likely to benefit.

Amid the very record, however, of the improvements thus achieved, it is interesting to note evidence of the risk involved in inclosure of releasing the bad and lazy farmer from all restraint. Thus in the case of Wilts it is pointed out that the soil of the downs might in unskilful hands be made worse, and that therefore a state of severalty might sometimes be injurious. Much the same is observed with reference to the wolds in the East Riding of Yorkshire where rapacious cultivation led to exhaustion of the soil and to ultimate loss.[2]

The foregoing investigation of the general impressions and views of contemporary writers, as well as of the facts which they record with varying degrees of accuracy, opens the way to some general summary, and to an attempt to disentangle from the mass of detail the more permanent economic principles which underlay the movement and determined its results at different epochs. These principles may be considered at the various epochs as they operate sometimes in unison, sometimes separately, and sometimes in obvious antagonism. At times, too, they or any of them are overlaid by particular causes which serve to obscure or even for the time to counteract their natural operation.

Firstly, the natural suitability of the land for a particular crop demands attention. As we have already seen the importance of this was recognised by some observers as when at an early time the claim is urged that inclosure allows land to be put to the particular use for which it is best suited, or again when the difference in results of an

[1] Large drainages, *Agric. Report*, *Derbyshire*, ii. (1813), 485. Irrigation, *Gen. Report*, pp. 93-95.

[2] *Agric. Reports*, *Wilts*, p. 46, "Severalty makes a good farmer better and a bad one worse"; *East Riding*, pp. 93, 94; *History of Worcester*, T. Nash (1781), *Introduction*, p. xii., "A bad tenant may plunder and impoverish an inclosed farm much easier than he can a common field farm."

inclosure, whether beneficial or not, is ascribed to the nature of the soil. Obviously the consequences are different when under the old system the land is already, though possibly less fully, under the same crops or in the same use as will occur when it falls into individual cultivation. In this sense the supersession of the common system is most conspicuous in result when it takes place in respect of land which is not fitted for so great a dependence on arable as was its former lot. In this connection it is well to remember that inclosed pasture was not an original or a very leading feature in the open field system.

Secondly, the nature of the inclosure whether of waste and common or of cultivated land is important. No doubt this distinction was in large measure due to geological differences, but with these were conjoined other differences. Distance from the village, the need of outlay in drainage and the presence of forest, all play their part. The reclamation of waste or partial waste and the inclosure of even good sheep commons have one particular effect. Consequent on it, some arable cultivation usually ensued, and this in its turn often allowed or even occasioned the conversion of other land already in arable to grass. This dislocation of employment might take place without any concurrent diminution in the food supply.

Thirdly, progress in the method of cultivation not only causes the demand for separate control over land, but allows land to be profitably turned to purposes for which previously it was not available.

Fourthly, the growth of population, and in particular the local growth in towns and districts filled with home industries, affects the use of the land. In the neighbourhood of such a district or town there is a natural tendency to bring land under inclosure, mainly in order to meet the needs of the town population: while on the other hand the growing industries offer ultimate employment to those who in its course may be deprived of rural work. In the early period the chief effect of town development upon the district lay in its adverse influence on the self-contained village which led to the retention of so much land in arable; in later times the requirements of the town for milk, meat, and local necessaries, were of great importance.

Fifthly, the state of the country with regard to locomotion and transport determines the extent to which the land can be used for other purposes than those necessary to supply the daily needs of those who dwell on it.

Lastly, the circumstances of any crop both as regards its cost of production and the demand for it, produce an effect not only on the progress of inclosure but on its locality and its results.

It remains to trace the relative effect of these influences at the different periods which have passed under our consideration.

In the early period, during the fifteenth century and well into that which followed, the exciting cause of inclosure was the remarkable coincidence between a want of profit from arable and the growth of profit from wool. On the one hand hired labour had become scarce and costly, while the land, exhausted by too frequent cropping, was in many parts ill-suited for arable use. This defect, indeed, was not uniform, the soils naturally suited to arable being apparently less affected. On the other hand, the demand for English wool had increased. It is true that the export of raw wool had been restricted, but that had taken place specifically on account of the home manufacture, and with the intention of substituting for it the export of cloth. The manufacture of this, though no doubt widespread, so far as the local supply was concerned, had led to the development of certain industrial districts where industry was busied in the production of fabrics of the better order, or of special kinds, needed both at home and abroad. Hence arose in these neighbourhoods an increased demand for wool, while, in addition, the self-maintaining village with its necessary common agricultural system was yielding.

The requirements of the industrial population produced an inevitable result. Locomotion had increased, but, as far as the transport of wool was concerned, it seems probable that the main line was still from west to east. The industrial growth of the eastern counties is too well known to need emphasis; but, undoubtedly, a like growth was taking place in the west. The wool pastures of Gloucester were of old standing, but there had been increase. Somerset and, at any rate during the sixteenth century, Devonshire had achieved a new importance. In both these latter manufacture had developed. Memorials of this still remain in the yarn marts and the evidences of a considerable population as in the churches dating to the fourteenth and fifteenth centuries. In the beginning of the seventeenth century we are told that Devonshire was too busied in manufacture to provide its own corn, and that its industry consumed not only its own wool, but that of Somerset, though possibly Somerset may be included with it, and that from further off, from Cornwall, Dorset, Warwick, and Worcester.

Now, as to the inclosure; that, if Fitz Herbert's account be taken, consisted in the inclosure of demesne accompanied by license in many cases to tenants to inclose their lands, the object being conversion to pasture. It is further evident from the re-enactment of the Statute of Merton that an attempt was made to enable approvement to be carried on. Probably from the reference to the wastes at the end of the century, and the demand for their use, this was not very effective. No doubt where the soil was more or less suited to inclosed pasture considerable local conversion of its use from arable to wool took place; but, as already pointed out, this was not invariable. In many cases excellent corn was still produced in the inclosures. Again, some woodland was brought into agricultural use, thus increasing the area under cultivation and in many cases being employed for corn. But, in addition to the general change thus experienced over a wide area, the change which took place in the use of the land in particular districts was more marked. In the west and the east, where both the demand for wool and the requirements of the urban and manufacturing population combined, and in the districts round London, the movement towards inclosure was, it may be asserted, much greater than elsewhere.

Towards the end of the sixteenth century new factors present themselves, which during the succeeding century become of increasing force, and dethrone the use of land as pasture from being so prominent an aim and concomitant of inclosure. Arable agriculture enters on a period of progress, and new methods of cultivation are within the power of the careful and enlightened tenant. To pursue these necessitates departure from tradition, and security against the depredations and bad farming of neighbours evilly disposed, or more slovenly and less progressive in their methods. Again, with the general progress locomotion and transport diminish the extent to which a locality, often a small locality, is dependent for the satisfaction of its wants upon its own produce. Further, new crops as fruit offer a prospect of gain in certain parts of the country.

In addition to these positive changes, certain of the causes which formerly operated in the encouragement of pasture at the expense of crops disappear or become of less influence. The land which had suffered from exhaustion till its crop-bearing power had been but slight, regained fertility, and was available for use. Not only so, but the wastes and uncultivated lands attracted attention. Partly because distance is no longer an impassable barrier and partly by reason of awakened interest, their cultivation in some one or other form is both advocated and attempted. As has been said, one writer indicates them as a source from which the required arable products may be obtained without the difficulties which must accompany the reconversion of lands, once arable but then in pasture, to their original use, while the movement of the *Diggers* is in large measure a claim to their use by those either dispossessed or unemployed. Side by side with this we have the great enterprises, such as the draining of the Bedford level, and in the Fens further woodland inclosure occurs. Nor are these all. The scarcity of labour, once important, apparently exists no longer. Where once a lord sought tenants, now tenants seek a lord and the land in the manor.

Hence, in this period, inclosure takes on a new aspect, and is attended by different results than those formerly described.

In the first place, inclosure undertaken in view of a variety of aims and under differing conditions takes place over a wider area, though not necessarily to a greater extent. In particular, it occurs in many districts in the interests of better arable and the progressive farmer, and very often on land previously lying almost waste, or affording at best scant pasture for a few half starved sheep, some of the land thus treated being turned to arable, and some to meadow or inclosed pasture.

In the second place, when change in use takes place, conversion to pasture is by no means the only form. In the home counties lying round the metropolis, where the town exercised its usual influence, and where, as can be seen from a comparison of Ogilby's travels with those of Leland, the inclosed land had greatly increased, the proportion between the various uses of land does not seem to have been seriously disturbed. No doubt in any locality some land in arable had been put to pasture, and some purely under pasture to arable, with probably disturbing results on the local employment. But there is no evidence of any dominant conversion to one or the other use. Elsewhere, however, this was not the case. Where the soil offered particular advantages, farming followed these, and land was turned to its best use. The Midland grass lands take on more and more the appearance of pasture. The same was true of North Wilts. On the other hand, in East Norfolk, and in the East Anglian counties, arable attracts the farmer.

In towns the question of storing grain is prominent, and granaries are erected in London, Oxford, and doubtless elsewhere. Even early in the century we hear of Devonshire, no doubt the district abutting on Somerset, as drawing its food supply from elsewhere, while, according to Blith, in 1652 many counties, as Hertfordshire, Essex, Kent, Surrey, Sussex, Berkshire, Hampshire, Wiltshire and Somerset not only raise their own corn but contribute to the supply of the metropolis.

Thus, in the third place, where conversion is a feature, it probably takes place far more thoroughly and uniformly than was previously the case. Districts suitable for corn became corn districts, those suited to sheep or cattle, respectively sheep districts and cattle districts. In particular, a part of the Midlands is turned more and more to pasture, and in the east, land begins to bear its present aspect in respect of grain. Taking the compositions for depopulation for the years 1635-8, the only counties where these bear a high proportion to area, are in their order, Leicester, Northampton, Rutland, Hants, and Lincoln. Very much below them stand Hertford and Nottingham, while in the other counties mentioned, these payments are insignificant.

At the end of the century there was, we are told, immense activity in inclosing with, as its result, a large increase in the arable area.

By this time, as during the eighteenth century, the introduction of fresh crops, as clover, new grasses, and later, turnips, combines with the general improvement in method to render inclosure imperative in the interests of arable. The same takes place when careful and scientific breeding supersedes the former casual methods of dealing with the live stock. Greater use and better means of transport further increase the tendency to inclosure. Nor must the force of habit be ignored. Imitation, which was a factor in the seventeenth, grows with the increase in the proportion of inclosed to uninclosed lands.

One particular matter, namely, the time of the inclosures

in the districts which were suitable for arable rather than pasture, and now are under arable, or, at any rate, mixed farming, calls for remark here. There seems little room for doubt that much inclosing in the early period took place in view of conversion to pasture; there is also no doubt that during the period of inclosing by private act, many of the counties standing high in the proportion of land inclosed are pasture counties. Further, it must be remembered that much of the complaint raised against the new movement was directed rather against the result of depopulation and want of rural employment, than against the movement itself. These facts point to the conclusion that during the seventeenth and the early years of the eighteenth century very considerable progress was made in the inclosure of the districts naturally suited by soil and other reasons to crops. This question will be considered further on.

In the main, it is evident that it was by means of inclosure that the differentiation of land to the use for which soil, aspect and climate rendered it suitable took place. As during the early period, however, sheep farming stands almost alone as a motive instigating change in the use of land, differentiation only rises into prominence as this phase ends. On the other hand, in the eighteenth century, the increased demand of large town populations for animal products, as milk and meat, has to be met in great part from the neighbourhood, a circumstance which has some effect upon the use to which the land, when inclosed, is put.[1]

[1] *Letters of First Earl of Malmesbury* (pub. 1870), p. 144. Letter from Mr. Hooper to J. Harris, M.P., 1766. "A notion prevails that a Bill will be offered for inclosing Enfield Chase and Epping Forest and dividing them into small farms as a means of adding considerably to the supply of provisions wanting for this overgrown metropolis." This of course does not restrict use to animal produce. Cf. *Agric. Report*, *Wilts*, p. 87. Inclosure sends people into towns and increases supply of food for towns. *Derby*, 174, results of increased demand for meat and animal produce on use made of the land. *Lancashire*. In this county much conversion into grass at end of century. Drain of population into towns noted, p. 393.

III

PARTICULAR PRODUCTS

ON turning from the effect of the inclosures upon cultivation in its general aspect to that produced on the things cultivated, fresh considerations come into count and new means present themselves for estimating the consequences if not for testing the benefits or injuries of the movement. Some writers seized on this as a positive and absolute test, and any diminution or increase in some one or other article was hailed as direct proof of the disadvantages or advantage of inclosure, ignoring too often the concurrent change necessarily occasioned in something else. Apart, however, from this error, it is important to examine the results thus occasioned.

Inclosure needs to be examined in respect of its effects on minor products, on the growth of timber, on cattle and sheep and their products, and, lastly, on grain.

So far as minor or miscellaneous agricultural products were concerned, it is probable that considerable alterations were caused. Thus, in the eighteenth century it seemed probable, or at any rate possible, to Horner, that the economy in carriage had led to some direct decrease in the number of horses, and so, as he adds, in the quantity of land laid down in horse beans.[1] Again, certain products peculiarly suited, in the existing and disordered condition

[1] Horner. *Essay upon the Nature and Method, etc.*, p. 17. Cf. Fitz Herbert's *Book of Husbandry*, p. 15. "Whereas is no several pasture, there the horse plow is better, for the horses may be tethered or tied upon leys, balks, or hades, whereas oxen may not be kept." Cf. *Inquiry into reasons for and against inclosure, etc.*, p. 19, as to draught horses.

of the commons must have been greatly affected when the land was separated, and when, in consequence, land could be turned to other uses. One writer complains of the decrease of hogs in Leicestershire, some hundreds, he says, " were kept in the open field parishes, ... which, since they have been inclosed, have not kept any,"[1] and further notes the decrease in geese or poultry from the inclosure of large commons.[2] On the other hand, the inclosure, we are told, affords an opportunity for the cultivation of commercial plants, as hemp, flax, and the like, as also of cattle foods and other food substances, as turnips, carrots, and potatoes.[3] But after all what do such complaints and assertions amount to, but that given the opportunity to employ the land for new purposes as well as old, in some instances and to some extent the old crops which once held on by reason or right of monopoly, must give place to the new. Permanent decrease, however, was not necessarily involved, since though less space was devoted to them, the former crops or stock might increase owing to the inclosure. With the general development of agriculture, too, the demand for horses must have speedily reached, and even exceeded, the earlier requirements.

Somewhat different from the above were certain products directly encouraged by the very circumstance of inclosure. Among such were to be included the fruit trees which in some districts, as in Worcester, Hereford, and Gloucester were planted in the hedges, a feature well recognised in the seventeenth century.[4] Orchards, it is needless to add, involved inclosure.

[1] *An inquiry into reasons for and against inclosing*, p. 19.

[2] *Id.*, also *Agric. Report, Derby* (1811), iii. 179.

[3] Erasmus Darwin, *Phytologia.* Forster (*England's Happiness Increased*, 1664, p. 22), advocating the planting of potatoes, urges in their favour as a food-stuff "there hath been of late years divers whole lordships and towns inclosed and their earable land converted into pasture ground, which practice being still continued, and more and more land inclosed every year," will lead in time to a rise in the price of corn.

[4] "Inclosures, nevertheless, have this advantage (which perhaps is peculiar to Hereford, Worcester, and some parts of Gloucester), that in the hedges fruit

The growth of wood and timber was a matter of great general and, in some respects, national importance, and one in which, owing to the length of time required before any profit could be obtained, the interests of the individual cultivator and of the community might well be held to be at variance. Wood as fuel and timber for construction were necessary commodities, and the argument that inclosure led to their increase, or at any rate their maintenance, was strongly emphasised by those who advocated the division of the lands. To some extent the argument depended for its force upon the great feature of English inclosures, that is the hedges.

That open field cultivation had led and was leading to a dearth of wood of some kind or other in the sixteenth and seventeenth centuries, and that this was injurious is supported by evidence of undoubted strength. Leland in his tour throughout the country constantly refers to the presence of wood in the inclosed districts and its absence where " champaign " prevailed. On the borders of Leicester and Northampton where all or nearly all was open, he says that wood was scarce owing to this very reason.[1] In Somerset he writes that " near the shore there is no great store of wood that is all in hedgerows of inclosures,"[2] and passing through the inclosed districts notes, " the elmewood wherewith most part of all Somerset is in hedgerows inclosed."[2] Again, a pertinent contrast is drawn between the vale of Aylesbury which " for the most part is clean barren of wood and is champaign," and the Chilterns which are " well wooded and full of inclosures."[3] The accuracy of his observation, of which the above may serve as examples, is well substantiated by

trees may be planted." Nourse, T., *Campania Felix* (1700), p. 28. "The hedgerows in the highways are filled with fruit trees," cf. Worcester, *England's Remarques* (1678), p. 211. In Standish's *Commons Complaint*, p. 34, reference to the fruit trees in hedges and fields of Worcester, Gloucester, and Hereford. Blith adds great part of Kent; p. 127.

[1] Leland, *Itinerary*, vol. i. p. 15. [2] *Id.* ii. p. 65.

[3] *Id.* iv. p. 123; and cf. i. 41, 118, v. 9, etc.

others writing about the end of that century and later, whose testimony, referring as it does to different districts, enables his general conclusion to be taken as fairly applicable throughout the country.[1] The hedges of Kent[2] and Suffolk were notorious, but in both cases we find observers noting a lack of wood in those districts where the proportion of champion was greatest.[3] Probably at this period, that is the latter sixteenth and seventeenth centuries, it was the consequent lack of fuel which was of most concern. The constant complaint is the lack of wood and fuel, often of wood for fuelling, one writer in 1613 speaking of "champaign countries where land is barren and fewell so scant that they are constrained to burn the straw and manure."[4] Another writes that "the fuel which they want in the champion is supplied by inclosure."[5] This need was met in the inclosed districts by the ordinary hedges and more particularly by hedges in which trees were planted. The top wood of the hedges

[1] Standish, *Commons Complaint*, p. 9-10, asserts profit of planting timber in hedges seen in many counties, especially Essex, where more care taken of hedges and timber in the hedges than in Northampton, Leicester, Rutland, and other counties; where in consequence more need of timber and firewood than elsewhere. This emphasised *New Directions of Experience to the Commons Complaint*, 1613, where, p. 6, the writer speaks of champain counties where land is barren. Lansdown MS., 487, f. 433. Burton, *Leicestershire* (1622), notes, p. 2, want of wood and fuei in south-east of the shire where "it is almost all champain." Lee, *Vindication*, p. 21, gives as an important advantage of inclosure that it nourishes wood. *Moryson, Fynes* (1617) in reference to Kent "des verges et des hayes vines qui enferment les terres labourables et des prairies," p. 24. In the *Considerations concerning common fields, etc.*, 1653, p. 11, profit of hedges asserted, as also in the Summary given in the *Vindication of the Considerations*. Blome in *Britannia* (1673) speaking of Kent says, p. 122, "it is also sufficiently furnished with wood for fuelling and good timber trees, except towards the east where it is more champion." Thus Reyce, *Breviary*, says, p. 33, of Suffolk that wood is plentiful in all parts "save towards the champion." Further, see *A New System of Agriculture*, John Laurence, 1726, p. 47.

[2] Kent, *Moryson, Fynes*; Halstead's *Kent*; Blome, *Britannia*, p. 122. Suffolk, Reyce, *Breviary*, p. 133; also above as to Essex.

[3] See above. [4] Standish, *New Directions, etc.*, p. 6.

[5] Lansdown MS., 487, f. 433.

is mentioned as a source of profit.[1] But in addition to the supply of fuel the hedges where trees are planted is regarded by many as a source from which timber could be obtained. For this purpose trees are to be planted in hedges; while by some it is urged that inclosure leads in general to planting.[2] The effect on planting other than in hedges would seem, however, to become of importance later, and mainly in the eighteenth century when the value of regular plantations was better understood and when the impossibility of securing such under the common field system was recognised. That it might encourage plantation seems obvious for the very same reasons which apply to any other improvement in which the enlightened wishes of any one proprietor might be obstructed by the ignorance of others under the open field system; but the extent to which this opportunity was utilised is much more doubtful. In the case of two counties we have definite evidence to this effect, and Horner, writing more generally, claims that it has operated in this direction.[3] On the other hand in answer to him it was contended that as a matter of fact comparatively little plantation took place in consequence of inclosure.[4] To the effects thus achieved must be added another, due to the greater security furnished by inclosure against depredation and wilful destruction where trees existed. On the other hand the temptation to clear land and fell timber when such passed into individual ownership must be taken into account.

In this instance, as indeed in many others, it is necessary to distinguish somewhat carefully between the consequences of inclosure at different periods and under different circumstances. As cultivation extended the waste woods themselves the subject of common tend to be cleared and

[1] *Considerations, etc.*, p. 11; Standish, *New Directions, etc.*, *v. supra.*

[2] Summary given in *Vindication of the Considerations*, p. 42, etc.

[3] *Agric. Reports, Cambridge* (1813), p. 197; *Rutland* (1808), pp. 40, 107; Horner, p. 41.

[4] *Inquiry into reasons for and against inclosing, etc.*, p. 9.

brought into more definite use. Alike as a consequence and a cause of growth such a development was inevitable. But even apart from it, forests under common use would suffer from depredation and neglect, while the intermixture of interests would prevent their maintenance by replanting and other measures for preservation. Granted the extension of cultivation, inclosure operated undoubtedly towards the provision of wood both as fuel and as timber, in the early period largely by increase of hedgerows and the planting of timber trees on banks and in the hedges, but later on because it made it possible for those who desired to afforest or at any rate to maintain woods to do so without depending on the consent of others.

In respect of cattle and sheep inclosure was welcomed by many from early times as a means alike of improvement and economy. The language of Fitz Herbert in the sixteenth century who estimates profits as likely to be doubled is re-echoed in the seventeenth century and by none more strongly than Houghton who writes with indignation of "pernicious commons which have led to small and underfed and badly cared for cows."[1] The same general verdict is, of course, widely expressed in the eighteenth century when different observers furnish different illustrations of the defects of the commons and open field system and the corresponding advantages noticed or to be expected from its supersession. Thus one attacks the argument that commons are good as nurseries of young cattle,[2] another gives instances where inclosure has enabled a farmer to fatten his sheep instead of selling them, as formerly, for stores,[3] while others compare from their experience the sheep in the inclosures

[1] Fitz Herbert, *Book of Husbandry*, p. 77; *Considerations*, 12, etc. Five reasons given; (1) Less attendance required; (2) Cattle quieter and not harried by dogs and exposed to infection; (3) Cattle can be out at night; (4) Ground not spoilt by cattle being driven to and fro; (5) Kept on most suitable land; *Vindication of the Considerations, etc.*, 42, etc.; Houghton, *Collections* (1693), p. 110.

[2] Tucker, J., *Elements of Commerce*, pp. 52-3.

[3] *Agric. Rep.*, *Leicester*, p. 72.

with those in the open fields and on the commons.[1] On the general aspect of the case Bakewell, the celebrated breeder, expressed himself strongly to Arthur Young. His opinion is worth quoting and may be compared with that of Fitz Herbert, pronounced more than two centuries before. "He asserts," Young records, "from long attention that if two poor men buy each of them a cow in the spring, and one turns his into the forest, and the other pays a farmer 1s. 6d. a week for the food of his among the farmer's cows, and at Michaelmas if both are driven to the market and sold, the difference in the price will more than repay the weekly expense of the man who rejected the ideal advantage of the common. The difference of the product may be imagined. And in sheep the contrast would be still greater."[2]

In illustration and support of this position many and various advantages are mentioned as arising from inclosure. The shelter of the hedges in the inclosed fields is considered important by some, probably in districts where the situation was bleak,[3] the provision of adequate winter feed by others, a security greatly lacking under the common system,[4] while mention is likewise made of the risk to sheep in being turned out of the warm fold into the exposed common or open field,[5] and the natural difference in the forest district between sheep wandering about in the woods and those cared for in a field.[6] A point more

[1] *Agric. Rep., Rutland*, p. 129; *Agric. Rep., Bedford*, by Storie, 1794, pp. 31, 32.

[2] *Annals of Agriculture*, vi., p. 497.

[3] *Agric. Report, North Riding* (1800), 90-1; *A View of Devonshire, in* 1630, by T. Westcott, p. 60. *Tusser Redivivus*, 1710, Feb., p. 9, explanation of Tusser's meaning in note, when speaking of hedging, the annotator says, "this is an excellent way to improve bleak grounds."

[4] *Vindication of the considerations, etc.*, p. 42 etc.; *Agric. Report, Wilts.* (1813), p. 40; according to *a Political Enquiry into the consequences of inclosing waste lands, etc.*, 1785, p. 45; cottagers keeping sheep often send them to board with farmers in the winter.

[5] Stone, *Suggestions*, p. 17.

[6] *Agric. Report* (1798), *Nottingham*, p. 125.

frequently emphasised is the greater quiet of the inclosed pastures where cattle and sheep have not to be constantly driven to and fro, not only to the injury of the ground, but to their own detriment. Cows thus kept yield more milk, and the butter is better.[1] As to the results on sheep there is more dispute, as will be seen later on.[2]

But there are more important results than those thus alluded to, which call for more detailed consideration.

In the first place, the general condition of the common often led to insufficient feeding. Whatever may be thought of Houghton's epithet "pernicious" as referring to commons under favourable and original conditions there can be no doubt as to its applicability in the case of unstinted and overstocked commons. The difficulties of maintaining the former limitations on the beasts entitled to common have been described already. By gradual steps these had led in some parts to attempted regulation by number, and in others to a virtual abandonment of any control. There is little reason to believe in the efficacy of the former measure. Neighbours without rights invaded the commons lying by them. The rich crowded their beasts on and literally eat out the poor: while worst of all the sale of right of common to jobbers and rich graziers augmented the class of those interested only in the herbage of the land, whether in open field or in common, who seem to have pursued their ends recklessly and without consideration for others.[3] In the sixteenth and still more in the seventeenth century there is abundant complaint of this tendency. By the eighteenth century it is evidently irresistible. Even where

[1] *Considerations*, p. 12; more milk; cf. *An Essay on Ways and Means for inclosing, fallowing, planting, etc., Scotland*, by a Lover of his Country, 1729, p. 38. Butter, *Tusser Redivivus* (1710), April 12.

[2] *A Political Enquiry into the consequences, etc.*, 1785, p. 50, asserts fine wool on commons; but half starved sheep according to *Agric. Report, Warwick*, p. 62.

[3] In addition to those actually interested in agriculture there were, according to some writers, a host of undesirable characters. "The men who usually reside near a common are the depredators of the neighbourhood; smugglers, sheep stealers, horse jockies and jobbers of every denomination here find their abode." *Agric. Report, Suffolk*, pp. 146-7.

commons were rated or stinted they were often overstocked,[1] in too many places the restriction on numbers being merely nominal. Under these circumstances it is little wonder that there were widespread complaints of the small and underfed cattle and sheep reared upon them. Nor do the complaints meet with any adequate answer from those who still remained faithful adherents to the old system. What defence they could offer depended on the supposition that commons and fields could be effectively regulated and the stint rigidly observed. The experience of two centuries showed how futile was this belief.

In the second place, a new opportunity was afforded for keeping cattle and sheep on the land best suited to them. No doubt in the common system some rough attempt had been made in this direction, but custom as also the wishes of others had to be consulted. Under inclosure land could be apportioned to one or other use as seemed best. Moreover with the growth of means of communication a further extension of the same principle became possible. In the open field system the land subject to apportionment between crops and stock was that of the manor, or the village, or the hamlet. Some of that was arable, some was meadow, and some lay in pasture. Only when that system is superseded do we find pasture and cattle or sheep spreading throughout a whole array of parishes, while elsewhere there was little stock and much arable. As a consequence the relation between stock and crops differs in different districts. In the eighteenth century it made of Leicester a sheet of green sward, while parts of Norfolk were covered with grain. As a writer of an earlier date already cited, says "when tillage is more profitable than pasturage, men will break up their pastures to till; and why should they not have liberty then to lay down their arable to land for grass when pasturage is more profitable than tillage."[2]

[1] *Agric. Reports, Suffolk*, p. 149, "even the rated are overstocked." *Westmoreland*, p. 321.

[2] *Considerations*, p. 21.

In the third place breeding could be better carried on. The old system of promiscuous pasture when the cattle and sheep of all owners were herded together made even ordinary care in breeding difficult. It made scientific breeding impracticable. It was mainly in connection with this latter evil that complaint became prominent. Alike in the *Reports* to the Board of Agriculture and the writings of practical men like Stone, the common flock is condemned on this account, and for this, if for no other reason the claim is urged that the breed of sheep and cattle is improved by inclosure.[1] It is not necessary to emphasise the dependence on such inclosure of skilled breeding which then was first finding an assured place in English agriculture owing in large measure to the experiments of Bakewell.

Lastly, the danger from infectious and other disease was a common ground for complaint against the open-field system. So far as infection was concerned there was no doubt as to the risk involved unless precautions were exercised. The matter was so grave as to be dealt with by act. One early act provides against the putting to common pasture of any horse with scab or mange. The prevalence of the danger is shown by the fact that two years before the close of the eighteenth century it was necessary to prohibit sheep with mange.[2] The advantages of inclosure are obvious.[3] On the other hand, sheep rot, arising from the condition of the pasture, may be held to be in a somewhat different position. With regard to its connection with the open field, and its accompanying want of care, evidence is at hand from the seventeenth century. It is one of the causes alleged in the Chancery suits of inclosure.[4] After inclosure the sheep-rot in certain districts is said to be

[1] Stone, *Suggestions*, pp. 17-18; *Agric. Reports*, *Somerset* (1798), pp. 53-55; *Wilts.* (1813), p. 40.

[2] The early act, 32 H. VIII. c. 13; the later act, 38 G. III. c. 65.

[3] Some examples referred to, *Agric. Report*, *Oxford* (1813), p. 99, etc.

[4] *E.g.* Chancery Enrolled Decrees, 1658; Great Coxwell, *Roll*, 653.

lessened.[1] Houghton emphasises the comparatively lighter loss incurred on the inclosed lands during a particular period of disease.[2] Instances of the decrease of rot are given in the latter part of the eighteenth century,[3] while the counter assertion as to the danger of sheep rot in inclosures during the winter called forth a somewhat indignant denial from Young, who says that this, when it happens, is the result of individual bad management, a somewhat easy retort, as it seems.[4] The balance of evidence as to what happened in general is distinctly in favour of inclosure and against the open-field system.

The results of inclosure which have been described in the foregoing pages may be briefly summarised. The quality and breed of both cattle and sheep was improved. Again, in some instances, and especially where inclosure brought with it an improvement in the grass, or where more suitable pastures were substituted for less suitable land, larger numbers could be reared; on the other hand, in many cases the crowded and over-stocked common gave place to fields with only a due quantity of stock. In such cases there were, if less beasts, better beasts.[5] Concurrently, however, with this, the new crops of turnips and clover enabled larger flocks to be kept.[6] The economy of the new system was generally accepted, though, it must be remembered, that owing to the capital charges incurred in actually hedging and ditching the land, early years might quite possibly show an increase rather than a decrease in cost. Lastly, in sundry animal products, as milk and butter, improvement was noticed.

On the other hand, there was one product, wool, in respect of which the consequences of the change were

[1] Lee, *Vindication, etc.*, 'Advantages of Inclosure,' pp. 21-25.

[2] Houghton, *Collections* (1692), p, 30.

[3] *Agric. Report, Cambridge* (1813), p. 93.

[4] *Annals of Agriculture*, vi. 459.

[5] Lee, *Vindication, etc.* 21-25, 'Advantages of Inclosure.'

[6] Houghton, *Collections* (1681), p. 144; Tucker, *Elements of Commerce* (1755), p. 49.

severely criticised. In the comparisons drawn between the two systems of agriculture, it was constantly and confidently asserted by those opposed to inclosure that such tend to diminish the quantity of fine wool.[1] Such was in the main obtained from the breed of small sheep in the open fields and commons, which were able to rove about at will.[2] In this, an injury to woollen industry, or at any rate to certain of its branches, was espied.[3] Even those who advocated the change of system do not directly deny this charge,[4] or at any rate its possible truth, though sometimes doubting its extent, and sometimes urging alleviating circumstances. Inclosed pasture with rich, artificial grass, resulted, according to some, in larger sheep, though coarser wool.[5] Again, it is urged that the defect in quality will be compensated for by an increase in quantity owing to an alleged increase in sheep.[6] Elsewhere, the argument is put forward that this alteration, though in the main admitted, is not necessarily inherent in inclosure, and that it might be

[1] *Inquiry into the reasons for and against inclosing open fields*, by S. Addington (1772), pp. 28-9; *A Political Enquiry* (1785), p. 50.

[2] *Political Enquiry*, p. 61.

[3] As above; but Young gives instances to the effect that as many sheep kept and as much work required in woollen districts. Young, *Eastern Tour*, ii. 5, 26.

[4] Tucker, however, does. *Elements of Commerce*, p. 50.

[5] *Annals of Agriculture*, iii. 341. Young cites an abstract from Lord Sheffield. Here a decrease in fine wool said to have occurred in some parts of England. Case of Shropshire instanced. cf. Stone, *Suggestions*, p. 66. *Address to the Society for the Improvement of British Wool*, by Sir John Sinclair (1791), p. 9. Speaking of fine wool, the writer proceeds: "The sheep which produce this sort of wool are small, delight in an extensive range of pasture, and do not thrive in those narrow bounds with which the long-wooled and large-sized sheep are content. They were formerly to be found in those extensive commons in England of which so many have been inclosed." cf. Barnaby Googe, *Four Books of Husbandry*, p. 132: "The plaine and the champion fields and downs are best for the delicatest and finest wolled sheepe."

[6] *The advantages and disadvantages of inclosing waste lands and open fields*, by a County Gentleman (1772), pp. 66-7; Tucker, *Elements of Commerce*, p. 49; *Agric. Report*, *Somerset* (1798), pp. 69-70.

remedied by proper breeding.[1] A more radical attitude however, is taken by Tucker,[2] who, while doubting the fact, contends that fineness is not essential to English wool, and by Howlett,[3] who points out not only that fine wool is not a necessary product, but that other uses of the land may be more beneficial, concluding his argument with the caustic epigram, that after all "a fat oxen is better than a silkworm."

[1] Thus, author of *Advantages and disadvantages, etc.*, cited above, and Stone, *Suggestions*, p. 66.

[2] *Elements of Commerce*, p. 50.

[3] Howlett, *Enclosures, a Cause of Improved Agriculture, etc.*, p. 89; cf. *Agric. Report, Gloucester* (1807), Appendix, 403.

IV

ANIMAL PRODUCTS AND GRAIN

THE chief point of controversy, however, concerned the total effect of inclosure upon the number of animals, or, rather, the amount of animal products and the quantity of grain.

This must be distinguished, on the one hand, from the question of profit[1] to the owners of the land, since the acknowledged economy of the new system might well enable a larger profit to be obtained from a smaller gross produce; and, on the other hand, from either the number of acres devoted to a particular use, or, in the case of stock, from the actual number of beasts, since it would be of no harm to supplant a large number of poor and underfed beasts by a somewhat smaller number, if larger and fatter. Granted an equal production of wheat or of meat, milk, and other animal commodities, it was not, except so far as employment was concerned, a matter of profound public concern if the acreage was less. The land diverted from one or the other use might be turned to other purposes; but on this point more must be said when we come to the question of population and employment. Apart from this, the real matter for discussion is the result of inclosure upon the quantity of grain on the one hand,

[1] Testimony as to the general result in the increase of rent is too abundant for quotation. Exceptions, however, might occur in the case of rich meadow and pasture land (see above, p. 307). Also, good arable which might undergo no change in its use, owing to particular conditions, was probably less profitable for inclosure.

and of animals on the other, whether as food or material, or, in some instances, as means of working the land.

Decision on such matters is clearly dependent on time and district, and it was neglect of this fact which led to such striking diversity of opinion and to many of the random assertions encountered in the literature of the subject. Different observers generalised from the effect occasioned in a limited area or imagined that their experience was a type of all experience.

With regard to stock, one general remark may be made at the outset.

At no time was mere economy in management generally alleged as the sole ground for inclosure. Indeed it was fairly well admitted that improvement in stock at any rate in some one aspect was an aim and a result. It might of course be accompanied, as in the particular instance of wool, by deterioration in some other aspect.

But, granted this, the question still remains whether at any time there was so great a diversion of land from pasture to arable as to occasion a decrease either in animals absolutely or in animals to such an extent as to outweigh the improvement in quality. To arrive at any conclusion in this matter, it is necessary to glance at the various epochs of inclosure. Some of the evidence on this point, affecting the real or alleged conversion of land from arable to tillage, will be more appropriately dealt with when the effect of inclosure on grain is considered.

So far, however, as inclosing during the fifteenth century and the first half of the sixteenth century is concerned, it seems quite safe to assert that there was certainly no decrease in the number of sheep; and the same may be said, though with less array of testimony, as to cattle. The complaints as to the substitution of the sheep for the plough, and of a corresponding depopulation, though possibly and even probably exaggerated, are wide-spread as well as loud, and find some corroboration in revolutionary movements and in the great development of the wool trade. To them may be added the recognition of this change and the definite attempt at its control in the statutes for the retention of land in tillage, and for other similar purposes. All this evidence points in the one direction.

To some extent, at any rate, the same—so far, that is, as actual decrease of live stock is concerned—would seem to hold good of the latter part of the sixteenth century. At the end of that century, however, and in the beginning of the next, there are, it is true, signs at times of more effective attention to arable, a feature which seems responsible for the dropping of the tillage laws in 1594-5. But this merely led to an increased demand for regulation; as is shown by the already cited preamble to the new law passed in 1597-8, which is as follows: "Whereas from the 37th year of King Henry the Eighth of famous memory until the five and thirtieth year of her majesty's most happy reign there was always in force some law which did ordain a conversion and continuance of a certain quantity and proportion of land in tillage not to be altered; and that in the last parliament held in the same five and thirtieth year of her majesty's reign, partly by reason of the great plenty and cheapness of grain at that time within this realm, and partly by reason of the imperfection and obscurity of the law made in that case, the same was discontinued: since which time there have grown many more depopulations by turning tillage into pasture than at any time for the like number of years heretofore."[1] About the same time were published like complaints, as, for instance, that since the reign of Henry VII. matters in this respect had changed for the worse, the number of sheep leading to the disuse of the plough.[2] From the

[1] 39 Eliz. c. 2 (1597-8), cf. 39 Eliz. c. 1 (1597-8), "and where of late years more than in times past there have sundrie towns, parishes, and houses of husbandry been destroyed and become desolate."

[2] *Certain causes gathered together wherein is shown the decay of England* (Early Eng. Tracts), p. 98, complaints of change for the worse since time of Henry VII. This tract apparently dates towards end of sixteenth century. The inclosure complained of is in Oxford, Buckingham, and Northampton.

words of another writer in 1613 it is clear that in some districts at any rate inclosures were regarded as proving beneficial to the cattle;[1] while another, a little earlier (1576), asserts that "the fourth part of the ground that some time was agreeable in this realm to maintain the plough to breed corn is now in pasture to maintain sheep."[2] Even when the injurious effect upon corn is directly challenged and denied, as in the celebrated comparison of Somerset and Northampton, the increase of corn therein asserted is not considered as taking place at the expense of stock. On the contrary, a like increase of wool is alleged.[3] The renewed enquiries during the early years of the seventeenth century, even if they do not uphold the view taken of inclosures at this time as tending towards depopulation and the abandonment of tillage, are sufficient evidence that on the whole, live stock, and especially sheep, were not diminishing but increasing.[4] This too is generally borne out by the petitions received and the proceedings undertaken by the Privy Council.[5] Land now, as we hear, was hired by jobbers and grazing butchers.[6] During the controversy waged in the middle of this century as to the result in the Midlands, the change made is the decrease of arable and not of stock.

[1] Standish, *New Directions of Experience to the Commons Complaint*, p. 19, etc.

[2] Address by Alderman Box, Lansdown MS., cxxxi. 2, f. 2.

[3] Lansdown MS. 487, f. 433.

[4] *S.P.D.* ccxxix. p. 490 (1632), warrant for commission to inquire touching depopulation and conversion of arable since 10 Elizabeth in counties of Lincoln, Leicester, Northampton, Somerset, Wilts, Gloucester. Cf. Commission, 1606-7.

[5] *P.C. Register* gives numerous instances of complaint and of consequent inquiries, v. vol. iv. p. 100; v. 700; vii. pp. 506-7, 522; viii. 194, 351; ix. 301; x. 40, 197. As to directions to Judges of Assize, etc., and interviews or correspondence with them or Sheriffs, and especially ix. 267 (9 Oct. 1633); in the account of the interview, no mention is made of inclosures, however, p. 278 (18 Oct.); ix. 301 (31 Oct. 1633).

[6] Depopulation arraigned by *R.P.* (1636), p. 40. This points to a particular development apparently connected with the growth of stock for the meat supply of towns, etc.

Still it would seem clear that inclosure had gradually taken on another complexion from that observed, when it presents itself in the fifteenth and early sixteenth century. In the words of a quotation already cited, land is being put to the uses for which it is best suited ; and the writer in question refers to the breaking up of pasture to arable as well as to the laying down of arable to grass.[1] That there was a possibility of such conversion, together with restrictions introduced as to the stock kept to grass, turning to the disadvantage of the amount of stock became clearer as the century advanced. Even where fewer, or, if fewer, the beasts were better, is the argument of some ; and Houghton definitely recites the objection only to deny that inclosure would decrease the number of sheep. On the contrary, as already pointed out, he says that new sources of food for beasts are furnished by the new crops of clover and turnips.[2]

The language used by various writers, in addition to the above, about the end of this century and the beginning of the eighteenth, leaves no doubt that conversions or re-conversions to arable were taking place. It is immaterial whether such pasture was previously in common or not, the main point being that land, once used for grazing, was withdrawn from that use. Thus one writer, speaking of the assertion that inclosure led to land passing into arable out of pasture, as applied to his days, says, "the contrary is notorious,"[3] to which another adds that the tendency for some little time previous had been for land to pass out of pasture, and writes, "I think there are not more than thirteen counties at present where feeding and breeding cattle is as much encouraged as formerly."[4] Later on in

[1] *Considerations, etc.*, pp. 10, 21.

[2] Houghton, *Collections*, 1681, p. 144, where he definitely urges that cultivation of turnips, clover, etc., will enable some sheep to be kept. This view is substantiated by fact, and is emphasised in the controversy in the latter part of the next century, *e.g.* Tucker, *Elements of Commerce*, p. 49.

[3] *A New System of Agriculture*, Lawrence (1726), 46.

[4] *The Landlord's Companion*, William Allen (1742), p. 18.

the eighteenth century when controversy was hot, views were expressed on both sides, the fact being that in this active period, when much common and many large tracts of open field were inclosed, instances of either effect could be observed.[1] In Norfolk, for instance, where sheep walks were divided, some went to pasture and some to

[1] As to conversion to arable, *Agric. Report*, *Bedford*, several instances, pp. 249-50, 270-271. On p. 224, a case where opportunity for grazing much diminished. *Agric. Report*, *Essex*, p. 123, citing from original draft by Howlett, "our new inclosures which are neither very large nor very numerous, have generally been converted from pasture to arable." The same writer calls attention to like tendency in the case of coarse pastures of ancient inclosures.

The Committee appointed by the Common Council, 16th July, 1786, to consider the causes of the present high price of provisions, published their report in 1786. This is summarised *Annals of Agriculture*, vii. pp. 47-58, and criticised. Among such causes inclosures are included, and the report gives a table showing the acreage of land, open or closed to sheep, of the inclosures in recent years.

Years.	Acres into which Sheep cannot be turned.	Acres into which Sheep may be turned.	Total.	Number of inclosures unascertained.
1775	30.831	22.909	53.740	9
1776	45.157	30.143	75.300	11
1777	49.248	42.685	91.933	17
1778	23.025	8.213	31.238	10
1779	34.812	26.407	61.219	10
1780	17.634	33.213	50.847	5
1781	8.404	12.730	21.134	3
1782	3.310	11.197	14.507	2
1783	4.700	24.277	28.977	4
1784	8.610	6.507	15.117	2
1785	13.939	7.678	21.617	4
1786	15.448	7.563	23.011	4
	255.118	233.522	488.640	81

Leaving aside the adequacy of this table as any proof, on which Young makes some sarcastic comments, its figures, if reliable, certainly point to a large amount of land, when inclosed, being under crop. It does not prove conversion of pasture to arable, but it makes it probable that such took place in some cases and districts. Both Young (in the *Annals*) and Howlett (*Inclosures a cause of improved agriculture*) devote considerable space to the report.

A large number of writers consider that sheep have increased, see, for example, Marshall, *Midlands*, ii. 250; as to *Leicester*, Darwin, *Phitologia*; Tucker, *Elements of Commerce*, p. 49; *Agric. Reports*, *Leicester*; Orig. Report cited *Reports*, 1815, p. 393.

corn, but as was pointed out even then, that remaining to pasture not only might, but did, feed as many sheep.[1] In Yorkshire, as Marshall says, the two processes went on together, while of Leicester he writes, that not long ago it was an open arable county, but that then it had become "a continued sheet of greensward, a district of grazing lands." The conversion of land from one use to another was, as has been already observed, by no means a conclusive test as to the actual effects on either stock or crops. This is particularly true in the case of waste and many commons where, prior to inclosure, little or no cultivation was taking place. Nominally these would rank as inclosures from pasture, and thus their division between arable and pasture would suggest a partial conversion from one use to another, though in reality the part left to pasture was first brought into effective cultivation and might well produce food for very largely increased flocks or lands. Even in Warwick, by no means a bare and infertile county, we hear that "land that formerly kept a few half-starved sheep, is now yielding abundance of both grass and corn." The same is true, to an even greater extent, in the case of some other counties.[2]

Turning, however, to the actual quantity of stock, some definite inquiries give a basis for a conclusion as to the effect during this period. The results of these enquiries are given in the *General Report* to the Board of Agriculture in 1808.

	No. of Incl. Parishes making returns.	No. showing increase.	No. showing decrease.
Cattle	571	354	106
Dairy Cows	511	255	143
Sheep	721	467	157

Taking the separate counties, increase is the general rule.

Of equal, if not more, importance than the effect on

[1] Young, *Eastern Tour*, ii. p. 5.

[2] *Agric. Report*, *Warwick* (1815), p. 62. Cf. *Agric. Report*, *Berks*, as to land suited for turnips, pp. 527-8; *Dorset*, as to the heaths, p. 93; *Nottingham*, great improvement in sheep in forest districts, p. 125.

cattle and sheep is that produced on arable and grain. This, which now comes before us, occupied a far larger share of controversial attention than any other agricultural matter, and was, as can be readily understood, a matter of very critical importance. In the first place it touched the provision of the ordinary staple of life, while, in the second place, any alteration from arable to pasture or the reverse, might make a difference in the employment to be offered in the district, thus affecting, as indeed the provision of bread affected, the population of the country. With these results in view it is little wonder that in all discussions as to inclosure, the effect upon arable played a very prominent part. The material on which a judgment must be based has been partly dealt with, but something must be added to what has been said. So far as the way in which cultivation was concerned little, however, is necessary. The distinction may be emphasised which was previously drawn between the relief offered from restrictions and disadvantages incidental to the old system and the opportunities which grew with time of adopting new and improved methods. As these latter increase, the need of enabling the more progressive farmers to advance more and more outweighs the advantages of a custom or standard which coerced idleness and prevented negligence. The middle sixteenth century may be broadly taken as the period during which this factor makes itself felt. Prior to that, but for the inconvenience attending intermixt lands and the malpractices and trespasses of neighbours, grain might be grown as well, or nearly as well, in champion or open field as in inclosures. Even when the means of improvement were far greater, some do not hesitate to express opinions favourable to grain in the large open fields; and though probably, as things went in practice, and largely by reason of the above inconveniences, the inclosed fields offered some superiority even at the earlier period, such was neither great nor invariable.

In view of this the effect of inclosure in early years upon the actual acreage put to arable acquires great importance. Its decrease meant a diminished supply and often restricted employment. It has been usual to treat the inclosures of the fifteenth century, and at least the early sixteenth century as resulting fairly uniformly in a conversion of arable to pasture, and as was said there is abundant evidence that such often took place. On the other hand, however, it is not correct to assume that inclosures were all permanently used for pasture. In Leland's *Itinerary* there is mention of enclosed land in some sixty instances. Out of these sixty, in the case of twenty-six, it is expressly stated that corn was grown. Sometimes it is termed " goodly corn land," sometimes said to be fruitful or plentiful of corn, and at other times fruitful of grass and corn. But in all such cases the corn was obviously plentiful enough to attract Leland's notice, and in his opinion to deserve mention.[1] At the time of inclosure much land may have been converted to pasture, but this cannot be asserted with certainty. Further, from many references it would seem that after some years of needed rest land would often be reconverted to arable with remarkable results as far as fertility was concerned. The circumstances which surrounded the land and dictated its use had changed even before the end of the reign of Henry VIII. One writing then says that conditions had greatly changed since the time when landlords through a

[1] When the reverse was markedly the case Leland appears to call attention to the fact; thus of some land between Winchester and Southampton he says, "apter for cattle than corn" (iii. 89), of the land in Arden, "plentiful of grass but not of corn" (iv. pt. 2, p. 65). Such references, however, are rare. Taking, then, the occasions on which inclosures are mentioned, in twenty-six there is mention of corn, often in an emphatic way. In the case of the remaining thirty-four, in some very few instances the opposite is indicated. Occasionally it is said that there is much wood; but in the greater number of the cases the mere fact of inclosure is recorded, and it cannot be concluded that such were wholly or mainly in pasture. The fact of the land being in champaign is often stated, likewise without comment.

Pasture lands, however, were probably more often inclosed than arable in early times. Thus Aubrey writes (*Nat. History and Antiquities of Surrey*, ii. p. 3) "from whence to the River Thames the country, being pasture, is inclosed," cf. iv. p. 172, where he speaks of inclosed pastures, etc.

lack of tenants had been driven to sheep and wool, and that by that date the increase of population had led tenants to seek for landlords.[1] The greater profit of inclosures when put to corn is shown by the higher estimate of the yield per acre, and by testimony as to particular places and districts.[2] Sometimes reference is made to cases where land apparently has been directly inclosed for arable, at other times to places where inclosed pastures have been ploughed up with favourable results.[3] This tendency cannot be assumed as operative much before the close of the sixteenth century, and the efficacy of the frequent efforts of the state both by laws as those of tillage, and by direct action in their support will always remain a matter for speculation. The discontinuance of the Statutes of Tillage in 1593-4 was due in part to the abundance of corn while the demand for their re-enactment alleges that in the few intervening years further conversions to pasture, and with them depopulation, had taken place. On the other hand there were not wanting those who thought that these laws produced little if any effect. One writer finds a reason for this in the absence of any provision in the statutes definitely limiting the amount of common or meadow, "without which no limitation of common or meadow can be maintained." Further than that, he adds, the law is defective inasmuch as even with the scant allowance of land which is to be restored to tillage "there is no limitation set down either for fine or rent. But the poor that are to be restored are in both left to the will or hard conscience of him that hath destroyed the town, or of him that hath unconscionably purchased the town so destroyed."[4]

[1] *Conference between ploughman and clothier*, by John Green. Reg. MS. 7, cxvi. f. 235.

[2] This detailed statement is rare, but see comparison of Somerset and Northampton. Lansdown MS. 487, p. 433.

[3] *Considerations*, p. 10; Lee, *A Vindication, etc.*, pp. 8, 9.

[4] Lansdown MS. 83, p. 68. Sir Anthony Cope to Burleigh. The writer is evidently criticising the draft of 39 Eliz. c. 1. Cf. Lansdown MS. cxxxi. p. 22 (1576), Address by Alderman Box.

The complaints current at the time both as to the harm done and the want of effectiveness in the legislation devised in its remedy were due doubtless more to the question of agricultural employment than to any real lack of grain. Even where the supply of grain was secured by the reconversion of land to arable after a short rest in grass and by improved fertility, the labour of the district might be injured in two ways; firstly, during the time when the land was in pasture; and, secondly, by the improvement both in the land and in the mode of cultivation in the inclosure whereby the crops required were raised with less labour. This injury was unavoidable in the cause of progress, and it might be local rather than general; but none the less it was a real injury to the people concerned, the more so because migration was difficult. A better and more practicable remedy than that attempted by the statutes was contained in the proposal, that the difficulty should be met by carrying inclosure further in the compulsory division and cultivation of the wastes.[1] This, it is urged, might be so achieved as to provide a fresh source for grain, and at the same time secure to the tenants or cultivators their rightful share in the profits of the land. It was obvious that it would increase employment, though no doubt change of place and migration might still be involved.

Though the ineffectiveness of the legislation may be partly owing to defects in the provisions as enacted and partly due to the impotence of laws opposed to the economic tendency of the time, there can be little doubt that some part of the inoperativeness arose from the want of machinery to give administrative effect to what was decreed. In the seventeenth century, however, during the early period of Charles I. when the Privy Council became an active administrative body, the attempt was made to supply this defect so far as the conversion to pasture was concerned. It is difficult to determine the degree of success attending this attempt. Complaints still continue,

[1] v. *supra*, pp. 157-8, Address by Alderman Box.

but on the other hand they are met by statements that the land which has been inclosed is in arable. The action of the Privy Council though vigorous at times was somewhat spasmodic, and the period of such action soon came to an end. Again, in some cases those who had converted the land were allowed to compound for their sins, which thus became a means of replenishing the royal coffers. Moreover, in all probability the time during which conversion to pasture could be considered a grave menace was actually over, such conversion bringing about a natural reaction. Arable was certainly profitable,[1] and hence, land formerly thrown into pasture reverted to grain; while in addition a good deal of actual waste was brought into cultivation for the first time as in the drainage districts.

Reviewing contemporary evidence, certain conclusions seem possible. Firstly, the tillage laws did not produce the effect sought. Secondly, so far as the latter part of the sixteenth and the earlier years of the seventeenth century are concerned, conversion to pasture was only a temporary and not a permanent consequence. Thirdly, it is obvious that such conversion was deprecated on two grounds, not always clearly distinguished. On the one hand a dearth of corn was feared, on the other hand a diminution of employment. But the latter effect might be occasioned by different causes than inclosure, as for instance increased fertility or improved methods of cultivation. In some instances these were the immediate cause and the inclosure which induced them, the indirect cause.

The controversy as to the inclosures in the Midlands during the seventeenth century, despite any precise evidence as to the total results, is very instructive. It shows that by a certain large class the new system was regarded as detrimental to the best national interests, a view which is equally evident from the proceedings of the Privy Council, and from other testimony. This view, which may be called the official view, was vigorously combated by others, and no doubt found a steady opposi-

[1] On the profit of arable, Blith writes strongly. *Improver*, pp. 83-84.

tion in the strong personal and private interests of enterprising owners and farmers. The reasons alleged in its support are important. Sometimes the decay of tillage is put forward, at other times depopulation occupies the front of the stage. It is, however, probable that the former does not mean only a decrease[1] in the supply of corn, if indeed it means that at all. As has already been observed, that supply might well be maintained even were the area devoted to corn restricted. The more efficient methods, which are hardly denied, at any rate during this period, would secure this. The main thing meant was the decrease of the effective area of agriculture, and so agricultural depopulation. It is probable that even during the seventeenth century there was some specious ground for this apprehension. In the first place, inclosures during the early period and during the century in question must have worn the appearance at least of partial conversions to pasture. This was inevitable, since under the three field system the fallow field was included in the arable land, although its use was largely for sheep. Where inclosure took place, unless some of the land thus treated were put to pasture, the arable would have been unduly increased. Again, better methods may in some cases have diminished the need for labour. Thirdly, so far as particular localities were concerned, the reclamation of lands by drainage or otherwise affected the profits of grain. Lastly, as said before, migration was difficult and a readjustment of the labour supply without suffering impossible. Hence the suspicion of the change cannot be dismissed as wholly unreasonable. Taking into account the whole evidence, there is no ground, however, to believe that the total arable area was decreased during the first half of the seventeenth century, even if it be true that in certain districts, as the Midlands and North Wilts,[2] some lands once in arable

[1] Some, however, like Forster, *England's Happiness*, 1664, did take this view.

[2] As to the Midlands, see above. For Wiltshire, see Aubrey, *Natural History of Wiltshire* (Wilts Topographical Society, 1847), p. 104. While the preface was written in 1685, the studies for this book were begun in 1656.

had been converted to pasture. Still less was this the case during the latter part of that century, and in the early years of that which followed. During that period, the acreage under the plough was almost certainly enlarged, possibly at the expense of pasture. In reply to the vague suggestion of conversion from arable to pasture there is strong adverse testimony, to be summed up in the statement of one writer that "the contrary is notorious."[1] The best evidence points to increase of arable as following inclosure at this time, and as we hear inclosure was going on rapidly. Not only so, but apart from the question of acreage there was the increase of wheat from more effective tillage. In the words of another writer, "In Northampton and Staffordshire, and in several other inland counties, there is great difference between the common fields and inclosures. The last has seven, eight, or ten years' crop successively, when the other has them but two years in three."[2] In general, it may be concluded the area under effective cultivation was enlarged, even though there may have been some local decreases, particularly in the case of land yielding scant or occasional crops.

During the portion of the eighteenth century covered by the private acts, the question was still one of interest, though the two matters of depopulation and decrease in the acreage set apart from corn are more carefully distinguished. In respect of the latter, as far as opinions are concerned, there is considerable conflict. Certain general conclusions are, however, possible. It was acknowledged on all sides that considerable change takes place in the use of land, acres that were formerly used for one purpose being now diverted to another. Thus Leicestershire had seen pasture extend over much of the land once common field

[1] John Lawrence, *A new system of Agriculture*, p. 46. The author of *England's Improvement and Seasonable Advice to all Gentlemen and Farmers*, 1691, argues that as more corn is sown in England, and more cattle fatted this year, land should be converted for growing flax and hemp.

[2] J. Lawrence, as above.

arable,[1] in Bedford some of the best corn land fattened an improved kind of sheep and cattle,[2] while on some of the poor lands in Worcester arable had increased, a tendency observed elsewhere, as in the Isle of Wight [3] and Cambridge.[4] As Marshall writes, there is in Yorkshire considerable change in the economy of live stock, owing to the conversion of the lowlands to arable, the inclosure of the commons, and the laying of the arable fields to pasture. Such a result was but to be expected of a method which, among other things, aimed at allowing land to be used for the purpose for which it was best fitted; equally naturally it is the more prominently revealed as agriculture develops and the methods of cultivation become more scientific. Secondly, the acreage under wheat in some counties underwent diminution. Moreover, so far as *former open field* was concerned, the same was probably true of the whole country. Despite denial by some and somewhat hostile criticism by others, this conclusion is fairly deducible from a review of the opinions expressed on different sides. Competent and practical advocates of inclosure, as Horner and Stone, while they criticise the extravagance of writers like Addington, evidently hesitate to deny this as a general truth, or, at any rate, as true in respect of large districts. They deny, and very emphatically, the suggestion that less corn is produced. Thirdly, better cultivation in the arable inclosures led to an increase of corn from the land thus treated. More corn could be raised from fewer acres. But open field was not the only land passing under inclosure, and wheat was not the only arable crop. When the land converted from commons or waste to arable, and

[1] Marshall, *Midlands*, ii. 250.

[2] *Agric. Report*, *Bedford* (1808), as to Marston. Cf. *Agric. Report*, *Essex* (1807), i. 123, as to conversion from pasture to arable; ii. 448, Appendix, conversion from arable to pasture; *Lancaster*, p. 393, conversion to grass.

[3] *Agric. Report*, *First Report*, *Isle of Wight*, by Warner, p. 67; note by Arthur Young.

[4] *Agric. Report* (1813). General increase of grain, shown by examination of the replies to enquiries.

the use made of such inclosures, as also of inclosures from open field for barley and oats and other arable crops, are taken into account, the above conclusion does not seem tenable. This indeed is the broad contention advanced by careful writers like Horner, Stone, Young, and Marshall, all of whom were advocates of inclosure. Their argument, which was not adequately met by their opponents, was that, owing to the inclosure of waste, the better utilisation of fallows, and the employment of other than grain crops, more and not less land was under effective arable use, and that the produce of land in arable was greatly increased.

V

GENERAL CONDITIONS OF RURAL LIFE

THE effects of the inclosures on the conditions of rural life, and particularly on the employment and the nature of the employment of a rural population, though obviously affected by the changes in agriculture in its more technical aspects, are sufficiently distinctive to require separate treatment. Their importance is great and it by no means follows that the results incurred in this direction coincide in advantageousness or otherwise with those which mark the record of the advance in the process of agriculture. The social consequences of technical improvement must be studied apart from that improvement.

Leaving for the present the question of the quantity of employment which can be more fitly dealt with when we come to the question of the population, the chief social results present themselves under the two headings of the general conditions of rural life and the method or system of agricultural employment; and these two matters require to be considered as they affect respectively the cottagers or the poor living in the country, whether legally concerned in inclosures or not, and the farming and cultivating class, especially the small farmers.

One by no means unimportant consequence of inclosure was the diminution of the constant bickering and litigation which found its source in the attempt to secure the greatest individual advantage out of rights which existed in common. A long array of authorities has been already cited to show the positive detriment to agriculture from this cause. To the direct loss thus occasioned must be added the more undefined harm arising from a state of affairs where individual rights in a common property existed without any swift authoritative means of defining them. Under the strict manorial system some such means existed, but with the disappearance of the effective power of the lord of the manor and his court, abundant opportunity was offered for mutual discontent and trespass. It is easy to see from the complaints of writers in the seventeenth century that the small farmers leading, no doubt, a hard existence, were at once suspicious of each other, and turn by turn prone to justify this suspicion. In the struggle with their richer neighbours they were, in many instances at any rate, subject to much injustice, being often crowded off the common and unable to exercise their full rights. The *Agricultural Reports* show that the same tendencies were in operation at the end of the eighteenth century.

Again, the actual effect of small common rights or common usages was, to say the least, by no means necessarily beneficial to the cottagers and the poor. Not only are commons accounted the rendezvous of highwaymen, but it was urged by some that a disproportionate amount of the crime originated among those living near commons or in uninclosed parishes. Of still more gravity was the contention that, so far as these latter were concerned, commons, and to a lesser degree common right, increased idleness, proved an obstacle to industry, and led to greater poverty and wretchedness. This view is set forth at the beginning of the seventeenth, but it is during the latter part of the eighteenth century that it received most support. It may be summed up in the words of one writer, who says, " where wastes and commons are most extensive there I have perceived the cottagers are most wretched and worthless and accustomed to rely on a precarious and vagabond subsistence."[1] Despite some protest, and no

[1] A large number of writers take the view that the existence of commons is detrimental to social welfare by the encouragement given to idleness or the

doubt some exaggeration in the statement itself, its substantial accuracy is too well supported to be put on one side. A means of gain, inadequate in itself and valuable in the main as part of a coherent agricultural system, when separated from this, served to attract loafers and idlers, while further, by reason of its inconsequent and precarious nature, its very existence struck at the roots of steady industry.

The question as to the injury inflicted on the poor was

opportunity offered to the dishonest, etc. Thus in the seventeenth century—*Comparison between Somerset and Northampton*, Lansdown MS., 487, p. 433—"The miseries of beggars are enormous." But the chief testimony on this particular matter is in the eighteenth century. John Lawrence, *A New System of Agriculture, etc.*, p. 47, argues that the poor are lessened by the commons being lessened. A. Young, *Annals of Agriculture*, viii. 438, cites instance of commons at Sutton-Coldfield where, despite these liberal rights, much poverty and high poor rates; *Annals*, v. 222, bad condition of the poor round the great commons at Chailey in Sussex. Cf. *Eastern Tour*, iii. p. 153, high poor rates at Chailey "owing to plenty of commons which encouraged the poor to such idleness as to bring vast numbers to parish." *Annals*, v. 221, charity estate at Framlingham has not decreased poverty. *Northern Tour*, i. 175, where in cheap times commons etc., offers an opportunity of idleness. "Another that in cheap times, used to bask himself all day in the sun, holding a cow by a line to feed on a balk, in dear times betakes himself to the pickaxe and the spade." *Observations on a Pamphlet entitled An Enquiry into the advantages and disadvantages, etc.* (1781), p. 5, in comparing cottagers on commons with others "I have also, unfortunately, found the cottagers (generally speaking) more perverse and more wretched than the labourers of inclosed parishes." Stone, *Suggestions*, p. 75, observes that an allotment which stimulates to industry much better than a common right which leads to idleness. Tucker, *Elements of Commons*, p. 54, commons, "a rendezvous of highwaymen."

Agricultural Report, Cheshire, opinion of Boys in Kent *Report* to effect that commons draw poor away from regular industry is cited and denied. *Essex* (1807), 173, Young thinks that in many cases summer pasture means winter stealing. *Hereford* (1794), p. 28, "a cottage with a few acres of inclosed land, gives the occupier a right to turn stock to these common hills. The profits of that stock is expected to supersede the necessity of labour, in cultivating the few acres which he possesses." *Hertford* (1804), p. 53, in text, "where wastes and commons," etc., cf. Original *Report*, 1795. *Lincoln*, p. 99, where assertion cited that most part of crime originated with inhabitants near commons, etc. *Shropshire* (1794), p. 24, bad effect on poor.

Making an allowance for exaggeration these references disclose a defect in the common field system where commons and common rights existed no longer in due proportion to, and in connection with, arable.

one which figures very largely in the discussions during the latter part of the eighteenth century. Whatever may be thought of the effect of the possession of common rights and uses to these as a class, the sudden deprivation of these was bound to operate hardly on the individuals concerned. Even could it be shown beyond dispute that the poor as a class would benefit in the end from the removal of these precarious and inadequate gains, none the less would the individuals accustomed to such suffer from their sudden cessation. This was recognised in a general, though somewhat vague way, and measures were urged by way of its mitigation. These need description.

In the case of inclosure a distinction must be drawn between what happened to the neighbouring poor living in common right cottages and those whose former use of the common was by some reason of proximity and by sufferance and not legal right. Probably both gained about as much from the common before it was inclosed, but at the inclosure they were subject to very different treatment. Common right cottages received allotments, small, it is true, but still definite and separate; but whatever was done with respect to the claims of the poor as a class, separate allotment did not take place.

Taking the case of those living in common right cottages or having small legal rights themselves, it would seem that divers reasons sometimes operated to prevent the compensation from being an equivalent for that of which they were deprived. In some cases the allotments were too small to be of any value,[1] even when they came to the inhabitant of the cottage. In others the expense of fencing proved too great,[2] while in other instances the very inclosure might occasion a change in the actual as distinct from the legal ownership. This occurred when the inhabitant of the common right cottage, though not an owner,

[1] *Agricultural Report, Norfolk*, p. 158.

[2] This grievance was fairly general. It is admitted in the *General Report*, *q.v.* Appendix, iv. As to especial effect on small allotments. *Agric. Rep.*, *Gloucester*, p. 92; also *supra*, pp. 87-8, 312.

had been permitted to enjoy the small rights attached thereto without payment. When an allotment was made, the landlord took the allotment and thus the cottager necessarily suffered.[1] On the other hand, cases are cited where care was taken to assign to each common right cottage not less than three acres. So far, indeed, as the small *owner* was concerned, there was considerable difference of opinion. Such writers as Fitz Herbert and Lee inclined to the belief that the balance was one of advantage since the previous gain from the common was small. This view was shared by others of a later date, who stated that these gained, inasmuch as they obtained an allotment in exchange for rights which they had been unable to exercise.

To some extent the same arguments occur in the instance of the poor other than the above, the one difference being that in their case there were no specific allotments. Taking both together there is evidence that privileges and advantages were lost, even though these may, in the case of those legally entitled, have been more advantageous previously than should have been the case.[2]

[1] *Agric. Report*, *Bedford*, p. 224; *Cambridge*, 56, etc.; *Middlesex* (1798). After the inclosure the land apportioned is taken into account in fixing the rent, whereas the common right used to be enjoyed for nothing.

[2] Fitz Herbert, *Book of Husbandry*, p. 77; Lee, *Vindication*, p. 2, etc.; *Tusser Redivivus* (1710), March, p. 9. Some writers in eighteenth century concur, *e.g. Agric. Report*, *Somerset*. The general contention is that the rich would overstock and live near the commons.

In the *Agricultural Report on Norfolk* considerable attention is given to the effect on the poor of this class, and it is said that inclosure offers an opportunity of conferring either a benefit or an injury on the poor. Sometimes the one result obtains and sometimes the other. Thus at Sayham they were so liberally dealt with that only two people were against the inclosure from first to last (p. 156); at Salthouse and Kelling they were better off than before, the common left being freed from overcrowding, and stinted to all houses under £10, the large commoners being excluded (p. 152). At Markham the poor did not suffer at all. In other cases the poor are injured. At Fincham the day of cottage cow-keeping is over, the allotments going to the farmers (152). Many who had no legal right had hitherto kept cows on the common with little interruption, though, of course, if the common was driven and their cows discovered they might have had to pay. At Sedgford they suffered, since a common right

This general loss formed a large part of the plea raised against inclosures in the early and middle seventeenth century; and this too was urged with equal emphasis in the eighteenth century. Apart from a general statement of injury, specific allegations are made. Thus with inclosure, the number of geese owned by the poor are said to have decreased: cows were given up; the poor lost fuel, being deprived of the privilege of turf-cutting; the commonage in the stubbles which enabled them to keep pigs and geese is theirs no more; and with these went other small advantages such as gleaning, which came to be more carefully restricted. That these losses were considerable cannot be doubted. Even strong advocates of the change seem to admit this. The moot point was the extent to which they were indemnified by the general improvement of the land or by some special compensation. Allowances for the use of common where such was not a legal right, though they may have been conceded by those inclosing in individual instances, were certainly rare and of but little value prior to the time of the private acts. One indication of this new importance lies

cottage received no more than half an acre in allotment in lieu of shackage and rights over a common of one hundred acres, which together allowed, it was said, of two cows to each right (158). Ludham (135) and Shuldham (161) fared much the same as Fincham.

So far as common right cottage owners were concerned, it is concluded, that the allotments were, as a general rule, adequate.

In the case of old use of common without right, the poor often suffered as at Fincham (*v.s.*), Bintry (82), and Northwold (147). On the other hand, at Stokesby, an allotment in common of 18 acres made for poor without rights (169), and in somewhat similar manner at Letton (95). At Sayham allotments made in lieu of old usage of common (156), and at Shottesham right of keeping a cow on a small common reserved for the purpose, granted indiscriminately to all poor inhabitants.

Turbary rights were considered very carefully. At some places land reserved for turf cutting, as at Thornham (176), and Old Buckenham (89); at other places land let at a rent which is to be spent in providing coals, etc. This is in practice at Fincham (107), Sayham (156), Cranworth, where it does not work well, and Southborough, where it does (94, 95).

Norfolk inclosures appear to have been more carefully managed in this respect than was the case elsewhere.

in the discussion as to the way in which the claims of the poorer class should be proved before the Commissioners. Legal proof, if required, imposed a considerable hardship, a natural conclusion when it is remembered that many of the claims in question were not claims of right, but for privileges which had been permitted by the owners of the rights to common.[1] To avoid injury in some cases as for instance in certain of the Norfolk inclosures,[2] proof was required merely of the practice and not of the legality of claims, and allotments were made to the individuals losing. But this was by no means usual.

The general custom when ultra legal claims were taken into consideration was to treat them on a different basis from those forming part of a legal right, that is by setting aside some land or money for the use of the neighbouring poor. On the whole, this seems to have been the most equitable and the most advantageous method. Unfortunately there was no uniformity in the procedure. All depended on the individual Commissioners and to some extent on the custom of the district or county. Hence variety of action naturally gave rise to a variety of opinion as to the effect of inclosure upon the poor.[3] Taking a large number of awards throughout the country, the recognition of ultra legal claims seems to be exceptional. In certain districts, as in Norfolk, there was greater liberality than elsewhere, but even there, in many cases nothing or little was done, and hardship was possibly inflicted. It must, however, be remembered that want of recognition may be due often to an absence of such claims in any great number. Compensation when granted took many forms. The chief privileges which attracted most favourable attention were those of cow keeping and fuel, and in consequence we find efforts

[1] *Agric. Report, Cambridge*, p. 76. [2] *Agric. Report, Norfolk*, p. 184.

[3] As to geese, *Agric. Reports, Worcester*, 248; *Norfolk*, 94, etc. As to other advantages, *General Report*, Appendix iv. gives many instances. Cf. Addington, *An Inquiry, etc.*, p. 14 and elsewhere; Young, *Eastern Tour*, ii. p. 24; Tucker, *Elements of Commerce*, p. 52, etc.

in these two directions. Sometimes small commons for cows were reserved and handed over to the use of the poorer inhabitants of the village, in some cases a stint being imposed as to the cows which each might turn out. In certain places a restriction was made as to the rental which entitled to any use of such a common. The provision of fuel was secured either by setting aside of land for this purpose where turf or whins could be cut or wood taken, or else by the sale or letting of some land. In this latter case the capital or income was vested in the overseers or others, the proceeds to be spent in coal or other fuel.

The contention that inclosure in the eighteenth century led to an increase in the poor rates was denied by many, and is not adequately substantiated. In many instances the rates in the neighbourhood of large commons prior to inclosure were abnormally high, and growing laxity of administration towards the end of the century led to a very general rise throughout the country.[1] On the other hand there are some grounds which render it probable that inclosure played a part in the general agricultural change which increased local distress and led to the leniency in relief which wrought ultimate harm. In some places there was without doubt some local reduction in the employment; in others the subsidiary means which enabled the poor to eke out a hard livelihood were taken away; elsewhere the poor occupiers lost a definite means of support. Allotments were often too small; and when common allotments were made to mitigate the hardships of a class, they were unfortunately made in a form which partook in some measure of the old evils attaching to uncertain charity, and did little to foster habits of industry or to provide a means of a self-reliant life. But this, whilst in itself a matter for regret is of little moment in the decision of the present point since like results were attributed to the assistance received by the poor from commons. Probably in this respect the old system was

[1] On this point see pp. 415-27.

worse than that which replaced it. Two other consequences deserve attention. The old common right system undoubtedly tended to link people to a district. Further, in many cases it freed them from the position of mere wage-paid labour under supervision. Change took place in both these respects.

Any conclusion as to the direct effects of inclosure upon the particular poor included in its scope depends not only upon the period during which it took place, but also upon the nature of their claims, either legal or prescriptive.

In the case of those poor cottagers who, by ownership, possessed rights of common, a very marked distinction must be drawn between the private act inclosures and those occurring before their date. Before the eighteenth century, such cottagers were apparently rarely if ever able to influence the division. Their assent when required was often obtained by pressure, and it is certainly probable that their claims received scanty consideration. Apart from what may have the effects produced upon them indirectly, the direct compensation in their case cannot be taken as ensured. The only question is the value to them of the original common rights. The same cannot be said of the inclosures under act or by agreement during that period. Taking the awards, the Commissioners, as a rule, seem to have given very careful consideration to the claims of the poor owners; and it seems true that the compensation given was equal in value to the rights of which they were deprived. Their difficulties lay, however, in the comparative smallness of the land thus granted, which often rendered it unsuitable in size for inclosure and their lack of capital to make the requisite alterations and to work it under new conditions of competitive farming. Thus while as individuals they were treated fairly as a rule, as a class they may have suffered. Their suffering, however, was due rather to the changed economy of the times than to the inclosures themselves.

The case of the poor occupiers of cottages to which common rights attached was different. Allotments, when made, vested in the owners, to whom they were a more tangible property than the small common right, the use of which in many cases was allowed by grace to the tenants. As the owner usually possessed several of these tenements, the compensation in land added materially to his property; and he was not under the disadvantages besetting the poor owner who dwelt in his own cottage. To some extent these occupiers might share in the allotments or compensations next to be considered.

The poor who lost by inclosure, since it deprived them of advantages to which they had no claim by right but only by usage, are more prominent in later than in early times. The careful consideration of the effect of the movement on them in the eighteenth century not only by writers on both sides, but even by commissioners in framing awards in not a few cases, points to their existence in considerable numbers. Their presence and growth is alleged to be one aspect of the decay of the system of common. But whether this be the explanation or not, the comparative silence of early writers is in marked contrast to the notice their sufferings, real or alleged, obtain in eighteenth century literature. During this latter period there is no doubt as to their frequent presence, the only question being the value of the common incidents enjoyed by them. The acknowledgment of their customary though not legal privileges as worthy of compensation, though never very frequent during the eighteenth century, grew less uncommon with the lapse of years. Early acts and awards rarely contain any mention of provision for them, while at the end of the century such was far from common. Possibly in some cases commissioners acted like Mr. Algar in certain Norfolk inclosures, in requiring from the poor nothing more than a proof of practice of common rights.

When from the consideration of the cottager and the poor we turn to consider the general method of agricultural employment, the importance of the inclosures during the eighteenth century, and particularly during its close, may be seen to be very great. Even before this time they offered an opportunity, often deplored, for the growth of large estates and threatened the small farmer, but in the eighteenth they took place under conditions and in the presence of influences which were adverse to the whole system of small cultivation. In the first place, the inclosures of this period involved a considerable initial outlay of capital on the part of those receiving allotments. Doubtless with a view to efficiency, definite regulations were laid down as to the inclosure of the allotments by fencing and ditching. In many instances, too, considerable initial expenses were incurred in common as in the procuring of the act, the setting out of the roads, and in drainage or other improvements, which had to be met by all in due proportion. Land was sold in some cases, which caused a deduction from the various properties. In the second place, the inclosure was often but a step in the transition from the early methods of cultivation to more modern methods of high farming. Again capital was needed, this time indeed to enable the farmers to keep pace with the improvements which were being introduced. In the third place, the change in industrial production and the development of mechanical processes struck a heavy, and in the end, a fatal blow at the combination of small industries with small farms which afforded the means of living to a very considerable proportion of the rural population. Fourthly, and lastly, the new wealth created by trade at home or abroad ensured ready purchasers for those who desired to sell land.

With these causes in operation there is little room for wonder at the steady and widespread disappearance of the small farmer, and especially of the small owner cultivating his own little farm. The fact itself is beyond all doubt. From all quarters comes the complaint; and even those who rejoiced in the technical improvement in agriculture were constrained to join in the dirge over the yeoman farmer.

From all sides rose the cry that consolidation of

holdings and estates was in progress, and that the very valuable order of small yeoman farmers was vanishing. Small tenant farmers likewise were disappearing, and their farms, put together, were let to large farmers. The *Reports* to the Board of Agriculture from the various counties call attention to the change, though some hesitate, and no doubt rightly, to attribute it to the single cause of inclosure. The complaint, lament, or whatever it may be called, seems to proceed indifferently from all quarters. We hear it from Northern counties like Lancashire, from the West in Wilts and Dorset, from the East in Norfolk, and from the Midlands, as Bedford and Berkshire. That the tendency was general is fully endorsed by the language used by Arthur Young in the *General Report on Enclosures*, and by others, as Lamport, Stone, Howlett, and Addington. Different observers express the matter in different ways. One speaks of "the loss of that set of men who were called yeoman," another says that the diminution in number of farmers is undoubted, others even speak of the "extinction" of small farmers; from another proceeds the estimate that "the farmers are reduced to one-fourth of their number," but these, as he adds, are "very opulent."[1]

When, however, the causes and consequences come under consideration, there is difference of opinion. To

[1] The tendency towards an increase in the size of farms and the extinction of the small yeoman farmer is very widely recognised in the latter eighteenth century. Thus Young, in *General Report*, cites Sir G. O. Paul: "Without entering into the doubtful question of the good or evil tendency of large farms, it may be admitted, without contest, that in proportion to the population the number of those persons who cultivate at all for themselves is grievously diminished; of those who cultivate sufficient for the supply of their family and a little more, the class is nearly extinct." Pp. 16, 17; cf. pp. 32-36. To some extent this applies to tenant farmers. On the whole question, see *An Inquiry into the connection between the present price of provisions and the size of farms, etc., by a Farmer*, esp. p. 126; Stone, *Suggestions*, etc., pp. 6, 40-1; W. Lamport, *Cursory Remarks, etc.*, p. 59.

Agric. Reports: *Bedford*, 606; *Berks*, pp. 46-7; *Cheshire*, p. 80; *Derby*, p. 505; *Dorset*, p. 90, etc.; *Essex*, p. 64; *Gloucester*, p. 52; *Hampshire*, pp. 76, 83; *Lancashire*, p. 90; *Somerset*, p. 66-7; *Stafford*, p. 41; *Suffolk*, p. 255;

some, inclosure, if not the sole, was still the dominant cause, the others being but unimportant by its side; to others it was one cause among others. Some, again, regard the alteration as overwhelmingly detrimental, while others, though regretting it in some respects, regard it as partly, if not largely, compensated for by other consequences. In the view of some of these, the improved prosperity of agriculture would affect the whole country, including in the end those temporarily injured. Some, too, held that the temporary injury was rather in appearance than in reality, since, as Young urges in respect of Cheshire, "the little farmers in this county are reckoned more wretched than day labourers." Howlett, too, considered that the little farmers of Essex made but a "poor starved living."[1]

The actual connection of inclosure with the growth of large farming is differently treated by different writers, some minimising, others emphasising its importance. Its tendency in this direction was admitted by many.[2] Whatever view was taken as to its relative importance, direct denial of it as at least a contributory cause was rarely, if ever, attempted. Young admits it, while Stone, one of the most judicious critics of the time, when considering the objection thus urged against inclosures, attributes the change, which he fully recognises, to three causes. The first and most important cause was a fallacious idea on the part of large landowners that by reducing the number

Westmoreland, p. 302; *Wilts*, p. 49. In some of these counties there had been little eighteenth century inclosure, *e.g.* Cheshire, Essex. In others, *e.g.* Westmoreland, Lancashire, the inclosure was mainly of wastes or commons.

In the case of Kent and Huntingdon the reports doubt decrease in small farmers. *Agric. Reports*: *Huntingdon*, p. 24; *Kent*, 26. While the cases of the yeoman farmer and the small occupying cultivator must be distinguished, there seems no doubt that the latter also underwent at any rate comparative diminution.

[1] Young, *Northern Tour*, iii. 246; *Agric. Report*, *Essex*, p. 64.

[2] Thus *Agric. Report*, *Wilts*, first edition, by T. Davis (1794), p. 138; *Agric. Reports*, *Bedford* (1807), p. 606; *Lincoln* (1799), p. 16-17; *Northampton*, ii. p. 33, etc. Less definite; *Rutland*, p. 29; S. J. Nash, *Address to Board of Agriculture*, p. 15.

of buildings on their estates, the expenses would be diminished. The second lay in the sale of small estates by the yeoman farmers who hope to improve their condition by becoming sheep farmers. Thirdly, the expenses of inclosure operated in this direction, though, in his opinion, not very often. But his first two causes may have come into operation in some places on inclosure. Inclosure as a matter of fact had two very different effects. In some ways it directly led to the decrease of small holdings. In other cases it produced an undoubted effect in the same direction by the opportunity it afforded for the unrestrained operation of other causes. Improved farming, changes in cultivation, or ideas such as those mentioned above, while not due to inclosure, were impossible on any large scale while common rights existed. Where these had been previously abrogated, the changes demanded by them proceeded in due course, but over a large area of the country their fulfilment was impossible till a similar change was effected. In this respect inclosure might be looked on as allowing land to be put to its most profitable use. But whether this was so or not, whether in some cases temporary and specious advantages might not be mistaken for permanent advantages, the effect of inclosure was undoubted. It enabled consolidation where otherwise such could not have occurred. The more direct effects remain to be noted. By disturbing existing arrangements it gave rise to a new distribution of holdings to suit the convenience of the large proprietors. In some cases "most of the small tenements and farms having fallen into the lord of the manor's hands he has let the whole to one or two substantial farmers, and the village now resembles a place that has been sacked and plundered."[1] No doubt the latter description gives an exaggerated idea if taken as of wide application, but the charge more soberly stated in the opening lines happened often. The motives under which this action was taken were different. Sometimes, as indicated above, it proceeded from the

[1] *The National Debt no national grievance* (1768), p. 61.

desire to achieve better organisation and to secure economy;[1] sometimes the reduction of the need for building was the object;[2] while elsewhere the substitution for a number of small farmers of a few very substantial men, held out a prospect of less trouble and uncertainty in the collection of rents.[3] Again, the termination of the common field system often injured small holders by depriving them of certain advantages which they had been enjoying. With separate ownership they might not have sufficient pasture to keep a shepherd, or again they would have to buy manure; with their small amount of land the gain from laying lands together was little in comparison with that obtained by large holders. In some cases and especially on horse commons they had enjoyed more than their legal rights, since in the latter case large farmers had not the stock to put out.[4] In these and like instances they suffered, partly because the old system presented certain minor advantages for them, partly because under it they enjoyed in practice more than their right by law. On the whole the commissioners dealt very fairly with the small holders; but the allotments were, in the main, according to legal rights and as has been seen, the advantages referred to were in excess of these. Lastly, the expenses incurred both under the inclosure acts and on the inclosure of land often compelled small holders to sell their land. On the one hand there was the expense of fencing, on the other that occasioned either by the new demands for improved methods, new buildings[5] or in the conversion of arable to grass. In some cases

[1] *Agric. Report, Wilts* (1813), p. 49.

[2] *Agric. Report, Gloucester* (1807), p. 52.

[3] W. Lamport, *Cursory Remarks, etc.*, p. 55.

[4] As to these disadvantages, *Agric. Reports, Wilts*, pp. 40, 41; Horner, *Essay*, 70-71.

[5] The greater expense of farm buildings may to some extent be offset by the use of farmyard manure, is the plea of one writer, *Agric. Report, Somerset* (1798), pp. 62-67. In any case, however, capital outlay is required, a circumstance inimical to the small farmers. *Id.* 66-67.

the need for money to inclose led to debt;[1] while with the disadvantages attending small farming when in competition with large farming at this period, loans, if obtained, could achieve little.

On the other hand it must be remembered that at this same time the growth of large holdings and the extinction or diminution of the yeoman farmer or smaller tenant, were often occurring where no open field inclosure was in progress or had been in progress for a long time. As has been pointed out, statements as to the change came from counties like Cheshire, Essex, Lancashire, Westmoreland and Somerset. It is true, of course, that but for the existence of a state of individual or several property, their progress would have been very difficult if indeed possible. This is fairly obvious to us. It was less obvious to some writing at the time, who confuse the results of the movement then in progress with those of a state of ownership which may have been of long standing. In other words their denunciation of inclosure on this ground often proceeded from a desire for a system of property so complicated and confused under a network of mutual rights that no one could do with the land what the needs of a progressive population required, that is, turn it to the most productive use. No doubt in other cases the incidents of inclosure itself led to the sale of small holdings and the consolidation of farms for reasons already discussed.

The evidence given relates to the latter part of the eighteenth century. It remains to be seen if much is offered in earlier years. This has been partly dealt with when the question of conversion was considered, since the substitution of pasture for arable no doubt implied the decrease of the smaller farms. But in the eighteenth century there was a like tendency in the case of arable or mixed farms.

Provided only that the land remained in an arable

[1] *Cursory remarks on Inclosures by a Country Farmer* (1786), p. 7. They run into debt and may borrow on mortgage.

or mixed condition it would seem that in earlier centuries there was little grievance experienced by the small yeomen or tenant farmers. The absence of complaint in this matter during such periods, as compared with the eighteenth century, is in marked contrast to what took place in respect of many other subjects, since, as has been shown, in many matters the same note is struck in all periods. Here there is a signal difference. But then the conditions of the times were different. The conditions determining the effect of eighteenth century inclosure on small farms were largely wanting. Capital was not so great a necessity. Facilities in transport were lacking. The inclosure was less exacting in its demands for improvement or expensive hedging by those concerned, and also less costly in itself. While, lastly, the small holder was less likely to be tempted to sell. Taking into account the technical advantages of the change, and the poor condition of over-stocked commons, it is very probable that the small owner or occupier benefitted, provided that he was fairly dealt with, and that there was no great conversion occurring. As to the first point, the arbitrary element in early inclosures has been indicated; even in the seventeenth century the small farmer, if a party, was a very passive party in the agreements, often, it may be said, coerced into an agreement against his will, and into a consent to what he considered to be to his detriment. In some districts, and at times when the lands inclosed remained under mixed courses, or were employed in large measure for dairy purposes, he probably held his own, that is, if fairly treated. But sheep-farming would be to his detriment, and under its spread he must often have been driven out. Occupiers would fare badly. It should be remembered, also, that in the sixteenth century and earlier the exhausted state of the soil was an important factor in the change.

For these reasons it seems probable that putting aside acts of arbitrary and unjust treatment, and also the period when, and the places where, sheep-farming spread rapidly, inclosure had comparatively little effect upon the small cultivator and the size of the holding till the eighteenth century. Its effect then and afterwards was due largely to its relation to the changes in agricultural method, and to its own cost.

One matter, however, requires a few words, namely, the part played by the poor law system in the alteration in the system of labour. No doubt the increase in the poor rate added to the expenses of cultivation and of rural life. Its effect on the small as distinct from the large cultivator is more uncertain. Probably the very narrowness of their resources would make them less able to bear any increased strain, and hence they would be more likely to part with their land when, owing to the action of inclosure, it passed into their possession and alienation. But, on the other hand, to have been tied to the land under a new load of expense would have made their lot increasingly difficult. While this does not show that the increase in the poor rate fell more heavily over the whole country on the small holder than on the large holder, it points to the former as less able to bear such expense, because in the economic competition he was weaker than his neighbour. Under one set of conditions the burden was greater in his case, namely, where allowance-scales or labour-rate systems were in operation. Under the former some part of the normal payment of wages was borne by the parish, while the latter implied the allocation to each householder of labour irrespective of his demand. In both cases the small holder working himself and with the aid of his family, stood to lose. The allowance system, however, only becomes general towards the very end of the century and in the beginning of the nineteenth century; while the labour-rate was confined in the main to a few counties, and was certainly not of great influence before the nineteenth century. An over emphasis of the connection between the poor rates and the decrease in small farmers and owners has led to the dating of this latter very late in the century. But against this date, it must be pointed out, firstly, that there is much complaint of great diminution in the number of small tenants or owning cultivators at an earlier time ; secondly, that the writers mentioned above, who fully recognise the phenomenon, give other causes for its appearance ; thirdly, that at the end of the century the decrease is seen and lamented, not only in counties where the poor rates had reached so great a level, but also in counties like Lancashire where the increase had not been nearly so great. Furthermore, it should be noticed that it is incorrect to suppose that poor rates only increased at the end of the century. As a matter of fact there was a fairly general rise[1] from the middle of the century onwards.[2] With these facts in view, it would seem a mistake to treat this as more than one among several causes, and, especially, to regard it as mainly responsible. Doubtless it operated at times, and probably with most effect in certain districts where allowances and labour rates ruled in the first decade of the nineteenth century ; but even so it only accelerated a movement already in active progress, and one which prevailed not only in these localities but elsewhere.[3]

Another point in this connection has been raised by Dr. Hasbach in his contention that with the intermixture of open and inclosed parishes, the allowance system tended to bring about an increase of hired labour, resident in the open parishes and passing in gangs to work in those which were inclosed. The particular illustration he gives from Norfolk of certain parishes about Norwich is anything but conclusive, as Lakenham, which shows a marked increase in population after 1811, was becoming a suburb of

[1] Not involving the allowance scale or labour rate. [2] Appendix B.

[3] The effect of increased poor rates on the small farmers must not be confused with the question of the influence of inclosure on poor rates. The former, as is pointed out, would press as hardly, if not more hardly, on small common field farmers. The latter question is discussed in Chapter VI.

the city, and its increase is ascribed by the census as being due to new building. Furthermore the extent to which this parish was open is doubtful. If other parishes in the neighbourhood which were not inclosed till after 1810 be taken, the small increase they display gives no support to this theory so far as that region is concerned. As to the question itself, it is of course quite possible that the allowance system and in general the poor laws system may have had this effect in some places. On *a priori* grounds such a result seems possible. But its selection as a chief feature of the change requires much more proof. If the figures given in one of the Appendices[1] be consulted where the densities (1801) of parishes inclosed before and after 1800 are compared in the case of several counties, the serious operation of any such cause at that time seems, to say the least, *most improbable.*

The main fact of the decrease of the small holder is undoubted. He is passing from the land, sometimes emigrating, oftener seeking new work in the towns or near home, but in many, if not most districts sinking into the position of the wage-paid labourers. According to one writer the reduction in every county of that valuable order of men, little farmers "was responsible for the lack of really good domestic servants who had been largely recruited from their sons and daughters."

From a social point of view few changes could be more important than the substitution of wage-paid labour for the small independent cultivator, here depicted in the sphere of agriculture. No doubt tendencies in this direction had been manifesting themselves for some time. Capitalistic farming had been increasing, and with the opportunity for capital, the small owner had experienced increasing difficulty in holding his own. Owing to the circumstances here narrated, the struggle had now definitely gone against him. The yeoman farmer who had owned and cultivated his land, though not wholly driven out, survives as from the past to remind a new age of a

[1] Appendix G.

time when he and his fellows constituted the strength of the country. The small tenant farmer likewise undergoes decrease. Their place is taken by large proprietors and large farmers. No doubt it is true that in many technical respects the new men were superior to the old. They were, so we hear, "quite different men, men of ideas."[1] They were richer and not in need of the small subsidiary gains[2] yielded by the home industry, and to be found in the loom and the spinning wheel. But they are few, whereas the others were many, and the class of small independent producers is merged into the growing class of wage-labourers who stand out in contrast to the few who employ them.

A further matter remains for examination. The class of labourers was, as has been indicated, increased though the full effects of the change was not experienced for some little time. How, it must be asked, was their employment affected. On this subject too there was much difference of opinion. It can be considered best in conjunction with the alleged effect on population.

[1] *Agric. Report, Oxford*, p. 269. [2] *Cursory remarks, etc.*, p. 20.

VI

EMPLOYMENT AND POPULATION

Of the complaints raised against inclosure the two which have left the most marked impression in the literature of the day, and which were rated most highly both by the public and by statesmen relate to the alleged decrease in the food supply, and in the amount of employment in the country. Nor is the reason for this difficult to find. In both cases the population of the country would be affected; and with a decline in population, the strength of the country might suffer.

Separate attention has been given to the effect on the various articles of the food supply. The general conclusion reached was adverse to the suggested defect. With the exception of the earliest years there seems no initial ground for the belief that arable production, to take the chief charge, was seriously and widely discouraged in the country. Even in those districts, and there were such, where it is partially superseded by pasture, the supply of meat and animal products was increased.

But the matter of employment is different. Put broadly the contention was that under the changed system of cultivation, the yield of the land was produced in such a way as to involve a less amount of labour. This might take place in various ways. Better organisation and greater economy in method might enable the same amount to be produced by less labour, or again the interest of the landlord and employer might be served better by certain uses which required little labour than by those which required much. The question was not always the same, and it will be necessary to examine different periods separately in order to ascertain how far at any time was there justification for the charge. But before entering upon this somewhat detailed investigation it will be well to glance briefly at the various arguments used on the one side and the other. Despite a difference in emphasis, there is considerable sameness in these throughout the whole time.

Firstly, there was, so far as this particular question of employment was concerned, a general admission that the inclosure of wastes and commons, of moor, heath and forest, was the reverse of detrimental to the general interest. This was evident at all times, and is shown both in the general tenour of the criticisms and accounts of the movement, and in particular references to particular cases. As was pointed out during the controversy in the seventeenth century, Mr. Moore's attack was not on all inclosure, but only on those which might occasion depopulation,[1] while the inclosures referred to both then and in the sixteenth century relate in the main to land lying in open field which might be diverted from one use to another. The distinction between the two kinds of inclosure was clearly drawn by advocate and opponent alike in the eighteenth century. But though some writers of this time point to the increase of population occasioned by inclosure of waste or land similar to waste, as in the forest inclosures in Nottingham, the open commons in Norfolk, and the wastes in Durham,[2] sufficient attention was not paid to the effect of the cultivation of waste lands on the agricultural area, and the consequent conversion of other lands to pasture.

Secondly, the change in the open fields from a use predominantly arable to a use predominantly pastoral is

[1] *Considerations*, p. 2.

[2] *Agric. Reports*, *Nottingham* (1794), p. 44; *Norfolk* list of parishes given; also cf. 168 "the utilization of commons" was the usual object of Norfolk inclosures, that is, during the late part of eighteenth century; *Durham* (1794), pp. 43, 44.

clearly the main matter at issue. There were, it is true, other ways in which the amount of rural employment might be affected. Thus the increase in the average size of farms might well produce some effect. The large farmers whose numbers were augmented by inclosure were accused by some of neglecting the small market towns for the sale of their goods, with the result that these were impoverished and tradespeople and others thrown out of work.[1] Again the very ingrossing of farms necessarily, we are told, diminished the number of people engaged in cultivation;[2] while at the time of the inclosure the rich according to others, seized the occasion to deprive the poor of rights and to drive them from the land.[3] Consequences such as these were, however, of little general importance, and may be regarded as merely incidental or occasional in the movement. A more important factor tending towards the immediate decrease in certain kinds of farm labour lay in the better and more economical methods introduced. The mere consolidation of distant lands into a compact holding necessarily lessened the labour previously required in carting manure and produce. Its effect on the use of horses has been mentioned. Very similar, it is argued, must have been its effect on the labourers. With the new farmers, there was an improvement in the general organisation and the working of the land.

It was not, however, on results such as these that the attack on the inclosures in respect of their effect on work, and so on population, rested. The main point which nearly every writer had in mind was the diversion of land from arable to pasture. Sometimes this was stated bluntly, sometimes it was put obscurely, but in nearly all cases where serious depopulation was alleged it was the real basis of the charge. In full accord with the oft-cited description in the early sixteenth century of the sheep

[1] *Agric. Report, Hereford* (1794), p. 70.

[2] This opinion expressed to Young by an opponent of inclosures, *Annals of Agriculture*, vi. p. 454. Cf. Lansdown MS. 487, p. 433.

[3] *Vindication of the Considerations.* Summary at end.

devouring or supplanting, we hear at the beginning of the seventeenth of the simple and gentle sheep "now become so ravenous that they begin to devour men, waste fields, and depopulate houses,"[1] and of the people "driven out by tyrants who would dwell by themselves in the midst of their herds of fat wethers."[2] The same complaint, though less picturesquely clad, meets us in the controversy in the middle of that century,[3] and again in the eighteenth century. Even those fully convinced, as was Howlett, of the essential desirability of the inclosure, had to admit that where the consequence was the wide extension of pasture, decrease in population would occur, though this admission was qualified by instances from other counties, where the very reverse followed on inclosure.[4] As the author of the *Report* on Leicester says, where the full effect of conversion to pasture is felt, many cultivators are dispossessed, and "the rejected occupier and his family must migrate into towns."[5] According to some, population was affected because less food was produced,[6] but this view, though in harmony with the contention that alterations of the food supply, even in the direction of increase, and alterations in population necessarily coincided, and of course obviously true so far as any great decrease in production was concerned, was not the aspect emphasised.

[1] *Geo. Description of England and Wales* (1615), under Northampton.

[2] *Diggers' Petition*, Harl. MS. 787, p. 9.

[3] *Depopulation arraigned*, by R. P. (1636), p. 84.

[4] Thus Howlett (*An Inquiry into the effect which Inclosures, etc.*) gives a few instances from Leicester, where there has been decrease, and then adds that he has many instances of parishes in Buckingham, Bedford, Derby, Wilts, and Hampshire, where an increase of population has ensued on inclosure, pp. 12-15; the author of the first *Agricultural Report on Rutland* (1794) states that in the first great run of inclosures, about 1760, labourers lost employment in certain parishes owing to conversion to grass, and sought shelter in other parishes or else resorted to other kinds of employment. Of late, owing to better methods, the population, in the opinion of the writer, has increased on inclosure, p. 31. Cf. *Agric. Report*, *Warwick* (1794), p. 21; *Northampton* (1809), pp. 58-63.

[5] *Agric. Report*, *Leicester* (1809), p. 16.

[6] Darwin, *Phytologia*. The general grounds given here are fanciful.

Some do not refer to it at all, and while it forms part of the general case put forward by others it is obviously not the part to which they attach importance. The contention which was treated as of far greater moment was that by inclosure the land, or at any rate a large part of it, would pass into uses involving a less amount of employment; in other words, the conversion into pasture was the anticipated peril. For at least three centuries the existence, probability, or extent of such change occupied the public mind. Despite the differences between the various periods both as to the degree to which conversion from arable to grazing really took place, and as to the opinions formed by contemporaries, there is a strong likeness between the arguments employed. The resemblance is made the more interesting because of the modifications introduced as time progresses. Taking the main point, it is generally admitted that where conversion to pasture takes place to any great extent there is risk of depopulation, unless the loss of employment directly on the land is compensated for in other ways. At all periods we find keen controversy as to the extent to which any such conversion took place, and as to the degree in which the population was affected. From the beginning of the seventeenth century the extent to which compensation is secured by new employments is likewise a subject of discussion. Of these matters the two earlier require little illustration. They lie at the root of the difference of opinion, and will consequently be involved in the attempt which will be made to determine the facts of the respective periods. The last stands in a somewhat different position. Increase of employment was suggested as likely to take place in two ways. In the first place, the inclosure would create work at the time. More labourers will be needed for hedging and ditching is the statement of a writer in 1607, and his opinion is re-echoed in the eighteenth century,[1] when it must be remembered inclosures

[1] Lansdown MS. 487, p. 433. Cf. *Agric. Report, Northampton* (1794), p. 60. Horner, *Essay upon Nature and Method*, p. 30, but in criticism, *Inquiry into the reasons for and against, etc.*, p. 24.

were taking place under strict conditions as to their fencing. But some part of this labour, as was clearly seen at any rate in the later century, was only temporary. The making of the inclosure created unusual activity for a time, but that would not continue. On the other hand, some hedging and ditching would continue. But of course the end sought in many inclosures would have been partly frustrated, if this latter employment had been sufficient to counterbalance the economy elsewhere achieved. In the second place, as industry progresses observers begin to take into account the new employments to which the increased production of wool might give rise. Even when industry was carried on under the domestic system compensation in this way was quite possible. At the end of the seventeenth century Houghton asserts that the new employment thus created was very considerable. A very similar view finds expression at the end of the eighteenth century.[1]

The modifying influence of changing conditions may be observed even more clearly in the attitude taken as to the effect of lessened employment on the lands converted to pasture upon the absolute amount of employment, and so of population. In the earlier times the complaint implies an actual depopulation. During the early sixteenth century this was probably the well-nigh universal view. Dissent from it was probably due to a recognition that inclosure did not always bring about a diminution of the arable area, owing either to its taking place on wastes hitherto uncultivated, or in order to facilitate improved agriculture, this latter aspect becoming of more importance at the end of that century. But with the seventeenth century the possibility, due no doubt to increased opportunities for locomotion, obviously suggests itself to some observers, that the decrease of employment in agriculture in one place may be offset by the increased work offered elsewhere, though not necessarily due to inclosure. Such

[1] Houghton, *Collections* (1692), No. 16. He has, he asserts, a calculation by him which proves this. Pennington, W., *Reflections, etc.*, p. 19.

seems the general tenor of the argument of the author of the comparison between the counties of Somerset and Northampton. It is put more clearly in 1656, when Mr. Moore writes: "I complain not of inclosure in Kent and Essex, where they have other callings and trades." From that time the absorption into other work, often in the same locality, of those driven out of agricultural labour, gains increased prominence, owing without doubt to the growth in industrial employments of all kinds. Consequently emphasis is laid, particularly by those who questioned or opposed inclosure, on the hardships involved in the change of employment.[1] Some, of course, amongst whom Dr. Price occupies a special pre-eminence, still remain faithful to the more pessimistic interpretation of the situation, as is shown by the pertinacious declaration of the absolute decline in the population. The new industrial growth was responsible for another point. Change of work often meant change from the country into town,[2] and, as some saw, the conditions of the town, through lack of sanitation and owing to overcrowding, were prejudicial to health and physique. On the other hand, there were not wanting those who viewed the industries and the towns as in part the cause of the drift out of the country. According to one, agriculture was suffering because the best labourers were attracted into other employments,[3] while another speaks of the great difference in habits between the early part of his century and the later, to him the present part, when "people are no longer content to remain in the country."[4] A third says that migration out of inclosed parishes was often due to prejudice and dislike to the new conditions.[5]

It is quite possible that alterations in the method of cultivation in some cases in the eighteenth century may

[1] Addington, *Inquiry into reasons for and against*, p. 24.

[2] *Agric. Report, Leicester* (1809), p. 166. Cf. Addington, *id.* p. 32.

[3] *Agric. Report, Hampshire* (1813), pp. 384-5.

[4] *A general view of England*, by M. V. D. M. (1766), p. 25.

[5] Stone, *Suggestions*, p. 39.

have occurred because of a decrease in good labour, owing to the offer of other work and the specious attractions of town life. In addition to the field of industrial employment, inclosure under and in the service of progressive agriculture operated in the direction of new work. Not only was there less waste in unnecessary fallow as already indicated, but the labour connected with the new crops, as for instance turnips, must be taken into account. Even without an increase of the land under cereals the total employment was increased in many districts.

The question of fact still remains. To determine it, a somewhat detailed consideration of different periods is necessary.

With regard to it, certain preliminary matters must be borne in mind with regard to the evidence as to depopulation. The mere fact of inclosure cannot be regarded as evidence, since, as has been seen, under certain conditions no such effect or even the very contrary effect would be occasioned. In addition to what has been already said, it must be remembered that in many cases new land from the mountain side or the forest was being taken in while the more settled village land was inclosed, with the result that the conversion of some of the latter from arable to pasture produced little effect in the directions under consideration, and further that in the very process of inclosure the reduction of fallow and other causes involved an increase in the amount of land in effective use.

(*a*) *Till middle of sixteenth century.*—In the early period, that is before the middle of the sixteenth century, the indirect evidence tends almost uniformly to substantiate the general charge that inclosure led to a diminution in employment and a decrease in the population of certain large districts. Sheep and sheep farms grew very rapidly and at the expense of land previously in arable. In support of this we have not merely public clamour but the detailed assertions of men like Latimer and Fitz Herbert, the latter of whom, at any rate, was no indiscriminate opponent. Side by side with this may be placed the great development of the English wool and cloth industry. But of course depopulation, even if only local, remains to be shown. That such was produced in certain districts at any rate is well authenticated. Dugdale, for instance, in the case of Warwickshire, supplies many instances of villages or hamlets stripped of their population in the time of Henry VII.,[1] and his statements find support from the passage in the history by J. Rossus where the writer, speaking of a district known to him as a boy, tells of the inconvenience now caused to a rider by having to dismount and open gates where once the land was open and uninclosed. Again, the risings in the time of Henry VIII. in Somerset and the eastern counties were partly due to inclosure of some order. The Commission of Hales and its findings prove that the movement was widespread. The fact, however, that these findings were sometimes reversed, as was the case, affects their value as evidence not indeed of inclosure but as to its results. In many instances complaint and popular discontent appear to have arisen by reason of a loss of common right and a consequent deprivation of advantages guaranteed by custom if not by law, rather than owing to conversion from arable to pasture. On the other hand, there is little actual evidence in support of the theory of compensation or of inclosure taking place for arable improvement. In some places, no doubt, waste was inclosed, probably, however, towards the end of the period, since the re-enactment of the statute of Westminster seems a proof that approvement which would, of course, have been the normal way of dealing with commons and wastes was not in frequent use. To judge from Fitz Herbert's language, the chief form of inclosure was an inclosure of demesne lands, accompanied by licenses to tenants to likewise inclose their lands, both allowing an increase of pasture. Agriculture, too, was at a low ebb. So little was the profit of arable that, as has been seen in a passage already quoted, there was more gain to be got

[1] For instances see Dugdale, i. pp. 24, Whitchurch; 51, Stretton, etc.

from land left in furse than when under corn. So far as can be seen the relentless use of the land in the common field system had led to its natural consequence. The soil, especially when light, was exhausted, and time and rest were needed for its restoration. Nor can it be said that available employment which might absorb those thus cut adrift, offered itself in other directions. On the contrary, save in certain districts, towns in the early part of the sixteenth century seemed to have been lacking in progress, while over the whole country a veritable flood of vagrancy was let loose. No doubt this latter feature was attributable to many causes, amongst which the growth of sheep farming was only one; but even if not occasioned by inclosure, its existence and magnitude indicate a condition of things when want was rampant and widespread. Hence, indeed, those who passed out of agriculture could find little employment elsewhere. Even if it existed it was in many cases too far off and quite out of reach.

There was of course little direct evidence as to depopulation,[1] except so far as the incidental allusions to different localities may be construed as such. Possibly, however, the Commission of John Hales should be added, since in the main the real concern of the State with inclosure lay in its general effect on the population.

It should be remembered, however, that most of the statements as to the general tendency of inclosure during this period are very general, and that in particular some part of the complaint, as already said, may be due to a deprivation of common. Further, there may have been *considerable* inclosure from a wild state, despite the later references to waste and unused land which point in an opposite direction. Probably there was some.[2]

[1] In a passage already quoted, p. 156, it is asserted by Sir Anthony Cope that those dispossessed are often driven into great towns where they may die in the streets. Lansdown MS., 83, f. 68. But this is a general and vague statement.

[2] Bk. ii. App. E.

(*b*) *From middle of sixteenth to end of seventeenth century.*—During the latter years of the sixteenth century, and in the first half of that which followed, anxiety as to the effect on the population is clearly shown. The same feeling which found expression in the preamble to the statute on "Husbandry" in 1597 instigates many pamphlets, and leads to communications to the Government by way of advice. Further, there is the inquiry at the end of the century with the returns of 1607, and the Commission of 1631-2, appointed as part of the continued policy of the Privy Council with regard to this matter. A clear distinction was drawn between inclosures which led to depopulation and those which, whatever other results they might have, had no necessary tendency in this direction. The action of the State was determined by this consideration. It formed the initial charge in respect to different cases disclosed to the Board, and was obviously the point on which they require to be satisfied. If satisfied that depopulation was not likely to ensue, the question of inclosure assumed a less important aspect, and in most cases further action in restraint was foregone. So much at least may be said of the recorded cases which were discussed before the Council, forming the subject of careful inquiry, constant communication and administrative action. That the Council could interfere, and, when deemed necessary on account of depopulation, did interfere, sometimes with immediate effect, is evident. On the other hand, the large number of inclosures of recent date, recorded in consequence of the Commission, and yet leading to few attempts towards the restoration of earlier conditions, requires some explanation. It may be that the approach of grave political trouble intervened to prevent remedy; it may be that the royal exigencies substituted punishment by fine to the king for punishment by restoration of the dispossessed, or by re-conversion to arable, but it is difficult to avoid the inference that, taken as a whole, the inclosures thus ascertained, had not resulted in the depopulation, which was the principal ground for intervention and action by the king and Council. Yet the list of compositions for inclosures imposed during the years 1635-8 shows how numerous and widespread were those open, at least, to this particular charge during the early part of the seventeenth century; but, of course, the system of composition, while adding a fiscal advantage to punishment, does not effect restoration. Nor is it accompanied by any attempt, such as that embodied in the old tillage laws.

The explanation here offered of this absence of any real attempt at remedial action receives additional support from its harmony with other evidence. The record of the cases brought before the consideration of the Council shows two things. On the one hand, the existence of inclosure, other than of wastes, without depopulation, is clearly recognised, and evidence on this latter point, altogether apart from that relating to the inclosure itself, is required; on the other hand, in certain instances, the testimony on this last matter is clearly inadequate. Further acknowledgment of the two kinds of inclosure is abundant. Observers taking different views join in the admission, though, of course, they do not agree as to the extent to which each kind has prevailed. Thus, the author of the *Considerations* (1653), both in that pamphlet and in his Rejoinder (1656), and Joseph Lee, urge that depopulation is not a usual accompaniment or consequence, while Moore,[1] on the other side with Powell and others,[2] obviously consider as rare, cases where this evil result has not ensued. Fuller, in *The Holy State*, writes of the good landlord that he "detests and abhors all inclosure with depopulation." Differing opinions, such as these, cannot be construed otherwise than as proving the occurrence of inclosures with

[1] The titles of Moore's pamphlets emphasise his attack on inclosures which "unpeople towns and uncorn fields."

[2] *E.g.* Joseph Bentham, *The Society of Saints*, p. 67, etc.; Fuller, *Holy State*, bk. ii. c. 13.

different results as regards the population, and of these, in both cases, in no inconsiderable amount. Like testimony is at hand in the lists and mentions of places where the presence or absence of depopulation has been observed. Moore says of the hundred or more townships, which he declares to have been inclosed in Leicestershire, "how few among them are not unpeopled or uncorned or both";[1] but he gives neither names nor details. In the same strain is Bentham's[2] statement of eleven manors in Northamptonshire which lost their population. On the other hand, a list of nineteen townships is given by Lee[3] where no depopulation has taken place, taken from the area of South Leicestershire and the adjoining counties, which, he says, ought to be added to. Indeed, he himself gives a further list of places in the same district where the inclosures either have been or are now about to be plowed. Moore's querulous complaint of writers who "fish out some few examples of inclosure not followed by evil result," carries little conviction, especially in view of the fact that where he speaks in general terms his opponents give precise instances. Aubrey, in his account of the inclosures in North Wilts, says definitely that in that case there was depopulation. The only general conclusion possible is that both results could be perceived in fairly considerable amounts in the districts treated of. But there were many other districts where the charge of depopulation does not occur.

A more important matter than the local result occasioned in each particular case, is the general result in a district, a county, or the country at large. Here the evidence seems more harmonious. Thus, Moore's statement already quoted: "I complain not of inclosure in Kent and Essex where they have other callings and

[1] This statement by Moore is cited in the *Vindication of the Considerations*, p. 14, as from a "Reply" in a printed sheet.

[2] Bentham, *Christian Conflict*, cited "Considerations," p. 40.

[3] Lee, *A Vindication, etc.*, pp. 5, 8.

trades to maintain their country by, or of places near the sea or city," may be compared with Lee's words: "Are there not many places in England, Essex, Hereford, Devonshire, Shropshire, Worcester, wholly inclosed and yet no such results follow?" and with the vindication of inclosure in the case of Somerset. As will be seen other counties or parts of counties might be added, as far as inclosure is concerned, but there is no record even of this general kind, as to their condition with regard to population. In some of the cases mentioned, the conditions at the time were such as to secure the easy employment, and so the reabsorption, as it were, of even large numbers thrown out of agricultural work, if such there were. It seems certain that some local disturbance must have taken place, and it is possible, though improbable, that the total agricultural employment in some counties underwent diminution. In Devonshire the busy woollen industry obviously offered increased employment, since, at the beginning of the century, wool had to be brought in for manufacture from many other counties, as from Dorset and Cornwall on the one side, and on the other from Worcester and Warwick. So busied were the people in industry that food also had to be imported into the county.[1] To some extent this was probably true of Somerset, but here inclosure had partly taken the form of bringing common and waste into general cultivation. The cases of Essex and Kent are sufficiently explained. In Shropshire and Hereford land had been taken in and inclosed from a state of waste, or something very like waste, and the same was true of districts in other counties formerly under wood, as is stated both by Blith, a supporter, and the author of *The Humble Petition of Two Sisters*, an opponent of inclosure. The actual date of inclosure in these counties is doubtful.

As a matter of fact, a careful distinction must be made between the circumstances of counties like Devonshire, Kent, and Essex and those of many others, including those

[1] Thomas Westcott, *A View of Devonshire in* 1630, p. 60.

inland counties "where inclosure is now so much inveighed against." In the former case, a decrease in one form of agriculture, if such occurred, might be shorn of effect by the growth of new forms of employment within reasonable reach. In the more agricultural counties where "the great manufacture and trade . . . is tillage," such means of remedy was not present. But even in the then agricultural circumstances of the country certain new opportunities for those deprived of farm work in one or other township, offered themselves elsewhere. In the first place, it must be remembered that by the very inclosure the effective area of cultivation was enlarged. Unnecessary fallows were abandoned, and the cultivation of these offered new work.[1] In the second place, the draining of the Fens and of the Bedford Level added so largely to the land under crop that deduction elsewhere might take place without any diminution in the total arable amount. In the third place, during this period, some of the land formerly laid down under grass was now being ploughed up, having regained its fertility with rest. The greatest yield of corn, according to the suggestion of one writer, is from old inclosures now broken up to tillage.[2] In the fourth place, land in many different regions was taken in from a wild and forest state. While the extent to which this took place is difficult to estimate, there is no doubt that it was very considerable. The period was one of progressive agriculture, and the spirit of reclamation which exhibited itself in the great drainage schemes was likely to encourage the utilization of land lying in an unreclaimed condition. Careful observers like Gibson and Morton, elsewhere cited, writing respectively of Warwickshire and Northamptonshire, employ this as the true cause of conversions from arable to pasture which took place in other parts of these counties. While not peculiar to the seventeenth

[1] Lee, *Vindication*, 21, etc. In the Summary affixed to *A Vindication of the Considerations*, strong complaint is made of the loss of ground for the crop of corn under the open field system. See answer to objection i.

[2] *Considerations*, p. 10; Lee, *Vindication, etc.*, pp. 8, 9.

century it was probably more operative on a large scale in that century than previously. The exhaustion of the woods and forests during this period lends probability to this view, and it may be that some of the inclosure which took place in the west and elsewhere without the intervention of any common field system, as suggested by Marshall, may be ascribed to this time.[1] At the end of the sixteenth century, it was suggested, as has been already pointed out, that the easiest remedy for the decay of arable was not the reconversion of the land now and recently laid down to pasture, but the bringing of the wastes largely overgrown and of little value into cultivation; and the extent of these was stated to be very great.[2] Taking into account the nature of the inclosures during the eighteenth century, about which good information exists, the reclamation of waste in that century, save in the north of England, does not seem sufficiently extensive to account for an area of waste, as large as would be gathered from the above account and also from Leland's *Itinerary*.

From the various accounts dealt with, and in the various ways described, it may be concluded that the whole area of cultivation was greatly enlarged.

The results on employment and population may be summarised. Local disturbance took place without doubt, a process which occasioned suffering and poverty, and combined with other causes to bring about migration, thus aiding the movement which the Act of Settlement of the Poor (1662) sought to restrain. But this disturbance was

[1] It is difficult to speak precisely as to dates. The author of *The Humble Petition* makes his attack on inclosure in 1604 "not condemning the inclosure of Essex, Hartfordshire and Devonshire, and such woodland counties." Blith in 1652 gives as the places where "woodlands now enclosed are grown as gallant cornfields as be in England," western parts of Warwick, the northern parts of Worcester, Stafford, Shropshire, Derbyshire, Yorkshire, and all the counties thereabouts. But neither of them say anything to show whether the inclosure referred to was novel and in progress, or past, but yet not too long past to be forgotten.

[2] Address by Alderman Box, Lansdown MS., cxxxi. 22.

not uniform and was probably confined to particular villages and districts, and even then not operative to any very great degree save in the inland, or rather the midland, counties. Any wide general effect in the direction of depopulation was checked in many counties by the large addition made to the total land under cultivation, and in other cases by the development of local industries and occupations.

From evidence already adduced as to the course of inclosure towards the end of the same century, there is even less probability of depopulation. Some change in the use of particular fields and farms must have taken place, but the balance of testimony is in favour of an increase of arable at the expense of pasture. During this time there is little complaint about inclosure,[1] and little if any suggestion of a decrease in the population, arising from this or any other cause. Gregory King and Davenant both asserted an increase.

(*c*) *Eighteenth Century.* When, with the growth of private acts, open field inclosure becomes a predominant feature of the movement, at least in many parts of the country, complaints as to the effect upon employment and population are revived. Certain differences distinguish the outcry at this time from that of an earlier date. Clearer knowledge as to the results of the movement restricts the attack to particular forms. Though still the gravest complaint, others are added to it, while further it is urged with more discrimination and less as a general charge. Again, save in a few instances, the real complaint is rather that local depopulation injures those thrown out of one trade and forced to emigrate or to resort to some other calling than that the number of the people in the country is diminished. Lastly, the social and unhealthy lot of those forced into towns insanitary in their condition and prematurely increased, occupies attention. Dr. Price, of course, was conspicuous among those who

[1] J. Cowper in *An Essay proving that inclosing commons and common fields is contrary to the interests of the nation*, 1732, furnishes an exception.

asserted depopulation.[1] His denunciation of inclosures had this peculiarity, that unlike that by others, it proceeded less from objection to them than from the evident desire to assign some adequate cause for what was then his favourite doctrine, the decline of the population. The inaccuracy of his calculations on this point, often exposed, were finally disposed of by the census of 1801. But his pertinacity had the merit of evoking able criticism which extended beyond the bare statistical matter to the question of cause, and hence the effect of the inclosures on population during the latter part of the century was very effectively examined. It was kept well to the front in all discussions.

Very fortunately during this period there is more direct evidence as to the result of inclosure, both in the country at large and in different districts, than in earlier times. Thus the amount of inclosure and its nature in the various counties can be at least approximately determined from the investigation of the acts and awards. Next, the evidence of the writers of the *County Reports* and of other observers gives the views entertained by those who had specific knowledge derived from inspection. In the third place, a detailed attempt made by Howlett to arrive at an estimate of the effect upon population in certain counties, was published in 1786; while, in the last place, data exist for a more complete calculation at the end of the century and the beginning of the nineteenth century.

Dealing with the first matter, it is obvious that in certain counties the amount of land which may be estimated as inclosed under private acts before 1800 was too slight to occasion any great or serious change, as may be seen from its percentage to the area of the counties in question.[2] This is certainly the case in Westmoreland, Lancashire, Cheshire, Shropshire, Hereford, Cornwall, Devonshire, Kent, Essex, Suffolk, Surrey, Sussex. In

[1] The exaggerated popular view is well illustrated in Goldsmith's *Deserted Village*, esp. Preface.

[2] Bk. ii. Appendix D.

other counties, Hampshire, Stafford, Somerset, Dorset, Westmoreland, the quantity, though about 5 per cent., is not great. In nearly all these cases the characteristic was inclosure of commons or waste. Only in some few did the movement affect land in open field. In Suffolk and Hereford the two are about equal, in Stafford inclosure was mainly of common, while only in Hampshire and Dorset did open field predominate. In the remaining counties mentioned above, commons and wastes formed the land thus dealt with. But to the districts where little if any effect on population could thus be produced, a considerable addition must be made when account is taken of counties where inclosure was large in amount and yet wholly or largely of waste, wild land or commons. To the above must be added the northern counties, Northumberland, Cumberland, Durham and part of Yorkshire. In Norfolk the two kinds had been going on simultaneously. In both Nottingham and Derby, a considerable amount of common was taken in, while in both Worcester and Lincoln[1] inclosures of this kind were neither infrequent nor in their total amount unimportant. Even this does not exhaust the matter. On many soils inclosure had but little effect so far as labour and population were concerned, for the simple reason that it affected the use of the land slightly if at all. In these instances it would have, in the main, a beneficial effect, since more continuous cultivation was introduced and a new call for labour was made in respect of the turnip crop and of artificial grasses. It is probably due, at any rate in part, to these causes, that in Huntingdon and Cambridge, in Nottingham and Derby, in Lincoln and in Gloucester, the complaint of rural depopulation does not appear to have been raised. The result of the above is to restrict to narrow and somewhat particular

[1] A good deal of fen land and comparative waste remained in Lincoln. Probably the appearance of this led one traveller to urge that the Lincolnshire inclosures must be beneficial to the nation even if hurtful to a few, and that they would increase population; "Tour in Midland Counties in 1772," *Gentleman's Mag.*, xliv. p. 206.

limits the regions where any very marked results might be apprehended. Thus we have Wiltshire, together with probably some portion of Dorset. Again, the midland counties, Leicester, Northampton, Bedford and Rutland, and in another group, Oxford, Berkshire, and some part of Buckingham, present themselves for separate examination. Possibly, too, Warwick and Worcester on the one hand, and Nottingham and Derby on the other, require a word.

With regard to these latter it should be remembered that they were necessarily affected by the growth of manufacture and the needs of a manufacturing population. In counties abutting on the new industries conversion from arable to pasture often took place by reason of the immediate demand for milk and meat, but this might be wholly independent of inclosure, as, for instance, in Lancashire.[1] Further, in them as in the home counties and in Lancashire and Cheshire, growth in manufacture produced new employments, which tended to attract people away from the more rural districts in the immediate proximity.

Turning to the midland group first mentioned, namely, Leicester, Northampton, Bedford and Rutland, information is to be found in the evidence of contemporary observers. So far as Leicester is concerned, there was little doubt among contemporaries that a marked conversion into pasture, resulting in the diminution of the labour on some farms and of population in some rural districts, took place. With very few exceptions, indeed, the inclosures by act up to 1800 were of land in cultivation, and thus in large measure of open fields. Both the direct evidence of careful observers of all kinds and the acknowledged development in the county of breeding point in the same direction. It is no doubt true that the growth of manufacture in certain centres provided additional work throughout the county, but this does not disprove the results on rural employment and population. In North-

[1] *Agric. Report, Lancashire* (1813), p. 393.

ampton these results are not so uniform. While the nature of the inclosures was the same as in Leicester, the results differ at any rate as far as one part of the county is concerned. According to the *Report* to the Board of Agriculture a difference in soil was in large measure responsible for this; one part becoming a great grazing district,[1] from which, the writer surmises, many had to migrate, while the others still continued in mixed cultivation. Where arable continued, improved methods and new crops may have led to an increased demand for labour.[2] In Rutland few wastes or separate commons were inclosed, and we are told that there was a decrease in the arable area. The case of Bedford remains. There is no doubt that in certain places conversion took place on a sufficiently large scale to attract observation. Of this instances occur in the north of the county, but the writer of the *Report* to the Board of Agriculture doubts if there was much effect produced on the population as a whole.[3] He agrees that it has taken place in certain cases. If the area under wheat can be taken as a trustworthy index of the land under arable, the returns to the inquiry instituted by a Committee of the House of Commons in 1800 can be adduced in corroboration of the conclusions thus arrived at. In all four counties, as far as returns reach, the acreage under wheat on the inclosures concerned during the periods 1760-1800 had undergone, after the inclosure, a diminution, amounting in Leicester to 37 per cent., in Northampton to 29 per cent., in Bedford to 13 per cent., and in Rutland to 54 per cent.;[4] in the last case the amount taken into account is perhaps too small to justify any very definite conclusion. The

[1] *Agric. Report, Northampton* (1809), p. 137, forming a great grazing district, supplying the towns and London with meat.

[2] See Stone, *Suggestions*, p. 30, etc.

[3] *Agric. Report, Bedford* (1807), pp. 270-1.

[4] These percentages relate to the inclosures in parishes in respect of which returns are made. It is far from certain that they can be taken as representative of inclosure throughout the entire country.

position of the various counties, showing decline in the wheat area as alleged, may be set out as follows:

INCLOSURE BEFORE 1800.	Decrease in Wheat acreage in Parishes for which returns are made.*
Bedford,	1157
Berkshire,	122
Buckingham,	3297
Cambridge,	297
Leicester,	3793
Northampton,	5787
Nottingham,	984
Oxford,	112
Rutland,	498
Warwick,	2180

These figures relate to the net effect on the wheat acreage of the inclosures of all land, not common field alone, in respect of which returns were received. In certain cases the decrease forms a considerable percentage of the area for which returns were made. As a general rule decrease occurs in counties where the amount of inclosure was great, and often, as a reference to the table shows, where inclosure took place mainly before 1780.

Another list gives the effect produced on the wheat acreage in open field inclosures in 646 cases. Of these 646 places increase occurs in 239 of 14,507 acres and decrease in 407 of 30,894 acres.

	Barley.			Oats.		
	Number of Returns.	Places showing Increase.	Places showing Decrease.	Number of Returns.	Places showing Increase.	Places showing Decrease.
Bedford,	23	8	7	21	10	5
Berkshire,	8	4	2	8	6	2
Buckingham,	28	18	6	28	13	12
Cambridge,	10	8	0	10	6	2
Leicester,	72	28	37	69	59	8
Northampton,	78	36	29	74	50	14
Nottingham,	50	33	9	46	34	5
Oxford,	29	14	13	31	29	2
Rutland,	9	3	6	6	4	2
Warwick,	35	14	18	35	19	11

To determine the land under some form of grain requires some account of the land under barley and oats both before and after inclosure. Though figures in acres are not given, some estimate as to extent of change may be formed from the number of inclosures in which either increase or decrease took place. These are set out for the counties enumerated above.

When these figures are taken into account, the total acreage under grain in certain of these counties may be regarded as not having decreased. This would seem true of Berkshire, Cambridge, Oxford, and probably of Nottingham. Further, the decrease in grain acreage is certainly considerably less than that in wheat acreage in Buckingham and Northampton. The position in Bedford, Leicester, Rutland and Warwick is not greatly modified. Now, taking into account the great increase in stock displaying itself in most of these counties, especially where that increase includes dairy cows, the probability of decrease in employment cannot be said to present itself in many cases.[1] The additional labour required for root crops must also be borne in mind.

The increase of stock is so great in some cases as to compensate for some decrease in arable if such took place. The counties where there is initial ground for treating diminution in rural employment and population as probable are Bedford, Leicester, Warwick, and also Northampton, Buckingham and Rutland. In the latter three cases the probability is much less strong than when wheat acreage alone is considered, while in the former three there is some modification. It is doubtful if sufficient instances are given in Rutland to justify much conclusion.

The matter may be approached from another point of view. A further list in the *General Report* furnishes the quantity of waste or common included in the inclosures, whether of open field or not, in the various counties. Taking these, and comparing the amount thus stated for the different parishes with open field inclosure with the

[1] Opposite page.

total acreage of such inclosures, the percentage of commons or waste in open field inclosure works out at 20 or 25 per cent. In Bedford it is 20 per cent., in Leicester 28 per cent. But this represents an addition to the land capable of close cultivation. If to this be added some 25 per cent. of the remainder for the fallow,

---

	Cattle			Dairy Cows			Sheep		
	Number of Returns.	Places with Increase.	Places with Decrease.	Number of Returns.	Places with Increase.	Places with Decrease.	Number of Returns.	Places with Increase.	Places with Decrease.
Bedford,	18	6	7	22	6	9	25	13	6
Berkshire,	3	3	—	4	3	—	7	5	—
Buckingham,	23	17	3	30	23	3	34	20	13
Cambridge,	5	1	2	7	1	5	9	4	3
Leicester,	57	51	4	47	39	7	65	59	5
Northampton,	33	28	4	3	—	—	43	39	3
Nottingham,	34	19	5	26	16	3	41	29	8
Oxford,	13	9	1	18	13	1	26	20	2
Rutland,	6	5	—	2	1	1	8	8	—
Warwick,	23	17	4	29	19	7	34	30	3

the increase of land brought at any rate within the sphere of cultivation will be seen to be considerable. In the case of Rutland, the writer of the *Agricultural Report*, seeking an estimate of the amount of land in existing open parishes actually under crop, points out that 76 per cent. of the total was in actual open field, and then deducts one-third for the fallow. On the basis of these two calculations a deduction of two-fifths from open field inclosures for land not under crop seems a fair though not an excessive allowance. If this method be adopted, and if the pastures, wastes or commons inclosed outside the open field inclosures be added, the result is different from that before the mind when in the various counties the amount of open field inclosure is given. The bare statement of this often reads as though this amount were composed of land actually in arable at the time.[1]

Taking the counties where there was much open field inclosure before 1800, the estimate on this plan reads as follows in round figures, for inclosures before that date:

	Percentage of land inclosed out of actual arable.	Percentage inclosed not out of arable.
Bedford, - - - -	15	10
Berks, - - - -	6	4
Bucks, - - - -	13	8
Cambridge, - - -	4	6
Derby, - - - -	5.5	5.5
Gloucester, - - -	7	5
Huntingdon, - - -	18	12
Leicester, - - - -	23.5	18.5
Lincoln, - - - -	12.5	11.5
Middlesex, - - -	2.5	2
Norfolk, - - - -	4.5	4.5
Northampton, - - -	23	14.5
Nottingham, - - -	14	11
Oxford, - - - -	14.5	10
Rutland, - - - -	24.5	16
Warwick, - - - -	12	9
Wilts, - - - -	7	6
Worcester, - - -	4.5	5.5
Yorkshire, E.R., - -	14	12.5

[1] Some part of the error involved in this was most clearly indicated by Blith in the seventeenth century.

Apart from the foregoing considerations some attempt may be made to classify the various counties so as to show those in which the charge of depopulation or decreased employment arising out of inclosure has *some initial* probability. The possibility of decrease in either of these two directions must be distinguished from the possibility of migration within the county—that is, of increase in one parish at the expense of another. That subject will be discussed later. Moreover, as far as causes or results of change are concerned, conversion of arable to pasture, and so decrease of population, if such be associated with it, might arise from the growth of industry and the attraction of labour to such employment and away from rural pursuits and districts.

I. Counties where amount of total inclosure up to 1800 small. Common field inclosures given in brackets where such occur.

A. Inclosure mainly or wholly of uncultivated lands.

Cheshire,	.4		Lancashire,	2.2	(*)
Cornwall,	.0		Shropshire,	2.1	(.2)
Devonshire,	.1		Sussex,	.3	(*)
Essex,	.1		Westmoreland,	.4	
Kent,	.0				

B. Inclosure partly or mainly of open fields.

Dorset,	4.3	(3.7)	Hertford,	5.3	(3.8)
Hampshire,	4	(3.7)	Suffolk,	1.5	(.7)
Hereford,	.8	(.7)	Surrey,	1.7	(1.3)

II. Counties where amount of inclosure up to 1800 considerable.

A. Inclosure largely or wholly of waste.

Cumberland,	5.8	(.2)	Somerset,	7.5	(.3)
Durham,	15	(.1)	Stafford,	5.7	(2.5)
Northumberland,	5.8	(.8)	Yorkshire, N.,	6.7	(3.7)

B. Where though inclosure of open field considerable, little change in cultivation probable.

Cambridge,	10.1	(7.1)	Lincoln,	23.8	(20.4)
Gloucester,	12	(12)	Norfolk,	8.9	(6.4)
Huntingdon,	30	(30)			

C. Change in cultivation possible.

(i) Change largely associated with urban growth.

Derby,	11.3	(8.6)	Warwick,	20.7	(19.8)
Middlesex,	4.7	(4.7)	Yorkshire, W.,	11.6	(4.6)
Nottingham,	25	(23)			

(ii) Considerable change possible.

Bedford, -	- 25.1 (25.1)	Northampton,	37.6 (36.9)
Buckingham,	- 20.9 (20.9)	Yorkshire, E.,	26.7 (23.4)
Leicester,	- 42.2 (39.6)		

(iii) Change, though less marked.

Berkshire,	- 10.2 (10.1)	Wiltshire, -	13.1 (12)
Oxford, -	- 24.6 (24.6)	Worcester, -	10 (7.6)
Rutland, -	- 40.7 (40.7)		

As, however, the complaints as to the evil results of inclosure, and especially as to the effect upon population, date from 1780 or thereabouts, the counties requiring attention are obviously those in which the movement had made itself felt in some perceptible degree prior to that date, 1780. These may be stated as follows, distinguishing the amounts inclosed, which include common fields and those which are from common or waste.

County.	Common field.	Common.
Leicester,	31.2	1.2
Northampton,	30.8	.7
Rutland,	20.4	—
Yorkshire, E.,	19.7	2.7
*Huntingdon,	17.9	—
Warwick,	16.3	.4
Oxford,	15.1	.1
*Lincoln,	14.9	1.7
Nottingham,	14.3	.9
Buckingham,	12.5	—
*Gloucester,	7.6	—
Bedford,	7.6	—
Berkshire,	6.4	.1
Worcester,	5.9	1.4
Derby,	3.9	2.1
*Durham,	—	8.4
*Yorkshire, W.,	2.4	7.1

If those marked with an asterisk be left out, the remainder, omitting the East Riding, correspond with the list already determined. Those left out are counties where, for sundry reasons, the change, though considerable, cannot be held to have affected the use of the soil as between crops and pasture. It is very doubtful if any but the first seven are sufficiently subject to inclosure to justify the gloomy prognostications met with in contemporary literature, even could it be shown that inclosure was attended with the alleged evils. But be that as it may, it will be well to consider all in our inquiries. The question is not whether some diminution of population was probable, but whether there is any ground for alleging that such took place.

The statistics and facts in respect of which these need to be examined can be placed under two headings, those affecting the whole county areas, and those where inclosed parishes in the various counties can be compared with those which did not pass under inclosure at this date.

Taking the first we may compare the counties subject to inclosure and those not subject to inclosure according to their estimated increase of population between 1750 and 1801 and the increase 1801-11, and the rate of increase in the expenditure on poor relief.[1] Something, however, must be said as to the value of these tests. Whatever they prove as to the counties, they cannot be conclusive as to the more local migration within the county areas, since diminution in one or more districts may be compensated for by increase elsewhere. But on the other hand it would be a remarkable coincidence if such were to occur so systematically as to nullify conclusions as to the influence of the factor of inclosure as shown in a considerable number of cases. Again, other factors must not be ignored. Both alterations in population and variations in the expenditure on the poor are due to many and various causes, of which inclosure if one is only one. Hence, indeed, the absence of any apparent connection between this factor and the changes in either of these two departments may be offset by the intrusion of other elements. But here a careful inspection of the various conditions of the respective counties should enable us to arrive at some, though perhaps only a general result. A more difficult point is raised when the position of all

[1] Appendices A and B.

inclosed counties is considered, irrespective of the date of inclosure whether effected during this half century or before. Old as well as recently inclosed land is obviously more liable to an alteration in its use than land which remains open. The difference, however, between the two is that land inclosed during the period under survey is more likely to exhibit a marked change because the obstacles to change are suddenly removed. At the same time in examining counties in respect of these particulars it will be well to note if inclosed counties in general show less increase of population or greater rise in poor rates than counties where more of the area is still open and so less liable to any alteration in its use. Other criticisms may be advanced. Thus it may be urged that whereas inclosure up to 1780 was more liable to conversion to pasture, the reverse was true of the inclosures towards the end of the century. This is possibly true in some measure. It is, however, shown elsewhere that of the inclosures made during 1780-1800 much took place on land which was undoubtedly used for grain and arable in general.[1] It is improbable that any considerable portion of the land turned to pasture at the earlier epoch was reconverted or that when inclosure continued on similar land to that inclosed before 1780, other results than those previously experienced ensued. The lists of parishes given in the Appendix to the *General Report on Inclosure* indicating the alteration in the wheat area show on examination that in such counties as Leicester, Northampton and Warwick, to take the more prominent, the inclosures during the two periods are attended with much the same results in this particular. The wheat area does not decrease in one period and increase or remain the same in the other. Further, as is shown later, the slow increase of population, 1801-11, in the great pasture district of Leicester and Northampton does not indicate reconversion to arable if that is attended with rapid and marked change in population. Likewise, the same complaints as to population are repeated, though

[1] See pp. 226-8, 237, 413.

less importance must be attached to this since an outcry once raised is always liable to repetition. So far as the population estimate for 1750 is concerned there is undoubtedly room for criticism. The estimate of population from the related baptisms, marriages, and burials is not certain; but in this case where the figures are collected from the parishes included in the counties, the error is not one likely to seriously impair the comparison between county and county. On the average the error, if any, in each county is likely to be much the same. As to the validity of the returns of the early expenditure on the poor much may be said. Very probably there is some inaccuracy, but when all is said, when broad results alone are sought, comparisons such as the above may be expected to afford some general trial of the accuracy of the statement that inclosure was followed by a decrease in the population and in the general employment of considerable districts.

Turning to the tests suggested under the second heading where the cases of parishes inclosed by act and those not so inclosed are compared, a more precise method is undoubtedly afforded in one respect. On the other hand the statistics at our command are different and in certain respects less satisfactory. In the first place, the tables[1] compiled by Howlett from replies to some 500 letters sent out to the clergy in parishes both recently inclosed and not inclosed may be taken. From the answers received he constructed a table comparing the two classes of parishes in each county concerned in respect of the baptism for the two quinquennial periods, 1760-5 and 1775-80. Despite the comparatively small number of parishes the table is of value as affording some test of the accuracy of the assertion that inclosure led generally to a decline in the population.

In the second place the census returns of the population in 1801 as compared with 1811 can be utilised for a comparison between the parishes inclosed during the

[1] Appendix C.

eighteenth century and those not so inclosed in certain counties, including those singled out above. This is attempted in two ways. On the one hand open field parishes inclosed during the eighteenth century are compared with the county and with open field parish subsequently inclosed, that is, after 1800, in respect of density.[1] If population decreased owing to inclosure, parishes subject to this process may be reasonably expected to show some trace in their density not only when compared with parishes where open fields remained but also with the county at large, care being taken of course to exclude so far as possible parishes of urban rather than rural characteristics. This latter necessity involves some little trouble, as no precise definition can be laid down; but this matters less when the same method is applied in the case of a large number of counties. On the other hand the parishes inclosed and the county may be compared with regard to the increase in population from 1801-1811.[2] This is not so certain a test, as reduction might take place to be followed by increase. Some light, however, is thrown on the truth of the statements that inclosure involved wholesale conversion and that conversion implied lack of progress and development in population and occupation. In this connection the possibility of some change in the results following inclosure during the latter years of the century from that encountered in the period 1750-1780 must be borne in mind, but for reasons already given this is of much less moment when counties or districts are taken separately than it would be if the inclosures of the whole country were taken together.

Taking the tests considered under the first heading where the figures for population and poor relief are treated together, a table[3] is appended giving (*a*) the amount of open field land inclosed under act in the whole eighteenth century, that prior to 1780, and that

[1] Appendix G. [2] Appendices D, E, F.
[3] Appendix A.

for 1801-1810 inclusive; (*b*) the rates of increase in the population from 1750 to 1801 and between 1801 and 1811; (*c*) the poor rates per head of the population for 1748-50 (average), for 1803 and for 1813. Another table[1] gives the increase of poor law expenditure between average of 1748-50 and 1783-5, between 1783-5 and 1803, and from 1803 to 1813.

An examination shows that there is no close, if indeed any, correspondence between the amount of inclosure and the rate of increase in the population. No doubt with the many factors at work this is but to be expected; but if it be true it shows that so far as the county areas are concerned, decline in particular places if due to inclosure was compensated for by increase elsewhere. In other words the matter at issue is rather one of local migration than of decrease in population and restriction in amount of occupation. Nor is it possible to assert that but for this alleged decline in the inclosed parishes the total population for the county would have been greater, since that ignores what is, after all, one of the most important questions at issue, that is, whether the inclosure was not necessary to secure for the population, increasing from other causes, its necessary supplies. That there is no general connection between inclosure during this century and population becomes more evident if the figures be looked at in more detail. For this purpose it will be well to single out the counties where the inclosure both in amount and kind was likely to produce an effect on the population, distinguishing between those where any appreciable decrease in the wheat area is noted in 1800, on the basis of the returns received, and those where no such appreciable decline presents itself or when an increase is noted. This list may be compared with one of the counties where the amount of inclosure is too small to affect the population of the whole. Counties where marked industrial causes of increase exist are denoted by an asterisk.

[1] Appendix B.

Counties in which population might conceivably be affected by inclosure (percentages in round figures).

With decrease in wheat acreage.	Open Field inclosure to 1800.	Increase of Population 1750-1801.	*Without perceptible decrease or with increase.*	Open Field inclosure to 1800.	Increase of Population 1750-1801.
*Leicester,-	40 %	32 %	Huntingdon,	28 %	15 %
Rutland, -	41	30	Oxford, -	25	14
Northampton,	37	9	Lincoln, -	21	26
Bedford, -	26	6	*Yorkshire,	8	50
*Nottingham,	23	53	Wiltshire,	12	9
Buckingham,	21	22	*Derby, -	9	48
*Warwick,	20	55	Cambridge,	7	14
			Berkshire,	10	17
			*Worcester,	8	35

Counties in which such effect would not be produced.

	Open Field inclosure to 1800.	Increase of Population 1750-1801.		Open Field inclosure to 1800.	Increase of Population 1750-1801.
Cornwall, -	—	33 %	Suffolk, - -	1 %	23 %
Devon, - -	—	4	Cumberland, -	—	36
Essex, - -	—	17	Durham, -	—	15
Northumberland,	1 %	5	Somerset, -	—	15
Shropshire, -	—	24	Westmoreland,	—	8
Hereford, -	1	18			

While the length of the period and the presence of other and varying factors render any very definite and positive conclusion impossible, these tables are, as a whole, against the alleged general connection between common field inclosure and decline in population. They do not even support the view that population in these counties progressed as a rule at a less rapid rate. The two counties where there are at once high percentage of inclosure, considerable apparent decrease in wheat area and a small rate of increase in population are Northampton and Bedford; but then, on the other hand, we have Wiltshire, where the wheat acreage increased with a rate of increase in population about the same as that of Northampton. Still, these two counties deserve attention when we come to other considerations, and it is, of course, possible that the same should be said of Leicester, though industrial causes of population were probably operative, even if to an uncertain degree, in that county. In both Rutland and Buckingham the rate of increase of population is very fairly high for non-urban counties.

Two other matters require a word. Even were it possible in the face of these lists and of the conclusions stated above to assume a connection between inclosure and population, these tables and calculations afford no means of determining the question as to the existence or non-existence of a tendency towards the end of the century either to reconvert to arable, land laid down to pasture on its inclosure earlier in the century or to retain land at that time in arable which would have been converted to pasture if inclosed earlier. It is known that much of the inclosure towards the end of the century was of land obviously suited to arable, and certainly used for what it was suited; but the matter raised relates not to land such as this which is the main subject of the period of inclosure, but to the land well suited for grazing, as, for instance, in Leicester or in the breeding and grazing district of Northampton. It is quite possible that the higher prices of grain prevalent at the end of the century may have affected the use made of such of this land as came into inclosure at that time; but these tables afford no evidence one way or the other. Moreover, it should be remembered that it has already been pointed out [1] that, taking the lists of inclosed parishes which show alteration in the wheat area, diminution occurs as often towards the end as earlier in the century, even in such counties as Leicester, Northampton and Warwick. Secondly, what evidence, it may be asked, is provided as to any difference between inclosed counties, whether recently inclosed or of old inclosure, and those where some land is open? The only conclusion which can be reached appears to be this, that there is no uniform distinction. Despite recent changes, the counties in which there is much land in

[1] Above, p. 408.

open field at the end of the century are fairly numerous, the chief being:

Huntingdon, -	25.7.	Middlesex, -	14.3.
Cambridge, -	25.2.	Norfolk, - -	12.8.
Berkshire, - -	20.1.	Buckingham, -	11.9.
Bedford, - -	18.9.	Wiltshire, -	10.7.
Oxford, - -	16.3.	Hertford, -	8.1.
Northampton, -	14.5.		

Now, if it were true that the existence of inclosed land, which, of course, being in separate properties, is more amenable to the use most profitable at the time, and that, further, the result of such an exercise of individual power results in a use coincident with a diminished population, these counties would exhibit in general a greater rate of increase in population than those where all the land is inclosed.[1] This is not the case. Indeed, the reverse tends to hold good. The matter, however, is undoubtedly complicated by the fact that many, if not most, of the counties appearing in this list occupy a prominent place among those showing a high percentage of inclosure prior to 1800.

Counties with open field Inclosure at or exceeding 5 per cent. (1801-10).			Counties with little or no applicable Inclosure.		
	Inclosure.	Incr. Pop.		Inclosure.	Incr. Pop.
Huntingdon,	16 %	12 %	Suffolk, - -	1 %	9 %
Cambridge, -	12	15	Somerset, -	1	11
Bedford, -	11	10	Hereford, -	2	6
Berkshire, -	9	8	Shropshire, -	—	9
Norfolk, -	7	6	Devon, - -	—	12
Hampshire,	7	9	Gloucester, -	2	14
Yorkshire, E.R.,	7	19	Dorset, - -	2	8
Buckingham,	6	10	Cornwall, -	—	14
Lincoln, -	5	13	Northumberland,	1	9
Oxford, -	5	7	Cumberland, -	—	14
Wiltshire, -	5	4	Westmoreland,	—	12
			Rutland, - -	2	-.7
			Leicester, -	2	15

[1] See Appendix A.

The theory that inclosure led to a less rapid increase in population, or even to depopulation, derives no support from the comparison of these two factors in the first decade of the nineteenth century, as may be seen from the table[1] appended. But to make this still clearer, on the previous page, the counties with an appreciable amount of inclosure are set out and contrasted with some of those where the variation in population could not be due to inclosure by reason of its complete, or nearly complete, absence.[2] Counties with an industrial development are, so far as possible, excluded.

Of the counties with little or no inclosure given by way of contrast, there are some which probably should be excluded. In the northern counties land wholly or little cultivated was coming into use under the influence of high prices, and the same was probably true in some measure of Devon and Cornwall. Leicester, again, may have been affected by this time by the spread of the textile industry. If we compare the more purely agricultural counties in both lists, it would seem that the inclosing counties present a slightly higher rate of increase in population. No doubt this was a time when prices added a stimulus to cultivation, to the advantage of those able to cultivate as they chose, and without hindrance from tradition or the bad habits of their neighbours.

The next matter calling for attention is the position of the inclosed counties, and especially of those specially indicated, in the matter of the expenditure in the relief of the poor, since it may be taken as probable that a lack of agricultural employment and the consequent need of migration in search of work would be reflected in the need and demand for relief. The statistics are of two kinds. On the one hand, the percentage increase of the total poor relief is given in round figures for three periods —1748-9-50 to 1783-4-5, 1783-4-5 to 1803, 1803 to

[1] Appendix A.

[2] Inclosures 1801-10 inclusive; population 1801 to 1811.

1813. This leaves out of account the population, and variations in population naturally affect the amount of pauperism. On the other hand, the amount expended in relief is distributed per head of the population, taking the returns for the above years, with the exception of 1783-4-5, and for population the estimate for 1750 and the actual census figures for 1801 and 1811. In the case of the latter half of the eighteenth century, perhaps the best method of comparing the counties is to view their state as regards poor relief expenditure in 1803 per head of the population with reference to the extent to which they underwent inclosure in the preceding century, the figures for the middle of the eighteenth century being more open to criticism. In the case of the first decade of the nineteenth century, when the figures both of population and of relief are much more certain, it is possible to compare the amount of increase in population with that of increase in poor relief. But it must be remembered that, quite apart from inclosure, there were other factors operating differently in the various counties and capable of affecting the poor relief very greatly, the most important being the changes in industrial method and the localisation of industries, and the alteration in the system of relief. Consequently only marked and definite correspondences and results can be taken as indicative of a connection between inclosure and the state of pauperism as shown in these figures. To assist in the comparison, certain counties are set out below:

I. Counties with decrease in wheat acreage at 1800.

	Common Field Incl. percentage		Poor Rate Expenditure per head.	
	before 1800.	1801-1811.	1803.	1813.
Leicester, - - -	40	2	12.8	15.4
Rutland, - - -	41	2	10.5	14.1
Northampton, - -	37	7	14.8	20.3
Bedford, - - -	26	11	12.0	17.9
Nottingham, - - -	23	3	6.7	10.4
Buckingham, - - -	21	6	16.5	23.6
Warwick, - - -	20	2	11.8	14.7

II. Counties without decrease in wheat acreage or with increase at 1800.

	Common Field Incl. percentage before 1800.	1801-1811.	Poor Rate Expenditure per head. 1803.	1813.
Huntingdon, - - - -	28	16	13.2	17.2
Oxford, - - - - -	25	5	16.6	24.5
Lincoln, - - - - -	21	5	9.7	11.8
Wiltshire, - - - -	12	5	14.2	25.0
Derby, - - - - -	9	5	7.2	10.8
Cambridge, - - - -	7	12	12.5	17.7
Berkshire, - - - -	10	9	15.6	26.8
Worcester, - - - -	8	2	10.7	12.5
Gloucester, - - - -	12	2	9.0	12.0

Taking these counties in particular, and also those others only included in the general lists,[1] certain conclusions may be indicated.

Firstly, while there is no close correspondence between inclosure and the state of poverty, as far as that is disclosed in the figures cited, there seems sufficient ground for the opinion that *considerable* inclosure tended to produce some increase in the amount of relief. Thus, if we take the first period, the counties in which inclosure before 1800 reached seven per cent. of the land, we have Bedford, Berkshire, Buckingham, Cambridge, Derby, Gloucester, Huntingdon, Leicester, Lincoln, Nottingham, Northampton, Oxford, Rutland, Warwick, Wiltshire and Worcester. Of these sixteen counties all save three, namely, Derby, Lincoln and Nottingham exhibit a poor relief expenditure in 1803 exceeding 10.0 shillings per head of the population. Derby and Nottingham were counties in which the new textile manufactures were advancing, and thus may be taken as not constituting exceptions so far as the particular relationship under consideration is concerned. The other counties in which there is a like expenditure are Dorset, Essex, Hampshire, Hereford, Hertford, Kent, Norfolk, Suffolk, Surrey, Sussex. Of these ten counties Norfolk has inclosure of six per cent. of its area. The three eastern counties, moreover, were affected by the

[1] Appendices A and B.

decline in the eastern woollens due to the rise of other districts and the development of the machine industry. Making allowance for these various causes, and also for the special position of the southern counties near the metropolis, this seems sufficient ground for the general conclusion indicated above. Further, of the twelve counties where the expenditure reaches 12.0 shillings per head of the population, all save Norfolk, Essex, Kent and Hertford had been inclosed above seven per cent. Turning next to the figures relating to the first decade of the nineteenth century, it will be noticed that there was a general increase in relief expenditure, due probably to bad administration, though it is possible that this was assisted by conditions of distress. An allowance being made for this, the counties may be taken where the increase exceeded 4.0 shillings per head of the population. This occurs in eight of the enumerated counties, that is, in Northampton, Bedford, Buckingham, Huntingdon, Oxford, Wiltshire, Cambridge, Berkshire. Of these all exhibit inclosure between 1801-1810 amounting to five per cent. of the area. To these must be added from the complete list Essex, Hereford, Suffolk, Norfolk, Hampshire, Kent, and Sussex. There are only two counties with inclosure amounting to five per cent. which show an increase in poor relief less than 4.0 shillings, namely, Derby where the increase is 3.6 shillings, and Lincoln where it is only 2.1 shillings. These results are somewhat similar to those obtained in the case of the earlier period. It is important to notice that the connection, such as it is, between inclosure and poor relief is quite as marked in the latter as in the former period.

Secondly, any such connection holds good, irrespective of the alleged conversion of land from arable to pasture. This is easily seen by a reference to the tables. Thus in the first period, the poor relief expenditure proportioned to the population is, if we take counties inclosing over seven per cent. of the area, slightly higher on the whole in the second group of counties, where there is no reason for apprehending net conversion than in the first group where such may have taken place to some extent; and it must be remembered that in this group, the latter, the average percentage of inclosure was greater. Of course there may have been conversion in some places compensated for by conversion in the contrary direction elsewhere. The above relates to the result on the county at large. Similarly, in the second period, the same result appears though here in a somewhat more marked degree. Moreover, it must be remembered that the soil passing under inclosure during these later years was more distinctly arable, and that the inclosures of this time appear to have been directed to its better arable cultivation. This is quite independent of the contention that at the end of the eighteenth century there was a tendency both to reconversion and of retention in grain of land which would have been converted to pasture at an earlier date. Irrespective of this contention, which has been criticised in earlier pages, the character of the soil was different. But if this is so, inclosure if it leads to an increase in poor relief expenditure, achieves this result from other reasons than because it occasioned, as has been assumed, conversion from arable to pasture.

Thirdly, in neither case do old inclosed lands appear to have been connected with increased symptoms of poverty. In other words, these symptoms if connected, and as far as connected with inclosure, are occasioned by the change and by its more recent results. Counties wholly or mainly inclosed before the movement in the eighteenth century had apparently settled into a stable condition and were not more susceptible to changes involving an increase in poverty than counties which remained to a much greater extent in the open field cultivation environed by custom and impervious to change.

The results arrived at in the foregoing pages, when taken together, appear to indicate the presence in certain agricultural counties of a force or forces unsettling the people and involving change and some increase in poverty.

It is impossible to interpret the facts as evidence of a general restriction on the amount of employment in the counties concerned, or even in all probability in any large areas within these counties. Had such been the case, population would have been more definitely affected, and this, as has been pointed out, was not the case in any considerable number of instances. Indeed, it is only in one of the two periods examined, and then only in the case of two counties, Bedford and Northampton, that any such result seems reasonably probable. Even these cases are doubtful. Moreover, the change occurs not only in counties where on other evidence a decrease in the grain area can be premised. A decrease in actual wheat area if small is no proof of a decrease in the total area under some course of arable cultivation as distinct from pasturage. It occurs as well during a later period when there is no ground for assuming conversion from arable to pasture, as during the earlier period when in some districts there was such a change. It is of course possible that while decrease in employment and population occurred in some parishes or districts within the county, such was fairly well balanced by a converse tendency in other parishes and districts. But this is mere assumption, and an assumption untenable save in conjunction with the further assumption that there was a connection between the two. If such existed, it existed because, as seems indeed probable, the tendency towards inclosure was the result of the increased demands made for the produce of the earth. In this sense, inclosure would be the means of maintaining a larger population, and one of the incidents in its growth, even if some decrease of population took place in particular and very limited districts or parishes. This will require some further investigation. Meanwhile other aspects require our attention. No doubt inclosure implied change. It implied considerable alteration in the methods of cultivation, and in the uses of particular lands or even of particular parishes. With this came the need for a change in work or in the habitation of those working on the land. Again, there is no doubt that considerable changes took place in the ownership of land, especially in its relation to farming. The small farming class received a grave blow, and the class of the simple agricultural labourer was increased and established. Hence, too, a new element of precariousness, and of precariousness most conspicuous at or about the time of the change. This aspect, however, is mainly of importance in conjunction with that previously delineated, since had the altered system of labour employment been the chief cause, it would have wrought its effects in old inclosed counties. In these, on the other hand, the results are not particularly apparent, if apparent at all. Inclosure then may be taken as involving a change of a somewhat twofold nature which probably affected the condition of life.

It remains, however, to canvass the point raised above, that is, the existence of evidence, one way or the other, as to the effects produced on population and the amount of employment not only in the large districts in the county but in the smaller districts, or, speaking generally, in the parishes inclosed.[1]

We turn, then, to the examination of the results in respect of population in the parishes where inclosures took place. To assist such, two sets of tables have been prepared.

There are three tables [2] comparing the inclosed parishes in each of certain counties with the whole county in respect of the alteration in population between 1801 and 1811. The selected counties are those where inclosure was antecedently most likely to affect population, namely, Bedford, Berkshire, Buckingham, Cambridge, Huntingdon, Leicester, Northampton, Nottingham, Oxford, Rutland and Warwick.

In the first table [3] the increase, and in the solitary case of Rutland, the decrease, in population during the decade 1801-11 is stated in one column for all the parishes recorded as inclosed up to 1800, in the next column for those inclosed 1791-1800, and finally for the whole county. The county in this instance is the registration

[1] Inclosed, *i.e.* recorded as inclosed.
[2] Appendices D, E, F.
[3] Appendix D.

county, since the various parishes have been treated in their respective registration districts. As the aim of the comparison is to discover whether there is any suggestive difference in the movement of population between the inclosed townships and the whole area or region, the use of the registration county in place of the county proper is of no real consequence. As towns, except in special cases, and the more urban townships are included, and as these increase faster and also are generally more prominent in the whole area, that is, the county, than in the parishes or townships where inclosure occurs the rate of increase for the former is overstated. An examination of the table shows that there is no general tendency for population to increase less rapidly at this period in townships subject to inclosure than in the county at large. To facilitate a more thorough consideration of the matter dealt with, another table[1] gives the rates of variation both for the parishes inclosed up to 1790 and for those inclosed in 1791-1800 as they are grouped in the various registration districts, as also the rate of increase for the separate registration districts. About these tables there are several things to notice. The counties where the difference between the rate of increase in parishes coming under inclosure and the whole area is marked are Berkshire and Cambridge, and in a less degree Rutland, Buckingham and Oxford. In the first three of these the inclosure movement becomes more prominent after $17\frac{80}{90}$ than before. It is prominent also in the others, though here a considerable amount of inclosure had taken place before. In Buckingham, the districts where the inclosure after 1790 was most marked are Newport, Pagnell and Buckingham; while in Oxford, Bicester, Woodstock and Witney occupy a like prominence. In both cases it is in these particular districts that the inclosed parishes show a lower rate of increase than the whole. On the other hand, Bedford and Huntingdon, which mainly conform as to time of inclosure to the same type as Cambridge, are quite dissimilar in this respect. It should be

[1] Appendix F.

noticed that in Northampton, Warwick and Leicester, where very heavy inclosures ruled at an earlier time, there is but little difference in the rate of increase for the total inclosed parishes and that for the whole county. What difference, indeed, there is, is to the advantage of these parishes. Taking the detailed list of districts given in *Appendix F*, it is clear that the parishes inclosed, 1791-1800, oftener show a less rate of increase than do other inclosed parishes. This, however, is very far from being invariable. All that can be safely said is that inclosure effected during this period is in more cases coincident with such less rapid increase.

The counties singled out above are not, with the exception of Buckingham, counties where the wheat acreage in 1800 showed any particular decrease. Further, taking the general rate of increase in the population, they compare favourably with most agricultural counties. This, however, cannot be said of Rutland.

As to actual instances of decrease it will be seen from another table[1] that parishes or townships where the population declines, 1801-11, are often parishes where there is no recorded inclosure during the eighteenth century, and but seldom parishes undergoing inclosure, 1791-1800, or for the matter of that, 1811-20. In many cases decline occurs in parishes where such inclosure as occurs takes place after 1810.

In face of these tables, and the facts concerning them which have been pointed out, the only conclusions possible are necessarily of a tentative character. In the first place, if any disturbance of population ensued in the great grazing district as a whole no trace is left by this period. Secondly, the effect of comparatively recent inclosure is slight and mainly confined to certain areas, where there is no reason for assuming any decrease in the acreage under arable. The counties and districts where the soil is best or where agriculture had been most developed show the least signs. It seems indeed probable that much of the

[1] Appendix E.

land coming under inclosure in those counties where inclosed parishes increased less rapidly was land of poorer quality, and hence less likely to permit of much increase in population. Of consequent decrease in population over any fair sized area there is no sign whatever.

But it has been urged sometimes that this period affords little test; that, in the first place, the older inclosures had wrought their effect, and that, in the second place, at this time the increased demand for grain had led to the retention of land in grain, if not to the reconversion. If this latter hypothesis were correct, the former inclosures should show a uniform higher rate of increase in population, which they do not, while in addition the recent inclosures in counties, like Berkshire and Cambridge, ought to increase at a higher rate than the county at large where some open field land still remained.

To investigate this whole point, however, another table is required.[1] Here are set out for the above counties, the density of population at 1801 per 100 acres in the common field parishes inclosed by 1800, in the parishes where common field inclosure takes place after, and also in the whole county. In these tables care has been taken to exclude, so far as possible, towns and town population, including most market towns. This is of course a matter of some difficulty; but it is very obvious that unless such are left out the figures would not be pertinent, since in numerous cases a town parish, with its naturally higher population, would be included in an agricultural district. The same and like deductions have been made in the inclosed parishes and the whole county. Owing to the comparatively small number of inclosures, and the small amount of land inclosed under act after 1800 in Rutland and Leicester, the figures in the last column are of little value in these two counties. Speaking generally, the last column is less reliable than the two others.

These statistics point to the general conclusions, that, whatever the use made of inclosure, and whatever its

[1] Appendix G.

immediate result, in 1801 the total land which had been subject to this treatment was at least as thickly peopled as that in the rest of the county, and that, moreover, land where inclosure occurred after 1800 was as a rule less thickly peopled. This latter fact is easily explicable in certain counties, since in these where inclosure had been the fashion little land of value had escaped the process. This, however, was not invariably true, as may be seen from the Flegg district in Norfolk and the south-west of Middlesex, as also from the Amersham district of Buckingham. But a movement which tended towards depopulation, even though but local in character, would certainly not leave the districts affected by it more populated than those surrounding them.

It is possible to go one step further. In an Appendix to the *General Report on Inclosure* a list is given of the parishes in the respective counties where, as a result of the inclosure of open field, the wheat acreage had varied.[1] As the returns from the clergy do not cover all and often not many cases, the total inclosures before 1800 cannot be separated into the two classes. But in certain counties a sufficient number of instances is forthcoming to make worth while an inquiry into the respective density of those showing decrease and those showing increase in wheat acreage. This has been done for the following:

DENSITY PER 100 ACRES IN 1801.

County.	Wheat acreage (1800) Decreased. No.	Density.	Increased. No.	Density.
Bedford, - -	18	17.6	4	21.5
Buckingham, -	17	20.7	5	21.9
Leicester, - -	45	21	10	18.8
Northampton, -	60	20.5	10	25
Oxford, - -	10	19.1	8	18.6
Rutland, - -	9	16.8	—	—
Warwick, - -	—	17	—	—
Gloucester, - -	16	14·6	15	14.1

[1] *General Report*, Appendix.

These returns were not, it must be remembered, selected by the Board of Agriculture, and even when presented by them were not applied to any such purpose as the above. Where the number of parishes is small, they are of less importance, but this only holds in the main of the last column. The densities in the first column should be compared with the densities in an appended *Table*.[1] The correspondence between the two is sufficiently close to be important in itself, and it is significant that only in three cases do the total parishes, with a decrease in wheat acreage, show a lower density than that of the inclosed open field parishes generally, while in four cases the density is higher.

To complete this branch of the investigation a further table is added as to the increase of poor rates from 1776 to 1783-4-5 (average), and from 1783-4-5 (average) to 1803 for certain counties, distinguishing that for the whole county, that for open field parishes inclosed 1776-1782, and that for open field parishes inclosed 1783-1802. The counties chosen are typical counties—Leicester, Northampton, Buckingham, Berkshire, and Cambridge. In the last-named county the number of parishes inclosed 1776-1782 is too small to make any conclusion trustworthy.

TABLE showing comparative Increase of Poor Rates.

County.	Per cent. Increase of Poor Rates in period 1776-1783 (av.).		
	Total County.	Open Field Township inclosed. Years 1776-82 (inclusive).	Open Field Township inclosed. Years 1783-1803 (inclusive).
Leicester,	26	6	35
Northampton,	30	37	69
Buckingham,	42	59	40
Berkshire,	27	decr.	22
Cambridge,	45	—	97

[1] Appendix G.

County.	Per cent. Increase of Poor Rates in period 1783(av.)-1803.		
	Total County.	Open Field Township inclosed. Years 1776-82 (inclusive).	Open Field Township inclosed. Years 1783-1803 (inclusive).
Leicester, - - -	171	187	159
Northampton, - -	112	117	126
Buckingham, - -	95	76	118
Berkshire, - - -	74	73	98
Cambridge, - - -	115	—	66

These figures do not lend support to the view that inclosure was responsible for the increase of poverty in the parishes affected, the point now under consideration. Indeed, taken together, they are not significant of any causal relationship between inclosure and poor relief.

Before stating any general conclusions a few words may be devoted to summarise the position of the counties selected for examination, as being specially liable to any injurious effects of inclosure in respect of population or employment. Now, so far as the reports in 1800 concerning wheat acreage in *all* inclosures go, the only counties where decrease was really marked are Leicester, Northampton, Warwick, Bedford, Buckingham, and perhaps Rutland and Nottingham. The returns in the case of Rutland are too scanty to allow of any fair estimate. We may begin with these two, obviously the more doubtful cases.

Rutland, so far from showing any decrease of population, shows a high rate of increase from 1750-1801, taking the estimate for 1750. In addition Howlett gave for this county the militia returns for the decade 1769-79, according to which the population increased more or diminished less in the inclosed than in the uninclosed parishes. As the large inclosures were from 1791-1800 some reflection might be expected in the table, comparing the census returns of 1801 and 1811. In the Oakham union the parishes inclosed in the eighteenth century show a decrease of .4 per cent., while the others increase .5 per cent. On the other hand, in the Uppingham, while the inclosed parishes decrease about .6 per cent., the others decrease about 1.7 per cent. Taking the figures of parishes inclosed before 1790—for Oakham an increase of 3.2, and for Uppingham an increase of .4—it would seem that any initial tendency to decrease was followed by subsequent increase. The tables giving density of population show a higher density of population for all inclosed parishes than for the county; nor was decrease of wheat an apparent cause of reduction in the density of population when it took place. The density of the parishes passing under common field inclosure after 1800 is also higher. From the account given in the *Agricultural Report* (1808) it seems that inclosure in this county reduced the amount of land in arable.[1]

In Nottingham the industrial growth both augmented population and forced on inclosures, adding to those made under the sanction of law, many made by private proprietors and without Act.[2] The population increases very considerably from 1750 to 1801. By the density tables we see that population in the inclosed parishes was denser than in the whole of the county. The increase in 1801-11 is also greater.

Turning next to Bedford and Buckingham, the rate of increase in Bedford for the estimated period 1750-1801 was unusually low. On the other hand, in the returns presented by Howlett, the three parishes with recent inclosures show a marked increase, and the six parishes

[1] *Agric. Report, Rutland* (1808), pp. 2-10, 31, etc.: From the figures given of nine parishes remaining open, it appears that 76 per cent. is in arable field. Deducting for fallow this leaves a minimum of 50 or 51 per cent. under crop. The percentage of land in the rest of the county in arable crop is 43. According to this, some diminution probable in land in active arable. The number of parishes open is, however, small. It must be remembered that this small diminution would not necessarily imply decrease in work or population, since increased stock and keener cultivation must be put on the other side.

[2] *Agricultural Report, Nottingham* (1798), p. 180, Appendix iv., a list given of thirteen inclosures, totalling over 10,000 acres, achieved without Act.

without such a total decrease. At the end of the century the increase in the inclosed parishes, both in all those inclosed during the eighteenth century and in those inclosed in the last decade, is considerably higher than in the whole county. Moreover, the density of these inclosed parishes is greater than that of the whole or of those where inclosure subsequently occurred. In the detailed account of increase in the unions for 1801-11, it will be noticed that in Luton and Leighton Buzzard, the increase for the whole union is greater than that for inclosed parishes. This may, of course, be accidental as the number of inclosures in this district prior to 1800 is small; otherwise it is distinctly curious since these districts lie on the chalk substratum where inclosure was late, and usually implied more arable use than before. Population in the parishes recorded with a decrease in wheat acreage does not increase so rapidly, but these do not occur in Luton or Leighton Buzzard. That certain inclosures affected population detrimentally seems probable; the writer of the *Agricultural Report* admits some decreases, but deems them unusual. There is certainly no sufficient evidence of any such general results. In Buckingham the rate of increase (1750 to 1801) compares favourably with other counties; on the other hand, the four parishes with recent inclosures returned to Howlett show a slight decrease, while in the eight not inclosed there is a considerable increase. For the decade 1801-11 the increase for the whole county is rather greater than for the total parishes inclosed in the eighteenth century, though less than for those inclosed 1791-1800; but if Eton, Amersham, and Wycombe, where few inclosures before 1800 occur, be excluded the increase is practically the same in both. On the other hand, the more detailed tables show that in most unions the rate is somewhat greater than the rate for the inclosed parishes. In the district of Buckingham there is very considerable increase all round. The density of population is less for the county than for the inclosed parishes, and particularly so in the northern part of the county; and where the wheat acreage is returned as decreased, the density is but little affected.

The three counties of Leicester, Northampton, and Warwick may be taken next. In all, the wheat acreage in the parishes sending reports in 1800 shows decrease; in all the percentage of inclosure was high. On the other hand, in all three the density of population for the parishes inclosed before 1800 was greater than for the whole county or for the parishes where common field inclosures occurred after 1800; and, finally, in all, the rate of increase 1801-11 for the county is about the same, if not lower than for the inclosed parishes. The important differences between these counties lie in the greater influence and importance of industry in parts of Warwick and Leicester, and the differences in soil. Where the counties adjoin, these causes of variety are less potent. As to the detail of fact, Northampton does not figure in the accounts returned to Howlett. The rate of increase for the half century 1750-1801 is certainly lower than in the best agricultural counties. Against this must be set the greater density of the inclosed parishes over the county, and the absence of any tendency on the part of these in general towards any falling off from the average increase of 1801-11. Contrasting the densities of parishes with a decline and with an increase in wheat acreage, it appears as if the latter, where such could and did take place, produced a decided effect on population. It may seem anomalous that the rate of increase 1801-11 and of density of population was so high in the inclosed parishes. One explanation offered for this, namely, the possibility of a reconversion to grain on inclosed land, which, it must be remembered, was largely inclosed before 1780, seems hardly tenable in face of the population of the districts where wheat acreage had diminished. The most probable explanation lies in the marked difference between districts in the north-east and districts in the south-west. The increase in inclosed parishes is less than that for the district, in Brackley, Northampton, Potterspury and Daventry. The two are about the same in Hardingstone and Wellingborough. It is greater in Peterborough, Oundle, Kettering, Thrapston, Brixworth and Towcester. On the north and east the soil was different from what it was on the south and west, perhaps more markedly so from what it was on the northern side of this particular region, that is on the confines of Leicester. This latter was the grazing district, while the soil in the east was suitable also for wheat and the new rotations.

Though Warwick offers some variety within its borders, facts seem to show that in no considerable district or area was any detrimental result on population effected by inclosure. The rate of increase for the period 1750-1801 is on the estimated population a high one, but that is to be expected from the urban growth in the west of the county. Twelve parishes recently inclosed are returned to Howlett, showing an increase of some twenty-six per cent. The parishes, seven in number, without recent inclosure also increased. The rate of increase 1801-1811 for all inclosed parishes was 7.3, and for the county, excluding Birmingham and Aston parish, 7.1. Of the districts, the rate for the southern and eastern districts is lower than that of the parishes, so far as parishes inclosed to 1790 are concerned, but some recent inclosures, that is, 1791-1800 are higher in Shipston and Southam, but lower in Rugby, Warwick and Stratford. The density of population for parishes inclosed up to 1800 is slightly greater than that for the county. On the other hand, parishes with wheat acreage decreased, according to the returns of 1800, are lower. There is little compensation for decrease of wheat acreage in an increase of land under other cereals, the barley land diminishing and that under oats rising. According to the *Report* of the Board of Agriculture, "land that primarily kept a few half-starved sheep is now yielding abundance of both grass and corn." This, of course, can only apply to some of the land, but the facts and figures given above certainly do not indicate decrease of population, but rather increase, even if there was temporary decrease after some of the inclosures.

Leicester, like Warwick, has a high rate of increase 1750-1801, also exhibiting increase in the recently inclosed parishes returned to Howlett. The population of the inclosed parishes considerably exceeds in density that of the county in 1801, while the parishes with decreased wheat acreage have a high density, higher than that of the county. This was probably due, as may be judged from the *Report* to the Board of Agriculture to the stocking trade, which in certain places both provided increased employment, and, like other urban developments, led to inclosure and sometimes to inclosure for pasture. In addition to the decrease in wheat acreage, there appears to have been a decrease in barley. There was, however, an increase in the land used for oats. It is clear, however, that a distinction must be made between the inclosure in the west and north-west and that in the east, and especially the south-east.

The four counties which remain may be most conveniently considered in two divisions, Berkshire with Oxford, and Cambridge with Huntingdon.

Berkshire and Oxford have many points in common. Both present a considerable and somewhat similar variety of soil, though of course an exception must be made as to south and west Berkshire. In neither county are there initial grounds for believing that the wheat acreage was seriously diminished. The amount shown in such returns as were received in 1800 is insignificant, while there was a marked increase in Berkshire in the cultivation of both barley and oats, and in Oxfordshire of oats. In both counties a large amount of inclosure took place after 1800; indeed, in Berkshire by far the greater quantity is after that date, but this was largely due to the inclosure in the chalky lands. Both exhibit a somewhat average rural rate of increase for the period 1750-1801.

The statistics both of density in 1801 and of increase 1801-11 show certain particular features. In Berkshire the density rate for the parishes inclosed by 1800 is considerably lower than for the county, in Oxford it is very slightly lower. Likewise, too, parishes increase in Berkshire at a much slower rate, and in Oxford at a somewhat slower rate. In both counties it should be noticed that inclosure before 1800 takes place but rarely in the districts bordering the Thames, and that in those districts, more especially in those belonging to Berkshire, the population runs high in many parishes. There is more inclosure in this area after 1800. Berkshire is the more marked in these respects throughout, the difference in both density of population and rate of increase being correspondingly greater, and the Thames districts playing a more dominant part. These facts make some separation of the very different regions essential. If this be done, and if, as is shown in the table, Henley, Thame, Headington and Oxford be withdrawn from Oxfordshire, and similarly the districts running along the Thames valley from Berkshire, a great difference is perceptible. In both counties the difference between the county rate of increase and that for the inclosed parishes is much reduced, while so far as density is concerned all significant difference vanishes. In Oxford, where inclosure and decrease of wheat acreage occurred, the density was higher than where there was increase in wheat acreage recorded.

In neither Cambridge nor Huntingdon are there any grounds for suggesting that inclosure affected the population detrimentally. The returns of 1800 even suggest an increase of arable. In Cambridge there is a very slight decrease in wheat acreage, while the land under both barley and oats seems to increase. In Huntingdon, while this latter remains much as it was, there is a slight increase in the acres under wheat. In both cases, the increase in the population, 1750-1801, is normal for agricultural counties. Howlett's table does not add to our knowlege. In Cambridge, while the density of the inclosed parishes is greater than that of the county, this latter increases more rapidly. In Huntingdon, both density and rate of increase are much the same, what difference there is indicating a slight superiority in the parishes inclosed.

To further illustrate the points raised in the foregoing pages, an investigation may be attempted of two very different agricultural districts, one in the midlands and one extending along the Thames valley.

The Midland Region is one to which contemporary evidence points as the scene of very considerable conversions from arable to pasture. It is marked by a high rate of inclosure, mainly achieved in the eighteenth century, and largely before 1780-90. It consists of that region covering the junction of the counties of Warwick, Northampton, Leicester, and Rutland, its area being that of the following registration districts:

LEICESTER, -	Market Harborough.	WARWICK, -	Meriden.
	Melton Mowbray.		Foleshill.
RUTLAND, - -	Uppingham.		Rugby.
NORTHAMPTON,	Brixworth.		Warwick.
	Kettering.		Southam.

In all these districts, with the exception of Melton Mowbray, the percentage of parishes which show an actual diminution in population, 1801-11, is forty or over. In Melton Mowbray the percentage is lower, taking the district as a whole, though in the southern sub-district it is as high as in the other districts.

The following table shows the density of population and the percentage of parishes diminishing in population, 1801-1811, respectively for the whole district and for those parishes affected by eighteenth century inclosure and those affected by inclosure after 1800. It should be observed that urban areas are excluded from the figures of the inclosed parishes as well as from those for the districts. In the tables only common field inclosures are taken into account.

District, Etc.	Density of Population.	Percentage of Parishes decreasing in population 1801-1811.	Increase of population 1801-1811.
Whole district, urban areas and towns *included*, -	20.2	—	—
Whole district with urban areas excluded, - -	16.2	44	2.6
Total parishes with inclosures before 1800, urban excluded, - - -	19.1	40	—
Parishes with inclosures after 1800, urban excluded, - - -	17	56	—

From these details one thing at least is quite clear. The inclosures of the eighteenth century which occurred in over one-third of the parishes in this region, excluding town parishes, which are indeed few, cannot be held responsible either for a decline in population, which does not take place, or for a lower density of population. There is, indeed, no ground for attributing to this phase of the inclosure movement any particular importance in the changes which occur in respect of local migration. The number of parishes showing decline, 1801-11, in this region, is very large. The degree of inclosure is high. But, on the other hand, it is not in the inclosed districts that these local decreases are most marked. If the parishes with inclosures of open field after 1800 were more numerous the difference in density in these parishes and in those where inclosure had preceded the census would be even more important.

Turning west, to the Region of the Thames valley, the following districts are dealt with:

Oxford, - -	Henley.	Berkshire,	Abingdon.
	Thame.		Wallingford.
	Headington.		Bradfield.
Buckingham, -	Amersham.		Wokingham.
	Eton.		Cookham.
	Wycombe.		Easthampstead.
			Windsor.

Here the following table presents the chief features of interest.

District, Etc.	Density of population.	Percentage of parishes decreasing in population 1801-11.	Increase 1801-11.
Whole district (towns *included*), -	23.6	—	—
Whole district, towns and urban excluded, - -	19.2	28	9.5
Total parishes with inclosures before 1800, urban excluded, - - -	19.6	31	—
Total parishes with inclosures after 1800 (urban excluded), - - -	—	31	—

The same conclusion as to the relation of the eighteenth century inclosure with the rest of the district holds good. It should be noticed that there is comparatively little difference between the population of the eighteenth century inclosures in this district and in that previously considered, while the difference in the two districts is considerable.

The two districts were different in character, and this difference is reflected in the figures given above. In the one, that is in the North Midlands, where grazing and feeding was in the course of development, the district was lower in density and less rapid in increase than in the other portions of the counties into which it extends. In respect of density an exception must be made for Rutland, where the district itself is obviously below the average density. In the other, that is in the Thames valley, the conditions are reversed. Soil and agriculture are alike different, the latter being more mixed. The district, both in respect of density and rate of increase, surpasses the other and surrounding parts of the three counties. Yet in neither case are the parishes inclosed in the eighteenth century less dense and more marked by parishes with a decline, 1801-11, than in the respective district.

The fact and figures adduced and the considerations brought forward point to some general conclusions.

The general ideas as to the effects of inclosure, gathered from the utterances of those who criticised and condemned the movement, can be stated under three headings. They regarded the inclosures as implying, at least, as a rule, large conversions from arable to pasture. These conversions in their turn are treated as the cause of a lack of rural employment and of a decrease in population, which, if not apparent in the total population, was not apparent because outbalanced by the growth of industrial population and by the rise of the towns into which people formerly employed on the land were now driven by a want of occupation. Lastly, emphasis is laid on the hardships occasioned by change and consequent migration.

With regard to these contentions, the first two cannot be substantiated in anything like the sense in which they were put forward.

In the first place, quite apart from the possibility or probability of such wholesale conversion to pasture, a change curiously coupled by some with complaints as to the rise in the price of meat, any such tendency, where it did exist, was subject to modifying influences. It was checked or partially checked in many cases by concurrent inclosures of commons or wastes. From former tables[1] the counties where such inclosures took place may be seen. In Stafford and Derby the two kinds of inclosure are fairly well balanced, while in Norfolk, Suffolk, Lincoln, Warwick and Worcester, the quantity of inclosed wastes and commons is sufficient to be of importance in this respect. Further, in Cambridge, Berkshire, Nottingham, Hampshire and Dorset, commons or wastes, though not in large quantities, are still apparent. Again, in the so-called open field inclosure, common, waste and pasture were frequently and in a great many instances conspicuously included. Judging from the returns obtained in 1800,[2] the extent

[1] pp. 405-6. Cf. Bk. II. Appendix D.

[2] *General Report*, pp. 184-209, Appendix vii. As those wastes are given in detail for the different inclosures in respect of which figures are returned, the total of the inclosures has been taken and the total of waste or common in those inclosures for certain counties. It works out as given in the text. Cf. p. 404.

of such included wastes or commons has been put in most counties at something like one-fifth or one-fourth of the open field inclosures. Thus, in Leicester and Halifax, it has been reckoned at something like the fourth; in Bedford it was about 20 per cent.; while there is some ground for surmise that it was particularly important in Norfolk and Cambridge.

But even where there was conversion and where the finger of pessimistic triumph could be pointed to a decrease in the wheat acreage, the situation was not necessarily bad. So far as the actual supply of wheat was concerned, it was generally conceded, though not of course conceded by all, that as a rule the actual quantity and quality of wheat was increased. But when this was so, and when at the same time land once lying to some extent in waste, was now used for more skilled breeding, and for dairy purposes, and for inclosed pasture, there was no probable decrease in rural occupation. As Stone pointed out, there was a considerable growth in the need for labour for purposes before little known and largely neglected. To secure this larger yield, more labour and not less was required on the land in close cultivation. Even where wheat decreased in acreage, such decrease might be accompanied by an increase in other grain crops, and in root crops. Taking the counties mentioned above for a decrease in wheat acreage, and taking the returns made in 1800, both barley and oats increase in Berkshire, Cambridge, Northampton, Nottingham; oats increase in Bedford, Leicester, Oxford, and Warwick, while in Buckingham there is an increase in barley. Outside these counties a quite perceptible increase in both barley and oats takes place in Derby, Gloucester, Hampshire, Lincoln, Norfolk, Shropshire, Somerset, Stafford, and Yorkshire, while many other counties, and especially those of the north, show some increase in one or other, but usually in oats. Again, there were root crops to take into account, for these crops, it must be remembered, call for labour, whatever their purpose. Except in particular districts, and possibly in the case of one or two counties, the assumption as to a wide conversion of land from general arable purposes to pasture seems not only improbable, but, so far as can be seen, incorrect. Of course much land in any locality, now freed from restrictions, varied in its use, being put to the purpose it was best fitted for; but this did not always mean pasture instead of arable use. Of county areas, there are comparatively few where there is any reasonable ground for the suggestion that inclosure was attended by conversion to such an extent as to involve a diminution of the land under arable. Leicester, Warwick and Rutland are all accredited with decrease in wheat acreage, but in the first two there appears an increase in the land under oats. The position of Bedford is much the same. In Northampton there is increase both of barley and oats, and in Buckingham an increase in barley.

So far as rural employment was concerned, the comparison of land under wheat in common field and inclosure is quite inconclusive, since one of the objects actually sought was relief from exhausting cropping by the substitution of a rotation in which wheat appeared less frequently. Hence it was only to be expected that common field would contain a larger proportion under wheat. Any diminution in the food supply was offset either by the bringing of other land under wheat or by an improvement in the quantity or quality of the crop. Employment, however, would not be diminished by an actual decrease of the land under wheat, but only, if then, by a decrease in the amount under all arable crops. As previously pointed out, other cereals and crops besides wheat must be taken into account. The reasonable view is that put forward by Stone, namely, that on inclosure without conversion agricultural work was considerably increased. On open fields, he adds, a comparatively small amount of labour is required, as there are no hedges to keep up, no peas or beans to drill, and no turnips to hoe; thus labourers are mostly wanted for harvest and threshing. In some counties, and particularly in Cambridge, Huntingdon, and some parts of Northampton as the hay harvest advanced, labourers proceeded down to the fens to take up mowing. Further, account must also be taken of the care required for the improved stock, and in the dairy districts.

In the second place, we have to consider the evidence of actual diminution of employment on the land, and of the population. So far as whole counties are concerned, there are no signs of actual decrease; and the only counties indeed among those affected by inclosure which exhibit any unusually low rate of increase, from 1750-1801, are Bedford and Northampton. On turning to the density Table[1] for 1801, it will be seen that, comparing the parishes inclosed during the eighteenth century and the whole county, and excluding as far as possible the urban places, the parishes thus inclosed are almost invariably the more densely peopled. This is so in Bedford, Cambridge, Huntingdon, Leicester, Northampton, Nottingham, Rutland and Warwick. It is so also in the districts of Berkshire, Buckingham, and Oxford, outside the Thames valley, where comparatively few inclosures took place in the eighteenth century. It is equally true, however, of the more thickly populated Thames valley. Again comparing with those parishes inclosed before 1800, those in which there was some common field inclosure after 1800, the former are again the more populated, except in Huntingdon, Cambridge and Rutland; and in the two latter there is very little difference. Oxford, Berkshire and Buckingham must be left out of the reckoning, as the earlier and later inclosures take place so largely in different districts. Even in respect of the rate of increase, there is comparatively little significance in the differences, and here in most counties,[2] the towns are

[1] Appendix G.

[2] In Berkshire, Buckingham and Oxford, for reasons given previously in the text, certain districts are excluded in some figures, and this involves the exclusion of certain towns. In Warwick, Nottingham and Leicester, the industrial cities are excluded, namely, Birmingham (with Aston), Nottingham and Leicester.

reckoned in the rate of increase in the county, thus increasing it unduly, since the parishes with inclosure are rarely town parishes. There is no general rule either in the county table or in that dealing with the districts. According to the county table Cambridge and Berkshire are the two counties where the county rate of increase is most conspicuously in excess of that of parishes inclosed in the eighteenth century. One interesting feature is disclosed in the detailed tables. It is possible to compare the parishes inclosed before 1790, and the whole union districts in 57 cases, and in 23 the parishes inclosed increase less rapidly than the district, that is, in some 40 per cent. of the cases. On the other hand, if the comparison be between parishes inclosed 1791-1800 and the whole unions, which can be made in 47 cases, the former increase less rapidly in 30 instances, or in the percentage of 63. The conclusion does not favour the theory that on like soils the inclosures very late in the century were more favourable to arable and rural population than those of an earlier date. Indeed, the general indication points to temporary disturbance followed by more regular and equal development when matters settled down.

But inclosure as a movement deserves to be treated from another point of view, as a consequence rather than as a cause. When it is said that, if inclosure had not taken place, changes in employment and in the use of certain soils would not have occurred, it may well be answered that in that case other features would have been different, and that many demands would have gone unsatisfied. These demands were often those of the district or the neighbourhood. If we take the dictum of Moore, who particularly said that he did not object to inclosure when other means of employment existed, and apply it to many of the districts affected by the movement in the eighteenth century, it will be seen that the question at issue is the locality where such employment existed. In some cases, indeed, inclosure was the response to a demand felt locally, and a demand often involving some conversion. Elsewhere the close connection of the movement in general with the growth of population and of home industries has been dealt with. According to Horner, in his time the use of animal food was on the increase, a view shared by the author of the *Agricultural Report on Derbyshire.* The latter says that some conversion in that county was due to the local manufacture of cheese and to the local demand for animal food. A like statement is made in the case of Lancashire. Both dairy work and careful breeding implied a not inconsiderable amount of work. When this took place, as they necessarily had to take place, in the districts rising in manufacture, largely in home industries, it is difficult to see how any diminution of work would occur. Moreover, it seems quite conclusively shown by the various statistics adduced that, so far as any considerable area was concerned, the inclosed parishes held their own either with those inclosed long ago or with open field still remaining. This was true alike of the Midland district, where no doubt breeding did increase and conversion occur, and of the Thames valley.

In connection with the assertion that people were driven into the towns, an assertion which had been made at different times during the preceding two centuries, it must be remembered that with the divorce between agricultural and industrial occupations, and the early growth of factory organisation, towns both by reason of the sole opportunity offered for manufacture and also of a growing and specious difference in wage were beginning to exercise that force of attraction which subsequently becomes the great cause of rural depopulation.

While, however, there is no doubt that the general statement that inclosure occasioned depopulation is incorrect, so far as this period is concerned, there may well be cases in which tendencies in this direction were caused. These were within somewhat narrow limits. Depopulation or at any rate a lower comparative rate of increase in population, might well occur where the inclosure of common field was accompanied by large conversions, and when such conversions were not in response to local needs nor offset by other inclosures of commons or wastes. If the various counties be passed in review, it will be seen that cases of this kind were by way of exception. There is no reason, for instance, to endorse the assertion that they occurred in the great grazing district of the North Midlands. There conversion took place, but conversion to pasture used for careful breeding, itself employed some labour, both directly and indirectly, as for instance in root crops, and further, owing to coincident industrial growth, implied local demand. So the evidence of statistics is substantiated. Similarly, when we turn to the more southern counties along the Thames, where, however, the greatest development of inclosure occurs when the chalk and brashy lands come under the influence of the movement, to a great extent after 1800, with a corresponding development in their arable use. In Cambridge and Huntingdon, also, there seems little ground for attributing a lack of increase to the effects of inclosure for pasture. The two counties where there seems most ground for the suggestion, so far as large districts are concerned, are Bedford and Rutland, where possibly there were fewer causes of other local growth.

The matter may be briefly summarised. So far as the counties, or even large districts or portions of counties are concerned, there is really no evidence of depopulation. Nor indeed, save under certain circumstances, does the inclosure of this period occasion a lower rate of increase. On the other hand, it is probably true that in certain places inclosure did restrict increase, that in many townships there was actual decline owing no doubt to change in the use of land, and so a need for population to migrate to neighbouring townships, and, further, that on land converted to pasture the subsequent rate of increase was lower than elsewhere, as, for instance, in the North Midland district.

With this cause of local migration, that is within a district rather than from a district, was another feature further tending to change and unsettle a population previously organised on a basis of unyielding custom. Inclosure was at once a cause in itself and a step in a general movement, leading to larger farming, the disappearance of the small farmer and the growth of a large wage paid class of labour less certainly attached to the land than was previously the case. The direct effects of inclosure are dealt with elsewhere. Here it is only necessary to indicate firstly, that a considerable temporary unsettlement was occasioned; and secondly, that as in manufacture so in agriculture changes occurred which accelerated the development of two classes, a very small class of employers and a very large class of employed. The results of the change at the time seem to be reflected, though, it must be admitted, somewhat uncertainly in the returns as to poor relief. The new system is one of change and competition instead of custom.

The real results of inclosures, wholly apart from those either merely alleged and incorrect, or those erroneously attributed to them, must be distinguished into those which were not necessary, and those which were necessary. Among the former must be placed the great assistance lent to the consolidation of farms and holdings and the incidental difficulties imposed upon the small farmers, largely arising from the expenses involved either in obtaining the act or at the time of allotment. Among the latter, however, rank the changes made in the use of land. With regard to this latter matter, the attacks made at the time and the criticism of the movement even by some later writers appear unjustifiable. The old open field system while suited to a period of local isolation had one inevitable defect in that it prevented land being put to the use to which it was best fitted either by soil or climate. It was not to the interest of the people at large that land should not be put to its best use. That change might result in some local distress is true. But facts, so far as they exist, show that this was not the case of the movement in the eighteenth century in general, or indeed so far as any moderately large district was concerned.

No one of the tests employed to investigate the truth of the general allegation as to the effect of inclosure on population is, perhaps, absolutely conclusive; but taken together they form very strong evidence. In general, they are mutually corroborative; and it is quite clear that a decline in population or occupation far less marked or widespread than that depicted by the adverse critics of the day would have left definite traces in these statistics. Moreover, their strength is made the more apparent by the singular paucity of the testimony adduced on the other side. Those who decried the movement based their case either on personal observation of a very limited number of instances or an assumption of an *a priori* character which leaves out of sight the many counteracting tendencies. The statistics show a disturbance of a restricted character and a variation within narrow limits; they do not show anything like a decline in the counties or regions where inclosure was most frequent, and they give no reason for believing that had such inclosure not occurred either these counties or these districts would have been a whit the better off in respect of total employment.

On the other hand there were certain positive results associated with and largely due to inclosure.

In the first place, local change in the use of particular soils was made easier and so encouraged. This was largely the immediate result of the change in system, and when, owing to the nature of the soil or the nature of local demand, the need arose for a change towards pasture there was some alteration in employment, certain parishes decreasing and others increasing.

In the second place, some pasture districts when formed tend to increase at a slower rate than elsewhere. Of this the North Midlands furnish an excellent illustration.

In the third place, the alteration in the system of farming accentuated by the temporary results of inclosure introduces a new uncertainty into employment.

In the fourth place, districts when once inclosed are more free to be converted to any agricultural use which the circumstances of the time may make advantageous, and hence inclosure in a certain far off sense may be held responsible at any rate in part for the decline or comparative decline in rural population which was to ensue a half century or even a century after their date. Here, however, it is but one among several causes.

The careful examination of the truth of general statements as to the effect of inclosure on population and employment in the latter part of the eighteenth century, in the light of statistics is important for a particular reason. It emphasises certain defects in the evidence of contemporary observers. Unless they exercised great care they were liable to be misled by appearance, as when arable strips were succeeded by pasture land. Moreover, they obviously argue too much from particular instances within their knowledge, taking little note of compensatory factors even when these were operating near at hand. But these defects are equally if not more important in earlier periods, when the range of observation was equally if not more restricted. In the seventeenth century in particular caution is required in accepting these statements. New land was coming into the cultivated area with the result that change in the use of old land was necessary, and yet depopulation or lack of work except in a very narrow sense was no necessary consequence. New employment in other words might be afforded within reasonable reach. Further, the spread of domestic industries occurring at that time was of importance in two ways. Not only was demand increased, and the best use of the land made more pressing, but it is probable that the inclosed system was more compatible with the circumstances of people largely occupied in industry and only partially employed in agriculture.

In the eighteenth century especially, it must be remembered that the general economic movement in the country could not be without influence. As Horner said, in a passage already quoted, agriculture from being "a means of subsistence to particular families," had become "a source of wealth to the public," a change which he considered of importance in examining the results of inclosure. Local production for home use yielded to localised industries and differentiated agriculture, and inclosure played its part in the development.

APPENDIX A.

Inclosure, Population and Poor Rates.

	Percentage of Common Field inclosure in round figures during			Percentage Increase of Population in round figures.		Poor Rates per head of Population in Shillings. Approximate for Years		
	18th Century -1800.	Before 1780.	1801-10.	1750-1801.	1801-1811.	Average of 1748-9-50.	1803.	1813.
Bedford, - -	26	8	11	6.6	10	2.8	12.0	17.9
Berkshire, -	10	6	9	17.1	8	3.4	15.6	26.8
Buckingham, -	21	13	6	22.3	10	3.8	16.5	23.6
Cambridge, -	7	1	12	14.5	15	2.4	12.5	17.7
Cheshire, - -	—	—	—	65.8	17	2.6	7.2	10.8
Cornwall, - -	—	—	—	32.9	14	1.3	6.0	8.2
Cumberland, -	—	—	—	34.6	14	.5	5.0	7.2
Derby, - -	9	4	5	48.8	15	1.4	7.2	10.8
Devonshire, -	—	—	—	4.1	12	2.1	8.6	11.8
Dorset, - -	4	1	2	21.5	8	2.5	11.6	18.0
Durham, - -	—	—	—	14.7	10	1.0	6.8	10.4
Essex, - -	—	—	1	16.8	11	3.9	16.2	25.7
Gloucester, -	12	8	2	15.0	14	2.2	9.0	12.0
Hampshire, -	4	1	1	52.4	12	2.8	11.7	18.7
Hereford, - -	1	—	2	17.8	6	1.3	10.7	18.3
Hertford, - -	4	1	3	18.9	12	4.0	12.0	14.3
Huntingdon, -	28	18	16	15.7	12	2.0	13.2	17.2
Kent, - -	—	—	—	69.7	18	4.6	14.0	18.3
Lancashire, -	—	—	—	97.0	22	1.2	4.7	8.1
Leicester, - -	40	31	2	32.1	15	1.5	12.8	15.4
Lincoln, - -	21	15	5	26.7	13	1.7	9.7	11.8
Middlesex, -	5	1	6	47.9	18	2.9	8.9	11.0
Norfolk, - -	6	3	7	15.0	6	2.5	12.8	20.6
Northumberland,	1	1	1	5.2	9	.5	6.9	8.4
Nottingham, -	23	14	3	53.6	16	.9	6.7	10.4
Northampton, -	37	31	7	9.7	9	2.0	14.8	20.3
Oxford, - -	25	15	5	14.3	7	2.6	16.6	24.5
Rutland, - -	41	20	2	30.2	−.7	1.3	10.5	14.1
Shropshire, -	—	—	—	24.0	9	1.1	8.3	12.0
Somerset, - -	—	—	1	14.5	11	2.1	9.2	12.8
Stafford, - -	3	1	3	58.3	21	1.2	7.4	9.1
Suffolk, - -	1	—	1	22.7	9	3.2	11.8	20.0
Surrey, - -	1	—	2	87.6	13	3.7	10.5	14.1
Sussex, - -	—	—	1	57.1	19	4.8	23.3	34.0
Warwick, - -	20	16	2	55.3	10	1.5	11.8	14.7
Westmoreland, -	—	—	—	7.8	12	.9	6.8	10.1
Wiltshire, - -	12	5	5	9.6	4	1.6	14.2	25.0
Worcester, -	8	5	2	35.4	14	1.9	10.7	12.5
Yorkshire, E., -	23	20	7	71	19	1	6.5	11.5
,, N., -	4	3	2	36	11	.9	6.4	8.7
,, W., -	5	2	2	73	16	1.2	6.9	10.5

APPENDIX B.

Increase of Poor Rates in certain periods given in percentages.

	1748-9-50—1783-4-5 Average. Average.	1783-4-5—1803 Average.	1803-13.
Bedford,	145	81	66
Berkshire,	194	82	92
Buckingham,	164	95	57
Cambridge,	185	114	59
Cheshire,	129	77	75
Cornwall,	195	102	87
Cumberland,	376	155	63
Derby,	198	155	71
Devonshire,	130	84	52
Dorset,	157	112	68
Durham,	173	180	58
Essex,	147	95	76
Gloucester,	152	74	52
Hampshire,	187	119	79
Hereford,	231	187	80
Hertford,	199	79	36
Huntingdon,	268	105	46
Kent,	153	102	55
Lancaster,	245	119	109
Leicester,	308	172	39
Lincoln,	190	134	39
Middlesex,	141	87	44
Norfolk,	227	85	65
Northumberland,	447	163	42
Nottingham,	313	163	100
Northampton,	272	112	47
Oxford,	180	154	51
Rutland,	310	145	33
Shropshire,	328	106	58
Somerset,	158	91	53
Stafford,	317	116	52
Suffolk,	147	79	87
Surrey,	148	115	60
Sussex,	199	154	74
Warwick,	470	106	37
Westmoreland,	212	154	63
Wiltshire,	162	110	81
Worcester,	255	116	40
Yorkshire, E.,	276	187	99
„ N.,	235	172	45
„ W.,	227	195	76

APPENDIX C.

Table exhibiting rate of increase in Baptisms in certain parishes in certain counties, distinguishing between those lately inclosed and those not lately inclosed. (Howlett, *An Enquiry*, *etc.*)

	Baptisms in Parishes lately inclosed.			Baptisms in Parishes not lately inclosed.		
	No. of Parishes.	1760-65.	1775-80.	No.	1760-65.	1775-80.
Northumberland, -	2	349	441	32	5977	6302
Durham, - - -	3	525	600	10	2735	3202
Cumberland, - -	3	956	1147	20	2431	2823
Shropshire, - - -	3	390	517	17	1729	1782
Norfolk, - - -	8	447	558	69	4384	5224
Essex, - - - -	2	165	248	19	1517	1920
Bedford, - - -	3	151	221	6	981	935
Buckingham, - -	4	343	335	8	1490	1748
Leicester, - - -	7	1255	1450	8	1021	1340
Stafford, - - -	2	320	356	10	2394	2860
Warwick, - - -	12	1269	1609	7	1154	1446
Derby and Berkshire, -	5	546	621	25	2135	2413
Middlesex, - - -	1	34	47	4	827	1073
Worcester, - - -	7	1490	1946	17	2011	2493
Gloucester, - - -	10	463	588	175	13,163	14,639
Wiltshire, - - -	13	1888	2187	48	5774	4210
Hampshire, - - -	4	213	267	15	3008	3374

APPENDIX D.

Rate of increase of population (1801-1811) in all parishes inclosed during eighteenth century, in parishes inclosed in decade 1791-1800, and in whole counties.—*Registration Counties.*

[In this table towns not excluded save in instances noted.]

PLACE.	All Parishes inclosed in Eighteenth Century.	Parishes inclosed 1791-1800.	COUNTY.
Bedford, - -	13.8	16.7	10.8
Berkshire, - -	3.1	2.9	[1] 8.2
Buckingham, -	7.5	10.0	[2] 9.1
Cambridge, -	7.7	4.9	14.8
Huntingdon, -	12.0	14.7	11.9
Leicester, -	12.1	*d.*	12.4 (Excluding Leicester.)
Northampton, -	8.0	8.6	7.4
Nottingham, -	17.2	20.1	15.4 (Excluding Nottingham.)
Oxford, - -	5.7	.4	[3] 7.5
Rutland, - -	*d.* .5	*d.* 8.1	*d.* 1.0
Warwick, - -	7.3	5.5	7.1 (Excluding Birmingham with Aston.)

APPENDIX E.

Parishes with decrease in populaton 1801-1811 distributed.

PLACE.	Total number with decrease.	In parishes not inclosed 18th Century and up to 1840.	PARISHES INCLOSED.			
			Before 1790.	1791-1800.	1801-10.	1811-40.
Bedford, -	23	11	3	3	5	1
Berkshire, -	88	53	7	3	14	11
Buckingham, -	57	32	10	7	5	3
Cambridge, -	27	7	—	6	4	10
Huntingdon, -	20	8	5	2	1	4
Leicester, -	89	52	26	8	2	1
Northampton,	91	52	23	2	11	3
Nottingham, -	74	54	11	2	5	2
Oxford, - -	73	46	11	9	1	6
Rutland, -	29	18	4	4	3	—
Warwick, -	95	46	23	6	5	11

[1] Excluding districts of Eton, Amersham, Wycombe, the rate for county is 7.4.

[2] Excluding Henley, Thame, Headington, Oxford, the rate for county is 6.9.

[3] Excluding Abingdon, Wallingford, Bradfield, Reading, Wokingham, Cookham, Easthampton, Windsor, the rate for the county is 5.2.

APPENDIX F.

Rate of increase of population in inclosed parishes and registration districts of various counties—1801-1811.

County.	District.	Increase of Population in percentages.		
		Parishes Incl. - 1790.	Parishes Incl. 1791-1800.	Total District.
Cambridge,	Caxton, - - -	12.3	*d.*	3.4
	Chesterton, - -	—	6.1	11.0
	Linton, - - -	10.6	4.6	12.2
	Newmarket, - -	—	9.4	8.3
	Ely, - - -	9.4	—	14.0
	N. Witchford, -	10.4	—	16.5
Bedford,	Bedford, - -	*d.*	10.3	10.8
	Biggleswade, - -	12.2	4.6	7.0
	Ampthill, - -	11.0	10.8	9.0
	Woburn, - - -	17.9	8.8	5.8
	Leighton Buzzard, -	.5	*d.*	8.8
	Luton, - - -	*d.*	18.7	19.9
Buckingham,	Eton, - - -	21.0	10.5	16.6
	Wycombe, - -	—	10.7	9.6
	Aylesbury, - -	6.9	.2	7.2
	Winslow, - -	4.1	3.2	4.3
	Newport Pagnell, -	3.5	13.6	5.3
	Buckingham, - -	9.1	10.8	11.6
Huntingdon,	Huntingdon, - -	4.8	2.4	11.3
	St. Ives, - - -	12.3	14.5	11.8
	St. Neots, - -	12.8	15.7	12.8
Oxford,	Henley, - - -	—	*d.*	9.7
	Bicester, - - -	4.8	15.11	7.6
	Woodstock, - -	10.3	12.8	11.7
	Witney, - - -	7.8	*d.*	3.3
	Chipping Norton, -	7.0	*d.*	5.7
	Banbury, - -	7.7	*d.*	4.1

County.	District.	Increase of Population in percentages. Parishes Incl. – 1790.	Parishes Incl. 1791-1800	Total District.
Northampton,	Brackley, - -	3.3	4.6	5.1
	Towcester, - -	9.3	5.1	6.1
	Potterspury, - -	*d.*	—	2.3
	Hardingstone, -	12.9	—	12.5
	Northampton, -	9.5	—	15.0
	Daventry, - -	4.4	—	4.8
	Brixworth, - -	9.8	*d.*	6.4
	Wellingborough, -	15.3	9.1	13.9
	Kettering, - -	1.1	—	.5
	Thrapstone, - -	2.0	9.0	6.8
	Oundle, - - -	4.8	38.3	3.2
	Peterborough, -	33.1	—	9.9
Berkshire,	Newbury, - -	13.8	—	11.8
	Hungerford, - -	*d.*	4.0	.5
	Faringdon, - -	7.9	*d.*	6.0
	Abingdon, - -	7.2	6.5	8.7
	Wantage, - -	6.8	*d.*	2.6
	Wallingford, - -	10.9	37.2	4.6
	Bradfield, - -	*d.*	—	7.0
	Reading, - -	—	—	13.5
	Wokingham, - -	.9	—	8.0
	Cookham, - -	*d.*	—	*d*
	Easthampstead, -	—	—	7.7
	Windsor, - -	—	—	26.8
Rutland,	Oakham, - -	3.2	*d.*	*d.*
	Uppingham, - -	.4	*d.*	*d.*
Warwick,	Aston, - - - -	—	*d.*	17.5
	Meriden, - -	9.4	5.9	3.3
	Atherstone, - -	10.2	—	8.3
	Nuneaton, - -	3.7	1.9	3.7
	Foleshill, - -	2.3	27.9	3.2
	Rugby, - - -	8.7	*d.*	4.6
	Solihull, - - -	6.9	*d.*	3.7
	Warwick, - -	16.4	5.6	9.9
	Stratford, - -	7.9	*d.*	6.9
	Alcester, - -	12.0	—	11.4
	Shipston, - -	4.9	4.3	2.7
	Southam, - -	4.4	13.5	3.8

County.	District.	Increase of Population in percentages.		
		Parishes Incl. – 1790.	Parishes Incl. 1791-1800.	Total District.
Leicester,	Lutterworth, - -	12.2	—	10.5
	M. Harborough, -	.9	—	*d.* .7
	Billesdon, - -	4.5	—	4.8
	Blaby, - - -	18.2	—	20.8
	Hinckley, - -	16.3	—	18.1
	M. Bosworth, - -	13.0	—	9.8
	Ashby de la Zouch,	13.8	—	11.6
	Loughborough, -	17.4	—	16.0
	Barrow, - - -	10.0	—	11.9
	Melton Mowbray, -	8.8	—	8.6
Nottingham,	E. Retford, - -	11.0	6.3	6.8
	Worksop, - -	13.5	—	7.5
	Mansfield, - -	22.1	—	14.4
	Basford, - - -	21.1	29.4	22.6
	Radford, - - -	50.4	56.7	48.8
	Southwell, - -	10.4	3.9	10.3
	Newark, - - -	8.7	7.2	8.9
	Bingham, - -	16.4	2.6	13.7

Note 1.—In 75 cases it is possible to compare rates of increase, etc., in parishes inclosed before 1800 and those for the related unions. In 29 cases rate of increase greater for the union than for the included inclosed parishes, that is in 38 per cent. of the cases.

In 53 cases it is possible to compare rates of increase, etc., of parishes inclosed 1791-1800 and those for related union. In 34 cases rate of increase greater for union than for included inclosed parishes, that is in 64 per cent. of the cases.

Note 2.—Taking the three counties Leicester, Northampton and Warwick comparison of parishes inclosed before 1800 and the union feasible in 33 cases. In 10 the rate for the union greater than for included inclosed parishes, that is in 30 per cent. of the cases. These are counties in respect of which much conversion is alleged.

Note 3.—In the foregoing tables the number of parishes in the union affected by inclosure 1791-1800 often inadequate to allow of a fair average. So in many cases the percentage is omitted. The parishes are of course ncluded in all cases in the figures for inclosure before 1800.

APPENDIX G.

Density of population to 100 acres. (1801.)
[In this table towns are deducted.]

Name of County.	Parishes incld. before 1800 (common field).	Whole County.	Parishes incld. after 1800 (common field).	Incl. Parishes with decreased wheat acreage.	Incl. Parishes with increased wheat acreage.
Bedford, - -	20.0	17.5	19.0	17.6	21.5
Berkshire, - -	14.8	18.0	16.8	—	—
Do. [1]	14.4	15.2	—	—	—
Buckingham, -	20.1	19.2	21.1	20.7	21.9
Do. [2]	19.7	17.6	—	—	—
Cambridge, - -	14.3	12.7	14.5	—	—
Huntingdon, -	14.4	13.7	17.2	—	—
Leicester, - -	21.8	19.9	17.7	21.0	18.8
Northampton, -	20.0	17.3	18.5	20.5	25.0
Nottingham, -	18.8	17.2	16.2	—	—
Oxford, - -	16.7	17.3	19.3	19.1	18.6
Do. [3]	16.9	16.9	—	—	—
Rutland, - -	16.2	14.5	16.9	16.8	—
Warwick, - -	19.0	18.3	18.4	17.0	—
Gloucester, - -	—	—	—	14.6	14.1

[1] Excluding districts of Abingdon, Wallingford, Bradfield, Reading, Wokingham, Cookham, Easthampton, Windsor, in which total number of parishes inclosed before 1800 is ten.

[2] Excluding Amersham, Eton, Wycombe, in which total number of parishes inclosed before 1800 is two.

[3] Excluding Henley, Thame, Headington, Oxford, in which total number of parishes inclosed before 1800 is six.

The present 1800 and past 1800 inclosures in these counties take place in different parts of these counties.

In Berkshire many inclosed parishes or hamlets are omitted because population not given separately.

APPENDIX H.

INVESTIGATION OF TWO SPECIAL DISTRICTS.

(*a*) *N. Midland Pasture*—

LEICESTER.—Market Harbro.
Melton Mowbray.

RUTLAND.—Uppingham.

NORTHAMPTON.—Brixworth.
Kettering.

WARWICK.—Meriden.
Foleshill.
Rugby.
Warwick.
Southam.

All showing *many* instances (1801-11) of Parishes actually decreased in population.

Table (Towns omitted)—

Whole District Density, - - - - - -	16.2
Per cent. of Parishes, decrease in population,	44
Increase of population, 1801-11, - - -	2.6
Inclosed Parishes (c.f.) Density, - - -	19.1
Per cent. of Parishes, decrease in population,	40.6
Parishes with subsequent c.f. Inclosure Density,	17
Per cent. decrease, - - - - - -	54
Density of District with Towns, - - -	20.2

(*b*) *Thames District*—

OXFORD.—Henley.
Thame.
Headington.

BUCKS.—Amersham.
Eton.
Wycombe.

BERKS.—Abingdon.
Wallingford.
Bradfield.
Wokingham.
Cookham.
Easthampstead.
Windsor.

Table (Towns omitted)—

Whole District Density, - - - - - -	19.2
Per cent. of Parishes, decrease in population,	28
Increase of population, 1801-11, - - -	9.5
Inclosed Parishes c.f. (?too few) Density, - -	19.6
Per cent. of Parishes with decrease, - -	31
Parishes with subsequent Inclosure, per cent. of Parishes with decrease, - - - - - -	31
Density of District with Towns,- - - -	23.6

APPENDIX J.

Increase per cent. of Poor Rates in certain Counties during periods 1776–1783-4-5 and 1783-4-5–1803, distinguishing total County—Townships c.f. inclosed 1776-1782 and Townships inclosed 1783-1802.

County.	Per cent. increase Poor Rates during period 1776-1783.		
	Total County.	Township c.f. inclosed during period 1776-1782 inclusive.	Township c.f. inclosed during periods 1783-1802 inclusive.
Leicester, - - - -	26	6	35
Northants, - - - -	39	37	69
Buckingham, - - -	42	59	40
Berkshire, - - - -	27	decr.	22
Cambridge, - - - -	45	—	97

County.	Per cent. increase Poor Rates during period 1783-1803.		
	Total County.	Township c.f. inclosed 1776-1782 inclusive.	Township c.f. inclosed 1783-1802 inclusive.
Leicester, - - - -	171	187	159
Northants, - - - -	112	117	126
Buckingham, - - -	95	76	118
Berkshire, - - - -	74	73	98
Cambridge, - - - -	115	—	66

INDEX.

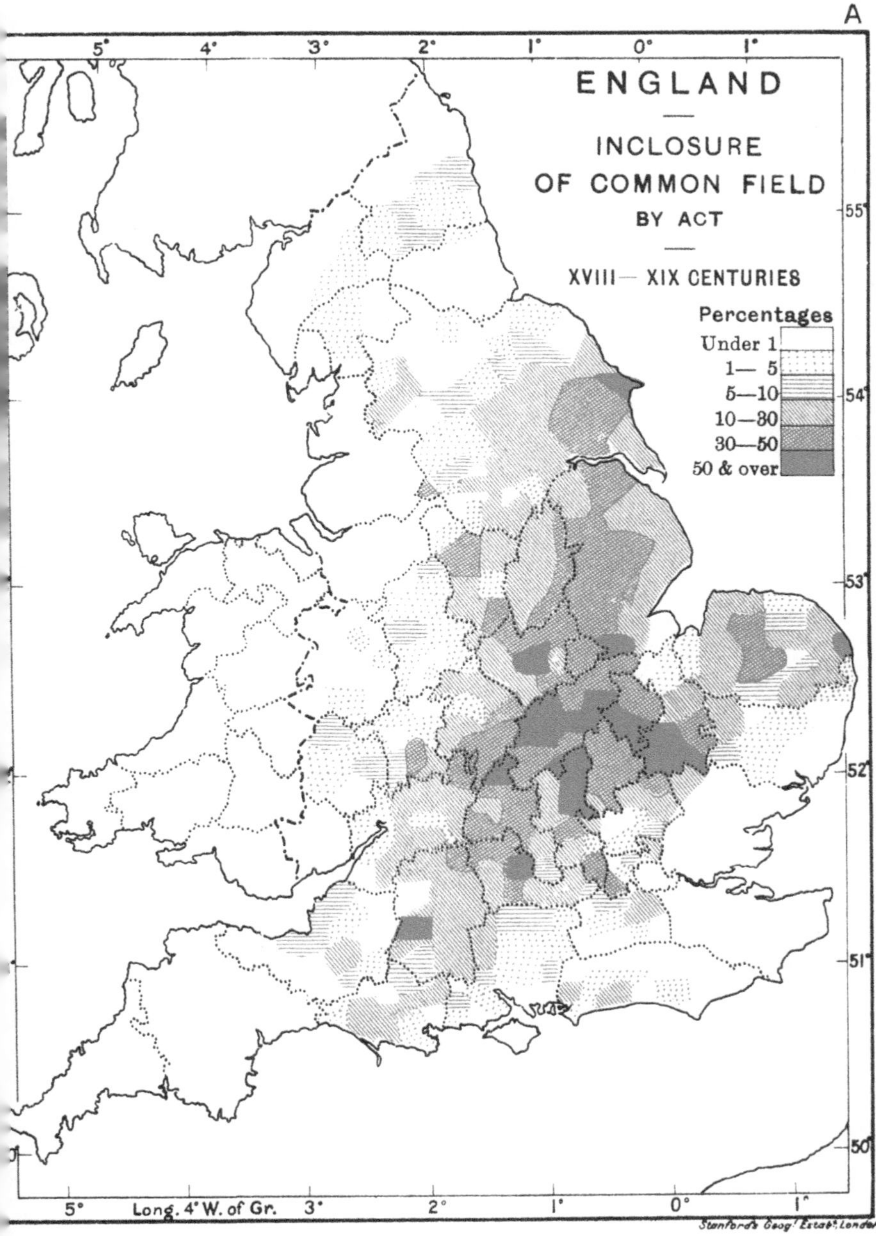
A
ENGLAND
INCLOSURE
OF COMMON FIELD
BY ACT
XVIII — XIX CENTURIES
Percentages
Under 1
1— 5
5—10
10—30
30—50
50 & over
Long. 4° W. of Gr.
Stanford's Geog! Estab! London.

B

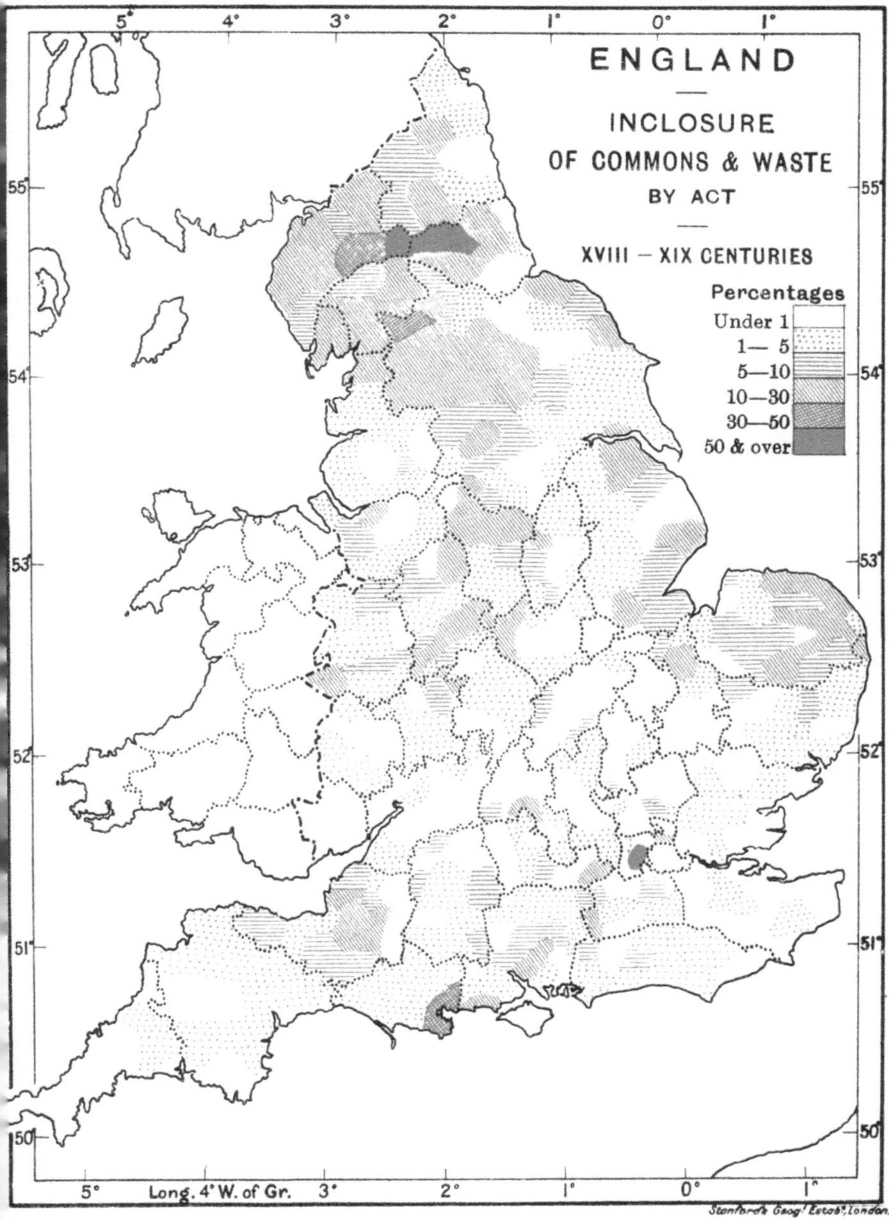
ENGLAND
INCLOSURE
OF COMMONS & WASTE
BY ACT
XVIII – XIX CENTURIES
Percentages
Under 1
1— 5
5—10
10—30
30—50
50 & over
Long. 4° W. of Gr.
Stanford's Geog! Estab!, London.

C

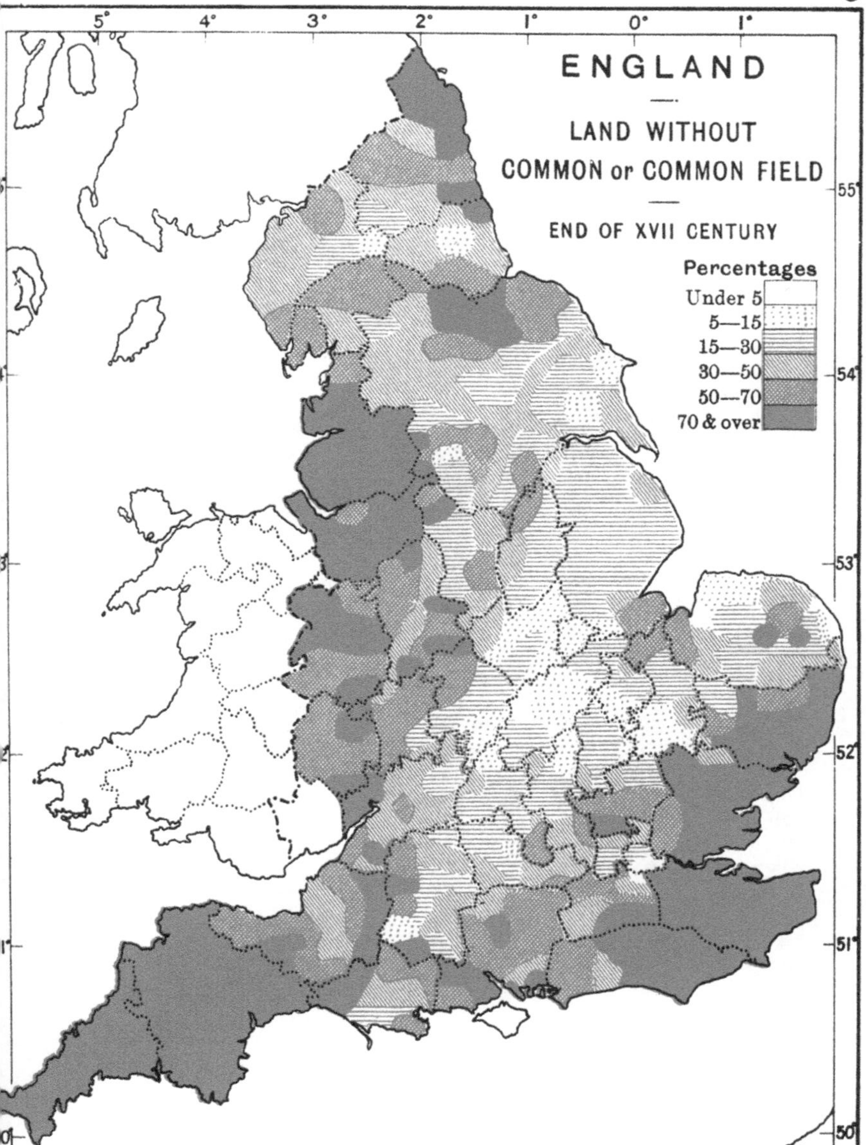
ENGLAND
LAND WITHOUT
COMMON or COMMON FIELD
END OF XVII CENTURY
Percentages
Under 5
5—15
15—30
30—50
50—70
70 & over
5°
4°
3°
2°
1°
0°
1°
55°
54°
53°
52°
51°
50°
Long. 4° W. of Gr.
Stanford's Geog¹ Estab¹, London.

D

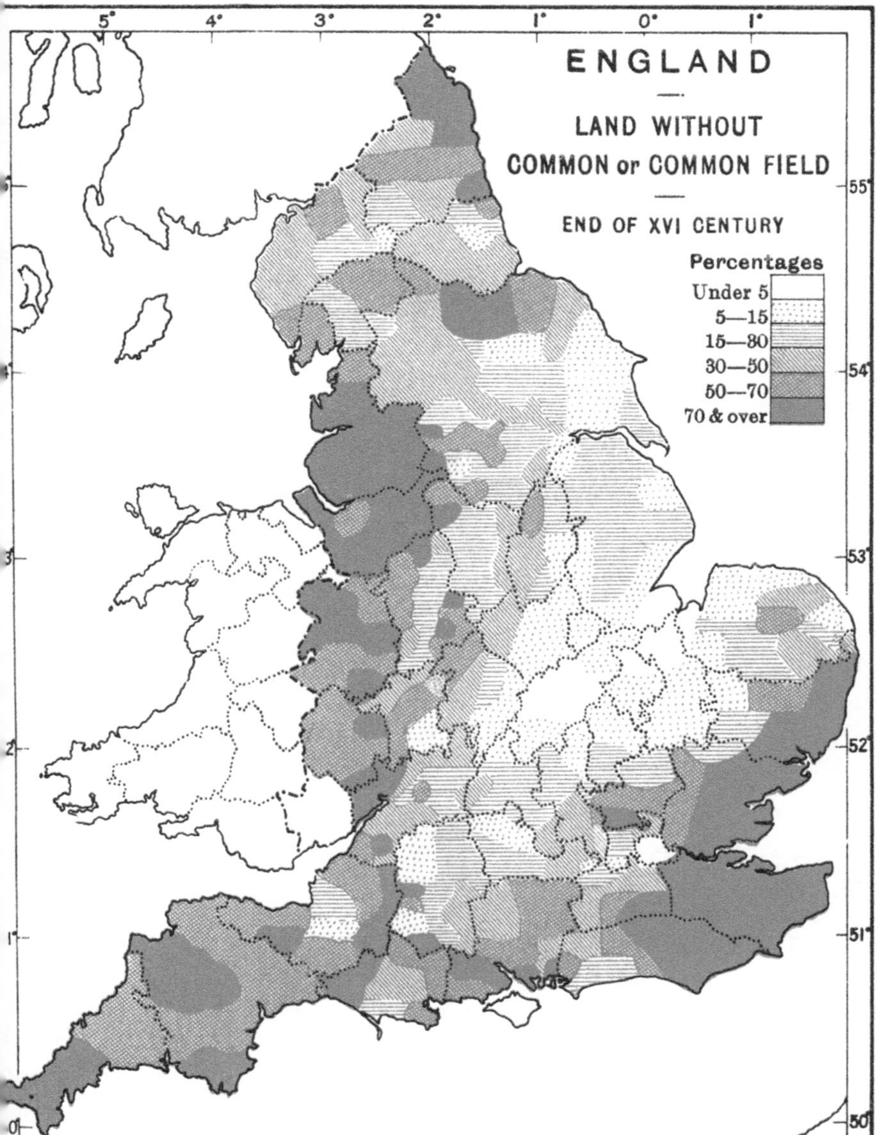
ENGLAND
LAND WITHOUT
COMMON or COMMON FIELD
END OF XVI CENTURY
Percentages
Under 5
5—15
15—30
30—50
50—70
70 & over
5°
4°
3°
2°
1°
0°
1°
55°
54°
53°
52°
51°
50°
Long. 4° W. of Gr.
Stanford's Geog! Estab! London.

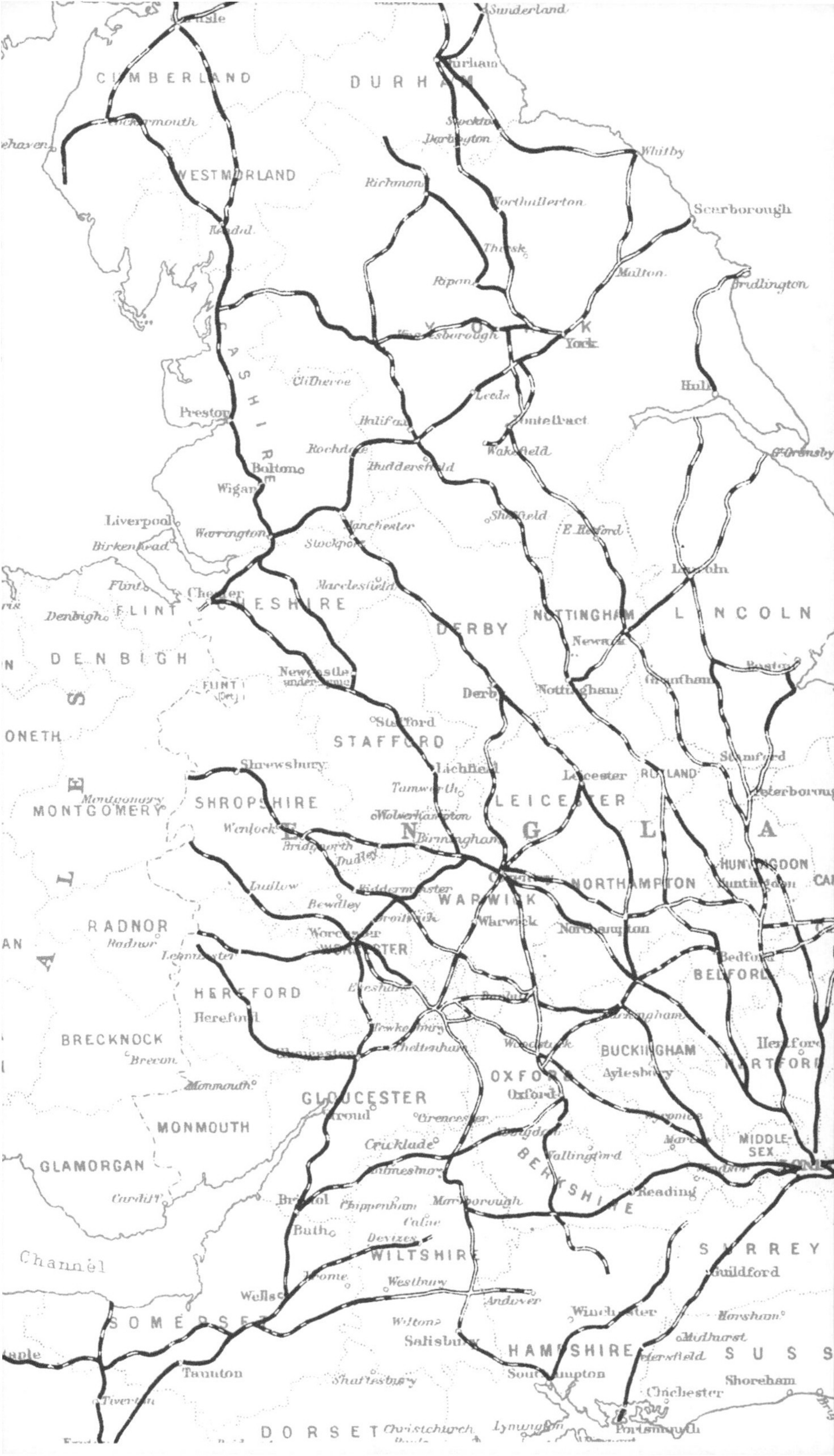

Sunderland
Durham
CUMBERLAND
DURHAM
Cockermouth
Stockton
Darlington
Whitby
WESTMORLAND
Richmond
Northallerton
Scarborough
Kendal
Thirsk
Malton
Ripon
Bridlington
Knaresborough
York
Clitheroe
Leeds
Hull
Preston
Halifax
Pontefract
Rochdale
Wakefield
Bolton
Huddersfield
Wigan
Liverpool
Sheffield
Warrington
E. Retford
Birkenhead
Stockport
Manchester
Lincoln
Flint
Macclesfield
Denbigh
FLINT
Chester
CHESHIRE
NOTTINGHAM
LINCOLN
DERBY
Newark
DENBIGH
Newcastle under Lyme
Boston
Derby
Nottingham
Grantham
STAFFORD
Stafford
Stamford
Shrewsbury
Lichfield
Leicester
RUTLAND
Tamworth
Peterborough
Montgomery
MONTGOMERY
SHROPSHIRE
LEICESTER
Wolverhampton
Wenlock
Bridgnorth
Birmingham
Dudley
HUNTINGDON
Huntingdon
Ludlow
Kidderminster
NORTHAMPTON
Bewdley
WARWICK
Droitwich
Warwick
RADNOR
Radnor
Worcester
WORCESTER
Northampton
Leominster
Bedford
HEREFORD
BEDFORD
Evesham
Banbury
Hereford
Tewkesbury
BRECKNOCK
Cheltenham
Woodstock
BUCKINGHAM
Brecon
Aylesbury
OXFORD
Oxford
Monmouth
GLOUCESTER
Stroud
Cirencester
MONMOUTH
Abingdon
Cricklade
Wallingford
MIDDLE-SEX
GLAMORGAN
Malmesbury
Cardiff
Bristol
Reading
Chippenham
Marlborough
Calne
Bath
Devizes
WILTSHIRE
SURREY
Channel
Frome
Guildford
Westbury
Wells
Andover
Winchester
SOMERSET
Horsham
Wilton
Salisbury
Midhurst
HAMPSHIRE
Petersfield
Taunton
Southampton
Shoreham
Shaftesbury
Chichester
Tiverton
DORSET
Christchurch
Lymington
Portsmouth